UNIVERSITIES AT **RISK**

HOW POLITICS, SPECIAL INTERESTS, AND CORPORATIZATION THREATEN ACADEMIC INTEGRITY

CAUT SERIES TITLES

UNIVERSITIES AT **RISK**

HOW POLITICS, SPECIAL INTERESTS, AND CORPORATIZATION THREATEN ACADEMIC INTEGRITY

EDITED BY JAMES L. TURK

James Lorimer & Company Ltd., Publishers

Toronto

James Lorimer & Company Ltd., Publishers acknowledge the support of the Ontario Arts Council. We acknowledge the support of the Government of Canada through the Book Publishing Industry Development Program (BPIDP) for our publishing activities. We acknowledge the support of the Canada Council for the Arts for our publishing program. We acknowledge the support of the Government of Ontario through the Ontario Media Development Corporation's Ontario Book Initiative.

Canada Council   Conseil des Arts
for the Arts   du Canada

ONTARIO ARTS COUNCIL
CONSEIL DES ARTS DE L'ONTARIO

Library and Archives Canada Cataloguing in Publication
        Universities at risk : how politics, special interests and corporatization threaten academic integrity / edited by James L. Turk.

Includes bibliographical references and index.

ISBN 978-1-55277-040-5

        1. Academic freedom — Canada.   2. Academic freedom — United States.
3. University autonomy — Canada.   4. University autonomy — United States.
5. Education, Higher — Political aspects — Canada.   6. Education, Higher — Political aspects — United States.   7. Business and education — Canada.   8. Business and education — United States.
I. Turk, James, 1943–

LA184.U56 2008   378.1'2130971   C2008-905575-6

Cover design by Meghan Collins

James Lorimer & Company Ltd., Publishers
317 Adelaide Street West, Suite 1002
Toronto, Ontario
M5V 1P9
www.lorimer.ca

Printed and bound in Canada

FOREWORD

Howard Pawley
President, Harry Crowe Foundation

The present collection of essays grew out of a conference sponsored by the Harry Crowe Foundation in November 2007. The theme chosen for that conference, "Protecting the Integrity of Academic Work," reflected the foundation's concern to preserve and advance all that is best in higher education.

The foundation approaches academic issues with an eye to international trends. Conflict of interest in sponsored research and third-party intrusions into academic processes are problems that know no national boundaries. They are symptomatic of the global privatization of public services and the commodification of higher education. Such trends may be beyond our control, but they are not beyond our influence. The community of scholars, writ large, must play a central role in protecting the integrity of scholarly inquiry and the education of students. This is our public obligation.

In choosing which issues we would address in these pages, we selected those that promised broad, international relevance. Whether addressing a general condition or problems at a particular institution, the articles should resonate widely, precisely because each of them points to a significant and systemic impediment to the search for or the transmission of knowledge. In my ideal world, ideas and information circulate freely across a boundless intellectual commons. Sadly, in the real world, there are many forces that want to restrict open and critical inquiry and education.

Hence, the Harry Crowe Foundation. Better understanding our institutions and practices is, we believe, the first step to improving those institutions and practices. Our foundation is young. We only began receiving donations as a registered charity toward the end of 2003. Still, this will be our second substantive contribution to the public discussion of higher education policies and standards. Our previous collection, *Free Speech in Fearful Times: After 9/11 in Canada, the U.S., Australia & Europe*, drew attention in 2007 to another threat to the scholarly exchange of ideas, the national security environment and so-called "war on terror."

Two books in as many years. The task of making things better is off to a good start, yet there is so much more to be done. In the coming months we will be announcing new conferences, new publications, and new projects. If you want to keep yourself apprised of our continuing activities, I would urge you to check our Web site www.crowefoundation.ca from time to time or, better, find out how you can become involved in our work directly.

Inquiries about the Harry Crowe Foundation may be emailed to hcf@crowefoundation.ca.

ACKNOWLEDGEMENTS

The idea for this book grew out of discussions with Jon Thompson, Arpi Hamalian, Howard Pawley, John Hoddinott, and Brenda Gallie.

I especially want to thank Marcus Harvey for his consistently excellent advice and counsel. Jean Lawrence's editorial assistance is greatly appreciated. Finally, I want to acknowledge Louise Desjardins, my long-time assistant, without whose help and support this book would never have been possible.

J.L.T.

INTRODUCTION

James L. Turk

It is difficult to talk generally about universities as, throughout their long history, they have assumed a variety of forms and have fulfilled different missions. At any historical moment, there has been considerable variation across universities and within any particular university. Nevertheless, some generalizations can be made.

Medieval universities, initially with some measure of independence, largely became instruments of the church and the ruling elites. Early North American universities trained future clergy and those destined to be leaders of society. To the extent these early universities were theological, they also were inextricably linked with study of the arts.[1] The complexity of North American universities through the nineteenth and twentieth centuries derived, in part, from influences of British and German counterparts.

American research universities, starting with Johns Hopkins, drew directly from the changes to German universities that were shaped by Wilhelm von Humboldt's university in Berlin, which emphasized the integration of teaching and research, training in research as a fundamental component of the university, academic freedom for faculty, and an emphasis on critical thought.[2]

Universities in Canada were shaped more by the British tradition with its emphasis on undergraduate education, academic self-governance, and academic free speech.

During the latter half of the nineteenth century, the American government adopted legislation that established land-grant colleges to
teach practical arts, such as agriculture, mechanical arts, military tactics,
and home economics, while not excluding other scientific or classical
studies; thereby adding a new dimension to the mission of the
university.

Harold Shapiro summarized this complex mix that shaped the
American university:

> The particular institutional structure of the modern American
> university emerged from the Colonial colleges, from land-
> grant colleges, and from a set of new private universities, as
> well as from a complex set of influences. These influences
> included not only different European models . . . but also
> some distinctly American needs and traditions such as the
> rather universalistic outlook of liberal Protestantism; a cultur-
> al preference for meritocracy; a commitment to increasing our
> material welfare; a certain kind of egalitarianism; immigra-
> tion; industrialization; and the economic forces emanating
> from a rapidly industrializing nation whose economy was
> organized around private markets.[3]

Over the first sixty years of the twentieth century, Canadian universities increasingly were influenced by the patterns developing in the
United States. Although Robin Harris points to some distinctive characteristics of Canadian universities, the growing similarities with their
American counterparts are more notable.[4]

Despite this mixed brew of traditions and influences, North
American universities are remarkably similar in characterizing their
fundamental purpose as serving the public good by preserving, transmitting, and advancing knowledge. For the most part, they recognize
that this requires institutional autonomy so that their educational and
scholarly work cannot be redirected or halted because it offends powerful interests, be they state, religious, ideological, or corporate. Also,
universities widely acknowledge that academic staff must have

academic freedom: that is, the right to teach, undertake scholarly work, publish, and participate in the work of the institution and the community without restriction by prescribed doctrine or institutional censorship.[5]

There has, however, been a growing concern over past twenty years that universities and their mission to serve the public good are being compromised by commercialization. Lawrence C. Soley, in his 1995 book *Leasing the Ivory Tower*, argued that "corporate foundation and tycoon money has had a major, deleterious impact on universities. Financial considerations have altered academic priorities, reduced the importance of teaching, degraded the integrity of academic journals, and determined what research is conducted at universities."[6] A decade later and a bit more colourfully, Jennifer Washburn wrote: "Since 1980 . . . a foul wind has blown over the campuses of our nation's universities. Its source is . . . the growing role that commercial values have assumed in academic life."[7] In *Universities in the Marketplace*, Harvard's former president Derek Bok reflected on how the trend to commercialization developed, the dangers it poses for universities, and what academic leaders could do to limit the risk to their institutions.[8]

Similar concerns were first seriously addressed in the Canadian context in Janice Newson and Howard Buchbinder's thoughtful 1988 analysis *The University Means Business*, and subsequently by others.[9]

While the quantity of writing on this subject may be relatively recent, the concern has a long history. Clyde Barrow reminded us of Marx and Engels's observation that "the class which has the means of material production at its disposal has control at the same time over the means of mental production."[10] In reflecting on American higher education in the late nineteenth and early twentieth centuries, Barrow argues: "The corporate ideal as applied to the university was actually a class-political program designed to conquer ideological power. . . . In this respect, the emergence of American universities is best understood as a cultural component of the Industrial Revolution, related transformations of class structure, and the culmination of these upheavals in the social rationalization of the progressive era."[11]

Thorsten Veblen, in his 1918 critique, *The Higher Learning in America*, observed that "the intrusion of business principles in the universities goes to weaken and retard the pursuit of learning, and therefore to defeat the ends for which a university is maintained."[12] Writing during the ascendancy of the anti–Vietnam War movement, Theodore Roszak argued that "the academy has very rarely been a place of daring. One might perhaps count on the fingers of one hand the eras in which the university has been anything better than the handmaiden of official society: the social club of the ruling elites, the training schools of whatever functionaries the status quo required."[13]

The reality of universities is more complex. While their failures to be places that honour and protect the human quest to advance, transmit and preserve knowledge are notable, they remain the one institution in contemporary society that explicitly claims as its mission (in the words of the University of Toronto's statement of purpose) a dedication to be a place:

> in which the learning and scholarship of every member may flourish, with vigilant protection for individual human rights, and a resolute commitment to the principles of equal opportunity, equity and justice . . . [including the right] to raise deeply disturbing questions and provocative challenges to the cherished beliefs of society at large and of the university itself. It is this human right to radical, critical teaching and research with which the University has the duty above all to be concerned; for there is no one else, no other institution and no other office in our modern liberal democracy, which is the custodian of this most precious and vulnerable right of the liberated human spirit.[14]

This book provides a more intimate look at the reality of today's universities where the idealism expressed in statements like the University of Toronto's is at risk — living uncomfortably with the realpolitik of coping with underfunding, a society dominated by a market mentality, an increasingly interventionist state, and aggressive special interests determined to shape what the university is and does.

Part I, "Corporate Sponsorship and the Loss of Integrity," begins with a look at the relationship between the university and two industries that have sparked considerable concern in the academic world — tobacco and pharmaceuticals. Joanna Cohen asks if the academic world can retain its integrity and credibility when it associates with the tobacco industry — an industry responsible for so much suffering and death and for manipulation of scientific research. She explores how the tobacco companies benefit from their association with universities and the inadequacy of conflict of interest and disclosure policies that are put in place to protect the integrity of academic research supported by the tobacco industry. She ends by posing key questions that the university community should be asking before accepting tobacco industry research money.

Arthur Schafer looks at the implications of the extensive funding for scientific research from the pharmaceutical industry, noting that university partnerships with industry have grown significantly as academics are under increasing pressure to bring in research funding. Schafer suggests that university researchers put themselves in a conflict of interest when they accept corporate research funding. He is careful to say that this does not mean they will consciously allow their work to be corrupted, but argues that there is a real danger of an unconscious bias. His provocative essay suggests that the most promising solution to this problem is an outright ban on corporate funding for university research.

Some universities have responded to issues raised by Schafer and Cohen by refusing to accept research money from certain funders, such as the tobacco industry. This has been welcomed by some as long overdue and rejected by others as a gross violation of the academic freedom of researchers at those universities.[15] Sheldon Krimsky looks the conflict between the broader university community setting funding policies that apply to all researchers and the academic freedom of individual academics to research and teach as they wish. He proposes a novel framework that identifies two types of normative standards — those that should be common across all universities and a second set that are university specific, enabling each institution to set additional standards that reflect its own traditions and its own academic culture and values. He tests this framework by looking at tobacco research and weapons research.

In Part II, the focus shifts to the experiences of individual scholars who challenge powerful interests. David Healy, a leading authority on psychopharmacology, has long raised questions about how the pharmaceutical industry influences medical research — suppressing unfavourable research findings, ghost writing articles for leading medical journals, and blocking funding for research that questions the industry's claims about its products. He provides a riveting autobiographical account of the challenges he has faced from colleagues, scientific journals, and the industry, especially after raising questions about the efficacy of antidepressants and about whether, for some patients, antidepressants can induce suicidality. He contemplates how academics become part of the marketing operations of the pharmaceutical industry, and what can be done to recapture scientific integrity.

Brenda Gallie provides another autobiographical view into the experience of an eminent researcher who upheld her ethical principles in the face of institutional opposition. As a distinguished professor of medicine at the University of Toronto and head of the Cancer and Blood Research Program at the Hospital for Sick Children's Research Institute, Gallie became aware of the problems being faced by one of her staff, Dr. Nancy Olivieri, whose own case subsequently became international news.[16] Assuming the Hospital administration had misunderstood what was at issue in Olivieri's case, Gallie spoke with her administrative colleagues, only to have her own position put in jeopardy when the institute's head wrote her that her accountability to him required her to put aside what she saw as her moral duty. Subsequently, families requiring testing for a rare cancer gene (a test Gallie's lab had developed — and one of two places in the world where the test could be reliably done) were told that the Ontario Government would no longer fund the test. Over the next five years, Gallie had to borrow more than half a million dollars to personally cover the costs of testing, so that Ontario families could have the same access to care as others across North America. She reflects on these experiences, how they were resolved and what lessons can be learned.

In a very different context at the First Nations University of Canada, Blair Stonechild, then the head of indigenous studies at the university and a leading authority on aboriginal post-secondary education in Canada, relates an incident following his criticism of the unprecedented actions of the university's board chair. Created by the Federation of Saskatchewan Indian Nations (FSIN), the First Nations University was thrown into disarray when the board chair, who was first vice-president of the FSIN, arbitrarily suspended three senior administrators and seized and copied the university's computer records. Learning that Stonechild was to be keynote speaker at Canada's Assembly of First Nations' National Symposium on Post-secondary Education, the FSIN intervened to have him removed as the speaker. Because of a strong union contract, his post at the university was secure and his faculty union was able to take the matter to arbitration as a violation of Stonechild's academic freedom.

In the third part, attention turns to threats to the integrity of academics and academic work that come from special interests that infiltrate the academy and use it to give credence to their ideas. Canadians frequently are bemused and troubled by the foothold creationism and its progeny, intelligent design, have gained in the United States through the efforts of pseudo-scientific initiatives like the Discovery Institute[17] with its stable of scientific "fellows."[18] Gary Bauslaugh, Pat Walden, and Brian Alters tell the embarrassing story of how Canada's national research funding agency for social sciences and humanities responded to Alters's research proposal to examine the detrimental effects of popularizing intelligent design theory. In rejecting the proposal, the granting agency's peer-review committee said it did not feel "there was adequate justification for the assumption in the proposal that the theory of Evolution, and not Intelligent Design theory, was correct." Through the exchange of correspondence that followed this decision, the authors explore the steadfast refusal of the funding agency to retract or explain the committee's position in regard to intelligent design. The authors question the wisdom of decisions about funding for scientific education being in the control of those who may know little science.

Donald Gutstein examines how well-funded libertarian and neocon-servative think tanks are financing the work of sympathetic intellectu-als who are changing the face of universities in the United States and Canada. He examines the pioneering ideas of former US Supreme Court Justice Lewis Powell who, in 1971, called on the business com-munity to establish a staff of highly qualified scholars to counter the criticism of capitalism and write and speak for the business communi-ty. Gutstein traces the aftermath — right-wing charitable foundations giving hundreds of millions of dollars to create libertarian and neocon-servative think tanks in the United Kingdom, the United States, and Canada. He details the work of key think tanks and major donors and their efforts to transform the academic world.

Shadia Drury drills deeper into this changing character of academia by looking at the work and influence of Leo Strauss, the University of Chicago's legendary neoconservative guru, and his students. She exam-ines how Strauss cultivated an ideological elite who challenged the embrace of other cultures and values within higher education and who became key players for the right wing in the administration of George W. Bush in the United States and Stephen Harper in Canada.

Marcus Harvey opens Part IV with an examination of how Middle Eastern politics is playing out in the university world. Against a back-ground of the efforts of David Horowitz[19] and the American Council of Trustees and Alumni to challenge what they perceive to be the anti-Americanism on US campuses, Harvey explores the concerted (and often successful) efforts to attack leading academic critics of American Middle Eastern policy, including Norman Finkelstein, John J. Mearsheimer, Stephen M. Walt, and Joseph Massad. He considers the damaging effects of these culture wars on the university community and how academics should respond.

Broadening the focus, Kevin Mattson puts into historical perspective David Horowitz's current attack on the university. Taking the reader on a brief trip through the relationship between American conservatives and the academic world, Mattson shows how Horowitz has abandoned the conservative traditions of William F. Buckley and Allan Bloom, with their disdain for what they perceived as the pervasive relativism of the left. He argues that Horowitz sounds a note of postmodernism, stressing the indeterminacy of knowledge, while carrying over the older conservative distrust of intellectuals and the professoriate into his efforts to get state legislatures across the United States to adopt his academic bill of rights, which empowers the state to monitor classrooms. Mattson concludes with his own ideas on how to deal with this challenge to the future of higher education and the future of democracy.

Challenges to the integrity of academic work come not only from outside the academic world but also from within the academy. The most notable example is the production-driven research culture that the academic community has created and maintains, often to its own detriment. Sometimes a truly horrific event is required to cause self-reflection. After Concordia University engineering professor Valery Fabrikant, feeling thwarted and deeply angry at the failure of all his legitimate and illegitimate efforts to secure a tenured professorship, killed four colleagues and gravely injured a fifth, a University-commissioned report examined the circumstances of this tragedy. While making clear that nothing in their findings diminishes Dr. Fabrikant's responsibility for the murders, the report usefully shines a light on the production-driven research culture, common across North American universities, that was an important part of the context at Concordia. In fields like physical sciences and engineering, where research is highly specialized and very expensive and access to funding is limited and highly competitive, success depends on the ability to produce results. As noted in the independent committee's report for Concordia:

> "Production" . . . can come to be measured primarily in terms of the quantity of units of output, rather than their quality, and to be maximized for its own sake, without regard to externalities — which it generates. . . . Too often university honours, research grants and industrial contracts are awarded on the basis of numbers of publications, rather than on their quality and significance.

> . . . Strong pressures to be prolific . . . may in turn lead to
> the adoption of strategies for being as prolific as possible, and
> . . . some of these strategies may promote undesirable behav-
> iour.[20]

The authors provide a thoughtful discussion of undesirable behaviours generated in such a culture.[21]

Mary Burgan brings these issues to Part V of this volume by addressing how they apply in the humanities. In her article, Burgan notes that the risk-averse, quantity-driven culture of many university humanities departments has led to reliance on outside opinion and tabulation of numbers rather than internal evaluation of content and quality. She suggests that faculty hustle to show their wares like car salespeople vying for Seller of the Month, and departments compete for superstars, making the university more like the National Football League in its approach — meaning there is no longer room for merely good faculty. She examines the various inquiries into these issues by the Modern Languages Association and finds them wanting. Burgan encourages consideration of Ernest Boyer's work as pointing in the right direction. She concludes with a number of suggestions for changing the production culture.

Part VI turns attention to the university being run in a corporate manner. Rosemary Deem reports on her ongoing research on the new managerialism in British universities, rightly noting that many aspects will be familiar in higher education elsewhere. According to Deem, the new managerialism brings private sector organizational practices into the public sector, including the primacy of management over other functions and a concentration on doing more with less. This approach, as she notes, is very different from the collegial self-governance that has been traditional among academics. She explores the implications for teachers and researchers of the managerialist focus on efficiency, performance, targets, outcomes, markets, and rankings. Her findings show that the integrity of academic work is being threatened, as creative aspects of teaching and research are being subordinated to other considerations, and as workloads are increasing with the growth of both internal and external audit systems. Deem concludes with recommendations of what can be done by both academics and those in administrative positions to maintain academic integrity in the current climate.

From the perspective of a Canadian university president, Michael Higgins issues a clarion call for the university to recover earlier notions of collegiality and subsidiarity, the latter meaning appropriate independence, institutional integrity, and freedom of choice, so that the university is neither subservient to nor wholly disengaged from a larger accountability. He thoughtfully points to John Henry Newman's conceptions of a university, including that management should not be in the sole hands of the rector, but shared with the professoriate. He also notes Newman's view that the purpose of the university is the enlargement of sensibility, cultivation of the mind, and uncompromised pursuit of excellence, not to be held hostage to the demands of economic pragmatism or political whims. Higgins calls for meeting the challenges of higher education in the twenty-first century by looking to those essential elements of the past that can be revitalized and put into the present context.

In the final chapter of that part, I examine the restructuring of academic work as universities and colleges are redefined (and redefine themselves) as servants of the market and commerce. In this context, public funding declines, and senior administrations turn increasingly to private-sector managerial models that prize lower labour costs and greater managerial "flexibility." The chapter reports on the dramatic transformation of academics from tenured and tenure-track staff to contingent workers, with low pay, few benefits, no tenure, compromised assurance of academic freedom, and no voice in the governance of their institutions. I argue that universities and colleges cannot fulfill their role in democratic society — offering high-quality education to their students and undertaking valuable scholarship for the benefit of their communities and society — when academic staff are reduced to closely managed production workers. Options are explored.

The book concludes with Jon Thompson's broad-ranging consideration of the growing threats to scholarly integrity, the reasons for that growth, and what can be done. While considering some high-profile examples of ethical misconduct, Thomson notes that, however spectacular they may be, these individual cases are less damaging to the public interest than the wider systemic corrosion of scientific integrity. He cites examples of the latter, such as decades of use of public money to channel cancer research strategies into directions favourable to certain business interests and the state-orchestrated anti-communist hysteria of the Cold War years, which caused the effective disappearance of academic freedom and the arbitrary and improper destruction of academic careers and reorientation of scientific work in line with official ideology, not unlike pressures on some Middle Eastern scholars today. He argues that much can be attributed to the complex of inducements to individuals and their institutions by government agencies and private corporations, while pointing out that these inducements do not absolve individual academics from responsibility. He then examines how we can meet the challenge to reorient universities and colleges to serving the broader public interest.

I. CORPORATE SPONSORSHIP AND THE LOSS OF INTEGRITY

1

PRINCIPLES AND INTEREST: IS THE ACADEMY AN ACCOMPLICE IN A CORPORATE-CAUSED PANDEMIC?

Joanna E. Cohen

INTRODUCTION

Academic integrity is a fundamental value of the academy and is important for sustaining public trust in our universities. One challenge to academic integrity originates from pressures exerted from external sponsors. A key example of how an industry can exploit academia to pursue its own interests, with life and death implications, is tobacco. Can academia retain its integrity, and its credibility, when it associates with an industry responsible for so much human suffering — one that has systematically worked to distort the scientific record? This chapter begins by briefly describing the global burden of tobacco products, and presents the tobacco industry as the disease vector. It then provides an overview of the tobacco industry's malpractices vis-à-vis academia and science, describes how these companies gain from associating with universities, elucidates some of the recent links between tobacco companies and Canadian universities, and discusses the inadequacy of conflict of interest and disclosure policies in dealing with these relationships. The paper concludes with some questions that would be worth considering when taking action to address the links between tobacco companies and universities.

THE TOBACCO PANDEMIC

Despite over five decades of scientific evidence regarding the harmful effects of tobacco products, they remain the leading cause of preventable death and disease in Canada, as well as in many other developed countries. Cigarettes kill half of all lifetime users when used exactly as intended by their manufacturers, and half of these die in middle age (age 35–69).[22] Although smoking prevalence in Canada decreased from 35 percent in 1985[23] to 19 percent twenty years later,[24] there remain almost five million Canadians who smoke,[25] with an annual tobacco-caused death toll in this country of about 37,000 and economic costs of tobacco use and misuse estimated at $17 billion in 2002 alone.[26] What is even more staggering are the global statistics. Already more men smoke in developing countries than in industrialized countries. In 2000, there were an estimated 4.2 million deaths caused by tobacco products worldwide, with half of these occurring in developing countries.[27] It is forecast that worldwide annual tobacco deaths will jump to 10 million by 2030, with 70 percent of this burden placed on developing countries.

THE TOBACCO INDUSTRY AS A VECTOR OF DISEASE

In public health, the epidemiologic triangle (Figure 1.1) is a valuable framework for understanding the causes of disease and for determining useful entry points for intervening to reduce the prevalence and incidence of disease. The framework was originally used to understand infectious diseases but has since been applied much more widely. Although a triangle, this model has four components: (1) the agent (the what) — what actually causes disease; (2) the host (the who) — who gets exposed to the agent and who gets sick; (3) the environment (the where) — favourable surroundings and conditions external to the host that cause or allow the host to get exposed to the agent; and (4) the vector (the how) — a nonhuman entity that spreads the agent to the host. An example of how the epidemiologic triangle traditionally plays out is in the case of malaria: the malaria parasite is the agent, the host is the human susceptible to the parasite, the environment encompasses the external conditions that support the survival of the agent and vector, and the vector is the mosquito. Public health interventions can aim to reduce the toxicity of the parasite, reduce the susceptibility of the individuals to the parasite, and create an environment that discourages the survival of mosquitoes. Similarly, one can apply the model to the tobacco problem[28]: in this case, the agent is the tobacco product, the host is the individual susceptible to using tobacco products, the environment is the social norms and the program and policy interventions that aim to discourage use of tobacco products, and the vector — the entity responsible for spreading the agent to the host — is the tobacco companies. Viewing the tobacco industry in this light highlights the primary role it plays in the tobacco pandemic and underscores it as a legitimate and integral part of the disease process that must be dealt with.

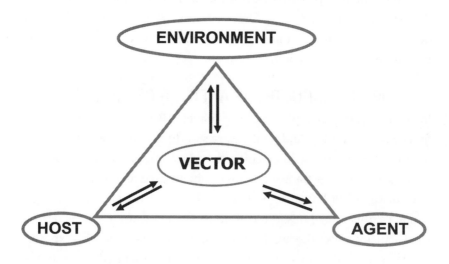

Figure 1.1 The Epidemiologic Triangle. The Epidemiologic Triangle consists of four components — environment, agent, host, and vector. The model implies that each must be analyzed and understood in order to predict patterns of a disease. A change in any of the components will alter an existing equilibrium to increase or decrease the frequency of the disease.

THE TOBACCO INDUSTRY HAS SUBVERTED SCIENCE

The foregoing Findings of Fact demonstrate that, over the course of approximately fifty years, different Defendants, at different times, took the following actions in order to maintain their public positions on smoking and disease-related issues, nicotine addiction, nicotine manipulation, and low tar cigarettes, in order to protect themselves from smoking and health related claims in litigation, and in order to avoid regulation which they viewed as harmful: they suppressed, concealed, and terminated scientific research; they destroyed documents including scientific reports and studies; and they repeatedly and intentionally improperly asserted the attorney-client and work product privileges over many thousands of documents (not just pages) to thwart disclosure to plaintiffs in smoking and health related litigation and to federal regulatory agencies, and to shield those documents from the harsh light of day.

— Honorable Gladys Kessler, United States District Court for the District of Columbia, *United States v. Philip Morris*, 2006.[29]

In 2006, after six years of litigation and nine months of trial, the Honorable Gladys Kessler rendered her ruling on the tobacco industry's fifty-year conspiracy to defraud the public. Importantly, the court found that the fraud continues to this day.

Notwithstanding the importance of Judge Kessler's ruling, documentation of the tobacco industry's history of scientific misconduct has existed for a number of years. Much of the evidence of tobacco companies' wrongdoings come from their own internal documents, documents that were made public following litigation by US states to recover the costs they paid for health care to treat tobacco-caused illnesses. Due to this litigation against tobacco companies, the public has access to millions of internal tobacco industry documents.[30]

Research has exposed the tobacco industry's attempts to deflect attention away from tobacco as a health hazard and to generate good publicity for tobacco companies.[31] Once tobacco companies realized they had lost the debate on smoking and health, their public relations and efforts to manipulate the scientific record turned to second-hand smoke (also known as passive smoking, or environmental tobacco smoke). This was a very important battle for the industry, because now the implications were no longer paternalistic: with second-hand smoke, tobacco products harm innocent bystanders — people who choose not to use these products. The tobacco industry has worked hard to conceal the harmful effects of second-hand smoke, and some of these efforts have been documented, ranging from sponsoring scientific studies showing no adverse effects of second-hand smoke, to discrediting reports reviewing the evidence on second-hand smoke, to working to prevent legislation protecting people from second-hand smoke.[32] There is also evidence that the tobacco industry has worked to subvert public policy protecting people from the harmful effects of tobacco products,[33] and it has attempted to undermine tobacco control efforts more generally.[34] Much of the research funded by tobacco companies has been strategically directed by lawyers.[35] Strategies have been systematic, calculated, and coordinated internationally.

One specific example of how the tobacco industry has worked to subvert normal scientific processes has been described by Ong and Glantz (2000).[36] In preparation for the release of the International Agency for Research on Cancer (IARC) European study on the link between second-hand smoke and lung cancer, Philip Morris led an inter-industry effort to undermine the study's findings. Their strategy involved:

1. A scientific component that included industry-sponsored research to counteract the IARC findings;

2. A communications component that planned to influence public opinion through manipulation of the media; and

3. A government component that aimed to minimize the introduction of increased restrictions on smoking.

While the IARC study cost $2 million over ten years, Philip Morris had planned to spend $2 million in one year plus up to $4 million on research. The IARC study found a 16 percent increase in the risk of lung cancer among non-smoking spouses of smokers and a 17 percent increase in risk among non-smokers exposed to tobacco smoke in the workplace; although the results were consistent with previous research, the sample size of the IARC study was too small to detect a statistically significant increase in risk with 95 percent confidence. The media portrayed the study as showing no increase in risk.

The World Health Organization (WHO) Committee of Experts on Tobacco Industry Documents published their report in 2000, documenting evidence of tobacco company efforts to influence and undermine WHO tobacco control policies and programs.[37] The expert committee discovered — based on internal tobacco industry documents — that the industry employed a range of strategies to weaken or prevent tobacco control efforts:

> The evidence shows that tobacco companies have operated for many years with the deliberate purpose of subverting the efforts of WHO to address tobacco issues. The attempted subversion has been elaborate, well financed, sophisticated and usually invisible. That tobacco companies resist proposals for tobacco control comes as no surprise, but what is now clear is the scale, intensity and, importantly, the tactics, of their campaigns. To many in the international community, tobacco prevention may be seen today as a struggle against chemical addiction, cancers, cardiovascular diseases and other health consequences of smoking. This inquiry adds to the mounting evidence that it is also a struggle against an active, organized and calculating industry.[38]

Indeed, the famous German pathologist, Rudolph Virchow (1821–1902), understood the political nature of disease, as illustrated by his observation that "Medicine is but politics writ large."[39] This underscores the need to consider and tackle not only the pathological causes of disease but also the political forces responsible for disease; treating only the pathological causes will not have a sustained impact. The WHO Committee of Experts on Tobacco Industry Documents made the following statement regarding the role of the tobacco industry in the tobacco pandemic:

> Tobacco use is unlike other threats to global health. Infectious diseases do not employ multinational public relations firms. There are no front groups to promote the spread of cholera. Mosquitoes have no lobbyists.[40]

Not only do public health efforts have to work toward minimizing the health burden caused by the use of tobacco products but also these efforts are actively countered at every turn by an industry that does all it can to maximize the sale of its products. The tobacco industry's links with academia are clearly one means by which these companies aim to resist strategies for reducing tobacco use.

Corporate social responsibility is a current trend whereby corporations take responsibility for the impact of their activities on customers, suppliers, employees, shareholders, communities, and the environment in all aspects of their operations. The intent is for organizations to voluntarily take steps that go beyond their statutory obligations. Tobacco companies have used corporate social responsibility as a strategy to minimize controls on these companies and on the use of their products. This is a worldwide systematic strategy in which universities play an integral role. In a 1999 British American Tobacco (BAT) internal document, Michael Prideaux states: "In addition, the process [the Social Reporting Process] will not only help British American Tobacco achieve a position of recognized responsibility but also provide 'air cover' from criticism while improvements are being made. Essentially, it provides a degree of publicly endorsed amnesty."[41]

Three years later, in 2002, British American Tobacco gave the University of Nottingham almost £4 million to establish an international centre for corporate social responsibility within their business school. That same year, St. Michael's College at the University of

Toronto took $150,000 from Imperial Tobacco Ltd. (a tobacco company owned by BAT) for its continuing education certificate program in corporate social responsibility. Michael Prideaux is currently the Director of Corporate and Regulatory Affairs for BAT. His photo is on their Web site on a page entitled "Operating Responsibly" along with the statement "If a business is managing products that pose health risks, it is all the more important that it does so responsibly." Academia plays an important role in a tobacco company's efforts to appear to be a responsible corporate citizen.

HOW DO TOBACCO COMPANIES GAIN FROM ASSOCIATING WITH UNIVERSITIES?

In our 1999 published commentary on "institutional addiction to tobacco," my colleagues and I proposed a schematic to assist in considering the many ways tobacco companies (as well as other corporate entities) can be linked with universities (Figure 1.2).[42] The schematic has four elements: universities, university boards of governors, researchers, and the tobacco industry. The arrows illustrate the types of relationships that can occur between a corporation and academia. For example, tobacco companies can give donations, endowments, and scholarship funds to universities. Universities can invest their pension plans in tobacco stock. There can be cross-ties on the boards of universities and tobacco companies; that is, senior officials of tobacco companies can sit on the boards or high-level committees of the university, and university officials can sit on the boards of tobacco companies. Tobacco companies can give research funding to researchers through their university, and researchers can produce research that is distracting or has the appearance of furthering the tobacco and health "controversy," and they can act as consultants or expert witnesses for tobacco companies.

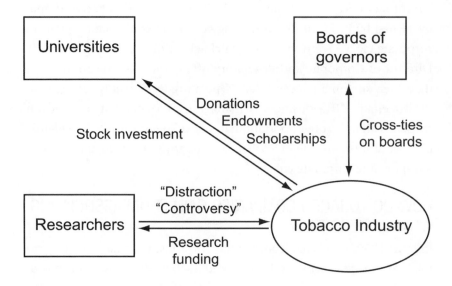

Figure 1.2. Relationships between universities and the tobacco industry. (J.E. Cohen et al., Tobacco Control *8[1899]: 70–4.)*

For a number of reasons, companies like to form associations with universities:

1. Companies Acquire Decency by Association
There was a turning of the tide of public opinion in 1994 when the CEOs of the top seven tobacco companies in the United States raised their hands and swore to tell the truth before a US senate subcommittee, and then testified that they believe nicotine is not addictive.[43] At that moment the tobacco industry lost much of its remaining credibility, and, as a result, had to rely more on other methods to gain credibility, respectability, and innocence by association. One way they attempt to do this is through relationships with universities and university faculty members.

2. Researchers Can Create Doubt about Harmful Effects
Tobacco companies develop relationships with researchers who help to create doubt about the harmful effects of smoking and second-hand

smoke and about the impact of bans on smoking in public places, among other topics. As a result of litigation, US tobacco companies have had to disclose all of their internal documents. Consequently, we now have information about many of their strategies for maximizing cigarette sales and minimizing the effectiveness of tobacco control efforts. A Philip Morris document from the 1980s lays out its project "White Coat" strategy, with the white coat ostensibly referring to the scientist's lab coat.

> Philip Morris presented to the UK industry their global strategy on environmental tobacco smoke [ETS]. In every major international area (US, Europe, Australia, Far East, South America, Central American and Spain) they are proposing, in key countries, to set up a team of scientists organized by one national coordinating scientist and American lawyers, to review scientific literature or carry out work on ETS to keep the controversy alive. They are spending vast sums of money to do so, and on the European front Covington & Burling, lawyers for the Tobacco Institute in the US, are proposing to set up a London office from March 1988 to coordinate these activities.[44]

Keeping the controversy alive creates doubt.

3. Distracting Studies Deflect Negative Attention

Tobacco companies also like to deflect attention away from the harmful effects of their products through the publication of research findings attempting to demonstrate that other non-tobacco exposures can result in tobacco-related diseases, such as studies reporting that owning a pet bird can cause lung cancer.[45] These studies imply that cigarettes cannot be all that bad for you, thereby serving the need to deflect attention away from the harmful effects of tobacco products.

4. Companies Gain Credibility with Decision Makers

By forging links with academia, tobacco companies can influence decision makers, including politicians, bureaucrats, and the courts.

Particularly in the courtroom, tobacco companies not only present the research they have funded that supports their position but also, importantly, they highlight all the universities and researchers they have funded. Juries, judges, and the public understand implicitly that these tobacco companies cannot be so terrible if universities are taking their money. Thus, it does not matter which specific study was funded — tobacco companies use their relationships and links with universities to influence decision makers by making them more sympathetic to pro-tobacco perspectives.

ASSOCIATION WITH TOBACCO COMPANIES CAN HURT UNIVERSITIES

While tobacco companies benefit from their relationships with academia in a number of ways, universities can suffer harm:

Academics Can Be Co-opted to Speak for Industry

University officers can act as spokespeople for tobacco companies. For example, in a debate in the *British Medical Journal* on whether Nottingham University should give back tobacco money it received, Richard Smith, the then-editor of *BMJ* and a Professor at Nottingham, argued that the university should return the money. However, the university's vice-chancellor argued the opposite. The tobacco company was able to remain quietly in the background, rather than be present in the limelight, because university officials took the tobacco company position and made the arguments on its behalf. In a similar vein, Dr. Mimi Morocco, Director of Continuing Education at St. Michael's College at the University of Toronto, took on the role of tobacco company spokesperson in dealing with the Imperial Tobacco donation toward the college's certificate program in corporate social responsibility: "Despite public views of the company's practices, it is a lawful and legitimate business. . . . I don't see any conflict between the program and the donation. . . . Cigarettes are not an illegal or immoral product. Sure it's unhealthy, but smoking is a personal choice."[46]

Providing Silence

A harm that can be worse than acting as a spokesperson is silence (because it is not visible, and thus, next to impossible to expose). Rather than speaking out on issues that are important to society, university leaders can be silent in such debates. John Ralston Saul has hypothesized that one reason Canadian universities have witnessed a significant decline in public funding is that the public sees them as less and less relevant to the issues that are important to society.[47] Part of the reason for this viewpoint is that the financial relationships between universities and the private sector make it appear that universities are more interested in serving the needs of companies than the needs of society. At the same time, against this backdrop, the public is not seeing universities sufficiently participating in societal debates. When universities do weigh in, all too frequently they do not seem to be on the side of truth and justice but rather on the side of their corporate funders.

Shirking

Universities have a mission for excellent scholarship, outstanding education, service to society, and the pursuit of knowledge with the ultimate goal of making the world a better place. When academic institutions do not acknowledge the broader impacts of their links with tobacco companies and that engaging in these links is a conflict of interest, they are shirking their responsibility.

Universities May Appear to Sell Out

When universities invest their pension plans in tobacco stock they have a financial interest in tobacco companies doing well financially. Tobacco companies profit when they sell more cigarettes. But when more cigarettes are sold, more people die and suffer. Thus, by linking with tobacco companies, universities are not only financially benefiting from death and disease but also implicitly supporting it.

HOW EXTENSIVE ARE LINKS BETWEEN TOBACCO COMPANIES AND UNIVERSITIES?

There are certainly potential problems associated with accepting money from tobacco companies, but is it really an issue in practice? Are researchers and universities taking tobacco money? The National Cancer Institute of Canada funded a descriptive study of the link between Canadian universities and tobacco companies during the period 1996–1999. The goals of the study were to describe the extent of the policies and practices of Canadian universities with respect to research, donations, and investments and also to examine the extent of cross-ties on boards. Nine percent of Canadian universities said that they received tobacco research funding, almost a third received tobacco donations, and 15 percent said that they directly held tobacco stocks or bonds in 1999 (not including those that were part of a mutual or pooled fund). Among faculties of medicine, 25 percent reported receiving tobacco research funding, and 27 percent received tobacco donations.[48] No university banned tobacco research funding or donations, and at that time, only one banned tobacco investments.

There was also evidence of cross-ties on boards. At the time of the study, Imasco was the holding company of Canada's largest tobacco company, Imperial Tobacco, which commanded about 60 percent of the cigarette market. There were several instances of directors of Imasco simultaneously holding positions in academia. For example, John Pritchard was director of Imasco and at the same time president of the University of Toronto (U of T), director of the Association of Universities and Colleges of Canada, chairman of the Council of Ontario Universities and a member of the U of T capital campaign. The Honourable Paule Gauthier offers another example: while serving as a director of Rothmans Inc., she was director and president of Laval University and the Laval University Foundation, and was a member of the board of governors of the Royal Military College of Canada. Additional examples include Charles Hantho, who was a Director of Imasco while holding the position of chairman of the board of governors at York University, and Rob Parker, who was president of the

Canadian Tobacco Manufacturers' Council (the trade and lobbying organization on behalf of Canadian tobacco companies), while being on the Board of Directors of Women's College Hospital Foundation. These are prime examples of leaders in the university community having a fiduciary responsibility to maximize the tobacco company's bottom line. Not surprisingly, there was very little action on tobacco by the University of Toronto when Pritchard was the president.

Notwithstanding the harms listed above, there is some good news to report. A number of health institutions have, indeed, banned tobacco industry research support, including the University of Adelaide, the University of Melbourne, the University of Sydney, the University of Hong Kong, the Karolinska Institute, the London School of Hygiene and Tropical Medicine, the Roswell Park Cancer Institute, Brigham and Women's Hospital, the M.D. Anderson Cancer Centre; various schools of public health, including those at Harvard University, Johns Hopkins University, Columbia University, the University of North Carolina, and the University of Alberta just this year; various schools of medicine at Emory University, Harvard University, Johns Hopkins University; and the University of Alberta Faculty of Nursing.[49] The McCombs School of Business at the University of Texas at Austin has also rejected tobacco company support.[50] The cancer society research funding agency in Canada — the National Cancer Institute of Canada — and its counterparts in Norway and throughout Europe will not fund research teams that accept tobacco money. The UK cancer society goes somewhat further — they won't give money to researchers if anyone in their academic unit (faculty, school, or institute) takes tobacco money. In Australia, some state cancer councils will not fund researchers if anyone in their institution takes tobacco money.[51] In addition, there are at least three journals that will not review papers arising from tobacco-sponsored research.[52]

Several institutions have divested their tobacco interests, including Tufts, Harvard, City University of New York, Johns Hopkins, and recently, the University of Toronto. Tobacco divestment signals that profiting from tobacco sales is unacceptable. Clearly, such an action would undermine the respectability of the tobacco industry. Evidence from internal tobacco industry documents indicates that Philip Morris did respond to two cases of academic divestment and succeeded in minimizing the impact of these actions.[53] A key element of its anti-divestment strategy was to exploit university concerns about losing corporate research funding.

ARE CONFLICT OF INTEREST AND DISCLOSURE POLICIES ADEQUATE TO ADDRESS THESE CONCERNS?

People who oppose university or academic unit policies to stop taking tobacco money argue that conflict-of-interest and disclosure policies are adequate to ensure that researchers are not biased by the sponsors of their work. However, disclosure policies have been shown to be ineffective (see below), and there are at least two reasons to believe that conflict-of-interest policies are insufficient to deal with tobacco company sponsorship of research: (1) the evidence does not support this view, and (2) the harms from this sponsorship go beyond individual studies. Barnes and Bero studied review articles on the health effects of second-hand smoke and examined why investigators reached different conclusions.[54] Of the 106 review articles identified, 37 percent concluded that second-hand smoke is not harmful to health. Three-quarters (74 percent) of these "negative" reviews were written by authors with tobacco company affiliations. When the researchers ran a multivariate regression controlling for article quality, peer review status, article topic, and year of publication, having an author with a tobacco company affiliation was the only variable associated with a conclusion that second-hand smoke is not harmful.

Even if researchers were not biased by their sponsors, conflict-of-interest policies would still be insufficient for guarding against the misuse of studies.[55] To understand why, one must view this issue from a higher vantage point: not only do tobacco companies use the studies they fund to bolster their position, they also make extensive use of their links with researchers and universities to gain credibility and respectability by association. Even if tobacco company research grants were unrestricted, the scientist had full ownership of data, there were no constraints on publishing, and the funding source was fully disclosed in publications, the scientist's good name and the reputation of

School of Occupational Health
École de Santé au Travail
McGill University
(514) 398-4238

Postal address
Dust Disease Research Unit
1140 Pine Avenue West
Montreal, PQ, Canada H3A 1A3

October 28, 1988

Dr Dunn
Imperial Tobacco Limited
3810, rue St-Antoine Street
Montréal, PQ
H4C 1B5

Dear Dr Dunn,

Here is our review of the paper by Collishaw, Tostowaryk and Wigle
published recently in the Canadian Journal of Public Health.

The epidemiological and statistical issues were quite complicated;
we hope we have dealt with them clearly. If further explanation is
needed please let us know.

As agreed, our fee for this work is $10,000. We would be grateful if
the payment could be made to McGill University, Account # 743-53 and
the cheque sent to Dr Nicola Cherry at this address.

With kind regards.

Yours sincerely,

J Corbett McDonald, MD FRCP
Professor

PS. I would wish to emphasis that there must be no publication of any
    part of this review under our name, and if any part of it should
    be published no reference should be made to us by name.

JCMcD/rc

enc.

Figure 1.3. Agreement for work between Imperial Tobacco Ltd. and a McGill professor.

the institution would be used to further the goals of the funder. And when the tobacco industry profits, the public's health suffers.

Conflict-of-interest policies do not guard against "distracting" research, nor do they protect against all forms of financial relationships. A letter to Dr. Dunn at Imperial Tobacco Ltd. from a McGill professor describes the agreement they had: Imperial Tobacco was to pay the professor $10,000 for a review of a four-page journal article (Figure 1.3). The professor took the money, despite knowing that knowledge of this work would not be good for his reputation: "PS. I would wish to emphasize that there must be no publication of any part of this review under our name, and if any part of it should be published no reference should be made to us by name."[56]

A front-page story in the March 26, 2008, issue of the *New York Times* provides an accounting of the limitations of disclosure policies.[57] In 2006, Dr. Claudia Henschke of the Weill Cornell Medical College published a study in the *New England Journal of Medicine* indicating that 80 percent of lung cancer deaths could be prevented through the widespread use of CT scans. The disclosure indicated that the study was funded by the Foundation for Lung Cancer: Early Detection, Prevention & Treatment. An investigation into tax records by the *New York Times* revealed the foundation was almost entirely supported by grants from the parent company of the Liggett Group, one of the top seven tobacco companies in the United States. The *Times* also reported that the study investigators did not disclose a patent and ten pending patents related to CT screening and follow-up in their articles and educational lectures. Although universities are responsible for ensuring adherence to conflict-of-interest policies, universities themselves can be conflicted. In this particular case, the academic institution was poised to benefit financially from Dr. Henschke's patent and pending patents, and university officials were on the board of the foundation. When universities themselves are conflicted, they can ignore the conflicts of interest of their faculty.

Not surprisingly, tobacco companies are among the strongest defenders of academic freedom, because of their need for the studies they sponsor to be credible. To this end, Philip Morris listed the following as a business objective in a 1998 internal document: ". . . [to] encourage ethics in science to promote academic freedom, so that research is judged on the basis of the science performed, not by who has performed the work, not by where the work was performed, nor who has funded it."[58]

MOVING FORWARD

While the evidence is clear that the tobacco industry has systematically worked to subvert the scientific process and continues to do so, and that the academy has (knowingly — at least, in some instances) played a supporting role in this deception, efforts by universities or academic units to sever their links with tobacco companies are often controversial and are opposed by those arguing that such efforts contravene academic freedom. Although a strong case has been made for dissolving university relationships with tobacco companies,[59] there are issues that do require further analysis and debate, particularly when considering whether the rationale for severing tobacco links can be generalized to other industries.

Some relevant questions include: When it comes to research funding, how clean is clean enough? How dirty is too dirty? How many degrees of separation are necessary for integrity to be protected? Is there ever a point at which minority viewpoints in society, such as the viewpoints of tobacco companies, should not be tolerated within academia? Does academic freedom go beyond freedom of expression, and should it extend to freedom to receive funding from any sponsor? How do different models of corporate funding of research and academia (for example, companies sponsoring research centres, contributing to departments, funding an endowed chair, or funding specific research projects) affect research integrity, faculty productivity, and technology transfer?

CONCLUSIONS

The tobacco industry has succeeded in sustaining and exploiting relationships with the academy that have undermined the scientific record while bolstering this industry's reputation, resulting in a maximization of tobacco sales, delayed implementation of evidence-based tobacco control interventions, and, consequently, a massive global burden of morbidity and mortality that is completely preventable.

Members of the academy, among others, have the duty to regularly ask ourselves "What do we know? When did we know it? What are we doing about it?" We now have sufficient evidence documenting how the academy has been, and continues to be, an accomplice in this corporate-caused pandemic. So, what are we going to do about it?

Universities have held a prestigious position in society. The public has looked to the academy for unbiased, just, and equitable guidance. Its response to issues, whether action or silence, has consequences. If universities fail to act on the knowledge that has accumulated about how they have aided and abetted tobacco companies in maximizing their profits at the expense of the public's health, they risk being seen as corrupt, arrogant, and irrelevant to issues of importance to the public. Their integrity and credibility are at stake.

2

THE UNIVERSITY AS CORPORATE HANDMAIDEN: WHO'RE YA GONNA TRUST?

Arthur Schafer

"Data is not information; information is not knowledge; knowledge is not wisdom."

— Frank Zappa

PROLOGUE: ANATOMY OF TWIN SCANDALS

I begin this essay by examining in detail a pair of research scandals whose genesis can, in significant ways, be traced to the new entrepreneurial spirit prevailing in our universities. Later, I will argue that, with the ever-growing importance of university-corporate "partnerships," scandals involving the integrity of university research may be expected to multiply in Canada, as they have elsewhere. The resulting loss of public trust is likely to be devastating to our universities and to the wider community they serve.

In this context, either the Apotex-Olivieri scandal or the Prozac-Healy scandal would have been entirely suitable as illustrative examples. In both the Olivieri and the Healy cases, the University of Toronto failed miserably to defend the academic freedom of researchers who spoke publicly about dangers associated with drugs they were investigating. In both instances, there were wealthy and powerful drug companies hovering in the background: Apotex, in the case of Nancy

Olivieri; Eli Lilly, in the case of David Healy. But, having written previously[60] about both of these shameful episodes in the history of Canada's largest research university, I have instead chosen the more recent Vioxx and Celebrex scandals to illustrate the ways in which the integrity of university research is threatened by the entrepreneurial university and the new class of entrepreneurial academics who labour in its laboratories and teaching hospitals. I am packaging together the Vioxx and Celebrex cases because they nicely illustrate the perils that may befall university research when it is funded by for-profit corporations. Sadly, there is no shortage of other examples one could have chosen instead.

THE VIGOR AND CLASS TRIALS: COX-2 INHIBITORS IN THE DOCK

The Celebrex scandal involved a drug trial with sixteen authors, eight of them employees of the drug company Pharmacia (later purchased by Pfizer, the world's largest drug company). The other authors were from eight different American universities. All sixteen, however, were paid consultants to the company. The Vioxx scandal encompassed the world's third largest drug company, Merck, and the world's highest impact medical journal,[61] the *New England Journal of Medicine (NEJM)*, as well as its editor, Dr. Jeffrey Drazen. It also involved, in the role of first author, a Canadian scientist, Dr. Caroline Bombardier, from the University of Toronto's Faculty of Medicine. Since this is the same faculty and the same university that were earlier implicated in the Olivieri and Healy scandals mentioned above and elsewhere in this volume, some readers may infer that the research environment at the U of T is ethically tainted to a degree greater than that which might be found elsewhere in Canada. Whether or not this conclusion is sustainable, it is certainly true that when it comes to attracting massive corporate funding, the U of T is far and away the most successful university in Canada. I shall argue that corporate funding of university research is at or very close to the heart of all these scandals.

In November of 2000, the *New England Journal of Medicine* published the VIGOR (Vioxx gastrointestinal outcomes research) trial. The trial appeared to demonstrate that those patients who were randomized to Vioxx experienced fewer stomach bleeds than those who received an older and much cheaper drug called naproxen.[62] Publication of the VIGOR trial in the prestigious *New England Journal of Medicine* (NEJM) launched Vioxx on its career as a blockbuster arthritis drug, with annual sales exceeding $1 billion. The University of Toronto was very proud of the fact that Dr. Bombardier was the lead author of this article.

A few months earlier, the *Journal of the American Medical Association (JAMA)* had published the CLASS (Celecoxib long-term arthritis safety study) trial, which purported to show that Pharmacia's drug, Celebrex, competitor of Vioxx, was associated with lower rates of stomach and intestinal ulcers when compared to two older and much less expensive drugs.[63] Based largely on this publication, again in a highly prestigious journal, Celebrex, like Vioxx, instantly became a blockbuster arthritis drug.

Vioxx (rofecoxib) and Celebrex (celecoxib), belong to a class of drugs known as COX-2 inhibitors. They are used for the treatment of arthritic pain. When these drugs were first introduced to the marketplace they were heavily promoted by their respective companies and were widely hailed by the mass media as "miracle aspirin." The miracle was alleged to be the comparative absence of serious adverse effects. Promotional advertising for each drug, aimed directly at both doctors and potential consumers, ran to well over $100 million annually.

Vioxx was not finally withdrawn from the market until September of 2004, when a second clinical trial, the ADVANTAGE (assessment of differences between Vioxx and Naproxen to ascertain gastrointestinal tolerability and effectiveness) trial, provided damaging evidence of the cardiac risks posed to patients taking the drug.[64] Tens of millions of Americans and millions of Canadians took Vioxx and Celebrex before both the VIGOR and the CLASS trials were exposed as being scientifically and ethically suspect.[65] Vioxx was withdrawn from the market in 2004. Celebrex was allowed to stay on the market, but was required to carry a "black box" warning on its label.

Vioxx was withdrawn entirely from the market, because it was shown to carry unacceptable risks of heart attacks and strokes.[66] The cardiovascular risks of Celebrex were comparable to those of Vioxx, and many critics thought that it, too, should have been withdrawn because of an unfavourable risk-benefit ratio.

The miasma of scandal that surrounds both of these drugs does not arise simply because they were found to be much more dangerous than first advertised. Rather, the scandal arises because the university (and company) researchers responsible for the conduct and publication of these two trials were discovered to have interpreted their data in an insupportable manner, and worse, to have suppressed vital data that would, if disclosed, have enabled doctors and patients to make a better informed choice about whether to recommend or use the drugs.

The Celebrex authors submitted data (for publication in JAMA) from the first six months of the CLASS trial. Based on these data, Celebrex appeared to be associated with lower rates of stomach and intestinal ulcers than the comparator drugs, ibuprofen and diclofenac. Significantly, however, but unknown to the editors of JAMA, the researchers, at the time they submitted their article, had possessed data for a full year. Equally or more significant, almost all the ulcer complications occurred in Celebrex patients during the second six months of the trial. When the full year's data were considered, the apparent safety advantage of Celebrex disappeared. In other words, the millions of patients who took Celebrex experienced no fewer gastrointestinal complications than those who took ibuprofen. Indeed, when one looks at the overall incidence of adverse side effects, one discovers that the people who took Celebrex experienced 11 percent more serious complications than those taking the older and much less expensive drugs. The safety advantage claimed by Pharmacia/Pfizer was illusory.

Dr. Michael Wolfe, the Boston University gastroenterologist who wrote a favourable editorial to accompany the JAMA Celebrex article, was upset when he discovered that the researchers had suppressed half the data. "We were flabbergasted," he said. "I am furious. . . . I wrote the editorial. I looked like a fool. . . . But all I had available to me was the data presented in the article."[67] The editor of JAMA, Dr. Catherine DeAngelis, commented: "I am disheartened to hear that they had those data at the time that they submitted to us. . . . We are functioning on a level of trust that was, perhaps, broken."[68] After reviewing the full year's data, the United States Food and Drug Administration (FDA)'s arthritis advisory committee concluded that Celebrex offers no proven safety advantage over the two older (and much less expensive) drugs.[69] Pharmacia/Pfizer unsuccessfully disputed this conclusion.[70]

At the time, the mass media virtually ignored the story. In consequence, most patients remained in the dark as to the true state of the evidence. Surprisingly, the medical profession seemed scarcely more attuned to the significance of what had transpired — possibly because much of the "education" doctors receive about drugs comes from representatives of the drug companies and from eminent medical colleagues who are paid consultants of these same companies. At all events, the public revelation of data suppression exerted no discernable restraining influence on the frequency with which doctors wrote prescriptions for Celebrex. The newly available data might have shown that it was very far from being "miracle aspirin," but these data had little impact on sales and profitability.

It is perhaps worth remarking that it was a Canadian clinical pharmacologist and drug evaluator from the University of British Columbia, Dr. James Wright, who first discovered and then reported the differences between the data presented in the *JAMA* article and the data presented by the company to the FDA. Dr. Wright is completely independent of the pharmaceutical industry.[71]

Returning now to the VIGOR trial, it is important to note that, as reported by Dr. Bombardier and her colleagues, the research subjects who took 50 mg of Vioxx per day developed significantly more serious cardiovascular complications than those taking naproxen. The VIGOR trial itself showed a 400 percent greater risk of experiencing heart attacks, strokes, and blood clots for subjects who were randomized to Vioxx, compared to those in the naproxen arm of the trial. The study's authors explained, or perhaps one should say "explained away," this elevated risk by claiming that Vioxx was not responsible for the surplus of heart attacks and strokes. Instead, they claimed, naproxen was protective. They also claimed that the serious heart and stroke complications occurred exclusively in patients with a history of cardiovascular disease. If true, this would suggest that Vioxx might have a favourable risk-benefit ratio for patients having no previous history of cardiovascular disease.[72]

Given the importance of the issue one would have expected the VIGOR authors to provide some evidence to support their hypothesis that naproxen was protective against heart attacks and strokes. In February of 2001 the FDA cast serious doubt on the claim that naproxen had been protective, which leads one inexorably to the conclusion that Vioxx was harming many patients. Curiously (and embarrassingly), the editors of the NEJM, when they were refereeing the article prior to publication, somehow failed to challenge the VIGOR authors to justify their sanguine hypothesis. Nor did the editors invite a more sceptical interpretation of the data from independent scientists.

Fortunately, rescue from company "spin" was at hand. Some alert scientists discovered that the VIGOR authors had failed to report several heart attack deaths in their NEJM publication, even though they had supplied the correct data to the FDA.[73] (As we will see later, it was a similar case of data suppression in the ADVANTAGE trial, discussed below, that proved to be the final straw for Vioxx.) These additional data showed that patients taking Vioxx were five times more likely to suffer from heart attacks and strokes than patients taking naproxen. Even worse, from the company's point of view, the Vioxx deaths that had been suppressed in the NEJM article were deaths that occurred in patients with no history of heart disease. This fact kicked the legs out from under the company's specious claim that only those with a history of heart disease were at elevated risk from taking Vioxx.

The investigators did not correct the scientific record. Their failure to do so was compounded when Dr. Jeffrey Drazen, esteemed editor of the NEJM, declined an opportunity to publish a letter submitted to the journal by independent scientists that would have alerted readers to the misleading nature of the data originally published. Years later, when the full extent of the harm done to tens of thousands of patients became undeniably clear, Drazen and his fellow editors at the NEJM justified their refusal to publish a timely correction with the intellectually (and morally) feeble excuse that it is the responsibility of authors, not journal editors, to correct data.[74] It must be conceded that the correct data were available on the FDA Web site; but the impact of the *NEJM* in promoting sales of Vioxx was incomparably more significant than the impact of data available on the FDA Web site.

Overall, if one considers serious complications — defining "serious complications" as those that lead to hospitalization, permanent disability, or death — the subjects who were given Vioxx had 21 percent more serious complications (of all kinds: gastrointestinal, cardiovascular, and other) than did those who were given naproxen. Tens of thousands of patients died unnecessarily because this salient fact was not adequately publicized; well over 100,000 suffered heart attacks and strokes.[75]

In sum, if all the data from the VIGOR study had been properly disclosed and properly analysed, the publication of the trial in the *New England Journal* would in all likelihood have dealt a death blow to the marketing and sale of Vioxx. Instead, the death blow came several years later with the publication of a second Merck sponsored Vioxx clinical trial, known as ADVANTAGE. The ADVANTAGE study displayed some of the same ethically dubious features as the VIGOR study, but is worth considering separately, partly because it helps to establish and reinforce the pattern of unethical behaviour in university-industry research partnerships and partly because it introduces some new and disturbing wrinkles to the already toxic mix.

The first point to note is that the ADVANTAGE trial was not a genuine scientific study.[76] Under the guise of science, the marketing department of Merck set up this "study" with the prime purpose of inducing an additional 600 doctors to prescribe the drug to their patients. In other words, the study was really marketing dressed up as science. Ironically, however, ADVANTAGE indicated — contrary to the company's strenuous denials since its earlier VIGOR trial — that Vioxx carried significant heart attack risks: five ADVANTAGE research subjects taking Vioxx experienced heart attacks, compared with only one in the naproxen arm of the study. Second, although Merck insisted that this number of heart attack deaths did not reach a level of statistical significance, the number of reported deaths was discovered to have been understated. In an instance of unethical data suppression comparable to that of the first-published VIGOR study, the ADVANTAGE study did not reveal that two additional Vioxx patients died from heart attack. Worse, the number of unreported heart attack deaths was likely three rather than two. Internal company records reveal that Merck's top scientist, Dr. Edward M. Scolnick, pressured a colleague to change his views about the cause of one patient's death, which was subsequently recorded as "unknown" rather than cardiac.[77] When all these additional Vioxx cardiac deaths are included in the study's total, they undermine the company's claim that there was no statistical significance to the number of deaths. As if these ethical breaches were not enough, it should also be noted that the lead author of the ADVANTAGE trial, Dr. Jeffrey R. Lisse, an academic rheumatologist from the University of Arizona, later admitted that he was little more than a ghost author: "Merck designed the trial, paid for the trial, ran the trial," Lisse admitted to a *New York Times* reporter. "Merck came to me after the study was completed and said, 'We want your help to work on the paper.'"[78]

University students are failed for "plagiarism" when they put their names to work that they have not done themselves. However, a surprising number of university scientists seem comfortable accepting drug company money in exchange for putting their names to studies that have been designed and carried out by drug company employees. Prominent academics thus pad their resumes and their wallets and, in the process, lend their scholarly prestige to the company's products. Frequently, these academic "lead authors" have not even had access to the raw data on which the study's conclusions are based. As a result of the Vioxx scandal and a host of others, many medical journals now require that the lead author take responsibility explicitly for the data presented.

In sum, almost no one emerges with much credit from the saga of the COX-2 inhibitors. The drug companies that massively marketed the drugs, both to doctors and directly to consumers, made billions of dollars; but, when the facts eventually emerged, the companies experienced a serious loss of public trust. Merck, in particular, is now facing a staggering number of expensive lawsuits. The company continues to insist that it took all reasonable measures to determine whether Vioxx carried undue cardiovascular risks and is defending its conduct in all of these lawsuits. Medical journals and their editors, in particular the *NEJM* and its editor Dr. Jeffrey Drazen, were seen by some critics as being incompetent at best and collusive at worst in what turned out to be a terrible human tragedy.[79] The medical community allowed itself to be "sold" on these miraculous new drugs, often persuaded of their merits over fine dinners at luxury resorts. The after-dinner talk would generally be delivered by a respected colleague who was also a highly paid consultant to the companies. In consequence of such "education," doctors wrote millions of prescriptions, and their unwitting patients paid a fortune for drugs that claimed to have a superior safety profile, but which, in fact, were inferior to older and much cheaper pain control drugs. This cannot have enhanced public trust in "evidence-based medicine" or the medical profession that claims to practice it. When the evidence on which evidence-based medicine relies has been massaged or otherwise tainted, it scarcely provides a reliable tool for medical decision making. In the interests of truth-in-advertising, perhaps the medicine practised in this era of corporate-university partnerships should be referred to as "pseudo-evidence-based medicine."

Finally, and from our point of view most significantly, university scientists, who are professionally obligated to pursue and to publish the truth, however embarrassing that truth might be to the corporate bottom line, were instead responsible for withholding data that was unfavourable to the products of their commercial sponsors. They withheld data and they also misinterpreted the data that they chose to disclose, spinning that data in such a way as to give the impression that their sponsors' drugs had a safety profile superior to older and cheaper drugs.[80] The opposite was true.

Although I have been focusing attention on one class of drugs, the COX-2 inhibitors, there is ample evidence that similar problems are to be found with respect to many different drugs and classes of drugs. York University drug researcher Joel Lexchin and colleagues have done a comprehensive meta-analysis of the tendency of drug company sponsorship to produce biased research results. They conclude: "There is some kind of systematic bias to the outcome of published research funded by the pharmaceutical industry."[81]

Canadian universities, like their American counterparts, tend to measure their success by the extent of the corporate financial support their researchers attract. Our universities and hospitals aspire to be world-class research institutions and, in pursuit of this objective, they vigorously solicit money (for research but also for new buildings and laboratories) from the world's wealthiest and most powerful drug companies. The pharmaceutical industry has come to be accepted by our research universities as a vital "partner." Handsome new buildings mushroom on campuses across the country, built with funds donated by these companies. However, when one discovers the cost to research integrity that seems to be an inescapable risk of such partnerships, the bargain may come to seem Faustian, with a terrible quid pro quo: the loss of research integrity and, eventually, the loss of public trust.

WHAT ARE UNIVERSITIES FOR?

I have been discussing some of the ethically dubious practices in which university scientists have engaged under the aegis of drug industry sponsorship. Now let's go back to basics for a moment to ask: What are universities for?

Universities are places where scholars pursue *knowledge for its own sake*. Hence, the venerable metaphor of the "ivory tower." University research is (primarily) curiosity-driven. Indeed, the intellectual vitality of universities derives from the fact that scholars are largely autonomous — beholden to no one, least of all the wealthy and powerful elites of society. The knowledge gained by university research is then freely disseminated to colleagues, students, and the wider community. For this reason, universities are a vital source of critical perspective on many of the issues that matter most to society. This critical perspective is possible only because universities and the scholars who work in them are fearlessly independent of governmental, church or corporate control.

This is the story we tell ourselves; or it's the story we used to tell ourselves. The paradigm of the university as a place of independent scholarship derives in some measure from the Enlightenment. We know, of course that the Enlightenment ideal of the university as a centre for pure scholarship, untainted by the pursuit of wealth, power, and status, was never entirely true. How could it have been true? As Immanuel Kant famously observed, "Out of the crooked timber of humanity, no straight thing was ever made."[82] Given our imperfections, it would be naive to deny that among the motives that inspire university research, there are some that are less than estimable. Career advancement, for example, would often be part of the motivational mix, along with competition for status and even hope for glory. When churches or other ruling elites/classes controlled universities and their finances, there was never a shortage of academics who sought promotion via scholarship that told power whatever power wanted to hear. La trahaison des clercs was a phrase made popular by Julien Benda (in 1928) to describe the kind of betrayal committed by intellectuals who advance their self-interest (by providing legitimation to ruling elites) at the expense of the more dangerous enterprise of devoting one's scholarly energies to the disinterested search for truth.[83]

Granting this point, and thereby conceding that there may not have existed at some indeterminate point in the past a "golden age" of scholarly purity, one might nevertheless insist that there was a time when the percentage of dross mixed in with the gold was less prominent than it is today. It is impossible to deny the claim — and many, within and without the university, want to trumpet rather than to deny it — that we are now living in an era when universities are regarded, perhaps first and foremost, as engines of economic prosperity. We constitute an important part of national "manpower policy." Our graduates, many of them, end up working in the corporate trenches. Our intellectual patents generate wealth for the biotech companies we have formed or with which we have struck up commercial alliances. Universities themselves often demand and receive an ownership share of these companies, from which arrangement they hope to receive substantial profits. It is now expected, indeed it is demanded, that university research findings should move rapidly from the academic laboratory or teaching hospital to the real world of bottom-line corporate profitability. Arguably, the modern university, in its role as corporate handmaiden, has acted in a way that restricts, rather than expands, the scope of researchers to engage in disinterested or critical scholarship.

Scientific research in Canadian universities is extensively funded by industry. This proposition is generally true, but it is especially true for pharmacological research, which attracts strikingly large sums of money from the pharmaceutical industry. As explained in the brief historical section that follows, it's important to remind ourselves that these university-corporate partnerships are a comparatively recent phenomenon. Thirty or forty years ago, most research funds came from governments and from quasi-governmental funding bodies (known as granting agencies). Today, although governments continue to invest large sums of money in scientific research (albeit a much smaller percentage of the total than in the past), the marked trend is towards private funding. Moreover, the importance of private funding is enhanced by deliberate government policies, which give strong funding preference to scientists and scientific projects that have also succeeded in attracting corporate sponsors. Often university researchers are not allowed to apply for public funds in support of their investigations unless they can recruit a private partner.

To put the point bluntly, this means that academics who seek to pursue a career doing scientific research at a Canadian university had better ensure that they and their projects will be attractive to potential corporate sponsors. University careers depend heavily upon the ability to bring in a continuous stream of research dollars. Pity the naive researcher who adopts as her research project a cancer treatment that depends on eating broccoli sprinkled with lemon juice. Which pharmaceutical corporation would fund such a profit-threatening idea? Which university would give tenure or promotion to a researcher who could not attract corporate funding, however brilliant and socially beneficial her research project might be? Which government agency would support such research in the absence of a legitimating corporate partner? It may be an exaggeration to say that universities have transmogrified into the R&D departments of economically powerful corporations, but the exaggeration, if any, is mild. In other words, the kind of research that is undertaken at our universities must nowadays be designed to please potential corporate sponsors by promising to produce results that will satisfy the profit-maximizing expectations of a lean, mean, competitive economy.

The gravamen of my argument, in what follows, is this. We have made a Faustian bargain. With the best of intentions, we have sold our souls for company gold and, in the process, have put the integrity of our research and the credibility of our universities into serious question. Data are fast accumulating which demonstrate that when corporations fund research, the results of that research are powerfully biased by the corporate agenda. A worrying series of academic scandals, two of which have been discussed in some detail above, shows that when universities become closely allied with the marketplace their vigilance in the promotion and protection of research integrity may be less than stellar. In other words, when the search for truth turns into the pursuit of profits, the end result is often very far from beneficial to society.

A BRIEF HISTORICAL PERSPECTIVE

The widespread public attention generated by the Olivieri and Healy scandals at the University of Toronto sharply focused public attention on the dangers posed by corporate sponsorship of universities and university research. Public concern about the growing commercialization of university research is heightened, almost on a weekly basis, by publicity given to the kind of data suppression engaged in by drug companies and their university collaborators. The Vioxx scandal received more media attention than most, partly because of the very large number of unnecessary deaths and illnesses that were associated with Vioxx use; but equally shocking revelations seem to hit the mass media almost on a weekly basis. One thinks here, for example, about the way in which drug companies suppressed vital evidence concerning the safety and efficacy of the SSRI anti depressant drugs, as David Healy has carefully detailed.[84]

A growing number of scholars and some thoughtful citizens, as well, are already persuaded that the commercialization of university research threatens to corrode, if not entirely to undermine, research integrity at our universities. But even among those who harbour such fears, a majority appears to hold the TINA view, popularized by former British Prime Minister Margaret Thatcher: There Is No Alternative. And if it's true that there is no alternative to the new entrepreneurial university, then the best we can do is to introduce reforms to restrain, even though they cannot altogether eliminate, the malign potential effects of the unholy alliance between universities and the commercial marketplace.

In this section I sketch briefly the history of corporate involvement as "partner" to university research.[85] Only when we understand how we got to where we are at present will we have an opportunity properly to consider whether there might, *pace* Margaret Thatcher, be an alternative.

Because the pharmaceutical industry has been in the vanguard of the movement to commercialize research at our universities, I am focusing my discussion on the so-called partnership between Big Pharma (as the pharmaceutical industry has become known) on the one hand and universities on the other. It should be noted, however, that university agricultural research has been captured (primarily by the petro-chemical industry) to an extent scarcely less worrying than university medical research.[86] And what is true for university medical and agricultural research is also true, to a greater or lesser extent, for university research in such disparate fields as climate change (funded by the fossil fuel industry) and foods and nutrition (funded by multinational food corporations).[87] Even such ostensibly humanistic disciplines as "strategic studies," nestled typically under the departmental aegis of "political studies," are often funded significantly by the military and by allied defence industries, on condition they produce research results that are pleasing to their military sponsors.[88] Those old enough to remember US President Dwight Eisenhower's warning, issued in 1961, of the dangers posed to American society by the rise of the "military-industrial complex" will now, almost half a century later, have a renewed appreciation of just how prescient Eisenhower was.

To pick any date as the point at which university research became a predominantly entrepreneurial activity would be somewhat arbitrary. There is widespread consensus, however, that a confluence of developments in the 1980s best qualifies as such a historic turning point.[89] This was the decade when the norms of science, as adumbrated by Robert Merton in his classic book, *The Sociology of Science*,[90] began to undergo a radical transformation.

The paradigm of scientific culture, as described by Merton, may be encapsulated as follows: the soundness of scientific research should be judged by impersonal criteria; research findings should be treated as open and shared rather than in a proprietary or secretive fashion; researchers should be motivated primarily by the desire to advance knowledge rather than by financial or careerist considerations; and research findings should be tested to death. That is, the scientific community should accept research claims only when they have been rigorously tested by disinterested scientists. Investigators can be counted on to communicate their results freely with each other because they share the same professional canon: a primary commitment to the advancement of knowledge.

These norms of scientific research were offered by Merton partly as descriptive of how scientists generally conducted themselves and partly as prescriptive of how they ought to behave *qua* professional scientists. Mertonian norms were still widely accepted at the mid-point of the twentieth century. It was at this point, however, that things began to change.

Much to the delight of the scientific community, the funding of scientific research became a top national priority in the United States during and after World War II. Prominent among the reasons for this development was the conviction that the advancement of scientific knowledge, via massive government research spending, was necessary for America's health, prosperity, and, most important, security. In consequence, the fifties and sixties in America were a golden age for government funding of basic science. During this period, less than five percent of university research funding came from private industry. Direct interaction between academic scientists and for-profit corporations was quite limited.

By the late seventies, however, university research came to be regard-ed as the means whereby America could achieve and maintain global industrial and military dominance. University science was now assigned the role of serving the nation as a potent commercial weapon in a highly competitive world economy. Passage in 1980 of the Bayh–Dole Act enabled universities and their researchers to patent dis-coveries resulting from federally funded research. As a result of these and other developments, corporate support for academic biomedical research escalated from less than $5 million in 1974 to hundreds of millions of dollars in 1989.[91]

By the standards of history, this transformation occurred in the twin-kling of an eye. The entrepreneurial scientist working in the entrepre-neurial university moved, almost in one fell swoop, from being an oxy-moron to being the way science was done and, or so it seemed, must forever be done. Within a mere few decades, the pharmaceutical indus-try became the major funder of clinical drug trials, and a major finan-cial contributor to medical schools and universities via donations of buildings and equipment.

Critics warned that these dramatically increased levels of corporate funding could produce, as an unintended side effect, a serious erosion of the norms of scientific research. What the discussion of the Vioxx and Celebrex scandals is meant to illustrate is that the critics knew whereof they spoke. Biomedical research at our universities has been absorbed, to an alarming extent, by the profit-seeking ethos of the mar-ketplace. The norms of commerce are now threatening to swamp the traditional norms of science. As Lexchin and others are demonstrating with persuasive empirical data,[92] when the disinterested pursuit of knowledge gives way to the entrepreneurial pursuit of financial self-interest, the result is a body of scientific evidence skewed towards the interests of the sponsoring corporation. It's as simple as the old folk-wisdom: He who pays the piper calls the tune.

The history of medical research in Canada followed a trajectory simi-lar to that in the US, though with about a ten-year time lag. In Canada, it wasn't until the late eighties that the federal government came to view the drug companies as a key to economic growth and moved to extend patent protection for drugs. By the 1990s, Canadian governments were either freezing or cutting funds for medical research under the rubric of fiscal responsibility. Caught in a squeeze between shrinking government funding and escalating research costs, Canadian medical researchers sought salvation in the welcoming embrace of the pharmaceutical industry. For many university presidents and medical faculty deans, commercializing university research by marketing universities to wealthy corporations was a realistic way, perhaps the only realistic way, to obtain the research funding necessary to compete on the international stage. Under the banner of "pursuing excellence" in research, universities became supplicants of the very corporations whose products and practices they had, in previous times, subjected to critical scrutiny.

At the outset of this chapter, two case studies, the Vioxx and the Celebrex scandals, were analyzed to illustrate the way in which powerful drug companies were able, via their funding of university research, to successfully develop and market drugs for which the risk-benefit ratio was known from the outset to be dubious at best. Investigators whose careers depend on drug company sponsorship seem to be producing research that often has greater affinities with marketing than with the pursuit of scientific truth. To understand how and why this problem arose, it will now be necessary to explore the key concept of "conflict of interest."

CONFLICT OF INTEREST

The best short definition of "conflict of interest" defines the concept as follows: "A person is in a conflict of interest situation if she is in a relationship with another in which she has a moral obligation to exercise her judgment in that other's service and, at the same time, she has an interest tending to interfere with the proper exercise of judgment in that relationship."[93]

My argument is that when university researchers accept corporate funding for their research projects, they put themselves in a conflict-of-interest situation. The same would be true of universities or hospitals that accept corporate donations and thereby allow themselves to become beholden to those corporations.

Drug researchers, for example, have an ethical obligation to put the interests of truth (and patient safety) ahead of the interests of the corporations funding their projects. When, however, the researcher's career depends upon the direction of her findings, there is a worrying danger that the researcher's view may be biased or skewed. Thus, if a researcher stands to gain monetary and/or career success by demonstrating the safety and efficacy of a sponsor's new drug, but stands to lose research funding and perhaps her job if she finds that the new drug is unsafe or ineffective, then she has a conflict of interest.

The suggestion here is not that researchers who have a conflict of interest will necessarily behave in a (consciously) corrupt fashion. Only a small minority of investigators is likely guilty of deliberately skewing their investigations so as to produce dishonest results that will be pleasing to their corporate sponsors. The real danger is that the unconscious effect of financial benefit or career self-interest has a marked tendency to generate biased research findings. Evidence from the social sciences demonstrates that "even when individuals try to be objective, their judgments are subject to an *unconscious and unintentional* self-serving bias [Emphasis mine]."[94] Moreover, we now have a substantial body of empirical evidence to confirm that when it comes to biomedical research, financial conflicts of interest are associated with significant effects.

The study that first drew wide attention to the issue of how research objectivity might be eroded by drug industry sponsorship was published in 1998 by Stelfox and colleagues.[95] Their goal was to investigate whether (and if so, to what extent) industry sponsorship of biomedical research might influence the outcome of that research. To answer this question they studied published articles on the safety of calcium channel blockers — a class of drugs used to treat high blood pressure. Stelfox and colleagues first divided authors according to their financial relationship with pharmaceutical companies and then, separately, classified (as "supportive," "critical," or "neutral") their research findings on the issue of whether these drugs were safe. What they found was that "96 percent of supportive authors had financial relationships with the manufacturers of calcium channel antagonists, as compared with 60 percent of neutral authors and 37 percent of critical authors." In other words, there was a striking association between the conclusions reached by investigators (with respect to the safety of calcium channel blockers) and the financial relationship of those investigators with pharmaceutical manufacturers.

The Stelfox study was unable to determine conclusively whether corporate funding came to the authors before or after they reached favourable conclusions about these drugs. However, more recent studies have repeatedly demonstrated that industry-sponsored studies are significantly more likely to reach conclusions that favour their sponsors' products than studies that are independently funded.[96] To cite Lexchin again: "Research sponsored by the drug industry was more likely to produce results favouring the product made by the company sponsoring the research than studies funded by other sources. The results apply across a wide range of disease states, drugs and drug classes, over at least two decades and regardless of the type of research being assessed — pharmacoeconomic studies, clinical trials, or meta-analyses of clinical trials."[97]

The proliferation of studies pointing to the important impact of funding source on the results of biomedical research should be of serious concern to those who support industry-university partnerships.

It might be helpful to reflect that in fields far removed from biomedical research there is a sharp awareness of the dangers posed by conflicts of interest. Referees are not permitted to accept benefits or gifts from team owners; police are not allowed to accept benefits or gifts from crime suspects; judges are not permitted to accept benefits or gifts from litigants; professors are not allowed to accept benefits or gifts from students. That's because referees, police officers, judges, and professors are obligated to exercise their judgment impartially, according to professional standards. When we hope for future benefits our self-interest may skew our professional judgment. Moreover, gifts and benefits make the recipient beholden to the gift-giver. The well-established anthropological phenomenon of reciprocity operates powerfully — though, again, often not in a conscious, deliberate manner — to motivate us to return kindness for kindness, gift for gift.

Although most people recognize that the powerful combination of self-interest and reciprocity can bias the judgment of others, often in ways of which the recipient of is scarcely aware, few of us are willing to acknowledge that we could ourselves be "bought" in this way. I have lectured on biomedical conflicts of interest at universities in Canada, the US, and Great Britain, but I have only once encountered a researcher who was willing to acknowledge that he had been biased by drug-company funding. The vehemence with which most researchers deny that they could have been biased by the acceptance of drug company funding or other financial benefits from these companies, such as consulting fees and stock options, reflects a common misunderstanding. Researchers become understandably indignant when they believe someone is accusing them of deliberate corruption. What many seem not to recognize, however, is that when one allows oneself to be placed in a conflict-of-interest situation — that is, when one has a vested interest (usually financial) in reaching a particular conclusion — one tends almost automatically, at a subconscious level, to weigh arguments and evidence in a biased fashion.[98]

PSEUDO-EVIDENCE-BASED DECISION MAKING

We pride ourselves on being a society in which important decisions of public policy are based upon (mostly) reliable scientific evidence. Across many domains, governments depend upon the research done at our leading universities, research institutes, and academic hospitals to guide policy. With respect to areas of great social concern, such as public health and safety, nutrition, environmental sustainability, employment, housing, foreign policy, and much else, governmental deliberations are framed and shaped by the work of university scholars.

What is true for us as a society is also true for most of us as individuals.

When we must reach a decision about such matters as whether to take medicine for a health problem and, if so, which medicine would be (comparatively) safe and effective, most of us rely upon the expertise of university researchers and the research findings they have published in scholarly journals. Some of us consult these research findings directly, but many learn of them and their significance indirectly both from the doctors and other professionals whose expertise we regularly consult and from popular reports in the mass media. When professionals dispense advice to us, they are meant to base that advice on research findings published by their academic colleagues in peer-reviewed scholarly journals.

We are similarly reliant upon university-based research when we deliberate about such disparate questions as which foods are nutritious, whether genetically modified crops pose an unacceptable threat to us or to the environment, and whether to have our children vaccinated against measles, mumps, and rubella. The list of personal decisions we make in reliance upon university expertise could be expanded almost indefinitely.

This is not to deny that we are also, most of us, influenced in our personal decision making by epistemologically less reputable factors such as celebrity product endorsements. For reasons best explored by social psychologists, we are more likely to buy life insurance from Company X or cough syrup from Company Y when a hockey superstar has lent his name and image to the brand. Still, all but the most naive of us understand that the celebrity in question very likely does not possess expertise in the relevant domain. Wayne Gretzky may be just the person to consult when buying a hockey stick — but life insurance? We understand, also, that he is being heavily remunerated for lending the star power of his name and image to the products whose virtues he publicly extols. We would not be shocked to learn that he has never actually used these products himself (except, perhaps, when they are given to him as free samples). So, we buy the stuff he endorses but, if questioned, we would readily admit that it is emotion of one sort or another (fear of this, hope for that), often below the level of full consciousness, which impelled our purchase.

Clearly, it would be foolish to deny that there is a deal of credulity among the general public. Ordinary folks seem prepared on occasion to believe in and/or act upon the most implausible propositions. Nor are elites immune from foolish irrationalities. University graduates can be every bit as credulous as hoi polloi when it comes to consulting the "expertise" of the astrologer, the medium, or the tarot card reader. It's sad to reflect, for example, that astrologers find a market among every stratum of society for the hokum they peddle.

GOVERNMENT POLICY-MAKING

Governments, too, have been known to base their policy decisions on factors other than scholarly evidence relating to "best overall net benefit." Nor is this aberration necessarily the result of an ignorant reliance upon superstition or other forms of irrationality.

The desire to obtain or to retain political donations from wealthy individuals and corporations has been known to induce governments to massage the available scholarly evidence or even to ignore or suppress it entirely when that evidence points to inconvenient truths. One does not need to be an inveterate cynic to recognize that manipulated data and consciously biased interpretations often form the basis of decision making. This is especially so when governments seek to placate major party political donors or to curry favour with influential segments of the electorate.

In short, whether we are speaking of individuals or governments, one must concede that the decision-making process on important issues is not always fully rational. Nevertheless, at both the social and the personal level, it seems reasonable to believe that our lives are likely to go better if we have access to accurate, reliable, honest, and disinterested information from experts whose commitment is to the truth rather than to their own financial or career self-interest.

Thus, when one thinks about how we, both as individuals and as collectivities, reach important decisions, one is confronted with a contradictory pattern of decision making. Sometimes we seek out the best available evidence and weigh it carefully; sometimes we follow our gut feelings or irrational prejudices (which, not infrequently, coincide). As well, our thinking is often distorted by self-interest, including especially financial self-interest, in ways of which we may be only imperfectly aware.

Information and advice offered by the scholarly professions is generally accorded considerable weight, although it must also be acknowledged that all professional advice is not accorded equal respect. Advice that is professionally mandated may be seen as suspect when the profession in question does not enjoy a high reputation for honesty and integrity. Advice from the medical profession is generally, though not always, thought to be trustworthy. By contrast, advice offered by lawyers is often greeted with cynical derision, owing to widespread public cynicism about the legal profession. Other professions, including accountancy and even medicine, are not immune from the perception that the professional advice they offer may be self-serving, and therefore unreliable, rather than public-spirited.

As an illustrative example of the potentially malign effect of such widespread public cynicism, consider the current widespread rejection of the MMR vaccine. Many parents, especially in Europe, refuse to allow their children to be vaccinated against potentially deadly childhood diseases such as measles, mumps, and rubella. They refuse because they disbelieve the reassurances offered by prominent medical scientists.

Scientifically unsubstantiated rumours abound to the effect that the MMR vaccine is responsible for an alleged increase of autism rates among children. The scientific community has strong evidence that points to the vaccine's having no such adverse side effect; but notwithstanding the fact that the British government has paraded a troupe of leading scientists before the media in an effort to reassure the public, the public remains sceptical. The public remains sceptical in large part because it has become known that virtually all the vaccine experts have had their research funded by the companies manufacturing the MMR vaccine and are themselves the recipients of substantial consulting fees from these same companies. The scientists in question are persuaded of their own rectitude but, understandably, the public questions whether their scientific conclusions may not have been shaped by some combination of career advancement and personal financial self-interest.

UNIVERSITY RESEARCHERS AND CONFLICTS OF INTEREST

At present, the public appears not fully to appreciate that such financial and career conflicts of interest have become the norm for university researchers in many different fields, including, but not limited to, such fields as academic medicine, agriculture, and climate change. Not only is it the case that most of our leading university scientific researchers benefit from sponsorship by industry, the universities and teaching hospitals in which these scientists work also accept very substantial amounts of money from the same corporate sources, usually in the form of "charitable donations." Indeed, it is these corporate donations that make possible the proliferation of many fine new research buildings on Canadian university campuses. They also fund the expensive equipment and technical staff without which the buildings would be empty shells.

This connubial relationship between universities and the world of business is seen by many, including a significant portion of university administrators and governing boards, as something to be welcomed and fostered.

Revenue generated by such partnerships (in the form of royalties on joint ventures, funds for salaries, equipment, and support staff, and the aforementioned donations for buildings) is seen as providing the leverage that universities and teaching hospitals need in order to achieve "excellence" or, even better, to become "world class." The alternative to such university-industry partnerships is seen as mediocrity and stagnation. University administrators are persuaded that if they do not aggressively pursue corporate research funds and corporate donations for their own institutions, then their competitor universities/hospitals, both nationally and internationally, will win the race for gold and glory.

This way of putting the case for university-corporate partnerships is misleading and incomplete, however, since it portrays the institutional imperative of the university as focused solely on growth for the sake of growth, or growth for the sake of status, fame, and fortune. Critics of the corporate university should, in fairness, acknowledge that university administrators typically see themselves as committed to the advancement of socially vital knowledge, both scientific and humanistic. This altruistic self-image should not be entirely dismissed. Human motivation is almost always complex, multiple, and ambiguous.

Doubtless, university administrators generally do sincerely believe their strenuous efforts to harness corporate wealth on behalf of university expansion make an important contribution to the promotion of the university's fundamental objective, the benefit of humankind through the advancement and dissemination of useful knowledge. It's also true, however, that in their ceaseless quest to raise money, university administrators may occasionally lose sight of the proper goals of a university. Means and ends are easily confused, with the means (rapid growth) coming to displace the end they were meant to promote (the advancement of knowledge), but that's not to say administrators don't sleep soundly at night, comfortable in their conviction that their corporate fundraising efforts are directed towards a noble cause.

CONCLUSIONS

Many members of the biomedical research community are persuaded that in this era of rapidly escalating costs, industrial sponsorship of university research is the best (and perhaps the only viable) path towards the advancement of science. They see or claim to see a synergy between the expansion of corporate profits and the flourishing of scientific creativity. The creation of beneficial new drugs is often cited as evidence to demonstrate that the commercialization of university research is a highly positive development for society as well as for science.

Critics tend to be less sanguine than university administrators about the outcome of increasingly close ties between universities and corporations. They argue it was government funding rather than corporate funding which promoted innovative and socially beneficial research. Corporate funding of university research has instead led us to a point where many of the new drugs coming to market are really "me-too" drugs: invariably more expensive than their predecessors (which have come off patent), but no more efficacious and often more dangerous.[99] Despite the very considerable sums of money invested by pharmaceutical corporations in university research, the US Food and Drug Administration reports that this money is producing fewer and fewer "new molecular entities."[100] In short, the number of golden eggs produced by the corporate goose is disappointingly exiguous. Even more

worrying, adverse effects from prescription drugs now occupy the number four place on the list of leading causes of death in the US.[101]

The critics worry about the marked divergence between the fundamental raison d'etre of industry, on the one hand, and universities, on
the other. If we ask, "What are corporations for?" the simple answer is
that corporations are for the maximization of shareholder profits. By
contrast, although today's multiversity may aspire to be all things to all
people, it nevertheless continues to be the case that the bottom line for
any university worthy of being so called must continue to be the pursuit of truth.

Corporations owe a fiduciary duty to their shareholders. That duty is
to maximize profitability. Realistically, given the competitive global
economy in which most corporations now operate, it is short- rather
than long-term profitability that often dominates the thinking of corporate officials. If quarterly profits don't satisfy market expectations,
stock values will decrease, sometimes precipitously, and heads may
roll. The fundamental commitment of the university, by contrast, is to
seek truth even when that truth may have an adverse effect upon the
corporate bottom line.

Once it is recognized that our current way of funding biomedical
research is vastly expensive but sadly unproductive of beneficial new
molecules and also demonstrably undermines the integrity of both our
researchers and our research institutions, then it becomes a matter of
some urgency to contemplate alternative funding arrangements.

Since the fundamental problem arising from university-corporate
partnerships is the problem of conflict of interest, and since many of
the reforms suggested as tools for "managing" this conflict — such as
disclosure of the conflicts — have proven ineffectual, the most promising solution to the problem turns out also to be the most simple: an
outright prohibition of corporate funding for university research. The
sequestration thesis insists that university researchers must be entirely
sequestered from the process of commercialization.

If we as a society want public science in the public interest, it will
have to be funded through public tax dollars.[102] The "partnership"
between universities and their researchers, on the one hand, and for-

profit corporations, on the other, is almost pre-ordained to produce research findings that promote the interests of the corporations even when, as not infrequently happens, those interests clash with the best interests of both patients and the wider community.

Hitherto, the community of university researchers has been viewed by society at large as an invaluable source of independent information and critical analysis. University-industry partnerships, as we have seen, threaten seriously to corrode the independence of university research and, thereby, its integrity. Once the true nature and extent of corporate financial sponsorship becomes widely recognized and understood by the rest of society, the credibility of university research is likely to suffer irreparable harm. Loss of public trust is a heavy price to pay for the short-term benefits that come when universities float on a sea of corporate largesse.

3

WHEN SPONSORED RESEARCH FAILS THE ADMISSIONS TEST: A NORMATIVE FRAMEWORK

Sheldon Krimsky

INTRODUCTION

Whenever the topic of dubious sources of external funding was raised in conversation, a former president at my university was known to have replied, "The only problem with tainted research funding is there t'aint enough of it." It is a curious statement by the president of a distinguished university, who, among other things, is the steward of the university's endowment, the torchbearer of its mission, and the moral placeholder of its values. This was also the same president who defended the university's policy against accepting grants or contracts for weapons research.

Like many other academic institutions, Tufts University has, on occasion, debated issues related to the ethics of sponsored research. Controversies have erupted over whether individual faculty or institutional policy should prevail in deciding whether sponsored research was acceptable to the institution. The individual researcher and his/her own institution are in a symbiotic relationship with respect to research funding. Sponsored research is awarded to the institution with the understanding that an individual faculty member, who is usually called the principal investigator (PI), is the responsible party to whom the research award is designated. If the PI changes institutional affiliation, frequently arrangements are made to transfer the sponsored funding to the PI's new institutional home. The PI works within a set of norms that have been incorporated into the university's bylaws and policies. Some of these norms are unique to the institution, while others are based on federal mandates and are, therefore, uniform across all institutions that receive federal support. Within the context of university sponsored research, I shall examine the following normative questions:

- Should universities be selective in approving grants or contracts applied for by individual faculty on the basis of ethical considerations?
- Is it acceptable, and if so, on what grounds, for university administrators to restrict grants or contracts sought by individual faculty based on a particular type of research activity?
- Is it acceptable, and if so, on what grounds, for university administrators to restrict grants or contracts sought by individual faculty based solely on the types of products manufactured by, or the business sector classification of, the sponsoring organization?
- Is it acceptable, and if so, on what grounds, for university administrators to restrict grants or contracts sought by individual faculty merely on the relationship of the investigator to the sponsoring organization?
- What rules of governance are appropriate in deciding which funding is or is not appropriate?
- What, if any, litmus tests can be used by university administrators for setting standards of acceptable research sponsorship without undermining the idea of a free and open university?

In this chapter I shall address these questions by first developing a framework that possesses generalizable elements, yet is capable of individuating the answers to specific cases by adapting them to variations in university micro-culture policies on sponsored research. I shall focus my framework on contracts and grants and set aside the issue of the standards for acceptable gifts to the university, which generally do not involve research. Second, I shall apply the framework to several cases where there has been controversy over the ethics of sponsored research.

THE UNIVERSITY'S MULTIPLE PERSONALITIES

Universities are unique institutions in the American landscape. The members of the professoriate have considerable autonomy relative to other professions, as characterized by what we teach, the types of research we do, and in our freedom to write and speak without having to meet a litmus test of the institution. And while all universities strive for the three major goals of education, research, and service, there is little homogeneity in the balance given to these goals. Within the research mission, universities express their goals quite differently. Even within the same institution, the concept of research takes different forms. I have previously described this as the university's multiple personalities.[104]

The four archetypal personalities or models that characterize university research are the classical, the Baconian, the defence, and the public interest. While universities have research portfolios representing each of these personalities or models, the weight of funding in any of these categories can affect a university's normative policies on acceptable sponsored research. According to the classical personality — identified with the phrase "knowledge is virtue" — research is organized around the attainment of knowledge for its own sake. Inquiry is internally driven by faculty, as captured by the expression "investigator-initiated research." Scientists/scholars adhere to the norms of universal cooperation, free and open communication, and the knowledge commons, where the results of research are freely available for everyone to use.

The Baconian model is described by the expression "knowledge is productivity." (Francis Bacon used the expression "knowledge is power".) The university's role is to provide personnel and intellectual resources to foster economic development. Professional education and corporate-related research is the key to this dimension of the academic mission. The work of the scientist begins with discovery, continues through application, and ends with intellectual property. Universities that emphasize the Baconian personality are typically more receptive to industrial contracts and corporate partnerships or faculty-corporate liaison programs. The agreements permit compromises on such issues as sharing of data, sequestered or confidential research, and single-party restrictive licensing of patents. The Baconian model implies that the pursuit of knowledge is not fully realized unless and until it contributes to productivity. As one study notes: "In recent decades universities have added a component of economic development to their missions, accomplished largely through transfer of university technology to existing or new businesses."[105] Therefore, the responsibility of the investigator includes both discovery and technology transfer. The term "translational research" is *au courant* for describing this process.

The "defence" model of the research university is guided by the dictum "knowledge is security." Universities devote their resources to capturing grants and contracts from the defence industry. The micro-norms of the research community adapt to weapons research, anti-terrorism and counter-insurgency studies, spy satellites, and code breaking, to name a few. Often, these projects involve research contracts that are fully or partially classified.

Finally, the public-interest model of science is framed around the aphorism "knowledge is human welfare." The university organizes its research facilities to address major societal problems such as the cure of dread disease, environmental pollution, global climate change, and poverty. Public-interest science is generally more favourable to the idea of the "knowledge commons" on the principle that when knowledge is publicly funded, it should be publicly available. This is the spirit of a bill introduced into Congress titled the Federal Research Public Access Act of 2006, which requires open access to research results funded by the federal government within six months of their first publication.[106] The norms attached to public-interest science can be expected to be different from Baconian and defence science. Traditionally, corporate science has had many more constraints and covenants embedded in its university contracts. As noted by Resnik, "Companies may suppress results, refuse to apply for patents, or keep research under a cloak of secrecy for many years. They may also refuse to share useful tools, resources or techniques."[107]

Because academic institutions are not homogeneous in their research personality, they choose a different balance in their research

portfolios, and as a result the norms that define their research programs will vary. The Baconian personality will tolerate more privacy
and confidentiality than the classical personality. Within the balance of
these multiple personalities, individual researchers are accorded a
degree of autonomy. Their autonomy is set against the norms of the
institution, which may limit some of their choices. It should also be
recognized that institutional factors can also impede faculty autonomy.
Faculty can exercise self-censorship on what they study or how they
study their field of interest, if they believe it will have a negative effect
on tenure or promotion. In the next section I discuss how faculty
autonomy can be in conflict with a university's policies on acceptable
sponsored research.

RELATIVE AUTONOMY OF FACULTY

Traditionally, faculties in universities decide the research questions
they pursue and the grants and contracts they apply for, as well as what
results are published and when. These choices are what we refer to as
faculty autonomy. Other rights of the faculty include academic freedom, or the right to speak and write on controversial or unpopular
subjects, and the right to define the content of a course.

The autonomy of faculty is a privilege associated with tenure, but it
is not an absolute privilege. It is largely modulated by two factors: the
local university rules and those of government agencies that apply to
all federally funded institutions. The federal rules are uniform,
although many are merely guidelines for which individual institutions
provide local content. In the case of conflict of interest, for example,
universities have significant latitude to meet federal compliance standards. Whether strict regulations or flexible guidelines, federal authority sets constraints on scientific autonomy, where autonomy is viewed
as "academic libertarianism."

As an example, US federal guidelines on human subjects research
has extended informed consent requirements to scholars interviewing
other scholars, hardly the intent of protecting vulnerable populations.

Many universities set limits on faculty consulting. If not universal, it
must be nearly so that a faculty member cannot simultaneously hold

tenure in two separate institutions. Some universities prohibit faculty from using their names, titles, and university affiliation on product advertisements — but it is certainly not a university-wide norm. No one claims that university faculty as teachers or scholars have absolute autonomy when it comes to academic-business relationships. When Nobel laureate and Harvard professor Walter Gilbert became the CEO of the BioGen Corporation, the university asked that he give up his professorship while he was in the corporate role.[108]

For some faculty, keeping the funding flowing is the lifeblood of their academic existence. Without this funding, they cannot support post-docs and technicians in their laboratory. On the other hand, it is the post-docs and technicians that are needed to maintain the flow of external funding and to produce publishable results. Increasingly, medical school faculty depend on external funding for their own salaries. As such, research faculty become small entrepreneurs who sell their research services in the form of grants and contracts to foundations, government agencies, or corporations. It is in the interest of the research faculty to be able to leverage their expertise and research skills to attract funds from any source that is willing and able to fund them. People with abundant sources of funding can be selective; those with fewer choices want the maximum latitude to bring in a grant or contract.

Universities benefit from the overhead that accompanies a grant or contract, regardless of its source. Some university administrators even discourage faculty from applying for funding from sponsors that do not honour the government indirect cost standard. From purely an economic standpoint, universities can benefit by having an open-admission policy for research funding, allowing their faculty to define the parameters of their research, with little or no restrictions on the substance of the grant or contract or the moral standing of the sponsor. But economics, while perhaps a central driving force behind university policies on sponsored research, is not the only consideration. Sponsored research programs are bound by norms other than maximizing cash flows to the university. For example, universities may decide that they will not accept research contracts that require sequestered student dissertations. When such contracts are opposed, the norm of open science communications trumps the interest in adding more research dollars to the institution. Similarly, universities are increasingly opposed to accepting sponsor control over publication.

Secret covenants that give the sponsor the final approval on publication was the issue behind the Betty Dong case. Professor Dong of the University of California at San Francisco signed a contract that gave the sponsor the ultimate authority for publishing results from the data collected by her research. Left without sufficient resources to take on the company in litigation, Professor Dong withdrew the paper at the eleventh hour from the galleys of the *Journal of the American Medical Association*.[109]

Under a libertarian view of faculty, the individual scientist alone decides what the contract conditions are between the faculty and the sponsoring organization. Where libertarian principles prevail in academia, the university is viewed as an enabler that fosters the interests of the autonomous researcher-entrepreneur while providing infrastructure for the research in exchange for overhead charges.

THE COMMUNITARIAN-LIBERTARIAN DIVIDE IN ACADEMIA

Within most universities there is a tenuous balance between communitarian and libertarian tendencies of the faculty. Under communitarian values, a faculty governance process decides on the rules and norms under which research takes place. At best, academic communitarianism functions out of a democratic process prescribed in the formal rules of the faculty governance structure consistent with the powers of the administration and board of trustees. Libertarianism affords faculty all rights not limited by communitarian norms. Thus, if a university has no constraints on faculty outside employment, then it is assumed that faculty may work as many hours as they wish outside the university while meeting their campus obligation.

The balance between communitarianism and libertarianism is calibrated for each institution. There is no reason to believe the balance should be identical across all institutional cultures. We may refer to this as the communitarian-libertarian balance, which speaks directly to the normative structure of research. The institution may decide that, in the overall interests of the university, some restraints are warranted on the type of grant money accepted. But the story doesn't end there. There are norms which are so deeply at the core of the university's mission and raison d'être that their retraction would bring into question whether the institution is still functioning like a university.

META-LEVEL NORMS

Universities share a family resemblance in their educational mission. However, not all institutions that claim to offer teaching and education would be considered universities. Thus, McDonald's has created "Hamburger University," which is only a university through false analogy and appropriated nomenclature. Other entities that use the term "university" are nothing more than diploma mills.

Not all universities can claim to focus on research. But of those that do, the communitarian-libertarian balance at universities helps to explain the diversity of norms guiding sponsored research. While acknowledging variations in the moral yardstick at different research institutions, I propose a second level of norms whose function it is to protect and preserve the unity of core values that capture the family resemblance across the micro-cultures we call universities. I refer to these as meta-level norms for research integrity. These norms should not be contingent on the calibration set for an institution between communitarian and libertarian values, which we may consider ground-level norms.

I shall argue that "meta-level" norms should be invariant across all universities. Insofar as the norms dictate acceptable criteria for accepting sponsored research, they shall not be traded away by rebalancing communitarian and libertarian interests (ground-level norms). To justify their invariance across the diverse university cultures, meta-level norms must stand up to critical scrutiny. When a meta-level norm is rejected, we must be prepared to argue that the institution falls short of meeting one of the essential qualities we associate with universities. Because they are invariant, meta-level norms are not subject to trade-offs. Sponsored research contracts that violate meta-level norms should fail the admissions test, however else the university calibrates its balance between communitarian and libertarian interests of its faculty. Ideological preferences should not affect the choice of meta-level norms. For example, the social and regulatory conservative Henry Miller of the Hoover Institute writes, "Universities must also ensure that he who pays the academic piper doesn't get to call the tune by influencing the results of research or by suppressing undesirable findings."[110]

As a start, I propose the following meta-level norms for externally funded research.

- The autonomy of the researcher must be protected. The researcher and his/her co-investigators must be in full control of the protocols, the data, the interpretation of results and the decision, venue, and time of publication.
- External research grants or contracts shall not place confidentiality requirements on the research outcome with the sole exception of a brief period to file a patent. Secrecy has no place in the open university.
- The purpose of external research funding should be to contribute to knowledge and not to produce public relations, promote products, or defend litigants in court.
- Transparency of the sponsor is essential to establishing trust in the university's role of a knowledge generator.
- No contractual constraints shall be imposed on the researchers for reporting results, however inconvenient or objectionable they may be to the sponsor.
- The principal investigators in a sponsored research project should be solely responsible for writing up the results; the sponsor should not play a role as co-investigator or contract with a ghost-writing company that is not cited in the publication.
- No external research grants or contracts should discriminate by age, race, religion, gender, political beliefs, or disability.

A few examples will illustrate these points. Let us suppose a sponsor issues a contract for research that takes away from the principal investigator his or her autonomy for publication of the results. This provision in a sponsored research contract is inconsistent with how we understand a research university is supposed to function. University research is not a product of public relations or advocacy but an independent pursuit of knowledge guided by the researchers' disciplinary canons and reviewed by peers.

While contracts that conflict with the autonomy of the academic researcher are inconsistent with the idea of the university, they are quite prevalent across academia. As noted by Resnik:

> Corporations that sponsor research frequently require scientists and engineers to sign contracts granting the company control over proprietary information. These agreements typically allow companies to review all publications or public presentations of results, to delay or suppress publications, or to prevent researchers from sharing equipment or techniques. The agreements are legally binding and have been upheld by the courts.[111]

In a second case, the corporate sponsor issues a contract in which an academic investigator permits his name to be used in a ghost-written article. The sponsor hires a firm that specializes in writing and placing medical articles in the literature. The firm locates a highly regarded scientist whom they consider a "thought leader" and offers him a contract to sign his name as author to an article written for the firm, which would then be placed in a medical journal. To the company, there is an advantage in having a prominent medical researcher write about, for example, off-label uses of a drug, which have not been approved by the US Food and Drug Administration (FDA). Companies are prohibited from promoting or advertising the use of a drug for some purpose that has not received FDA approval. Physicians, however, may prescribe off-label uses of drugs based on their own judgments, even as drug companies are prohibited from lobbying them in support of such uses. Through ghost writing, drug companies get around the prohibition of off-label lobbying by having doctors speak to one another about their "best" practices and observations. Journals are beginning to respond to ghost writing as a form of plagiarism and therefore a violation of scientific integrity.[112]

In both the previous cases, the focus of the sponsored research is on the nature of the contract language and not on the company sponsor or the type of research. Meta-norms against plagiarism or sponsor control of research outcome speak to the core principles of a research university. However, the boundary between ground-level and meta-level norms is dynamic and not invariant. As professional associations and accrediting groups reach unanimity over ground-level norms, those norms can rise to the meta-level.

Starting after World War II and continuing through the Vietnam War period, a number of universities in the United States accepted classified research from government agencies, most prominently the Department of Defense. Faculty and graduate students participating in a classified research project had to be investigated and vetted by the Department of Justice to determine whether they represented a security risk — a term that was broadly interpreted to include people who protested the war. Classified research divided the academic community. Some viewed it favourably as contributing to the "defence" model of the university, where academic scientists contribute to national security. Others, however, saw the system of classified research as an anachronism in the modern research university where free and open exchange of ideas is the hallmark of higher learning.

During the 1960s, student anti-war activists at the University of Pennsylvania (U Penn) learned that their institution hosted classified research on chemical and biological warfare, under the program names Spicerack and Summit, which had direct relevance to the US actions in Vietnam.[113] While students criticized the research for being immoral, most faculty criticism focused on the inappropriateness of secrecy at the U Penn campus. Eventually, after a split between the administration and faculty, the U Penn Board of Trustees voted to divest the university of the classified war-related research and refused to transfer the projects to its off-campus sites.[114]

By the Vietnam War's end there was a broad consensus among major research universities that classified or secret research was incompatible with the values of academic science. The pursuit of certifiable knowledge requires transparency to actualize the self-correcting function of science. Classified science was a recipe for perpetuating errors. Science could easily fall victim to ideology in a closed system built on secrecy, sequestered science, and loyalty oaths.

A number of research universities that had once accepted classified research spun off separate research centres that were not part of the core universities. For example, in response to student protests against secret research on campus in the 1960s and early 1970s, MIT turned Lincoln Laboratory into a semi-autonomous, off-campus entity where it located its classified research. Thus, the ground-level norm of "no classified research" adopted by some universities became the meta-level norm adopted by the vast majority of universities by the mid-1970s. However, secret research entered the university in another form: namely, business contracts that contained clauses about protecting confidential business information, including intellectual property. The campus political climate and public criticism that pressured universities to abandon classified research was not recreated to address business secrecy on campus when "academic capitalism" was ignited in the 1980s.

Another meta-level norm grew out of federal mandates that required universities to adopt ethical guidelines for human experiments, especially informed consent requirements for all persons participating as human subjects. By the mid-1970s it was no longer a matter of discretion for universities to protect human subjects in clinical trials. Human subjects research, whether from public or private funding sources, had to comply with federal guidelines on informed consent.

CASUISTRY AND QUESTIONABLE SPONSORED RESEARCH

The term casuistry refers to the use of cases to draw conclusions in ethics and law.

I shall use cases to draw out and test the normative principles developed in previous sections. The framework I described has two levels for building a normative structure of sponsored research. Meta-level norms provide unity, continuity, and invariance across research universities, while ground-level norms offer a degree of flexibility enabling localized balances of communitarianism and libertarianism values. The boundaries are not impermeable but respond to consensus-building processes of professional and university associations. In the United States, government regulations and congressional oversight committees can also create a broad consensus for negotiating ethical standards in conducting research.

TOBACCO INDUSTRY–SPONSORED RESEARCH

Let us begin with a case of prohibiting research from a particular industry. The University of California Board of Regents debated whether any of its faculty should be allowed to conduct research financed by the tobacco industry.[115] This proposal was not a restriction on the content of the research but rather on the funding source. Presumably, the same project supported for funding by Philip Morris, Inc. could be funded by another corporation. This proposal to ban any research contract or grant from an entire industrial sector, namely tobacco, from sponsoring research at any of the universities in the California state system grew out of the findings about the tobacco industry's unsavoury and rogue activities that were revealed in the state tobacco litigation.

Arguments in favour of "banning tobacco money" cite the health effects of tobacco, the industry's record in distorting research findings that were unfavourable to the sale of tobacco products, and the industry's lack of respect for scientific integrity. Critics of the tobacco industry characterize this sector as flagrantly dishonest and untrustworthy in claims about its products. For years the industry manipulated the amount of habit-forming nicotine in cigarettes and advertised directly to children. Universities, some believe, have an obligation to draw a scarlet letter on rogue industries who wish to gain credibility by funding research at a university. Bans on tobacco money are mostly found in certain schools, such as public health and medicine, because the mission of these schools cannot be reconciled with the reckless disregard of human health shown by the tobacco industry. The pretension that the tobacco industry had a true interest in science was nothing more than a ruse; all the time, it was seeking to buy itself fabricated knowledge. The misdeeds of the industry are well documented. The World Health Organization reports that, "the tobacco companies planned an ambitious series of studies, literature reviews and scientific conferences, to be conducted largely by front organizations or consultants, to demonstrate the weaknesses of the IARC [International Agency for Research on Cancer] study and of epidemiology, to challenge ETS [environmental tobacco smoke] toxicity and to offer alternatives to smoking restrictions."[116]

For over fifty years tobacco companies have placed articles in the medical literature, without revealing their support for the research. They financed a large number of studies intended to show that the research conducted by IARC was flawed, and they created an independent coalition of scientists to manufacture uncertainty on the link between tobacco and disease. The tobacco industry also funded international seminars to develop "good" epidemiological standards of scientific proof that would serve cigarette manufacturers by raising the standards of proof.[117] As noted in the journal *Science*, "The [tobacco] companies frequently killed their own research when it came to unfavorable conclusions, funded biased studies designed to undermine reports critical of smoking, and used the names of respected scientists and institutions to bolster their public image."[118]

Increasingly, studies have shown that health research funded by the tobacco industry is biased in favour of the financial interests of the sponsor. A report published in the journal *Addiction* found that "scientists acknowledging tobacco industry support reported typically that nicotine or smoking improved cognitive performance while researchers not reporting the financial support of the tobacco industry were more nearly split on their conclusions."[119]

Even with its legacy of deceit and malfeasance, there are reasons not to ban research funding from an entire industrial sector. First, some of the grants or contracts funded by the tobacco industry may lead to positive outcomes, particularly post-litigation, as the industry is under the social microscope. It can no longer get away with its unsavoury practices. If there is any redemption from past misdeeds, industry money could benefit society. Most of today's mega-foundations obtained their wealth by human exploitation and deceit. By placing a blanket ban on such funding, the university could be foregoing socially valuable research.

A second consideration is how to circumscribe the so-called tobacco sector. Tobacco companies are parts of conglomerates. If there is a contaminated branch of a corporation or industrial sector, does it implicate all other branches from the corporate trunk? If a university bans funding from Philip Morris, should it also ban funding from a food corporation that sits under the same corporate umbrella? To circumvent such restrictions, tobacco companies can provide support to a foundation which then doles out money for research. As an example, a cancer researcher at the Weill Cornell Medical College published a study stating that 80 percent of lung cancer deaths could be prevented through the use of CT scans. The study had been financed in part by a little known non-profit called the Foundation for Lung Cancer. Investigative reporters at the *New York Times* learned that this foundation was largely supported by the parent company of a tobacco group.[120]

Third, what makes tobacco's behaviour unique? Consider, for example, drug companies that have withheld important safety information from the FDA, resulting in preventable deaths. Or what shall we say about the asbestos, lead, and chemical industries that knowingly compromise workers' health in favour of maximizing corporate profits. Is there such a thing as tobacco exceptionalism? Failure to distinguish among rogue corporate behaviour is one of the reasons the American Association of University Professors issued a policy on sponsored research that opposed the idea of singling out the tobacco sector:

> An institution which seeks to distinguish between and among different kinds of offensive corporate behavior presumes that it is competent to distinguish impermissible corporate wrongdoing from wrongful behavior that is acceptable. A university which starts down this path will find it difficult to resist demands that research bans should be imposed on other

funding agencies that are seen as reckless or supportive of repellent programs. If the initiative in calling for these bans on the funding of faculty research comes from the faculty itself, our concerns about the restraints on academic freedom are not thereby lessened. A university at which the research is conducted should not be identified with the views and behavior of the tobacco industry because faculty members accept its funding, just as the university should not be identified as necessarily endorsing the content of the researcher's work.[121]

Some critics of tobacco exceptionalism question whether government sources of funding stand on higher moral ground than that of the cigarette industry. For example, funding from the US Homeland Security Agency or from the Department of Defense is said to be tarnished by an illegitimate war effort based on presidential malfeasance in claiming unsubstantiated weapons of mass destruction as justification to make a preemptive strike against an independent state. Once moral criteria enter the decision for determining which funding is worthy of entering the university, research libertarians argue that no clear line can be drawn.

Another opponent against banning tobacco research in universities was quoted in *Science* as opposing the use of moral criteria to evaluate sponsored research. "How do you avoid infringing on academic freedom, and what sort of slippery slope do you create by denying grants on moral grounds?"[122]

Where does the case of the tobacco companies sit with respect to the framework developed in this paper? The meta-norms of the framework are not intended to apply to the historical or current misdeeds of a company. Similarly, the use of guilt by association, which can blemish an entire industrial sector for the malfeasance of a few companies, is not justified for establishing a meta-norm. Neither a company's history nor its current market behaviour tells us anything about the quality of the research it could sponsor and its respect for independent and autonomous academic scientists who would plan and execute that research. Meta-norms are specific to the conditions under which research is conceptualized and executed under the sponsor's contract. In this framework, the meta-norms cannot be used to prohibit research dollars from an entire industrial sector, unless a specific action adopted by that sector violates one of the core principles of independent research: for example, if an industrial sector never allows a sponsored researcher to have autonomy over publication.

The framework leaves open the possibility that ground-level norms would bar tobacco companies from sponsoring research. The university community can decide that, regardless of the social value of the proposed research project, the commercial goals of the tobacco industry are in conflict with the values of the institution. Moreover, the university does not wish to lend its honourable name to a dishonourable industry that preys on people prone to addiction and whose product is responsible for untold deaths and illnesses. Forbidding any research sponsor should not be taken lightly, because it is restricting individuals from potentially funding their work. For example, in 1990 the University of Delaware refused to receive grants from the Pioneer Fund, which one faculty member described as an organization with "a long and continuous history of supporting racism, anti-Semitism and other discriminatory practices."[123] University president E.A. Trabant initially defended the ban on Pioneer Fund "so long as the fund remains committed to the interest of its original charter and to a pattern of activities incompatible with the University's mission."[124] After an independent arbiter ruled in favour of two professors who wished to apply for grants from the fund, the University of Delaware reversed its policy.[125]

The Harvard School of Public Health and the University of Glasgow prohibit their researchers from applying for tobacco funding. Some foundations like the Wellcome Trust (UK), the American Legacy Foundation, and the American Cancer Society will not fund researchers who have been awarded tobacco money.[126]

While such policies may conflict with an individual faculty member's funding opportunities, and in some cases their ability to maintain their laboratories, they do not rise to the level of infringement of academic freedom (meta-norm) as long as the policies follow appropriate university governance procedures and they do not constrain a faculty member's right to speak or write about a subject.

Those protesting any constraints on sponsored research cite the academic freedom of individual researchers to pursue areas of investigation of their choice. A resolution approved by the University of California's (UC) Academic Senate stated that "no special encumbrances should be placed on faculty members' ability to solicit or accept awards based on the source of funds."[127] Others correctly note that academic freedom refers to speaking, writing, and pencil-and-paper research. No professor has an unbridled right to engage in laboratory research or any research that requires sponsored funding independent of institutional or government norms. The investigator and the university administration are partners in the sponsored research. If an institution refuses to accept sponsored funding from a tobacco company, there are other options open to investigators who wish to pursue a research program. They could find other funding, pursue the study without funding, if possible, or collaborate with someone whose institution will accept the funding. There are no universal norms among universities which state that, "because I can get funding from company X for work Y in institution Z, then I *should* get approval from Z for such funding." Universities, however, should be able and willing to provide a justification, within the tradition of faculty governance, to prohibit a particular funding source. The burden for denial should be on the shoulders of the university.

In September 2007 the Board of Regents of the University of California took a middle-of-the road position between outlawing tobacco funding and giving total authority to individual faculty to negotiate research contracts with tobacco companies. The regents created a scientific review committee whose mandate it is to certify that a tobacco-industry funding proposal "uses sound methodology and appears designed to allow the research to reach objective and scientifically valid conclusions." Once the proposal is vetted and approved, the investigator will be allowed to apply for funds from the tobacco industry at any of the University of California colleges and universities.

WEAPONS RESEARCH

A second case that can be tested against the normative framework is the opposition to a class of research: namely, *weapons research*. Let us assume that a faculty senate is in agreement with the administration on proscribing any sponsored research involving weapons, including building or testing weapons or weapons systems, analysis of weapons, or protecting citizens or the military against weapons, as in the cases of developing vaccines for biological weapons or anti-missile systems. Let us also assume that the research contract does not violate the academic freedom or autonomy of the investigator in conducting or publishing the research, which usually implies that it is not classified. In this example, the contract language is not in conflict with other meta-norms. Because no meta-norms are violated, the decision on the suitability of the research would be made at the ground level. Can the university apply reasonable ethical grounds, based on its mission and core values, sufficient to gain support from the academic community for proscribing weapons research? Can the university establish a sufficiently clear demarcation between weapons and non-weapons research to avoid even the appearance that the decision is whimsical rather than being grounded on an accepted ethical norm?

It is likely that most, if not all, federally funded weapons-related contracts would have some degree of secrecy and, therefore, violate a meta-norm in the normative framework of this chapter. If the research is unclassified, it could be argued that it is fundamental in nature and does not have specific weapons application, such as a system of parallel computing that could be useful for radar tracking of a high speed projectile in the atmosphere. Alternatively, a novel method of vaccination against Rift Valley fever or anthrax could raise questions about indirect weapons research. If a country has a vaccine, then the biological agent for which citizens or soldiers can be immunized becomes a weapon. Although at various times in history biologists have signed pledges stating they will not work on biological weapons, the distinction between defensive and offensive weapons within the fields of bacteriology and virology can easily be blurred.[128] As a communitarian decision, a university can, on moral grounds, proscribe sponsored research on weapons. But the framework I have introduced does not imply that response as long as meta-level norms are not breached. In my view, the concept of the "weapon" itself does not elevate the research concern to a violation of a meta-norm, therefore making it inherently unfit for a university.

COMMERCIAL TESTING IN ACADEMIA

Throughout much of the twentieth century, during the growth of academic entrepreneurship and government-sponsored research, universities reexamined the standards for tenure at their institutions and debated the criteria for evaluating the quality of faculty productivity. In fields such as chemistry and chemical engineering, faculty were doing extensive consulting and participating in what Karl Taylor Compton, former president of the Massachusetts Institute of Technology (MIT), called "pot-boiling research." According to John Servos's account of industrial relations at MIT, "excessive outside work, 'pot-boiling' as Compton called it, would militate against [academic] advancement."[129] Compton and others warned faculty that they would not get promoted if their work involved routine testing programs, typically handled by consulting companies, rather than the engagement in fundamental advances in science. Those who opposed pot-boiling research considered it outside of the university's educational and research mission to be turned into corporate testing centres that are likely to be accompanied by contracts with confidential business information requirements, potentially violating the meta-norms of openness and publishing rights. However, even if the meta-norms are not violated, an institution is correct in exercising its fiduciary responsibility when it evaluates whether the sponsored project offers any educational value or contributes to new knowledge.

Today, a number of universities make income by selling their testing services to corporations. As an example, Clemson University hosts the Clemson University Packing Service, which "provides contract package/product testing and material evaluation for both food and non-food industries."[130]

Because the standards for what contributes to educational value and new knowledge may vary widely across disciplines and institutions, decisions about the proper place of testing programs in universities is best left to local governing systems. Nevertheless, extreme cases can easily be identified. For example, if the sponsored activity is not likely to yield published papers in refereed journals, the sponsored contract would fail the test of advancing knowledge. University public health departments have toxicology sections that accept industry contracts to test chemicals by in vitro or in vivo studies, applying standardized protocols that meet the criteria of regulatory bodies. There exist many refereed journals for publishing such studies.

I would include a meta-norm in my framework that sponsored testing activities that have no prospect for advancing knowledge or educational benefits for the university should be proscribed. This meta-norm protects universities, during times of financial exigency, from becoming contract research outposts for corporations. When the interpretations are ambiguous, the decision making should be left at the ground level, where local standards are applied.

During the past quarter-century, universities have found new lucrative income streams in running clinical trials for drug companies. Most of the new drug testing in the United States and Canada is supported by the pharmaceutical industry. Medical faculty benefit by acquiring publications from such trials, when such publications are approved by the sponsor. Published trial data can contribute to the applied knowledge of drug safety and efficacy, but rarely contribute to basic medical knowledge. From the public-interest perspective, universities may offer more quality control and moral accountability in managing clinical trials than one finds among contract research organizations, who hire private institutional review boards and have no accountability outside of their corporate structure.

MEGA-RESEARCH CONTRACTS

In 1980 the US Congress enacted the Bayh–Dole Act, which stimulated aggressive corporate research investment in universities. Under the act, the government gave up to the universities and their business partners all intellectual property rights assigned to discoveries made under federal grants. A host of new multi-year, multi-million dollar corporate grants and contracts were awarded to universities, targeted to academic units as opposed to individuals. These included British Petroleum's $15 million to Princeton,[131] Chevron's $25 million to the University of California at Davis,[132] and ExxonMobil's $100 million to Stanford.[133]

Recently, the University of California at Berkeley (UCB) has been at the epicentre of a controversy over corporate-academic partnerships involving sectors of the university. In the first of two partnership agreements, the dean of UCB's College of Natural Resources sent out letters of inquiry to sixteen agricultural biotechnology and life sciences companies, ostensibly to auction off a research collaboration with the Department of Plant and Microbial Biology. The dean selected Novartis, a $20 billion food and pharmaceutical company, as UCB's corporate partner. Under the contract Novartis provided UCB with $25 million in research dollars over five years. Among the benefits to Novartis were patenting and licensing rights as well as seats on UCB's internal research committee, which decided on the allocation of funds. All faculty members who signed on to the agreement (which it turned out was the vast majority of the department) were subject to restrictions. "Once a faculty member signed the confidentiality agreement, he or she could not publish results that involved data without approval from Novartis."[134] Novartis could request publication delays of up to 120 days and could obtain exclusive licensing rights of UCB patents — which has been argued by legal scholars is not in the public's interest. A second mega-contract with UCB came to fruition in 2007. British Petroleum (BP) signed an agreement worth $500 million in research funds to UCB, Lawrence Berkeley National Laboratory, and the University of Illinois to develop new sources of energy, with a primary interest in biofuel crops.[135] BP's funding supports a major expansion of UCB's clean energy research. The company gains the opportunity of assigning fifty of its researchers to the partnering institutions. Faculty at UCB raised questions about the impact of the agreement on researchers' academic freedom and the external control over the university's research agenda.[136]

Mega-contracts awarded to universities can compromise the autonomy of the institution or its faculty. Corporate partnerships typically involve joint corporate-academic committees that decide on the research agenda for use of the funds. With corporate funds amounting to hundreds of millions of dollars, there is a risk that it could create a monoculture of research in a department or even an entire school that is financially linked to one industrial sector or a single multinational corporation. The grass roots group Stop BP-Berkeley expressed a similar view in their protest literature: "We believe the proportion of corporate funding in public research must be carefully limited, to prevent the over-development of specific areas of research at the expense of others."[137] The academic unit in partnership and under contract with the company begins to take on the appearance of a research satellite of the sponsor. If the partnership lasts long enough, the size and influence of the sponsor's contract can violate the meta-norms that should be common to all universities. The prospect that mega-contracts can override the university's core values by violating meta-norms is, within the framework I have outlined, a reason to oppose them. The scale of the contract, not its specific content or the reputation of its sponsor, is at the root of the conflict. The quantitative changes arising from the size of the contract can result in qualitative changes that can impair the university's autonomy and diminish its role as a broker within the academic marketplace of ideas.

RACIAL OR ETHNIC DISCRIMINATION AND SPONSORED FUNDING

Universities are obligated to abide by national anti-discrimination laws. Let us imagine that a US university is offered a grant to become research partners with a university in a Middle Eastern country. The national science agency in the country is similar to the US National Science Foundation in that it funds basic science and operates under a system of peer review. There is one difference between the two agencies. Our hypothetical Middle Eastern science agency, following its national laws, prohibits anyone who is Jewish from working on the grant. The US university must decide whether it will adopt the standards of another country with regard to personnel on its grants when it considers sponsored research funded by that country. Would accepting such a grant violate US anti-discrimination laws? And if it were possible to get around those laws, would it be ethical to accept such funding? Both the US Constitution and the federal civil rights enactments are sufficient grounds for treating anti-discrimination as a meta-norm in the proposed ethical framework for sponsored research. An external grant that requires a university to violate a constitutional principle — equal treatment under the law — cannot be permitted, whatever national government is footing the bill. It should not be left to the discretion of a university to sign a contract for sponsored research that would prevent members of the university community from fully participating in the research project because of their race or ethnicity. Even the lure of healthy profits from oil-rich countries can not be an excuse for accepting such a contract or considering it under a fully deliberative communitarian process.

CONCLUSION

This chapter has explored the question: Are there ethical grounds for prohibiting university faculty from apply for certain types or sources of external funding? I propose a two-level normative framework, which I term the ground level and meta-level. The latter consists of a set of norms directed at the core epistemic values of independent and autonomous research institutions. The normative conditions outlined in the meta-level should be invariant across all research universities. Examples include norms such as that the investigators of a study are fully responsible for the data, the contents of published work, and the timing and venue of publication. The National Institute of Environmental Health Sciences journal *Environmental Health Perspectives* emphasizes such a norm in its instructions to authors: "all authors are required to certify that their freedom to design, conduct, interpret, and publish research is not compromised by any controlling sponsor as a condition of review or publication."[138] Another meta-norm should be that, under the conditions of external research, there shall be no discrimination of personnel with regard to race or ethnicity.

Ground-level norms include any factors of social and moral relevance to the institution that, in conjunction with faculty governance
standards, allow the institution to calibrate a balance between communitarian and libertarian interests. Under my proposed framework,
sponsored funding from tobacco companies, pro-Nazi organizations,
or radical animal rights groups could meet meta-level conditions if the
research contracts protect core values of the concept of the university.
However, to account for the diversity of interests and values across
American universities, the ground-level norms are set by proper governance functions at the individual institutions. The burden must be on
the university to provide transparency and deliberative justification for
taking from individual investigators the prima facie right to apply to
funding organizations for sponsorship of their research. In developing
this framework, I recognize that I depart from the policy adopted by
the American Association of University Professors (AAUP), with whom
I agree on many other issues. The AAUP has stated: "Denying a faculty
member the opportunity to receive research funding for such reasons
would curtail that individual's academic freedom no less than if the
university acted directly to halt research that it considers unpalat-
able."[139] In my view, as long as faculty members are neither suppressed
from nor penalized for writing, teaching, investigating, or speaking
about an issue, they retain their academic freedom. That freedom is not
extinguished in the case that a university community takes responsible
and transparent collective action, following accepted governance procedures, that prohibits certain funding from entering the university.

II. QUESTIONING POWERFUL INTERESTS — WHEN BAD THINGS HAPPEN TO GOOD SCHOLARS

4

COLLEGIALITY LOST

Brenda L. Gallie

INTRODUCTION

I discovered a very painful lesson about what can happen when one stands up for fundamental principles of science in support of a colleague who has been falsely accused by powerful interests within the academic medical world.

WHO WAS I?

Flashback to Dr. Brenda Gallie, Hospital for Sick Children, 1998. I was — and am — a clinician scientist and ophthalmologist, focused since 1974 on retinoblastoma, a rare tumour in children's eyes. I have contributed to the understanding of cancer as a genetic disease through delineation of the mechanism of tumour suppressor genes, genomic changes pointing to oncogenes and tumour suppressor genes contributing to tumour progression, and translation of that knowledge to improve outcomes for families affected by cancer.

Dr. Helen Chan and I have together applied basic knowledge of drug resistance to devise a novel protocol that improves chance of cure and saves vision. We mounted the first multicentre clinical trial in retinoblastoma. I have developed novel disease-specific electronic tools that improve patient care while providing the clinical data to basic science in multiple cancer disease sites. Together with survivors, volunteers, and professionals, I have initiated global collaboration to extend the benefits of our scientific work internationally.

My research has been continually peer-review funded since 1976, and from 1985 to 1999 this funding was awarded through the hospital. I have received no funding from the pharmaceutical industry. I contributed to, and benefited from, the commercial development of a novel gene sequencing technology that became a highly successful Canadian company. Application of that technology by my team achieved an efficient and highly sensitive system for clinical diagnosis of mutations; to deliver that knowledge to families, I founded a not-for-profit genetic testing company that serves as a global reference lab, providing results that improve care for families around the world. The data collected have repeatedly led to further cancer discoveries that we translate back to help patients.

In 1997 I represented the hospital with the hospital president, Mr. Michael Strofolino, at a presentation to the Canadian health minister, Mr. Allan Rock. The purpose of this meeting was to show the minister how important basic science is to health care, in order to increase the federal funding to research. We were effective in conveying this message: the federal allocation to the Medical Research Council of Canada was significantly increased in support of basic science. The Medical Research Council of Canada subsequently became the Canadian Institutes of Health Research.

In 1995 the hospital awarded program status to the Eye Genetics Program based on the scientific evidence from my group that molecular diagnosis for retinoblastoma families would save significant health-care dollars.[140] I assisted the hospital's Research Institute to apply for Ontario grants to translate our basic science into an economically viable business for the hospital in evidence-based clinical molecular testing for complex disease genes, when there was evidence that the test would change clinical care.

THE RESEARCH DIVISION — CANCER AND BLOOD

In January 1998 I became head of the Cancer and Blood Research Program within the hospital's Research Institute. The first issue that confronted me was a brewing controversy around the management of a clinical trial in thalassemia. I was aware that Dr. John Dick, senior scientist in the institute, had been assisting Dr. Nancy Olivieri, world expert in hemoglobinopathies, in discussions with the hospital administration around the safety of children on drug company–sponsored clinical trials. In May 1998 Dr. Olivieri brought to me, in my role as her division head, a stack of papers documenting the issues.

When I reviewed the papers, my first reaction was that the vice-president for research, Dr. Manuel Buchwald, and President Strofolino, despite the efforts of Dr. John Dick, did not understand the danger for the hospital, if patient safety and research integrity were not the foremost concerns in a health sciences research institute. I undertook to assist them in understanding this fundamental concept through several face-to-face discussions and then summarized my views in a strongly worded letter to Dr. Buchwald and President Strofolino, May 12, 1998:

> You must forthrightly deal with the escalating firestorm which threatens to consume HSC and threatens the confidence of our scientists and the public in HSC. I believe this matter is so severe and dangerous that you should **inform the Board of the Hospital** and request a **complete review of all aspects** by an independent, scientifically and ethically knowledgeable individual who has no conflict of interest. Recommendations from such a review may be wide sweeping, and are critical to the stature of HSC as an academic health science center. [Emphasis original]

My naiveté soon became clearly evident. The accuracy of my May 1998 predictions were borne out by the events most clearly described in the *Olivieri Report*.[141] In brief, Dr. Olivieri had developed a very promising therapy to remove excessive iron from patients who required regular transfusions to treat the anemia of thalassemia. When new data from her long-term trial revealed the medication potentially failed to protect a majority of the children and adults from excessive iron accumulation in the body — a potentially fatal condition — Apotex Inc., the drug company manufacturing the medication and supporting the clinical trials in order to license the drug, denied that the evidence showed risk. Dr. Olivieri's response to the possibility of a serious adverse reaction in the patients on the drug was to inform the Hospital Research Ethics Board. With their support, she revised the patient consent forms. The company then immediately and prematurely terminated the clinical trials, and strongly advocated locally and internationally against Dr. Olivieri, the principal investigator of the studies. The company also issued warnings of legal action should Dr. Olivieri disclose the risk to patients or anyone.

The hospital's board of directors, President Strofolino, VP Research Dr. Manuel Buchwald, Chair of Pediatrics Dr. Hugh O'Brodovich, and Dean Arnold Aberman of the University of Toronto Faculty of Medicine apparently felt that Dr. Olivieri's position was in some way extreme and encouraged "resolution" between her and the company. Privately, these people in positions of major responsibility, and Dr. Gideon Koren, head of clinical pharmacology and a co-investigator in the trials with Dr. Olivieri, told me the situation was not so simple, and I should not involve myself.

Dr. Helen Chan and Dr. Peter Durie joined Dr. Dick, Dr. Olivieri, and me to help the hospital to put safety first, in keeping with what we continue to feel is at the core of human research and clinical care. In August 1998, an open forum was held in the hospital auditorium for all staff. We sought to determine the responsibility of the hospital's research institute for safety of clinical trial subjects (Figure 4.1). The meeting deteriorated into a shouting match between senior hospital administrators and the staff, who demanded that Dr. Olivieri's point of view be heard. One week later, the *New England Journal of Medicine* published Dr. Olivieri's results.[142] The issue burst into public view and Drs. Olivieri, Chan, Durie, Dick, and Gallie became referred to as "The Gang."

In September the hospital appointed Dr. Arnold Naimark of the University of Manitoba to head an inquiry into the very public scandal. We met once with Dr. Naimark, but sadly, clearly understood from that

---

ISSUES RAISED BY THE CANCELLATION
OF THE LI CLINICAL TRIALS, MAY 1996

What is the HSC Research Institute responsibility for safety
of clinical trial subjects?

* When data suggesting toxicity is suppressed?

* To the academic community, MRC, the public, ETC who
  support our academic health science center?
  (analogous to the legal requirement to report child abuse, for which
  medical staff and the public is held accountable if they do not
  report their suspicion)

* To the study subjects who expect full disclosure of risks?

* Of the HSC expert on design and ethical conduct of clinical trials?

* To PROVE, not assume Safety and efficacy

* To complete clinical trials

* The legitimacy of the entire clinical process is imperiled

Figure 4.1. The overhead introducing the August 1998 Open Forum.

meeting that there would be no due process in his single-person inquiry, as the procedure he adopted was biased in favour of the hospital administration. Collectively, we decided not to participate further in the Naimark inquiry. Subsequently, the president of the Medical Research Council of Canada, Dr. Henry Freisen, also attempted to mediate between the Gang and the hospital, to no avail. The Naimark Report was made public in December 1998.[143] Our concerns were validated, as the report was severely biased against Dr. Olivieri and failed to put the safety of children foremost. The troubles for us escalated.

My own position as head of the cancer and blood program within the research institute was put in jeopardy. Dr. Manuel Buchwald, head of the hospital Research Institute, told me that my responsibilities as a leader within the Research Institute and my accountability to him and to the leadership of the Hospital for Sick Children, including its board, required me to not question their position on the issue. He wrote on December 7, 1998, "You apparently believe that your moral duty over rides your accountability to me as Director of the Research Institute and the formal leadership of this institution, including its Board. . . . "

My active support for Dr. Olivieri, as a scientist in the Cancer and Blood Research Program, and for the primacy of safety of children in research and under the care of the hospital, was not recognized by the hospital administration and its board to be part of my duties. In January 1999, I resigned from my position in the hospital research institute and moved the basic science portion of my program to the Ontario Cancer Institute within the University Health Network. I remain to the present the head of the Clinical Retinoblastoma Program within the hospital's Department of Ophthalmology.

The crisis further deteriorated with the imposition of "gag orders" — a prohibition of staff talking to the press. At this time we first met the executive of the University of Toronto Faculty Association. With further assistance from the Canadian Association of University Teachers (CAUT) and international experts in thalassemia, (Sir David Weatherall, Regis Professor of Medicine at the University of Oxford, and Dr. David Nathan of Harvard University), University of Toronto President Prichard stepped in to help achieve a settlement that was intended to resolve research activities for Dr. Olivieri within the hospital. Unfortunately, within days that settlement was breached by the hospital. Over the summer of 1999 further trouble ensued, and in September President Prichard's lobby of the federal government on behalf of Apotex was revealed in the *Toronto Star*, September 4, 1999.

Anonymous threatening letters to and about us were distributed widely in the hospital. By December 1999, we had determined by DNA testing that Dr. Koren was the author of the letters. He was later disciplined for this misconduct, which included repeated "lying" to conceal his responsibility.[144]

CAUT commissioned the *Olivieri Report*, which brought great clarity to the chaos and is a seminal document in health research ethics.

Throughout the ordeal, CAUT supported the primacy of academic freedom. With many more twists and turns involving both the hospital
and the University of Toronto, CAUT and the University of Toronto
Faculty Association brokered a "final" settlement in 2002.

ABOUT TURN

My advocacy for safety of children on clinical trials had surprising consequences for me in my own work. In December, 1999, based on evidence that I had presented to the Ontario Ministry of Health on the
importance and relevance of high sensitivity molecular *RB1* mutation
testing for retinoblastoma families and its positive impact on health
spending for care of these families, the Ministry acknowledged that this
specific genetic test should be covered by the Ontario Health Insurance
Plan (OHIP), so that it would be available to all Ontario families that
need it. I had conducted clinical testing over several years, first as
research and then in a new translational molecular diagnostic laboratory set up within the hospital research institute.

However, early in 2000, Dr. Buchwald informed me that the translational molecular diagnostic laboratory, translating the hospital's basic
research, had to leave, as he no longer considered our work "research."
Since there was no place to take the technology we had developed, we
formed a new company, Solutions by Sequence, and the molecular
translational laboratory moved to the University Health Network
(UHN). The translational laboratory became Retinoblastoma
Solutions, a not-for-profit company and charity. I remain to the present head of the clinical retinoblastoma program at the hospital.

On March 8, 2000, the Ontario Ministry of Health and the hospital
issued a press release announcing that the hospital's generic molecular
testing laboratory would undertake *RB1* testing. That announcement
remains to this day on the hospital's Web site (www.sickkids.ca /releas-
es/retino.asp), claiming: "This is another good example of Sick Kids'
ability to bring research bench breakthroughs quickly to the patients
and families who rely on the hospital. By moving this test into our day-
to-day laboratory operations, we ensure that every family in Ontario
who needs the service has access."

This claim was simply not true. The hospital lab to this day has refused to translate the science for which the hospital received large federal grants. Instead, they applied standard molecular assays for retinoblastoma with no demonstrated sensitivity or validation. On the advice of the hospital, until 2006, the now Ontario Ministry of Health and Long-term Care covered the costs of genetic testing for retinoblastoma families only if the tests were done in the hospital's unproven molecular lab.

As the ongoing head of the retinoblastoma program within the Department of Ophthalmology, I was faced with a dilemma. I could comply with the hospital administration and send the samples from children under our care to the hospital laboratory, where I was provided no evidence that the tests would be effectively performed but where they would be covered by Ontario health insurance. Alternatively, I could send the tests to Retinoblastoma Solutions in the UHN, where my group had formed a US-accredited clinical molecular laboratory that, with our colleagues in Germany, continues to establish the world standards for clinical *RB1* mutation tests. Outside of Ontario and internationally, insurance paid the costs of the tests for families. Ontario families had no such access. If I relied on an unvalidated test with unknown sensitivity, I risked putting children through needless, potentially dangerous, invasive procedures to detect early tumours that might grow in their eyes.

I chose to describe the situation to each individual family, both in person and in writing. I presented to them the choice of evidence-based testing at Retinoblastoma Solutions or the hospital's test with no evidence of validity. To ensure Ontario families could have access to proper testing, I personally covered the costs of the tests at Solutions, if that was what families chose. Through the spring of 2000, my colleagues and I worked hard to find a more appropriate solution. Dean of Medicine David Naylor and the hospital's vice-president of Surgery, Dr. John Wedge, attempted to mediate, but eventually gave up their efforts to bring the hospital to an evidence-based discussion of the children's best interests. When the Ontario Hospital Insurance Plan refused to designate our lab as the one at which it would cover the costs of genetic testing for retinoblastoma, rather than sacrifice my patients and the science I had developed, I borrowed about $500,000 to provide for those Ontario families' tests.

From 2001 to 2005, fifty-seven Ontario families were tested for *RB1* mutations at Retinoblastoma Solutions and the molecular results were utilized in their health care. Each of these families filed an "out of country service" request (the only process available) with the Ministry of Health for reimbursement of the test, on the basis that the hospital test did not provide a demonstrated level of care. All their requests were rejected by the Ministry, which claimed the hospital's provincial molecular lab provided *RB1* mutation testing. The fifty-seven families then appealed to the Health Services Appeal and Review Board of Ontario, arguing that their clinical care required evidence-based testing, not standard molecular assays with no demonstrated validity. The appeal process first involved nine pre-hearing legal conferences, with eight Ministry lawyers arguing against one lawyer for the families. At the first and only real hearing on September 8, 2005, the Appeal Board ruled that they could not hear the case, since the requested service was located in Ontario and not "out of country." The evidence for the importance of test accuracy and sensitivity in health of families with retinoblastoma was never heard.

Things began to change in early 2005 because of a major testing error in the hospital's molecular lab. The hospital lab reported in 2004 that they had identified an *RB1* gene mutation in a clinical sample sent to them by the clinical geneticist from one of the patients being treated in the Retinoblastoma Program. The child's siblings tested negative for this mutation. We relied on this result to stop clinical examinations of the siblings, as they were no longer considered to be at risk. One year later, an addendum report arrived in the mail, indicating that the lab had made an error and, indeed, had not identified any mutation in the child with retinoblastoma. Therefore, the siblings would be still at risk.

Until then, my concern had been that the false negative rate was high in the hospital lab, in the absence of evidence that the test was sensitive to identify the majority of mutations that were present. False negative tests are costly to the health system and impose unnecessary procedures on children in the effort to find any tumour at the earliest time, but conventional care ensures that tumors are not missed.

On the other hand, a false positive *RB1* test (falsely identifying a specific mutation) is a previously unheard of critical error that can lead to harm. When the relatives are tested negative for a false mutation that does not exist in the affected child, conventional clinical surveillance for tumours for the infant relatives of the affected child is discontinued. This false laboratory result falsely reassures that they are not at risk for disease, putting them at risk of late diagnosis and loss of vision — and even of life. I know of no other false positive *RB1* test in any lab around the world, since clinical laboratory practice guidelines require each identified mutation to be confirmed by a different assay. A false positive RB1 test result is much more dangerous than a false negative one.

At the urging of the child's family, the hospital conducted a "critical occurrence investigation" of the error. Over one full year multiple individuals were interviewed, but to the best of my knowledge and the knowledge of the family, no investigation of the technical failure at the laboratory has yet been carried out.

In response to this critical error, on March 1, 2006, the hospital molecular laboratory finally ceased *RB1* testing for Ontario families. Retinoblastoma Solutions conducts the tests for Ontario under the auspices of Mount Sinai Hospital Laboratory Medicine. The fifty-seven families, who found no process in Ontario to hear their request for evidence-based testing, have filed a complaint through the Office of the Ombudsman of Ontario. Extraordinarily, the Hospital for Sick Children continues to offer to non-Ontario families the test that they have agreed is not valid for Ontario families.

The abrupt withdrawal of the hospital's support for the translation of science for which they had applied and accepted funds over many years, even if it meant second-rate care for children, coincides with my support for Dr. Olivieri.

"AFTERMATH" (BUT NOT "AFTER")

Dr. Olivieri remains under attack by those who opposed her principled stand. She left the Hospital for Sick Children in 2002 for the UHN, leaving the Ontario children with thalassemia with no access to forefront care and international clinical trials. Dr. Olivieri remains a lead contributor to thalassemia adult clinical trials in North America and spends significant time on her global project (http://www.hemoglobin.org) building thalassemia centres in Sri Lanka and Bangladesh. Dr. Olivieri continues to suffer personally for her principled stand. She has been "stalked" and vilified in a bizarre book by a freelance psychiatrist purporting to examine the clinical trial process. It would be laughable in its ineptitude if it were not so nasty and hurtful of a courageous person who is still determined to put safety first.

Dr. Chan remains in the Oncology Division at the hospital and is the principal investigator of an international multi-centre trial of multi-drug resistance in retinoblastoma, with no industry funding. She has essentially closed her basic science research lab, which was highly funded prior to 1999, and has no allocated time for research protected from clinical duties. Prior to 1999 she was a career scientist whose mandate was 80 percent research time.

Dr. Peter Durie went on sabbatical, made a major gene discovery, and carries on providing global leadership in his field.

Dr. John Dick moved in 2002 from the hospital research institute to the UHN and continues with global leadership in cancer stem cells.

I moved my basic research laboratory in 1999 to the UHN, from which we continue to make cancer genomic discoveries. Retinoblastoma Solutions functions as a reference lab for much of the world, due to the high sensitivity and overall quality of our work. We regularly discover fundamental truths in the clinical work, showing that translation between basic science and clinical care is bidirectional. I have expanded my leadership role to global retinoblastoma, particularly focusing in Kenya, India and China, where most children with retinoblastoma are located. Although the province of Ontario finally agreed to fund at Mount Sinai Hospital the Retinoblastoma Solutions tests, it has so far refused to reimburse me for the half-million dollars I spent on behalf of patients between 2001 and 2006.

Dr. Koren remains at the hospital Research Institute, continuing to work closely with the hospital administration and the pharmaceutical industry.

WHAT HAVE I LEARNED?

1. Good scientists are hard to kill.
2. Power, driven by combinations of money and ego, has the potential to overwhelm ethics and concern for individuals.
3. People make a choice between what they know is right, and what they hope will serve their community and themselves best. The Gang individually and collectively chose what they knew was right and bore the consequences. We would all make the same choice in the same situation today.
4. Others chose differently. Harassment of colleagues with anonymous mail and lying to the hospital appears to have been considered a lesser offence than standing up for the safety of children against a drug company.
5. Many wonderful people stood by us and continue to support the principles that we could not give up. We are privileged to gain through this fiasco such close and honest friends.

The Gang, from left: Doctors Helen Chan, Nancy Olivieri, Peter Durie, Brenda Gallie, and John Dick

5

ACADEMIC STALKING AND BRAND FASCISM

David Healy

ACADEMIC STALKING: A CASE HISTORY

From the early 1990s, using the example of how companies had marketed antidepressants — in particular the then new selected serotonin reuptake inhibiting (SSRI) antidepressants — I had authored a series of articles that illustrated the marketing power of pharmaceutical companies.[145] This strand of thinking led to the publication in 1997 of a history of the antidepressants.[146] This book was favourably reviewed both by those supportive of pharmacotherapy and those against it, as well as by reviewers from the pharmaceutical industry. Company reviewers appear to have been pleased that industry involvement in the creation of the field was acknowledged instead of being overlooked, as typically happens in traditional histories of medicine that feature a series of "great" individuals or academic institutions and downplay the business side of science and medicine.

I had also from 1991 onwards written a number of articles and made a number of presentations on the issue of antidepressant-induced suicidality, especially as this linked to the SSRI antidepressants and in particular to Prozac.[147] In books written for general readers from 1993, I included the observation that antidepressants could cause problems of this type.[148] In response, Eli Lilly, the makers of Prozac, invited me to consult for the company, and otherwise invited me to meetings and were "friendly."[149]

The reception for another article, appearing in 2000, that combined these two themes was quite different. This article appeared in the *Hastings Center Report*, one of the leading bioethics journals in the field, whose spring issue in 2000 was entitled "Prozac, Alienation and the Self." This issue contained five articles on Prozac.[150] Two of these articles suggested that as Prozac was so wonderfully effective it would be a mistake to restrict its use simply to people who are depressed and that it should be available more widely to anyone who responded to it. Two further articles argued that even though Prozac was very effective, its use should be restricted to people who are depressed. The fifth article, by me, argued that Prozac was not particularly effective and that impressions of its efficacy stemmed in great part from the fact that negative trials went unreported, that data on the hazards of the drug were concealed, and that in part this state of affairs was linked to the fact that articles on Prozac and on other psychotropic drugs were increasingly being ghost written.

Following the publication of this issue, Eli Lilly, who at the time were the biggest single funder of the Hastings Center, withdrew their support, because the center had "published articles that Lilly felt contained information that was biased and scientifically unfounded and that may have led to significant misinformation to readers, patients and the community".[151]

In July that year, at the British Association for Psychopharmacology's (BAP) annual meeting in Cambridge, I presented data on a healthy volunteer study conducted in which two volunteers who had been blindly randomized to Zoloft (sertraline), one of the Prozac group of SSRI drugs, had become suicidal.[152] Professor Charles Nemeroff from Emory University was the guest lecturer at the meeting. Quite extraordinarily in the course of his lecture, he indicated there was research at the meeting which he felt did not have a place at an academic meeting. It appeared clear that he was referring to my work and it seemed likely that when the study was presented in poster format later that day he would be present.

He appeared at the poster, and in the course of a brief encounter he made it clear to me that he had been approached to get involved in

legal action against me. He also made it clear that he thought presenting research of this kind was unlikely to be helpful to my career, as
pharmaceutical companies roll over people who are awkward to them.

Finally, at the end of November 2000, the University of Toronto and
the Centre for Addiction and Mental Health hosted a meeting to cele-
brate the 75th anniversary of the university department and the 150th
anniversary of the mental health services in Ontario. I was one of the
guest speakers at the meeting. At the time I was scheduled to move to
the University of Toronto, having been interviewed for and offered a
post as professor of psychiatry earlier that year. The distinguished collection of speakers for the meeting included Dr. Nemeroff. The audience was invited to evaluate both the content and presentation of talks
afterwards. My talk was rated the highest on the combined scores.

During the course of that day, I gather Dr. Nemeroff made it clear to
members of the university that it would be a mistake to hire Healy.
Later that evening I had the first intimations that my appointment was
in jeopardy. The following morning, as I understand it, Dr. Nemeroff
told colleagues at meetings in New York that Healy had lost his job. A
week later I had an email confirming that my contract with the university was terminated.

STALKED

I contested the termination. The story broke in April 2001[153] and the
media approached me for my side of the issues. They also approached
the university, who declined to comment but directed reporters to a Dr.
James Coyne, then at the University of Pennsylvania, indicating that
Dr. Coyne would be able to comment on Healy.

I had never heard of Dr. Coyne. His remarks appear to have been
intemperate, and none of the outlets that covered the story featured his
views. This led him to write letters, the first of which was published in
the University of Toronto *Bulletin*, in which he indicated the only odd
feature of what has come to be known as the Healy affair was that the
university had seen fit to consider hiring Healy in the first instance, as
he had little research to his name and his healthy volunteer study was
poor from a methodological point of view and likely unethical.[154] Dr.

Coyne sent a number of comparable contributions to locations, including Web sites, where they could be posted without oversight.

Who was James Coyne? I later found that he had consulted for a number of pharmaceutical companies, including Lilly, and also that he had links with Chamberlain Communications, a New York-based PR agency working for Lilly. He was a psychologist who had previously been employed in Ann Arbor, working on depression, moving to the University of Pennsylvania in the second half of the 1990s.

From 2000 onwards, Dr. Coyne made regular and colourful contributions to a Society for Scientific Clinical Psychology (SSCP) listserv berating me and my research and anyone who offered me support on the issue of whether antidepressants could trigger suicidality.[155] This was not a listserv on which I was a participant. I only became aware of the contents some years later.

In a posting on 9/11/01, before other news broke that day, referring to Healy he stated: "He had not only BEEN an expert witness when he published that article, he was ACTIVELY a witness in an unresolved civil suit in which it was crucial that he be able to cite data for his otherwise unsubstantiated position that SSRI's make people suicidal. Releasing the paper to accomplish that was both timely and sleazy, and all the more so because he did not disclose his relevant financial interests in the study having a particular outcome. His testimony and soliciting of law suits was quite germane to any effort to make sense of his bizarre report and I doubt many readers understood the connection. . . . Incidentally, when it is convenient, Healy accepts considerable money from drug companies, more than most people I know."

Many of the claims made by Dr. Coyne in his postings and correspondence regarding the Healy affair contained claims and assertions about me that were only otherwise being made to my knowledge in briefings to the media by Lilly, Pfizer and GlaxoSmithKline (GSK).

The types of materials aired by Dr. Coyne found an echo in a posting by Pfizer on the US FDA's Web site in July 2004. This posting was linked to a drugs advisory committee meeting to consider the issue of suicidality on antidepressants given to pediatric patients. An earlier meeting in February 2004 had indicated there appeared to be a problem — antidepressants made minors suicidal. The FDA had deferred handling the issue further for a period of half a year on the basis that the agency needed to analyze the data further. Prior to the second hearing in September 2004, interested parties were allowed to make postings on the FDA's Web site and Pfizer did so.

The Pfizer letter was a fifty-page billet-doux extolling the character and science of David Healy in terms such as the following:[156]

> Dr. Healy has distorted and mischaracterized the evidence . . . many erroneous statements, unsupported contentions and data distortions. . . .
>
> Dr. Healy has been hired by lawyers representing civil-litigation plaintiffs and criminal defendants to criticize SSRIs in at least 8 cases. Although he is a psychiatrist and reader at the University of North Wales, he is primarily known for his work as a medical historian. He has little scientific experience in conducting and interpreting the results of controlled clinical research. . . .
>
> Before becoming a litigation expert witness testifying against SSRI manufacturers, Dr. Healy published views opposite to those he now espouses on the question of whether SSRIs induce suicide.

This material contains a number of claims that appear to me actionably false, but taking an action against a pharmaceutical company seemed counterproductive in that any legal effort would likely distract my attention from other important work, and it seemed to me quite likely that Pfizer and other companies had this possibility in mind. FDA denied me a right of reply, but I have since published a reply.[157]

Aside from postings on the SSCP listserv, Dr. Coyne's stalking took more concrete form in 2005. I was aware from postings on the listserv that he was writing or proposing to write an article on the Healy affair. When an article on the "Martyrdom of David Healy" finally appeared in the *American Journal of Bioethics*, it was only published online. There was no hard copy.[158] The journal refused a right of reply. The article is in many respects curiously unfocused, but from its title onwards it conveys the impression that Healy has a lot to answer for.

This article led the Collegium Internationale Neuro Psychopharmacologicum (CINP), the leading international psychopharmacological association, of which I am a member, to institute an investigation. Curiously this investigation and apparently a number of other investigations of the Healy affair have been able to proceed without consulting me at any point.

The Coyne article set up a debate, scheduled for Columbia University in October 2005, supposed to feature Dr. Coyne and myself. I turned up, but Dr. Coyne did not. Subsequently, Dr. Coyne posted on the SSCP listserv a series of comments on Healy and Healy's positions, which I presumed were the kinds of things that he would have said in the debate. These comments and my replies have been posted on the Alliance for Human Research Protection and healyprozac.com Web sites.[159]

The most ominous development in relation to the Coyne article came in March 2006 when I had a letter from the General Medical Council (GMC) in the UK, the body responsible for the registration of doctors. Investigation by the GMC can lead to a doctor being struck off. The letter from the GMC started "Dear Healy, . . ."

Letters like this from the GMC must also include the letter of complaint. The GMC is headed by Sir Graeme M. Catto. Ordinarily letters to Dr. Catto would be addressed "Dear Sir Graeme," but this letter of complaint was addressed "Dear Graeme, . . ." It was from someone I would have considered a relatively close professional colleague, Professor David Nutt, the Professor of Psychiatry and previously the Dean of Medicine at Bristol University. This letter referred Dr. Catto and the GMC to the Coyne article, which "raises serious concerns about the scientific and ethical conduct of Dr. Healy. . . . Is this something the GMC should be concerned about?"[160]

Complaints to the GMC often take years to run their course. Individuals being complained about find the process highly stressful. In this instance, the correspondence surrounding the complaint was fast and furious. It has been laid out in its entirety on healyprozac.com.

Using freedom-of-information provisions, I was able to establish that Dr. Nutt and colleagues had apparently drafted several letters to the GMC to complain about me but, it would seem, had lacked a clear focus for a complaint until the appearance of the Coyne article.

Dr. Nutt's closest collaborator in the exercise of drafting a letter to the GMC appears to have been Dr. Guy Goodwin, the professor of psychiatry at Oxford, another colleague I would have regarded as relatively close. In 2000, I had given a lecture in Oxford at Dr. Goodwin's invitation on the history of the antidepressants and issues to do with suicidality on these drugs.

In 2003 in the course of legal work, I had visited Pfizer in New York to look for documents the company might have on rates at which children in the clinical trials of their antidepressant, Zoloft, had become suicidal. Almost all of the documents related to pediatric suicidality were apparently missing from the archives when I was there, but a vast number of pages remained. There had therefore to be considerable odds against finding any single loose page amongst this material. But a loose page came to hand that appeared to be notes of a telephone call that had been made by an employee of Pfizer to Dr. Goodwin following the lecture on antidepressants and suicidality I had given in Oxford.

These notes may have been taken entirely without Dr. Goodwin's awareness. He appears to have been asked to give an account of what I had said in my lecture, and may also have been asked for, or volunteered, further information on issues to do with me that might be of interest. It seems likely to me that someone gets approached in this way after all my lectures, and that something similar probably happens when anyone critiques the pharmaceutical industry.

Presented with the evidence of serial complaints by Drs. Nutt and Goodwin and apparent plotting on this issue, together with information on Dr. Coyne's background and links and his failure to engage on the issues — and the co-incidental emergence of a letter from GlaxoSmithKline that conceded their antidepressant, Paxil, was linked to a two-fold increase in the risk of suicidality — the GMC chose to draw their investigation to a close some months later. Their letter informing me of this contains a phrase to be cherished: "The paper by

James Coyne represents an alternative view and perspective, which is encouraged in the arena of academia and research."

HANDLING ACADEMICS

This case history needs to be read in a context that includes the role of PR agencies such as Chamberlain Communications, with whom Dr. Coyne had links. When a new drug is launched or when an old drug needs to be defended, public relations companies like this have a brief to handle some of the problems in the field that the new drug might face, including perceived critics.

The kind of "handling" involved can be seen in the example of what happened to another clinician who questioned the received wisdom on Prozac, Joseph Glenmullen. In 2000 Dr. Glenmullen published *Prozac Backlash*, a book that details hazards linked to treatment with the SSRI antidepressants Prozac, Paxil, and Zoloft. On its launch Chamberlain Communications in New York, and other communications agencies working for Lilly, such as Rasky Baerlein in Boston, sent reviews of the book by eminent figures in US psychiatry including John Greist, Tony Rothschild, David Dunner, Graham Emslie, and Harvey Rubin to media outlets such as *Newsday* in New York and the *Boston Globe*. These reviews from some of the more eminent figures in American psychopharmacology broadly state that *Prozac Backlash* was an unfortunate book that emphasized the hazards of treatment without detailing the benefits. The reviewers feared that such a book would put people off seeking treatment and that the failure to seek treatment might lead to their suicide.

The reviews sent to *Newsday* arrived with a covering letter from Robert Schwadron of Chamberlain Communications, who asked *Newsday* to take these reviews into account. Schwadron went on to indicate that he could arrange for *Newsday* to have interviews with people from Lilly and with "independent researchers" to balance the views in *Prozac Backlash*.[161]

This system of controlling the message does not necessarily require people to change their views in return for money from a pharmaceutical company. The companies' power lies in their ability to select the views that suit their interests and to ensure a wide distribution of these views, rather than in their abilities to buy off opinion leaders, although the latter almost certainly also happens.

Even before I had lost my job in Toronto, both Dr. Glenmullen and I had become problems for Chamberlain to handle, in my case probably because of the fact that as of 1999 I had become an expert witness in legal cases against all three major SSRIs. It is possible that at least three different PR agencies working for the respective companies had Healy briefs.

Around that time, I became aware from colleagues as far away as Japan that American academics linked to pharmaceutical companies — who had never met me, heard me talk, or engaged with me on any of the issues I had raised — were spreading the word that Healy was trouble and likely to be in trouble and anyone linked to him risked being damaged by association.

A subsequent freedom-of-information request to Lilly UK threw up 109 items. The contents of items 103 and part of 104 are reproduced here:[162]

103: Healy long term strategy.

Thank you for the message outlining your strategy to counter-act Dr. David Healy's claims re: Prozac and violence.

Send a letter to Healy designed to get him to stop discussing a study that he has never done.

Have a third party expert in the audience at BAP to ask Healy questions when he presents.

Just last Thursday Healy was quoted in a Cincinnati paper saying Prozac causes violence and suicide . . . . X has asked that we go back to legal and determine if we can sue Healy under UK law.

104: Huge turn out. . . . Good talk. Lesson no sponsor if Healy
present in future.

I have been informed by several colleagues in pharmaceutical companies that they had been told they could not have me as a speaker at
meetings they organized. Efforts were made at meetings where I
was scheduled to speak, such as the International Society for
Pharmacoepidemiology, to have me disinvited right up to the last
minute. Funds already committed by pharmaceutical companies to
meetings were withdrawn in a manner that appeared linked to positions I was taking. None of this is unusual; others such as Adrienne
Fugh-Berman have reported similar experiences.[163]

I also learned through emails that a number of what were described
as national (American) meetings had supposedly been held to discuss
the Healy issues, and speakers or other materials at these meetings had
made it clear to participants that those who supported Healy were simply not aware of the facts. These meetings were held without any input
from me and even without my awareness.

Despite having good links to most major psychopharmacology
forums, it proved almost impossible to get the issues of antidepressant-
induced suicidality onto the agenda of any meetings. On the rare occasions when debates were set up, such as at an Irish psychiatric meeting
in 2003, my opponents and the chair were briefed by pharmaceutical
companies with material that overlapped heavily with Coyne and
Pfizer material.

Finally, in the midst of my difficulties with the GMC in 2006, I had
another difficulty. The Internal Revenue Service (IRS) in the United
States made it clear they thought I owed them over $30,000 for the
years 2001 and 2002. This covered tax they regarded as unpaid, the
interest on unpaid tax, and fines for non-payment. It seemed quite
likely that something similar would unfold for 2003, 2004, and 2005,
and indeed for subsequent years.

Britain and America have a tax treaty which allows an individual to pay tax in one jurisdiction only. Aware of possible developments of this sort, I had ensured that all of my accounts had been professionally handled from 1997 onwards, and that all tax had been paid. Within the UK, I had been subject to several reviews in the years from 2000 onwards, to the surprise of my accountant. My accountant was, however, unable to help me with the American tax authorities. I had to seek help from an American accountant. (The IRS ultimately concluded they owed me money, but I continue to have to file tax returns in both the US and UK.)

In 2004, at the time of the hearings on the risks of suicidality in pediatric populations linked to antidepressant intake, the FDA's associate commissioner for external relations was Peter Pitts, whose challenge it apparently was "to clearly define FDA's brand image."[164] Pitts later went on to be a prominent figure in the Center for Medicine in the Public Interest (CMPI). This proclaims itself as "a non-partisan, non-profit educational charity, whose Mission is to discuss, debate and demonstrate how exponential and accelerating technological progress coupled with smart public policy will enhance and advance 21st Century health care by predicting, preventing, diagnosing, and treating diseases with greater speed, more precision and less cost."

CMPI runs a Web site, http://www.drugwonks.com/. As the Internet has become a source of information on the development and the hazards of drugs and on health in general, pharmaceutical companies have learned how to ensure that pharma-friendly sites come up early on Internet searches and hostile sites do not. Drugwonks.com comes up early in searches for information on antidepressant hazards. A prominent figure posting here is Peter Pitts, who writes about critics of pharmaceutical companies, such as David Healy.

> Given the huge body of evidence that the decline in the use of antidepressants has fueled an increase in suicides, the fearmongers now blame the use of anti-psychotics. That includes David Healy, the well-paid expert witness for trial attorneys now suing the likes of Eli Lilly who make anti-psychotics. Can we say conflict of interest? Where will Healy, David Graham

and the rest go to wash the blood off their hands.[165]

Mr. Pitts is also a vice-president for Manning, Selvage and Lee. MS&L "is ranked among the world's top healthcare communications practices. We specialize in health policy, direct to consumer, health policy, medical education, third party alliances and strategic communications around key pharmaceutical benchmarks including medical meetings, advisory committee meetings, product approvals and launches."[166] Its clients include Eli Lilly, Pfizer and GlaxoSmithKline.

Conversely, other sites, such as http://furiousseasons.com/ or http://clinpsyc.blogspot.com, that may feature material on the hazards of psychotropic agents are regularly trawled by legal offices, PR agencies and other groups linked to pharmaceutical companies for, among other things, references to the views of or work of David Healy.

All of the experiences above find echoes in the accounts of what happened to Nancy Olivieri,[167] Aubrey Blumsohn,[168] and John Buse,[169] among others. The market arranges for critics of current products to be marginalized or silenced in a manner that fits well with fascist traditions of the 1930s, 1940s, and 1950s. Anyone who criticizes a brand is likely to have "friends" planted in the audience to monitor what they say and if need be challenge it; is likely to have their utterances or writings scrutinized for possible legal actions; is likely to find "friends" and colleagues have been mined for information; is likely to find "friends" complain about them to whatever body monitors their registration as a physician; is likely to have all their emails and telephone calls monitored; and is at distinct risk of losing their job.

CENSORING ACADEMIA

The current academic scene involves a number of other factors and forces. There is more involved than just individual stalkers operating in a climate facilitated by PR agencies. Whatever the fate of individual academics in the past, science in general has been viewed as relatively unaffected by passing commercial concerns, but the SSRI, osteoporosis, and other stories noted above involve a distortion of the science base. And it is this distortion, and the ability of companies to get the majority of academics to buy into distorted versions of the facts, that isolates academics from the herd and makes them vulnerable to being stalked.

For most academics it is probably close to inconceivable that scientific journals and meetings might be censored. Those a little wiser to the ways of the world might concede there is a certain amount of interference in areas that bear on commercial sensitivities but nothing that could conceivably be called censorship. Readers are likely to think the difficulties surrounding the *Hasting Center Report* mentioned above must simply have been an aberration, one that likely backfired on the company that withdrew its funding.

The alternate explanation, namely that the way Lilly treated the Hastings Center has come close to being the norm for the way companies treat academic journals and meetings, would need to be substantiated. With this in mind, consider the following eleven cases.

1. In 1999, having agreed to testify medico-legally in a case involving homicide and suicide on Prozac, I became aware of documents shedding light on the propensity of Prozac to trigger suicidality and of company efforts to avoid warning of the risk. The documents were in the public domain but few were aware of their existence. My immediate thought was to write an article outlining the material for the *British Medical Journal* (*BMJ*).

When the question of Prozac-induced suicide was first raised in 1990 and the first legal actions had been filed against the company, the *BMJ* carried an article with a company-only authorship line that, despite demonstrating a 1.9-fold increased risk of a suicidal act on Prozac compared to placebo, was widely spun as evidence that there was no risk from the treatment.[170] This article drew an intriguing response from a professor of psychiatry who had a history of difficulties with the pharmaceutical industry: "The *BMJ* is a journal of distinction and, dare I say it, perhaps also of some innocence. At a time when in the United States the manufacturer of fluoxetine is facing litigation, the corporate defense attorneys will be pleased by the journal having published a piece authored wholly by the manufacturer's employees."[171]

The initial *BMJ* response to my submission was encouraging. The editor suggested reframing the article for the education and debate section of the journal. A revised article was sent to a reviewer, who was apparently not told that it was an education and debate article about company behaviour and not an evidence-based assessment of the case for Prozac-induced suicidality. The reviewer suggested the article had not established the case for treatment-induced problems — which it had never attempted to do. The editor rejected the piece on this basis. Mystified at the mismatching messages, I appealed but in vain, with the editor in a phone call stating that no matter what revisions I made nothing would be published.[172]

This article was published unaltered in the *International Journal of Risk and Safety in Medicine*, whose editor, Graham Dukes, commented that "It seems to me your approach is original and fair. . . . I had not seen the issues of litigation, regulation and patents juxtaposed in this way before. . . . I agree entirely from my own experience with many of your comments; there are some striking examples of companies tenaciously hanging onto a profitable and patented drug despite the evidence that it is doing more harm than good. Their motives are a mixture of opportunism and genuine belief that the product is being wrongly accused. I also agree with your remarks about the failure of the present overall research approach to elicit a reliable picture of adverse effects and the sometimes unrealistic defenses put up by industry when their products are the subject of injury litigation." The article was given guest editorial status to emphasize its message.[173]

2. A year later, having conducted a blind and randomized trial in healthy volunteers, one in which two volunteers had become suicidal on an SSRI, I again contacted the *BMJ* about a submission but was told there was no point submitting the article. This was the research that so exercised Drs. Coyne and Nemeroff. My assessment of the situation suggested seeking publication instead in a journal whose editors had previously worked within the pharmaceutical industry, on the basis that this background would make them less rather than more nervous about offending industry. The paper was reviewed and rapidly published.[174]

3. Subsequently, I submitted a data-driven article to the *British Journal of Psychiatry* on ghost writing, whose key finding was a majority of articles that deal with pharmaceutical products in our leading journals are likely to be ghost written. This journal usually has two peer reviewers. In this case a clearly nervous journal used at least five reviewers and had the revised article re-reviewed. The article was subsequently referred to the legal department of the journal, and the copy editors for the journal spent a great deal of time working on the final version.[175]

4, 5, 6, and **7.** Around this time a much smaller journal, *Contemporary Psychology*, requested a review of Joseph Glenmullen's *Prozac Backlash*. My review outlined the key points made by the book, without endorsing the position of the author. It added that I was in possession of five highly critical reviews of the book by distinguished American psychiatrists, with accompanying documentation from public relations agencies working for Lilly providing these reviews to media outlets and encouraging them not to feature the book. I sent the review and the accompanying documents to the editors. The review was initially accepted but failed to appear. On enquiring I was told that the journal could not find a balancing reviewer and so they could not carry my review. The response made little sense.

When the issue of antidepressant-induced suicidality in pediatric populations emerged, *Open Minds* and *Young Minds* requested pieces on the issue. Both journals declined to publish on what I was told was legal advice. They made it clear the decision was entirely based on the assessment that they did not have the resources to handle any difficulties they might run into with pharmaceutical companies as a result of publishing the articles, and to invite such problems could put them out of business.

In 2005 the *Times Higher Education Supplement (THES)* featured a series of articles on Aubrey Blumsohn, who had "blown the whistle" on Sheffield University and Proctor and Gamble over company concealment of data on the response to therapy with risedronate, a treatment for osteoporosis (See Blumsohn's chapter in this book). A series of letters were submitted to *THES* commenting on aspects of the case.

Mine sought to make clear that Blumsohn's case was not unique. *THES* amendments to the letter stripped its meaning. I suggested their revisions made the letter pointless, to which they responded: "We have also had to run these letters past our lawyers as this is, as you are aware, a very sensitive issue, and there are certain legal amendments we had to make." They did not publish any letter from me.

8. In 2004 *Evidence-Based Mental Health* approached me to provide a 300-word commentary on a *Journal of the American Medical Association (JAMA)* article on antidepressants and suicide by Herschel Jick and colleagues.[176] This article, which appeared in the midst of controversy as to whether newer antidepressants might trigger suicidality in minors, appeared to exonerate these antidepressants of any risk. Following its publication, the FDA requested Dr. Jick to make available a further analysis that the published data obviously called for but which the manuscript did not include. This analysis suggested the newer antidepressants were riskier than older ones. My commentary used this new data from Dr. Jick as a comment on their methods.[177]

The publication of my commentary seemed to be an unusual development for the journal. Frontline staff invoked the senior editors. Despite my contention that the best way forward surely was to have new evidence made available, perhaps with an accompanying comment by any other party of their choosing, the journal decided instead to abandon any comment on Dr. Jick's article. In follow-up correspondence I noted:

> I think looking at the confidence intervals in the originally published version, it was pretty clear that a reanalysis of the figures would throw up problems for anyone who was committed to the view that SSRIs pose no problems. And that's just what a reanalysis did.
>
> *JAMA* has also published another article on the Treatment of Adolescent Depression (TADS) where again the abstract and headline and content are at variance with the data from the study, which by strict criteria is a failed Prozac study. But *JAMA* have turned down pretty well all correspondence on the Jick

article or the TADS, while running lengthy commentaries praising these same articles, both of which have also attracted front page *New York Times* and *Boston Globe* coverage. At the same time I and colleagues have sent a meta-analysis of all 677 [published] SSRI trials to *JAMA*, who have turned it down on the basis of a point that could be handled by a simple rewording. Make what you will of this. [Email D.H. to S. Vincent of *Evidence-Based Mental Health*, October 29, 2004.]

In my view and that of my colleague authors, the *JAMA* reviews had not pointed to any substantive problem with our article, and indeed the *BMJ* later accepted the same article essentially unchanged. It has been among the top-three cited articles in the *BMJ* in recent years.[178]

9. In 2005, *BMJ* had a new editor, and I submitted an article on how the data on suicide and antidepressants had been manipulated. The peer reviews were longer than the original paper. After I'd answered all queries from both a first and second round of peer reviews, the paper was accepted. In the middle of correcting the proofs, I received an email from the editor: "Thank you very much for all your hard work on this article. I'm afraid we've run into a legal wall with our libel lawyer reluctant for us to publish your piece. . . . I remain supportive of publication but obviously can't do this against legal advice."

Eventually, possibly because of my persistence, a year and a half later the article was published.[179] The wording had been minimally altered to emphasize the failings of the regulatory authorities for the corrupted data in the public domain and to de-emphasize any company failings.

10. Study 329 was the key study of GlaxoSmithKline's SSRI antidepressant, paroxetine, in depressed children. Faced with the results from this trial, company documents show GSK had concluded in 1998 that the drug didn't work and that the data could not be presented publicly, or even shown to the regulator. Nevertheless the "positive" aspects of the data would be selected for publication.[180]

In 2001 an article reporting the results of Study 329, apparently authored by some of the most distinguished psychopharmacologists in

America claiming paroxetine was safe and effective for children, appeared in the *Journal of the American Academy of Child and Adolescent Psychiatry (JAACAP)*, the journal with the highest impact factor in child psychiatry.[181] In fact the paper was primarily authored by a medical writer, Sally Laden.[182] The selected data and claims presented in this paper were presented at a series of meetings by the "authors," and sales of this drug, whose use in children was unlicensed, soared.

This is not the only case of its type. As of 2004, when concerns about antidepressants given to children blew up, from material available to me it appears that 100 percent of the published literature was primarily authored by medical writers or pharmaceutical company personnel. The ghost writing of these articles was, however, only a minor issue. The real problem is that there was a comprehensive divide between what the articles universally claimed, namely that the drugs were safe and effective, and what the raw data later showed. This is the greatest known divide in all of medicine between what the published literature and the actual trial data show, but the processes that gave rise to this divide can be reasonably assumed to apply as well to all other areas of therapeutics.

Asked baldly on BBC's investigative *Panorama* program whether she would retract Study 329 or regretted its publication now that it had been shown to be ghost written and misleading, the editor of *JAACAP* said No. More generally the editors of our leading medical journals have attempted to clean up the mess posed by ghost writing and lack of access to the underlying data from company studies by asking for authorship declarations and conflict of interest statements, rather than seeking to require companies to make raw data available.

11. In 2007 I was approached by *Index on Censorship* for a piece outlining evidence:

> That pharmaceutical companies are not transparent and that medical journals allow this to happen. The implications of this for doctors and the general public would also have to be spelt out. You put it very succinctly when we spoke — pharmaceutical companies get to publish articles in major journals

under the banner of science but they don't conform to the norms of science. The fact that there's this curious "gentleman's agreement" which means that pharmaceutical companies don't have to produce their data should also of course be mentioned. . . . I think to an outsider who has certain expectations of science (that data is widely available and that access to data is fundamental in terms of any credibility) it's a baffling and shocking state of affairs.[183]

The resulting article covered the evolution of ghost writing, and the lack of access to clinical trial data, focusing on Study 329. An iterative process began that finally got to the lawyers:

Our lawyer's just taken a look at your piece — and I do need to ask you for more chapter and verse on some points.
I realise this is taking up more of your time than you bargained for and do apologise — lawyers must make you weary by now — but am sure you'll understand that it's necessary.

The process ended with:

The documents made interesting reading — and certainly answered the concerns — along with the cuts. But I've still got worries about running the piece. . . . I regret how things have turned out very much. I've appreciated all your help in finding documents and in cooperating with all my requests. As I've said before — it's a hugely important subject and we should be covering it.

Index on Censorship self-censored.

12. The difficulties with publication of a critique of 329 do not seem to be solely due to its author. Following the emergence of evidence that SmithKline Beecham (later GlaxoSmithKline [GSK]) had viewed 329 as a failed study but nevertheless considered selecting the good bits for publication, the *Lancet* published an editorial, "Depressing

Research."[184] Subsequently, the journal published a letter from A. Benbow of GlaxoSmithKline claiming the company were transparent on all issues to do with clinical trials. Leemon McHenry and Jon Jureidini wrote to the *Lancet* taking issue with Benbow's claims in a letter, clearly stating that as an expert in a legal case involving Study 329, Jureidini had a conflict of interest. The *Lancet* agreed to publish their letter, but sent it first to GlaxoSmithKline, who replied that it would not seem appropriate to publish the letter given Dr. Jureidini's role as an expert witness involving these issues, implying that seeking publication in the *Lancet* was a tactic designed to achieve a legal advantage. On this basis the *Lancet* declined to publish McHenry and Jureidini's letter, even though the original Benbow letter could as readily be construed in this fashion, as New York State had taken a fraud action against GlaxoSmithKline for their lack of transparency in 329 and related studies, which the company later settled.[185]

McHenry, Jureidini and Peter Mansfield wrote a further paper on Study 329, "Clinical Trials and Drug Promotion: Selective Reporting in Study 329." The *BMJ* editor wrote to them saying she had heard of their paper and wanted to fast track its publication. Six months later, after revisions, the *BMJ* indicated their lawyers still had concerns and they would not publish.

In contrast to these difficulties in getting articles published, the process of publishing ghost-written articles in major journals appears to be straightforward. In a 2006 *JAMA* editorial, Catherine deAngelis tackled the issue of why leading journals could not ban further articles from those linked to tainted articles saying that "[l]evelling sanctions against an author who fails to disclose financial interests by banning publication of his or her articles for some time period would only encourage that author to send his or her articles to another journal; it cleans our house by messing others. So what about all editors, or at least a group, such as the ICMJE (International Committee of Medical Journal Editors), agreeing to share the information and jointly to ban the offending authors?" Those who suggest this approach have not considered the risk of an antitrust suit.[186]

This statement appears to concede that "scientific" journals cannot insist that contributors adhere to the norms of science by, for instance, being able to make publicly available the data on which their claims are based. This being the case, to avoid misleading a wider public, it might be better if publication outlets unwilling to commit to the norms of science were redesignated as periodicals rather than journals. Company power can be seen in the sequence above. Such pressure tactics are another means to ensure that views not favourable to company interests get closed down. There must be many other instances of journals self-censoring but where the authors have no idea why they have been rejected or no way of proving their suspicions. The effects on academic discourse can only be profound.

The process affects the most prestigious journals in the field — as does the ghost writing, which now affects the most prestigious journals in the field primarily. Where once ghost writing happened in obscure journals, the bulk of articles linked to pharmacotherapeutics appearing in *JAMA*, the *New England Journal of Medicine*, and the *Lancet* are now likely to be ghost written. The agencies responsible for writing these articles trawl the offices of academic journals to find out which journals might be interested in material on a particular issue in order to speed the publication of their product. Such articles will not be impeded on their way by any considerations about incurring a legal action.

On the one hand, companies appear to be able to block the publication of material inimical to their interests, even when this stems from clinicians or others doing what they are legally supposed to be doing — namely reporting on treatment hazards — while on the other hand our journals are ever more full of material that does not conform to the basic norms of science, namely to make available the data on which claims are based.

Systematic action on behalf of companies or related public relations agencies to damp down the effects of publications that do not suit their interests, added to the increasing willingness of journals to effectively self-censor out of fear of the legal consequences of publishing material that is not in the interests of the pharmaceutical companies, puts in place the conditions to recreate a climate not unlike that in Germany in the 1930s and the Soviet Union in the 1950s.

I grew up in Ireland in the 1950s and 1960s, a period when Catholic censorship meant that work by Joyce, Beckett, Kiely, Broderick, McGahern, O'Brien, Dunne, Moore and many others were banned in Ireland because they tackled sexual issues.[187] But it is a moot point as to whether that censorship was any more draconian than the current censorship. Having prided ourselves on finally overcoming Catholic, Nazi, McCarthyite or Soviet censorship, we perhaps think this could never happen again. We fail to see what is happening and to call it what it is. One symbol of the shifting forces is the contrasting experiences of John Cornwell, who wrote books on the risks linked to Prozac[188] and on the inaction of the Vatican vis-à-vis the extermination of Jews in the Second World War.[189] Where once incurring Vatican wrath, as the second book did, might have been a cause for concern but is no longer, as Cornwell found, incurring the strong displeasure of Lilly, as the first book did, led to warnings of legal action against Cornwell in multiple jurisdictions.[190]

BRAND FASCISM [191]

Since the 1950s, a wealth of new drugs has come into medicine. The 1950s also saw the emergence of randomized controlled trials (RCTs), and many thought these methods would help curb the excesses of the pharmaceutical industry. Finally the new drugs were made available as prescription-only from doctors, who it was thought were less likely to be influenced by industry than non-professionals and better able to understand research and its implications.

However, while in the 1950s these new treatments saved lives that would otherwise have been lost and extended the compass of human freedom, forty years later we have moved instead into a world in which pharmaceutical products appear to be contributing to reductions in life expectancy, a degradation of the scientific and academic base of medicine, and the emergence of a medico-pharmaceutical complex that is making the discovery of agents for illnesses that need to be vanquished less likely, while at the same time pathologizing a range of life's vicissitudes and variations.

Key to all this has been the emergence of the marketing departments of pharmaceutical corporations as one of the most potent cultural forces in our world today. They have been able to suck into their ambit the academics who were supposed to act as a counterweight to industry, as well as the apparatus that was supposed to regulate companies, and have in addition transformed those in the media, who distrust every politician whose lips move, into the willing bearers of the good tidings of salvation through pharmaceuticals. Their operations also engineer a situation in which most academics view the efforts of clinicians to fulfil their legal duty to draw attention to the hazards of prescription-only agents as an attack on clinical medicine. As a result, the most distressing attacks on clinical academics typically come from other academics.

THE LEVERS OF POWER

The new marketing has availed of the use of brands, a weakening of patent laws, an industrialization of the clinical trial process, the willingness of physicians to be sold diseases, and their inability to manage uncertainty. But above all it has been aided by physician ignorance of marketing.

While brands such as Nike and Reebok are household names, pharmaceutical brands are the oldest and most profitable brands. The industry turned to branding in the late nineteenth century with astonishing success, as evidenced by Aspirin and Heroin, which a century later still have greater recognition than their generic compounds. With the SSRIs, there has been a much greater investment in these brands than in any other branded products from non-pharmaceutical domains.

Companies brand more than the names of drugs. They can conjure into existence notions such as mood stabilizers, a term that did not exist before the mid-1990s but which is now among the most commonly heard terms within psychopharmacology. Diseases like manic-depressive illness can be rebranded as bipolar disorder, as part of a transformation aimed at persuading clinicians and others that a disorder that until recently was thought to occur at a rate of approximately ten new cases per million per year affects 5 percent of North Americans — 16.5 million people.[192]

Two developments in patent systems in the US and elsewhere made an increased focus on brands possible. First, where these patent systems once aimed at rewarding substantial novelty that clearly contributed to public utility, the US system in particular has moved toward rewarding even novelty with diminishing regard for evidence of benefit. Thus Abbott gained a patent on semisodium valproate for mania and created Depakote, even though the off-patent sodium valproate had already been demonstrated to be useful for mania since the 1960s.[193] Lilly was able to get a patent on olanzapine and create Zyprexa for schizophrenia and mood stabilization on the basis that it was less likely to produce lipid elevations in dogs compared to a never marketed compound, when in fact this drug raises lipids in humans more than almost any other drug in medicine.[194] This relaxation in the application of patent laws in the US to the point where compounds with no novelty and no utility can now be patented may be linked to a calculated attempt to seduce pharmaceutical companies to the United States.

Second, in the 1960s, older laws enabling companies to take out process patents were phased out in favour of patents on products, so that only one company could have a fluoxetine. This has enabled companies to embark on the creation of brand blockbusters such as Prozac, Depakote and Zyprexa. As a consequence, companies have a much greater incentive than ever before to aggressively defend their compounds and conceal their hazards.

Thus talking about early difficulties Lilly had with reports of suicidality on Prozac, one of their then senior scientific officers, Leigh Thompson, put the issues like this: "I am concerned about reports I get re UK attitude toward Prozac safety. Leber (FDA) suggested a few minutes ago we use CSM database to compare Prozac aggression and suicidal ideation with other antidepressants in UK. Although he is a fan of Prozac and believes a lot of this is garbage, he is clearly a political creature and will have to respond to pressures. I hope Patrick realizes that Lilly can go down the tubes if we lose Prozac and just one event in the UK can cost us that."[195]

More recently company marketing documents linked to Zyprexa

make the stakes clear: "The company is betting the farm on Zyprexa . . . the ability of Eli Lilly to remain independent and to emerge as the fastest growing pharma company of the decade depends solely on our ability to achieve world class commercialization of Zyprexa."[196]

World class commercialization has been achieved by, among other things, the following developments. First, companies gained control of clinical trials in the 1980s, when clinical research organizations (CROs) took over from academic physicians as the organizers of trials. As of 2000, CROs ran more than two-thirds of clinical trials undertaken by industry, worth $30 billion. Privatized research of this sort is profoundly different from previous clinical research. CROs have transformed human subjects research, restructured controls of disclosure and confidentiality, and managed intellectual property in an entirely new way by, for instance, sequestering RCT data in a way that did not happen when a federation of academic centres conducted trials.

CROs provide a privatized institutional review board system (ethics review) that grants ethical approval to company studies, when university centres might not. CROs have made it possible to move trials on drugs for Western markets into Asia or Africa, in a way that university departments could not have done. Whether this move has been prompted by concerns to avoid regulatory oversight or cost considerations is less clear. Even in trials done in Western settings, it is now clear that CRO-run psychotropic trials have included bogus patients.[197]

Second, as mentioned above, companies now control the production of the scientific literature. In the case of drugs on patent, a significant proportion of the trials undertaken that do not return the right result now remain unpublished, while a majority of those published are in all probability ghost written and bear an ambiguous relationship with their underlying data.

Third, a further problem for scientific developments lies in the very methods put in place to control the industry. Strapped into a supposed clinical trial straitjacket, pharmaceutical companies found the new methods meant that barely beating placebo would get a licence for all mood disorders or all psychoses or for other conditions. Where once clinical trials had been a method to debunk the claims of treatments that didn't work or didn't work reliably, they have since become the fuel for the therapeutic bandwagons of treatments that are not particularly effective — such as Prozac or Zyprexa.

Trials in which drugs barely beat placebo on rating scale measures are read as evidence that drugs "work," when philosophically it would be more accurate to state that in fact these trials offer evidence that it is simply not possible to say the drug does nothing but that most of whatever benefit there is stems from non-specific factors. The emergence of trial results of this kind should, almost by definition, have marked the point at which scientific investigation of the drugs began, not the point at which independent scrutiny of the drugs in fact finished. This should be the point where we ask if we can identify the small number of patients who benefit specifically and move on to develop other approaches for those who don't.

But having received marketing authorization on the basis of rating scale evidence that the drugs "work" rather than on outcomes such as saved lives or return to work, there is no incentive for companies to find treatments that have big effects on particular syndromes. If the drugs "work," surely it would be unethical for clinicians not to use them for all cases of depression or schizophrenia!

Fourth, clinical practice is increasingly constrained within guidelines issued by a variety of academic or semi-regulatory bodies. Faced with escalating costs and public bewilderment at variations in medical practice, the managers of medical services have turned increasingly to guidelines. Companies have been aware of this for some time and, through their control of the clinical trial and publication processes, they now effectively control the guidelines governing large swaths of medical practice. Although regulators have refused to endorse claims that newer agents — from the antipsychotics and antidepressants through to the antihypertensives — are superior to older agents, even those guidelines drawn up by apparently independent academics invariably endorse newer over older agents, making them among the most powerful marketing tools that pharmaceutical companies have.[198]

Of course, guidelines state that they are not law, but any commentary on whether one must adhere to them makes it clear that any deviations without justification dramatically increase the medico-legal risks of practice. The element of coercion may soon increase with payments being linked to guideline adherence. It is not too fanciful to see in this process a silencing of formerly independent physician voices by an una duce, una voce process.

Control of the scientific literature and the clinical trial process has enabled drug companies to monger diseases.[199] Disorders such as social phobia, panic disorder, and depression have been sold in the expectation that sales would follow. Epidemiological research that establishes how many people might potentially meet criteria for particular conditions provides some of the most valuable data for this disease mongering.

This selling of disorders has gone hand in hand with a marketing of risk and fear. Early hints of depression must be detected and treated in order to reduce the risks of suicide, alcoholism, divorce, and career failure, and treatment must continue to reduce the risk of relapse. Where treatment of a disease might mandate treating one person per hundred, with treatment stopping once the condition responds, treatment of those at risk of a disease or its consequences mandates the treatment of one in ten, and has no natural stopping point.[200]

But there is more to disease mongering than this. Company marketing is less and less about spreading recognition of established disorders and increasingly about pathologizing vicissitudes. A licence for Viagra, for instance, became a means for companies to question young men with normal sex lives as to whether things couldn't be better. Any of life's vicissitudes are now grist for the marketing mill, and companies with a licence do not balk at changing our understanding of what it means to be human, if it captures a niche for the product. There are no academics drawing this to wider attention, perhaps because physicians in general fail to understand where disease mongering comes from.

THE ROLE OF ACADEMICS IN THE NEW FASCISM

At the heart of these developments is the failure of academics to understand modern marketing. Despite regular surveys from marketing com-

panies about the properties of a desirable antidepressant or antipsy-
chotic, and despite the participation of clinical academics in opinion
leader (focus) groups, clinicians confuse marketing with the trinkets,
free lunches, lecture fees, and trips to conferences sponsored by company sales departments. They fail to see that they are the source of the
knowledge that goes into creating brands and fail to see their role in
virally transmitting new brands.[201] The actual differences between
modern antidepressants and modern antipsychotics are minimal; the
perceived differences come almost entirely from sophisticated consumer research aimed at understanding what physicians might
swallow.

In this process, academics have three roles. First, as repositories of
knowledge their role is to help companies understand what the average clinician might perceive as a development. Second, as opinion
leaders they help deliver the company message to non-academic clinicians. Third, they lend their names to ornament the authorship lines of
journal articles and programs of academic meetings reporting the
results of the most recent company studies.

These academic meetings have come to resemble political rallies,
where the faithful assemble to hear about the evils to be vanquished
and the new methods to do so. It has been some time since a trace of
uncertainty entered into any of our major meetings, even though we
are living through a profound medical crisis in that the health of our
patients is worsening and beyond medicine there is debate about the
corruption of our science.[202] Yet the adverse effects of drugs are only
aired if it suits the marketing interests of one of the competing companies. Meanwhile companies have commandeered most of our plat-
forms and journal space to present their products under the banner of
science, while flouting the basic norms of science — to make data publicly available.

Marketing of this sort does a great deal to create the Healy, Olivieri,
Blumsohn, Nissen, and Buse stories. Because the marketing copy for
drugs is derived from the most cherished notions of academics and clinicians, rather than support colleagues grappling with the pharmaceutical industry, clinicians perceive anyone who raises hazards of treatment

as attacking clinical care and the welfare of patients rather than attacking the pharmaceutical industry, and these academics and clinicians react accordingly, even if they have little or no connection to pharmaceutical companies.

What the Olivieri, Blumsohn, and Healy stories suggest is that academia and health care have been infected with an academic immune-deficiency virus (AIV). The defence reactions that might have been expected from prestigious journals and professional bodies in response to the virus seem to be paralyzed. Quite the contrary, the virus seems to have been able to subvert normal defenses to its own purposes. These defences have reacted almost as though it was their programmed duty to shield a few fragile companies from the malignant attentions of a pharmacovigilante.

But just as everything was crumbling behind the rhetoric of Stalinism, so also there is good evidence that outcomes within both mental and physical health are deteriorating. Within psychiatry, rates of hospital admission are rising and life expectancy for patients with serious mental illness is declining. [203] What we are seeing within mental health is not what happens when treatments work; it is not what happened to the dementia paralytica (tertiary syphilis) services after the discovery of penicillin.

It is difficult to see our professional organizations of clinicians, scientists, and academics being able to take stock of the current situation and engage with the new corporate campus. Our major journals and academic meetings have lost brand value.

Another way forward lies in the recognition that drugs are not made in company laboratories — chemicals are. In order for a drug to come into being, two things have to happen. First, healthy volunteers and later patients in clinical trials agree to take these chemicals to see what happens. Willingness to participate in these studies was borne out of the global calamity of World War, when conditions of scarcity mandated the development of the first controlled trials. We participated on the basis that taking risks might injure us but would benefit a community that included our friends, relatives, and children. We did so for free. At first this worked and extended the compass of human freedom from the epidemics and other scourges to which our ancestors had been subject for millennia.

But now this data freely given is sequestered by corporations who market selected parts of it back to us under the banner of science. This business model has made these corporations the most profitable on the planet, while increasingly jeopardizing the health and wellbeing of our friends, relatives, and children.

Second, companies take the inner aspirations and fears of both patients and clinicians to transform a chemical into a drug and also to mould a strategy designed to get patients to consume drugs more faithfully than they would if they were living in a totalitarian regime and ordered to consume them. This is what branding and patenting is about. It yields the biggest profit margins in history, significant amounts of which go to ensure a continuing hold on academic minds and through academics the public mind.

There are both ethical and scientific grounds for objection. It is not clear that companies own the data of clinical trials other than by force majeure. Whether they do or not, it is time for clinicians to consider whether it is ethical to enter their patients into such "exercises." The consent form should at the very least contain an explicit statement that the company may sequester any data from the trial, rendering it unavailable for scientific use. We should see whether patients would accept involvement in trials on that basis.

The scientific grounds to object lie in the fact that current academic practices breach the norms of science by not making data available. If we are to be scientific we must object. This can only be good for both health care and companies in that a medicine of the sort we now have will inevitably be sterile and is only capable of rescue by the serendipitous discovery of new agents. We were supposed to have left behind some decades ago the era of discovering drugs by blind chance.

6

ACADEMIC FREEDOM AT THE FIRST NATIONS UNIVERSITY OF CANADA

Blair Stonechild

Dr. Blair Stonechild was scheduled as the keynote speaker at the Assembly of First Nations "National Symposium on Post Secondary Education," in April 2005. Dr. Stonechild was to speak about the results of research he had conducted on First Nations post-secondary policy under contract with the Assembly. Approximately a week before event, he was advised by the Federation of Saskatchewan Indian Nations' director of higher learning that his services were no longer required.

The policy area I planned to address had been the subject of my doctoral research, published by the University of Manitoba Press as *The New Buffalo: The Struggle for Aboriginal Postsecondary Education*.[204] When I asked the director, whose MA thesis I had supervised, for an explanation, he confidentially told me that I had been removed from the program because of fear that I would make statements about the situation at the First Nations University of Canada (FNUC). This situation related to the period after Morley Watson, vice-president of the Federation of Saskatchewan Indian Nations (FSIN) and Chair of the FNUC Board of Governors, staged an unexpected takeover of the university on February 17, 2005. This action was taken without prior board approval and resulted in the removal of several senior managers, outcries against political interference, and eventual departure of a large number of faculty, staff, and students.

As a result of this information, I immediately submitted a statement to the board of governors, in which I stated:

> The Assembly of First Nations asked that I make a presentation to the National Symposium. . . . [L]ast week I received notification from Danette Starblanket that this action [being dropped from the agenda] was due to the fear that I would use my presentation to make statements about the current dispute at the First Nations University. . . . I am hereby making written confirmation that I would not be making any references whatsoever to the current situation during my presentation.

I asked to be reinstated to the agenda. However, my appeal was unsuccessful.

The FNUC collective agreement states, among other things:

> The First Nations University of Canada is a unique institution in both philosophy and mandate, and as such, has a distinct responsibility to safeguard and promote academic freedom . . . . Members of the University academic community are entitled to enjoy freedoms essential to teach, to conduct research and publish the results thereof, freedom to initiate and enter into dialogue and discussion in areas of interest and competence, as well as freedom to examine, evaluate, and make critical commentary on matters pertaining to, and subject to, the rigors of academic inquiry. . . . Each faculty member is entitled to freedom from institutional and political censure in conducting his or her activities relevant to the carrying out of his or her duties.

Finally, "the University will defend the academic freedom of members from interference from any source."[205]

In testimony before the arbitration panel that was convened, the FSIN director of higher learning provided a different account, claiming that it was solely her responsibility to determine the keynote speaker, and that she had had simply changed her mind at the last minute and decided that another individual from the University of Saskatchewan was a more appropriate choice of speaker. This conflicted with testimony from former FNUC president Dr. Eber Hampton and faculty representative Dr. Brent Galloway, who referred to his notes of the FNUC board meeting. Both confirmed that board chair Watson had ordered the director of post-secondary education to remove me from the symposium.

Nevertheless, in its March 26, 2006, judgment, the arbitration panel chose not to challenge the Federation of Saskatchewan Indian Nations' account of its decision-making process. Instead, the panel focused on "antagonistic" statements that Mr. Watson had made toward me during the board meeting. This in itself, the panel decided, constituted a violation of academic freedom as described in the collective agreement between FNUC and the University of Regina Faculty Association, which represents teaching staff at FNUC:

> We have concluded, nonetheless, that by suggesting that his dispute with Dr. Stonechild should affect the opportunity for Dr. Stonechild to appear at the Symposium to present his research, Vice-Chief Watson failed in his obligation to refrain from interfering in and to defend the academic freedom of a faculty member. In this respect, we find that the Employer violated the collective agreement, and we therefore uphold the grievance in part.[206]

Since he was acting in his capacity as board chairman of the First Nations University of Canada at the time, Watson was an official of FNUC, and therefore FNUC had violated academic freedom. The FNUC initially claimed that the judgement ruled in their favour, but soon after decided to appeal the panel's decision.

A judicial review conducted by Justice C. R. Wimmer of the Court of Queen's Bench was concluded on May 24, 2007. Wimmer upheld the panel's decision, stating "In my judgement, the reasons as a whole support that finding. The decision meets the reasonableness test."[207] The executive director of the University of Regina Faculty Association commented "We feel it's a pretty strong vindication of the original decision that the arbitration panel made."

FNUC's official response of May 31, 2007, to the judicial review confirmed that the institution did not intend to respect the notion of academic freedom as contained in the collective agreement as upheld by the arbitration panel and judicial review: "The issue in this recent judgement, dated May 24, 2007, was about the freedom of expression of board members: not about academic freedom, as was implied by the University of Regina Faculty Association. . . . In fact, since the events of February 17, 2005, there have been no findings of violations of academic freedom at the First Nations University of Canada." [208]

To those who have witnessed the political takeover of FNUC, the attempt to redefine academic freedom to include protecting the right of political leaders to speak is not surprising. The sentiment that academics are merely "technicians" akin to civil servants has been often expressed by the FSIN Directors. In the context in which First Nations governments lack true bureaucracies, there is often a propensity to view academics as surrogate civil servants.

Following its own in-depth review of governance issues and events at the university, in April 2007 the Association of Universities and Colleges of Canada placed FNUC on probationary membership, stating specifically that "the university's board of governors should not be chaired by the FSIN vice-chief responsible for Education and Training, nor should anyone elected to the FSIN Executive serve on the Board."[209] In April 2008, the association lifted its probation of First Nations University that required depoliticizing of FNUC's governance.[210] However, while the FSIN vice-chief resigned, unfortunately, the board of FNUC has not been de-politicized, as fourteen of the eighteen-member board continue to be chiefs or their representatives. Jim Turk, speaking on behalf of the Canadian Association of University Teachers, observed: "We are saddened that AUCC did not feel the First Nations University was worthy to be held to the same standards as Canada's other universities."[211]

There has always been reluctance to criticize chiefs in the past, and this certainly will not change. What is a professional academic to do if a chief interferes with research or teaching that is critical of First Nations government? In such an environment, academic freedom tends to be given short shrift. This unfortunate development lays the foundation for potential future troubles. Will what continues to be a highly politicized environment doom FNUC to continued upheavals and collapses of institution as happened in 2005, and, as well, occurred in 1990 when faculty organized in the face of arbitrary firings by the then board chairman? At that time FSIN threatened to close the institution rather than see it unionized, a threat it ultimately backed down from.

The Saskatchewan Labour Relations Board decision has been appealed to the Saskatchewan Court of Appeal. There needs to be effective resolution in this case of academic freedom, as well as in all aspects of the FNUC collective agreement. For example, the University of Regina Faculty Association reports continued frustration in attempting to have the thirty-five grievances launched by FNUC faculty and staff addressed. If anything is to be learned from this process, there needs to be an outcome that includes some sanctions severe enough to discourage this type of political interference from happening again.

III. INFILTRATING THE ACADEMY — THE STRUGGLE FOR CREDIBILITY

7

INTELLIGENT DESIGN AND SSHRC: AN EMBARRASSMENT FOR SCIENCE IN CANADA

Gary Bauslaugh, Patrick Walden, and Brian Alters

THE ORIGINS OF INTELLIGENT DESIGN

Thirty-six years after Charles Darwin passed away, Henry M. Morris was born. Primarily through Morris's efforts in the 1960s, he became known as the father of modern creationism — a belief that evolutionary science is fundamentally wrong. We will use "creationism" herein to mean an anti-evolution education position often holding views related to issues of teaching science in public schools, such as: (1) evolution should not be taught in science courses, (2) evolution instruction should be greatly diminished in science courses, or (3) evolution instruction should be modified to include supernatural cause as an explanation in science courses, instead of, or in addition to, evolutionary theory.

Morris was most responsible for popularizing "scientific creationism" — an oxymoronic juxtaposition of the natural sciences with the supernatural. Effectively, it was a delivery system to inject a narrow religious point of view into public school science classrooms. Despite virtually the entire scientific community finding it to be pseudoscientific at best, Morris was wildly successful in spreading a facade of scientific respectability concerning scientific creationism across the general public. High schools and parents throughout North America battled over whether to have scientific creationism in the science curricula until

1987, when the US Supreme Court found that creation science, by advancing the religious belief that a supernatural being created various forms of life, endorses religion.[212] That put an insurmountable legal roadblock between scientific creationism and the public schools; no longer could creationism proponents legally attempt to inject that form of religion into the science classroom. The discredited scientific creationism cannot be taught as science, but what about creationism by another name?

Almost right away the basic core of scientific creationism mutated into something called "intelligent design" (ID). As with scientific creationism, ID has at its core a religious proposition that some supernatural being (i.e., God) miraculously created various forms of life on Earth, an explanation that is extraordinarily different from that of the natural explanation of modern evolutionary science. As with creationism, ID is not only antithetical to evolutionary biology but also antithetical to the nature of science in general. Just as with scientific creationism in the previous decades, ID has been scientifically discredited by virtually every major scientific organization.

Nevertheless, following in Morris's footsteps, the proponents of ID have been widely successful in spreading a facade of scientific respectability concerning ID to the general public. As in the past with scientific creationism, high schools and parents throughout the continent have recently battled over whether to have ID in their science curriculum. In 2005, the most important and widely publicized US federal case since the 1987 case concerning science education took place. It was centred on the actions of the school board of Dover, Pennsylvania, where the board infused ID into the high school science curriculum. After a forty-day trial, the court determined that ID was a religious proposition (related to creationism) and not science.[213] Therefore, it could not be taught in their public school science classrooms. In court, ID was clearly and devastatingly discredited as science.

In the leading scientific journals the occurrence of evolution has not been seriously debated for more than a century. In today's modern society, not one secular university grants degrees — or even teaches classes — in ID-based biology, but all teach evolution-based biology.

There are no major scientific conferences that give sessions on ID-based biological sciences, but there are thousands of sessions given on evolution-based biological sciences. There are thousands of governmental scientific grants awarded to scientists doing work on evolution-based research, but none for ID-based research. To put it frankly, effectively all university biologists — whether personally religious or not — consider the science of intelligent design to be a joke. We may respect intelligent design as a particular religious or philosophic proposition; however, it is counterproductive for the general public — in public venues — to be misled by pseudoscience masquerading as science for a particular religious gain.

INTELLIGENT DESIGN IN THE PUBLIC SPHERE

Public business ought to be a secular matter, based upon reason, research, and analysis, not upon any particular religious belief. Most people of moderate religious belief, and of course all secularists, support this idea, which was designed not to suppress religion but for the very opposite reason: to guarantee freedom of religion. The allocation of special influence in the public sphere to any one set of religious beliefs would disenfranchise all others, including those who, as is their right as well, have no religious faith. And of all activities in the public sphere, education (and science education in particular) is the one that above all must be kept separate from religious interference. The science curriculum needs to illustrate the nature of scientific thinking — how theories are based upon evidence, how evidence must be collected so that it leads us toward greater accuracy rather than toward what we might wish to believe.

The religious idea of ID is essentially a device adopted by creationists to bring religion into the science classroom. It has support in many areas of society, including from many politicians who either have an inadequate grasp of science or who are seeking support from the religious groups that continue to fight against the teaching of evolution in schools or try to undermine that teaching with religious stories about creation. That support is not terribly surprising. But it would be astonishing to see, for example, a national research council, staffed and supported, one likes to suppose, with the best and brightest from our research community, apparently unable or unwilling to make the distinction between a religious and a scientific idea.

RESEARCH COUNCIL EMBARRASSES CANADIAN SCIENCE

On March 8, 2006, Canada's second largest research-granting agency, the Social Sciences and Humanities Research Council (SSHRC), which dispenses around $300 million a year for research projects, clumsily initiated a major controversy about evolution and ID in Canada. The problem centred on the rejection of an application by one of the authors of this chapter, Brian Alters of McGill University. Alters is head of the Evolution Education Research Centre at McGill and is a recognized authority on the topic. He appeared as an expert witness in the previously discussed landmark trial at Dover, Pennsylvania. The rejected application proposed to study "the detrimental effects of popularizing anti-evolution's intelligent design theory on Canadian students, teachers, parents, administrators and policymakers."

The rejection of Alters's application was not the problem, however. A majority of projects submitted to SSHRC are not approved, for any number of reasons. The rejection alone would have created not a ripple. However, the rejection statement was as follows:

> The committee found that the candidates were qualified. However, it judged the proposal did not adequately substantiate the premise that the popularizing of Intelligent Design Theory had detrimental effects on Canadian students, teachers, parents and policy makers. Nor did the committee consider that there was adequate justification for the assumption in the proposal that the theory of Evolution, and not Intelligent Design theory, was correct. It was not convinced, therefore, that research based on these assumptions would yield objective results. In addition, the committee found that the research plans were insufficiently elaborated to allow for an informed evaluation of their merit.[214]

In view of its reservations the committee recommended that no award be made.

The problem lay in the insertion of the gratuitous comment: *Nor did the committee consider that there was adequate justification for the assumption in the proposal that the theory of Evolution, and not Intelligent Design Theory, was correct.*

Shortly after receiving this notice, Alters was giving a public Royal Society of Canada address at McGill.[215] He illustrated a point about widespread support for the idea of ID by reading the rejection statement, including the strange clause about ID. Reporters who were there picked up on the statement, and soon it was reported worldwide in the press and in the media. Not only was it reported in leading scientific journals, such as *Nature*, and hundreds of popular newspapers and magazines, but also in venues as disparate as CBC Radio and MTV. It caused consternation amongst scientists around the world, but especially in Canada. Was SSHRC buying the creationist ploy of ID, a shallow and obvious strategy to bring religion into the science classroom? Did people at SSHRC really think that the religious idea of ID is equivalent to evolution, a cornerstone of science?

The immediate responses from SSHRC were anything but reassuring. A spokesperson claimed that Alters was taking the statement out of context (he read it in its entirety — exactly as written — without editorial comment), but gave no indication of how context could make the statement more palatable.

When contacted by the media about the letter of rejection from SSHRC, Janet Halliwell, executive director of the research council at the time, was quoted by Canwest News as follows: "Janet Halliwell has described the wording of the letter as 'misleading' and said the research council did not intend to cast doubt on the survival-of-the-fittest theories advanced in the 1800s by British biologist Charles Darwin."

This sounded odd but mildly promising, but then she added: "There is a growing belief among scientists that certain phenomena in the natural world 'may not be easily explained by current theories of evolution.' The research council supports 'critical inquiry' that challenges scientific doctrine," she added. "We don't make any blanket assumptions."[216]

This was disturbing. There is no growing belief among scientists that certain phenomena in the natural world "may not be easily explained by current theories of evolution." Some explanations have not yet been worked out, but there is no doubt among scientists that evolution will eventually work out the solution. And the idea that there are phenomena that "are not easily explained by current theories of evolution" is one that is often used by creationists to legitimize ID by referring to scientific differences about how exactly evolution works. The suggestion is that there are things we do not know (true) and that ID is a possible way of explaining some of these (highly dubious). Of course there are phenomena that are not now fully explained by evolution; natural processes are very complex. But all that we do know about the natural world — and that is very much indeed — is consistent with evolution. There is no good scientific evidence for ID, as much as creationists try to create the illusion that there is.

Halliwell's statement did not reassure anyone, at least not any of the scientists who were concerned about the adjudication committee's statement. In fact, it made things worse by revealing that the problem goes deeper than an inadvertent misstatement by the committee.

No more reassuring were comments made by Larry Felt, a sociology professor from Memorial University in Newfoundland, who was one of the committee members who reviewed Dr Alters's application. As reported by Canwest News, he, like Halliwell, allowed that there is some validity to the idea of evolution: "No one is disputing the theory of evolution," he said, calling it a "powerful tool not without some difficulties, but nothing that renders it obsolete."

But then, like Halliwell, his comments suggested a deeper problem: "There are features of the natural world including the rapid development of complex organs that 'evolution has some trouble accounting for.'"

He went on to talk about the "possibility of synthesis" between evolution and ID that "compels scholars to take an open mind." Felt recalled a general consensus on the panel that the proposal's research framework was flawed and would have yielded predictable results that "dump on the religious right."

We should be grateful to Felt for having the courage to speak up; three of the other four committee members remained silent, though all were subsequently approached by *Humanist Perspectives* (*HP*) magazine to respond. But what Felt did have to say was indeed unfortunate, because he essentially confirmed that the committee, like SSHRC's Executive Director Halliwell, believes that it is an unwarranted assumption that "the theory of Evolution, and not Intelligent Design theory, was correct."

Humanist Perspectives magazine did try to get other responses from SSHRC and the committee.

THE CORRESPONDENCE BETWEEN *HP* AND SSHRC

Email, April 18, 2006, to Susan Goodyear, media relations officer, SSHRC:

> Our magazine is doing a story on the reasons given by SSHRC for the grant rejection of the evolution/ID project. Could you please tell me:
>
> — how the statement on your website that "the theory of evolution is not in doubt" squares with the committee's statement that there is not "adequate justification for the assumption in the proposal that the theory of Evolution, and not Intelligent Design theory, was correct." Either you are repudiating the statement made by the committee, or you are saying that because evolution is not in doubt, and since according to the committee evolution and ID have equal justification, that ID is not in doubt. Can you tell me which it is?
>
> — I assume that the identities of the committee members is public knowledge. Could you please forward those names and contact information to me, or tell me where I can find them?
>
> Thank you very much.
> Gary Bauslaugh
> Editor, *Humanist Perspectives*

Response from SSHRC, same day:

Hi Gary,

The peer review committee that adjudicated Dr. Alters' proposal to the Research Development Initiative program were:

Dr. Susan Bennett, Dept. of English, Univ. of Calgary (Chairperson)

Dr. Lawrence F. Felt, Dept. of Sociology, Memorial University of Newfoundland

Prof. Ruby Heap, Associate Dean, Dept. of History, Univ. of Ottawa

Gilbert Larochelle, Département des sciences humaines, Université du Québec à Chicoutimi

Madame Ruth Rose, Institut de recherches et d'études féministes, Département des sciences économiques, Université du Québec à Montréal

I'd like to note that SSHRC's funding decisions are made by a peer-review process. Each research proposal is reviewed by a volunteer committee of independent Canadian experts, who then provide advice to SSHRC regarding the quality of the proposal and whether it should be funded.

In the case of Dr. Alters's recent proposal, the committee's decision was not based on doubts about the theory of evolution; rather, the committee had serious concerns about the proposed research design. We regret that the letter sent to Dr. Alters gave the impression that the committee doubted evolution.

Like all applicants, Dr. Alters may appeal the funding decision on the basis of factual or procedural errors in the adjudication process.

If you require further information, do not hesitate to get in touch with me.

                              Thanks,
                              Susan Goodyear

Response from *HP*, same day:

Hello Susan,

Thank you for the information, but as you probably realize I want to know if SSHRC repudiates the committee's statement. You say that SSHRC regrets that the letter gave the impression that the committee doubted evolution, and your website makes a similar statement about not doubting evolution. But that is avoiding the real question. The committee letter did not say, exactly, that it doubted evolution. It indicated that it considers evolution and ID to be more or less on an equal footing. Does SSHRC believe that? If not, then can we assume that SSHRC repudiates the letter?

I am sorry to press you for an answer, but I think it is important for the public to know if one of our leading Research Councils has lost the ability, or the courage, to distinguish between science and pseudoscience.

Regards,

Gary

Response from SSHRC, April 26, 2006:

Hi Gary,

My manager of external relations, Eva Schacherl, will be calling you today.

Thanks,

Susan

Message from *HP* to Eva Schacherl, Manager of Media Relations, SSHRC, April 29, 2006, two days after a phone conversation:

Thank you for speaking to me on the phone the other day. Since I will be reporting on this matter, and as I want to be as accurate as possible, I would like you to check on what I recall from the discussion.

— You said SSHRC regrets the wording in the Committee statement — it is not a proper formulation of the committee's position. SSHRC supports evolution, as expressed in its statement on its website.

— When I asked if you would disown or repudiate the statement in question, you said that SSHRC's role is not [to] make comments on the validity of statements like the one made by the Committee, particularly statements about scientific matters. "We are not scientists," you said.

— You said "SSHRC is a granting agency, and its role is to manage the peer review process." When I asked if that meant assembling competent committees you agreed, but could not comment on the performance of particular committees.

— I asked if SSHRC would refrain from comment if (as one of the commentators in this matter has suggested) a committee had said there was no adequate justification for the assumption that the notion of the Holocaust, and not Holocaust Denial (HD), was correct. You declined comment on this.

We will be covering this matter in our June issue, and I likely will mention our conversation. So if I have remembered incorrectly please indicate, instead, what you would like to say. And please take this opportunity to add any comments you would like to make.

Sincerely,

Gary Bauslaugh

Editor, *Humanist Perspectives*

Response from Eva Schacherl, May 3, 2006:

Hello Gary,

Thanks for giving me the opportunity to confirm and clarify my statements:

— When I asked if you would disown or repudiate the statement in question, you said that SSHRC's role is not make comments on the validity of statements like the one made by the

Committee, particularly statements about scientific matters. "We are not scientists," you said.

I believe I said "We are not biologists." Social scientists are scientists, and rightly want this recognized. I would nuance your statement. It is SSHRC's responsibility to comment on whether the summary sent to Dr. Alters by SSHRC was a correct statement of the committee's views, and we have done that and confirmed it was poorly formulated and did not reflect their views.

— I asked if SSHRC would refrain from comment if (as one of the commentators in this matter has suggested) a committee had said there was no adequate justification for the assumption that the notion of the Holocaust, and not Holocaust Denial (HD), was correct. You declined comment on this.

With respect to SSHRC, I answered your question in this way: SSHRC's focus is on having a quality peer review system that ensures that academic experts review all proposals in a fair and rigorous manner. The system includes checks and balances such as an appeals process that is open to any applicant. In addition, SSHRC is currently reviewing our quality control process to ensure that committees' views are expressed clearly in letters sent to applicants.

Sincerely,

Eva Schacherl

Response from *HP*, May 3, 2006:

Hello Eva,

Thank you for clarifying those points.

You say you have confirmed that the committee statement did not reflect the views of the committee. Can you tell me what part of the statement did not reflect their views? Specifically I and many others want to know if the committee believes that ID is a theory on the same footing as evolution. If the committee as a whole does not believe this, are we to assume that the Chair of the committee just expressed her own views in writing the letter?

What troubles many of us, you see, is that so far, to my knowledge, none of the responsible parties, SSHRC or the committee members (with the exception of Ruth Rose in an e-mail to me), has specifically repudiated the claim made about ID.

You say social scientists are scientists and want this recognized. Yet if the senior Canadian funding organization for social science cannot acknowledge that it recognizes the difference between the science of evolution and the pseudoscience of ID, then what are we to think? This is not just a question for scientists who call themselves biologists, this is a cornerstone in scientific thought, a case where nature has been revealed through extensive and critical observation and experimentation. Diminishment of this work, one of the great achievements in science, by equating it to the wishful thinking of ID proponents, is an attack on science itself.

You may be aware of the fact that science is under siege in the United States, with the growing influence of the Christian fundamentalist movement and its influence on the Bush administration. Many of us thought that Canada was not about to follow this example. We are heartened by the recent statement made by the Royal Society of Canada, putting ID in proper perspective. But we wonder still why SSHRC finds it so difficult to do so. If you do in fact have scientists in your midst, as you claim, this should be a simple matter. And you could very easily ease the worry of many thinking Canadians, and perhaps reduce the international embarrassment caused by SSHRC's refusal, so far, to repudiate the sentence in question.

And finally, your answer to the analogy about Holocaust denial, made by Pat Walden of UBC, misses the point. Would SSHRC remain silent if a committee report stated that it could see no difference between cases made for the reality of the Holocaust, and the case for denial? Would you just say that there is an appeal process for grant proposals? SSHRC would have to make a statement repudiating that claim. Why is it so difficult to repudiate the equally ludicrous claim made by this committee?

> Sincerely,
> Gary Bauslaugh
> Editor, *Humanist Perspectives*

There was no further correspondence from SSHRC. On receiving information about the committee members from Susan Goodyear on April 18, 2006, *HP* contacted all committee members by e-mail, with a version of this letter that was sent to committee Chair Susan Bennett:

> I understand you were the Chairperson of the SSHRC peer review committee that wrote the following explanation for the rejection of a grant application by Dr Brian Alters of McGill: [Committee rejection statement shown earlier.]
>
>   We intend to publish the names of the committee members, but would like to give you the opportunity to disown the statement, or to say anything you would like to say about it, if you are so inclined. If so, please give me a statement by April 30, since we will be going to press shortly after that.
>
> > Sincerely,
> > Gary Bauslaugh
> > Editor, *Humanist Perspectives*

Response from Ruth Rose, April 21, 2006, stating (among other things, including comments about an appeal procedure if applications are rejected),

> I would like to say that I am in no way a supporter of the theory of Intelligent Design and that, although I am not an expert in the biological sciences, I consider the theory of evolution to be correct in all essentials.

This statement was the only one received from anyone connected with SSHRC casting any doubt on ID. The other committee members did not immediately respond, so another e-mail was sent on April 28:

> I recently wrote to all members of the SSHRC Committee responsible for the controversial statement about evolution and intelligent design. I asked if any of you would like to make a comment about it, but the only response I have had was from Ruth Rose.
>
> Although she had the courtesy to reply, she missed the point in part — it is not that I am asking you to reveal anything about the application itself, and I am not interested in whether or not the application is reviewed. The query is not about the rejection of the application, it is about the statement made by the committee in making the rejection. That statement is not confidential. I only want the committee to explain the statements it made, particularly the part that appears to put ID on an equal footing with evolution. Is that really your position?
>
> Ms Rose did at least respond with "I would like to say that I am in no way a supporter of the theory of Intelligent Design and that, although I am not an expert in the biological sciences, I consider the theory of evolution to be correct in all essentials." Are the rest of you prepared to make even that modest statement?
>
> If I do not hear from you I will have to assume that the original committee statement does reflect your view of the matter. That will be disturbing news to not only the Canadian and indeed the international scientific community, but to any person minimally familiar with the difference between science and pseudoscience.
>
> And, Ms Bennett, as Chair of the Committee, I believe you have a particular obligation to clarify your views since, I presume, you were responsible for writing the statement that appeared.
>
> Sincerely,
>
> Gary Bauslaugh
>
> Editor, *Humanist Perspectives*

Response from Larry Felt, same day, stating (among other things, including what he recalled were the real reasons for rejection of the application):

> The one damn sentence is an unfortunate phrasing that some-times happened without any culpability. I wish I had seen it and I would have said something like "The committee feels that the proposed research did not allow for a careful and empirical assessment of any erosion intelligent design might have in the public's understanding of and support for evolu-tion as the scientifically acknowledged basis for understanding changes in the natural world" or some such thing.
>
> Anyway, that's it. It was just one of those unintended bit too general statements that opened up multiple interpretations including the one the proponent chose. Any sense of finality to the episode??

Response to Larry Felt, copies to other committee members, April 29, 2006:

> Hello Larry,
> As I said in my recent message to the Committee members, I am not pursuing this because the committee rejected the Alters proposal, but because of the reasons the committee gave for rejecting it — "the one damn sentence" as you put it. The issue now really has nothing to do with the Alters proposal, except that the proposal elicited the sentence in question. The issue now is, does the sentence reflect the thinking of this panel appointed by SSHRC? Does the Committee support the idea that Evolution and ID have essentially equal merit?
> It is not enough to say, as SSHRC keeps saying, that one sup-ports evolution, because many ID supporters, who are thinly disguised creationists, say that too. Nor is it enough to say the sentence was a mistake, because that does not make it clear what the mistake was. Clearly it was a public relations mistake,

but I want to know if what the sentence says was, in your view, and in the view of the other Committee members, and in the view of SSHRC, wrong.

In other words, do you believe that there is not "adequate justification for the assumption in the proposal that the theory of Evolution, and not Intelligent Design theory, was correct"? You may have been trying to disown this sentence in your letter, but I am afraid you were not very clear. You say you would have written the sentence in another way, but is that because you would have realized it was political dynamite, or because you thought it was wrong?

Finally let me point out that the problem with the sentence is not that "it was just one of those unintended bit too general statements that opened up multiple interpretations." The problem is the exact opposite of that. The "damn sentence" can mean only one thing — that ID has as much validity as evolution. That is why it is so disturbing to so many people, and that is why many of us want an answer.

I am afraid that until there are some straightforward answers, from all of those involved, there will be no "finality to the episode" in sight.

Sincerely,

Gary Bauslaugh

Conspicuously absent from all of the correspondence was anything from Susan Bennett, who, as Chair of the committee, might have been expected to make some comment, given the international embarrassment, and letters of concern from scientists all over the world, this incident was now causing. The following letter was sent on May 1, 2006, to Bennett and the other two committee members who had said nothing. The letters were sent by express post, requiring a signature on delivery:

Dear Professors Bennett, Heap and Larochelle,
I recently sent you the following e-mail messages in the hope that you would retract or explain the letter of rejection you

sent regarding Brian Alters' grant application. My question is not about the rejection but about the opinion, your opinion of ID and evolution, expressed in the letter.

Since I have not heard from you I assume that you have nothing more to say and the letter of rejection represents your actual opinions.

If you do wish to say something please contact me by May 8 — otherwise we will have gone to press.

Sincerely,

Gary Bauslaugh

Editor, *Humanist Perspectives*

NO RESPONSES FROM SSHRC COMMITTEE MEMBERS

No response from these three committee members was ever received.

As the controversy was growing in Canada and internationally, the SSHRC Web site posted an announcement saying that it did recognize that evolution was a "cornerstone of science." This was construed by some as a concession, but it was not so, and it (deliberately, many of us suspect) obscured the real issue. Of course evolution is a cornerstone of science — even many creationists would agree with that. But is it an idea that is any more scientifically sound than ID? Apparently the SSHRC committee didn't think so. Apparently SSHRC officials did not think so.

As of May 2008 SSHRC has steadfastly refused to retract or explain the position of its committee in regard to ID. Representatives of SSHRC have tried various gambits to take the heat off. They have repeatedly said that Alters could always reapply, but that was not the issue. They have frequently made reference to their subsequent statement about evolution, but that too avoids the point of concern.

We are still waiting for a satisfactory response from them. Various groups such as the American Sociological Association, the Canadian Society for Ecology and Evolution, and the American Institute of Biological Sciences, as well as many individual scientists in Canada and elsewhere, have expressed their concerns to SSHRC, but to no avail. Prompted by the SSHRC affair, one of Canada's most prestigious scientific associations, the Royal Society of Canada, issued a statement clearly differentiating the religious idea of ID from the scientific idea of evolution.[217]

ALTERS'S REQUESTS FOR CLARIFICATION

Following the rejection of the Alters grant application and the subsequent controversy, SSHRC has publicly stated that the committee statement did not accurately reflect the decision of the peer review committee and, apparently because of that, set a new policy that peer-review committee views are to be expressed clearly and unequivocally in letters to applicants.[218]

In an email on March 28, 2006, to SSHRC, shortly after the grant rejection, Brian Alters formally requested an explanation of the adjudication committee statement. He was not challenging the rejection, which he accepted as SSHRC's perogative, but he did wish to have an explanation of the extraordinary statement of the committee — a statement that reflects very badly on the state of science education in Canada. The program officer replied that he was not in a position to elaborate on the committee statement. After implementation of the new policy requiring that "peer-review committee views are to be expressed clearly and unequivocally in letters to applicants," Alters wrote twice to Chad Gaffield, President of SSHRC, on August 3, 2007, and November 19, 2007, requesting a clarification. All he has received is a terse statement from Gaffield on September 10, 2007, saying that "SSHRC has provided clarification in this matter, both publicly and in correspondence, on several occasions." Alters's last letter was not answered at all. The clarifications alluded to by the SSHRC president are unknown; nor were they specified in the communication.

In a letter sent to Patrick Walden on November 8, 2006, Gaffield stated "that one sentence of the decision letter sent to Dr. Alters did not accurately reflect the thinking of the peer-review committee." Regarding clarification, Gaffield explained the new policy, "that, in future, peer-review committee views are to be expressed clearly and unequivocally in letters to applicants." Walden has argued that these two statements obligate SSHRC to provide Dr. Alters a clarification in a letter sent directly to him: if the adjudication statement was inaccurate, then Dr. Alters must, by SSHRC's own policy, be given the committee views "clearly and unequivocally."

In this letter of November 8, 2006, to Patrick Walden, Gaffield also wrote, "SSHRC remains silent on Intelligent Design theory — simply because it is not our agency's mandate to take a position." At another point in the letter Gaffield wrote, "With respect to the reaction to this sentence, SSHRC's focus has been to ensure the impartiality of the peer-review process, not to enter into debates on the issues."

Like all of the responses SSHRC has given since this controversy started, these statements add no clarification to the central concern about the position of SSHRC and its adjudication regarding ID. Instead, they only heighten concerns. As Walden had earlier argued, the agency's supposed mandate regarding remaining silent would not likely hold if, for example, one of its committees had argued in favour of giving equal time to holocaust denial theory. Why does it feel so constrained in the case of the unscientific, religiously based ID theory? The comment regarding not entering into "debates on the issues" sounds like SSHRC and Gaffield are supporting the adjudication committee's apparent view that there is a legitimate scientific debate concerning evolution and ID. That is precisely the tactic being used by creationists to argue for bringing creationism, or its stalking horse, ID, into public school curricula.

Alters and the rest of the Canadian scientific community deserve a clarification of the adjudication committee's position on ID and, more importantly, the position of SSHRC itself. If SSHRC really does think there is a legitimate scientific debate on the relative merits of evolution and ID, then that body cannot be responsible for grants for research in science education in Canada.

SEEKING ALTERNATIVES FOR RESEARCH IN SCIENCE EDUCATION

As the prime government custodian of funds for science education research, SSHRC cannot remain officially impartial in regard to a matter of such fundamental scientific importance and of such overwhelming scientific consensus. The science community and the science education community that it serves regard intelligent design as a Trojan horse specifically designed by fundamentalist advocates to undermine science education and to bring religion into the classroom. The present impartial stance denigrates the prestige and regard SSHRC maintains as the granting agency for science education research. It questions the agency's competence and undermines confidence in its ability to execute its science education mandate.

Given SSHRC's refusal to state that it does not entertain any illusions whatsoever that ID is a scientific theory, alternatives must be considered. Researchers involved in science education need to know that their research will be reviewed by peers who understand the science as well as the educational methodologies.

To this end, a number of people have suggested that the mandate for research in science education be turned over to, or at least shared with, the Canadian agency responsible for grants for science and engineering research, the Natural Sciences and Engineering Research Council (NSERC).

On September 11, 2007, Louis Marchildon, president of the Canadian Association of Physicists (CAP), wrote to Chad Gaffield, president of SSHRC, informing him of the following motion passed on June 16, 2007, by the Council of CAP: "CAP Council recognizes that, in order to receive knowledgeable review, research applications in the area of science education be reviewed by SSHRC jointly with NSERC or CIHR [Canadian Institutes of Health Research] as appropriate."[219]

In referring to the Alters case, Marchildon wrote: "This decision and other experiences have highlighted the importance of knowledgeable scientific peer review when research proposals in science education are reviewed" and that "scientists involved in research in science education feel that decisions regarding their research are taken by peers who understand in depth the science, as well as the scientific and educational methodologies involved."[220]

On Nov. 28, 2007, the presidents of SSHRC, NSERC, and CIHR responded to the CAP initiative with the words "Given the importance of science education, we will ensure that your recommendation is included in the tri-council discussions currently underway regarding tri-council coordination."[221] The tri-council discussions have long been concluded, but at the date of this writing no further communication in this matter has been received from the tri-council.[222]

CONCLUDING COMMENTS

Brian Alters and others continue to speak about the strange SSHRC/ID affair. Patrick Walden has documented events in detail on the Web site http://tuda.triumf.ca/evolution. Gary Bauslaugh has followed the story closely in *Humanist Perspectives*, publishing reports in six different issues of the magazine and compiling the reports on the Web site http://humanistperspectives.org. Reports on the matter have appeared on the Richard Dawkins Web site,[223] in the *Skeptical Inquirer*, *Canadian Humanist News*, and in many other publications. As of this writing, however, SSHRC continues to stonewall and refuses to answer the simple question of whether or not it believes the statement made by its adjudication committee — that ID theory is just as good as the theory of evolution — and neither NSERC nor CIHR has felt inclined to comment.

SSHRC's refusal to address the issue of ID, by arguing that its role is "not to enter into debates on the issues," is fully in accord with the strategy of the creationists, who argue that there is a legitimate scientific controversy which in turn argues that both theories should appear, side by side, in school science curricula.

Why did all of this happen in the first place? Are the people at SSHRC fundamentalists? This possibility is unlikely, although some have suggested that SSHRC, a federal government agency, may be acting under the influence of Canada's current right-wing government. More likely is that this large public agency is in thrall to certain trendy ideas in the social sciences and humanities. There clearly is a large postmodernist contingent in those circles in Canada, as in the United States, which often holds that science is an ideology, no better and probably worse than other ways of knowing. In the US, Eugenie Scott, executive director of the National Center for Science Education, reports

"There exists an anti-science movement among postmodernists that views science as negative and even 'corrosive.'"[224]

Peter McKnight of the *Vancouver Sun*, in reporting on the SSHRC affair on April 22, 2006, had the following opinion of the matter:

> At the root of these complaints is the postmodern ideal — the notion that the religious right's knowledge claims are as valid as the claims of science, that all truth, and all methods for arriving at truth, are equal.
>
> By learning to speak the language of postmodernism, the religious right has therefore succeeded in gaining a foothold in the academy, and in influencing funding decisions in the social sciences and humanities. But it has paid a great price, a price that involves denying the existence of absolute truth.
>
> "Misery acquaints a man with strange bedfellows," wrote William Shakespeare, and nowhere is the truth of that nugget more in evidence than in the unhappy marriage of the post-modern left and the premodern right, a marriage made not in heaven, but consummated by the parties' mutual commitment to the relativity of truth.[225]

Our best guess is that something like this is happening at SSHRC, which unfortunately remains firmly in control of research funds for science education in Canada.

8

CONSERVATIVE THINK TANKS AND THE ACADEMY: CREDIBILITY BY STEALTH?

Donald Gutstein

The Fraser Institute is based in Vancouver but in 2004 held its 30th anniversary gala celebration in Calgary, signifying the importance of Alberta money and scholars in supporting the institute over the years. The scene was the glitzy Imperial Ballroom of Calgary's Hyatt Regency, where 1,200 adoring libertarians and conservatives paid $275 each — or $600 for a seat at the VIP table — to hear four politicians and one academic pay tribute to the Fraser Institute's success in pushing political ideas in Canada to the right.

All speakers were effusive in their praise for the institute. Alberta Premier Ralph Klein was the Fraser Institute's "teacher's pet" because he adopted so many of its ideas.[226] Conservative Party leader Stephen Harper showed off his $45 Fraser Institute Adam Smith silk tie and confirmed he was a big fan of the institute. Like the Fraser, he is dedicated to the ideas of Friedrich Hayek, the high priest of market fundamentalism. Former Reform Party leader Preston Manning said he was influenced by the institute when he was building his party in the 1980s.[227] And former Ontario premier Mike Harris lamented he should have gone farther and faster with Fraser Institute ideas.

The Fraser Institute's achievements were celebrated not only in the hotel ballroom but also in the pages of the Canwest Global papers owned by the Asper family. David Asper was a Fraser Institute trustee until he took over as publisher of the *National Post*. The *Calgary Herald's*

Danielle Smith, who emceed the evening, is a former Fraser Institute intern. In fact, the *Herald* sponsored the event.[228] Several Canwest papers went over the top in lionizing the Fraser. The *Province* proclaimed, "We're all 'right wing' now" and ended by congratulating the institute for "daring to dissent. May it do so for another 30 years."[229] The editorial was reprinted in the *Ottawa Citizen* and *Windsor Star*. Libertarian columnist Lorne Gunter reported in the *National Post* that "the Fraser Institute is so highly regarded, that not only was the room chock block full of prominent provincial and national conservative politicians, organizers, consultants, academics and volunteers, it was also full of financiers of conservative parties and causes."[230] Gunter didn't name any names. Nor did he, or anyone else, mention the reason for the Fraser Institute's success — the more than $100 million funnelled through the organization during its thirty-year existence.

With this $100 million directed at the Fraser Institute, and the billions of dollars pumped into scores of think tanks in the United States, Canada, and almost every country around the world, corporations and the foundations of wealthy businessmen are prevailing in the war of ideas with the message, as the politicians noted, that the market is always right and government almost always wrong. Working through think tanks like the Fraser, they're reversing the gains of the welfare state and putting business back in the driver's seat, a project they launched in the early 1970s. And by financing the work of sympathetic intellectuals, they're changing the face of the academy, populating university economics departments and law schools with pro-business, anti-government libertarians, and political science, philosophy, and history departments with the neoconservative students of Leo Strauss and his followers.

The fifth speaker at the thirtieth anniversary bash was University of Calgary political scientist Tom Flanagan. He is a Fraser Institute senior fellow who worked behind the scenes to help Stephen Harper consolidate his grip on the conservative right. Flanagan is the informal leader of the so-called Calgary School, a grouping of libertarian and neoconservative academics based in the political science and economics departments at the University of Calgary that has achieved significant influence over federal government policy directions under both Liberal and Conservative governments.[231] Flanagan spans libertarian and neo-conservative streams. He is best known for his *First Nations? Second Thoughts*, which won a Donner Canadian Foundation book prize for its claim that Aboriginals are simply the country's first immigrants and have no indigenous rights. He is a darling of the Fraser's resource-industry backers for his arguments that instead of enjoying self-govern-ment, Aboriginals should be assimilated into the Canadian economy and their lands opened to market access. Donner provided $20,000 for Flanagan's research for the book and an additional $5,000 to help him publicize his revisionist book, *Riel and the Rebellion: 1885 Reconsidered*.[232]

During the 1990s, Toronto-based Donner was the lifeblood of the war of ideas in Canada, providing nearly $1 million for Calgary School research and millions more to conservative efforts across the country. It helped political scientists Barry Cooper attack the CBC as being too liberal and Ted Morton and Rainer Knopff raise an alarm about femi-nists, gays, and lesbians taking over the courts. Donner money assisted in creating the tale that the Calgary School was inevitable because of Western alienation in a country dominated by the concerns of Ontario and Quebec. It was supposed to be the voice of the excluded. Yet a 1998 study by the Center for Strategic and International Studies, a neo-conservative think tank in Washington, D.C., concludes differently. This study claims that the West, acting through these professional intel-lectuals, exercises an overpowering influence on federal politics. Study author David Rovinsky reports that in the 1990s the West became the "motor of Canadian political thought."[233] The School helped shape the political direction of the Reform Party and Canadian Alliance and, through them, influenced the direction of the Chrétien and Martin governments. Calgary School-devised stealth campaigns helped Stephen Harper become prime minister, says Shadia Drury, who worked in the University of Calgary's political science department for more than two decades.[234] Harper selected Flanagan as his closest advisor and, as his chief of staff, Ian Brodie, who studied under Straussian-trained Ted Morton. Gone are the days when Canada's think tanks had to look outside the country for the intellectual heft of a Milton Friedman or a Friedrich Hayek, as the Fraser Institute did in its early years. The year the Fraser celebrated its thirtieth anniversary, a third of its senior academic fellows worked at the University of Calgary, while Barry Cooper directed the institute's Alberta office.[235]

One of Harper's first actions as prime minister was to amend the *Income Tax Act* to provide a larger tax benefit when donors contribute company shares to a registered charity. This is pure Hayek, promoting the voluntary sector while squeezing government. Many charities benefited from this change in the tax law. So did the Fraser Institute. Its revenues shot up by 60 percent in the next two years. With a budget of nearly $11 million in 2006, it could afford to spend over $1 million on its senior scholars.[236] It took the institute 30 years to burn through its first $100 million. It's likely to spend the next $100 million in less than a third of the time.

The project to roll back the power of government and boost that of business was launched in the United States in the early 1970s, in response to the threat of re-invigorated citizen activism in civil, human, and consumer rights, environmental protection, and the movement to control and regulate business. It was quickly exported to Canada and other developed countries. A key figure in establishing the corporate-sponsored think-tank system was Lewis Powell, a lawyer in Richmond, Virginia, who in 1971 was about to begin a fifteen-year stint as a justice of the US Supreme Court. Like his business colleagues — he was a member of eleven corporate boards, including the Phillip Morris Tobacco Co. — Powell loathed the progressive advances of the 1960s. He was convinced that people like Ralph Nader and the anti-business rebellion had to be stopped. Powell commiserated with friend and neighbour Eugene Sydnor, a department store owner and chairman of the education committee of the Chamber of Commerce. Powell and Sydnor agreed that a new type of national campaign was necessary, and Sydnor invited Powell to outline his ideas about the direction the project should take. The result was the so-called Powell Manifesto, which Powell turned over to Sydnor two months before he was nominated to the bench by Richard Nixon.[237]

The Chamber circulated the 5,000-word document confidentially to members, and it had an enormous impact. Titled "Attack of American Free Enterprise System," it began by claiming that "no thoughtful person can question that the American economic system is under broad attack." Powell's analysis of why the system was under attack and his recommendations to turn the situation around became a blueprint for corporate action over the next thirty years. Powell laid responsibility for the dismal situation at the feet of businessmen, who must "confront this problem as a primary responsibility of corporate management." Managers must concern themselves with "protecting and preserving the system itself" as well as with next quarter's profits. Business must go far beyond its traditional public relations activities. Individual corporate action would not suffice. "Strength lies in organization, in careful long-range planning and implementation, in consistency of action over an indefinite period of years, in the scale of financing available only through joint effort, and in the political power available only through united action and national organizations," Powell wrote presciently.

Powell recommended action on four fronts: the media, politics, the courts, and institutions of higher learning. In the battle for public opinion, business needed to monitor television, radio, and newspapers for content hostile to the free enterprise system and demand equal time. Today, a half-dozen well-funded media-monitoring organizations relentlessly attack mainstream media for being too liberal and successfully push them further to the right. On the political front, Powell urged business to cultivate and use political power "aggressively and with determination." Less than a decade later, Ronald Reagan was business's man in the White House, and fifteen years after that, a Republican-controlled Congress began to undo many 1960s-era laws. In the legal arena, Powell's recommendations inspired a thirty-year campaign to change the face of American law by: creating law firms to advance the business agenda in the courts; installing ideologically friendly faculty in law schools; and placing hundreds of conservative lawyers on the bench.[238]

Powell's most far-reaching proposals were on the battleground of post-secondary education. As he saw it, academia was infected by liberals, socialists, and Marxists, who were poisoning the minds of their students against capitalism. The main culprits were social science faculties that "usually include members who are unsympathetic to the enterprise system." Business needed to establish a staff of "highly qualified scholars in the social sciences who do believe in the system." They would counter the critics, evaluate social science textbooks, write scholarly and popular books and articles, demand equal time for guest lectures, and ensure balanced faculty appointments. These eminent scholars "will do the thinking, the analysis, the writing and the speaking" for the business community.[239]

Powell suggested the Chamber of Commerce should coordinate the corporate effort. This did not happen. Chamber members decided not to take on this role because they thought Powell's ideas were too ambitious and costly. But within a year corporate leaders created a new organization, the Business Roundtable, which did meet Powell's criteria for a coordinating body. This organization consists of the chief executives of 194 of the largest corporations in the country, representing about half the country's economic output.[240] The roundtable has a dual mandate to produce favourable research on public policy issues that affect business and to encourage the organization's prestigious members to speak out on these issues to government, unions, and the community. The organization was a success, partly because of its rich endowment from corporate members, which enabled it to hire resident scholars who seemed to uniformly support the business agenda. Within a few years, the roundtable became the voice of big business in Washington.[241]

A similar organization was established in Canada several years later. The imposition of wage and price controls in 1975 by the Trudeau government was seen by business as a sign the decades-long truce with the welfare state was over. Business needed an organization to take charge of a newly constituted agenda. The Business Council on National Issues (BCNI) was established within a year. It comprised the CEOs of 150 of the largest corporations in the country. With its deep pockets and political and economic clout, the organization quickly became Canada's chief business lobby.[242] BCNI later changed its name to Canadian Council of Chief Executives to better reflect its purpose, consigning the word "national" to the dustbin of history.

The Canadian chief executives' target audience is narrow: the prime minister and cabinet, senior mandarins, the rest of the business elite, and leading media pundits. They're not interested in obtaining broad public support for their proposals. Nor could they easily do so, since, as the voice of big business, they are limited in the claims they can credibly make. Most Canadians "immediately distrust the concerns raised by the [council]," C.D. Howe Institute president Jack Mintz argues. Canadians perceive the CEO council as the "fat cats" who are "pressing their agenda for tax cuts on high-income earners and businesses," Mintz wrote in *Canadian Business Economics*.[243] The professor of taxation at the Rotman School of Management at the University of Toronto argues that the debate is "sterile." It shouldn't be about tax cuts, yes or tax cuts, no but about the "optimal" size of government. Then, in a nifty piece of intellectual footwork, he concludes that government is too big, because it spends too much on "wasteful programs" and requires "too much tax revenue." Because government is too big, it needs to be downsized through tax cuts. Mintz reaches the same conclusion as the CEOs. However, this is no longer the fat cats saying they need tax cuts, but an "independent and reasoned" — the Howe's motto — academic. Because its self-interest is transparent, business requires the support of academics and professionals who can mask the corporate interest.

The tragic events of September 11, 2001, created a unique opportunity for Canada's corporate elite to further a project it had been working on since the 1980s — greater economic integration with the US. Within three months of 9/11, Paul Tellier, CEO of Canadian National and a vice-chair of the CEO council, was beating the drums for further integration. He told the Railway Club of Canada that integration of the two economies "will continue, it is inevitable, it is irreversible and it is taking place faster than any of us expected."[244] Four weeks after that, the CEO council held its annual general meeting. Tellier had been appointed co-chair of a North American policy committee to study

Canada–US economic interdependence, integration, and security. At the meeting, the CEOs agreed on a twelve-month research and analysis program to develop an integration strategy.[245] But, as Mintz pointed out, the CEOs would not get very far with the public in promoting their strategy. Instead, they focused their efforts on the politicians, government bureaucrats, and other corporate executives who might be wavering in support. Let the public be persuaded by the "independent and reasoned" arm's-length think tank.

Two months after the CEOs' meeting, Howe launched an extensive publishing program of more than forty reports and backgrounders it branded as the Border Papers. All the publications argued for deeper integration — of energy resources, security, trade, and regulation. With over $200,000 in funding from the Donner Canadian Foundation, the program supported publications by Howe policy analysts and by academics from the University of Toronto, Carleton University, University of British Columbia, University of Western Ontario, and York University.[246]

Howe may say it is independent, but its links to the CEO council are extensive. In 2002, when Howe launched the Border Papers, sixteen CEO council-member companies were represented on the Howe board, which was top-heavy with representatives from banks, financial institutions, and the oil and gas sector, the most integrated industry in Canada.[247] There is no question the integrationist voice was well-represented. And this view was reflected in Howe's work. This is not to suggest the institute's staff and academics write what the board tells them. But it does mean that academics whose views coincide with the corporate agenda and who are willing to lend their work to the corporate effort are selected and supported.

For its part, the Fraser Institute spent some of its $100 million to set up a Centre for Canadian–American Relations to promote deeper integration. It appointed Simon Fraser University political scientist Alex Moens as a senior scholar to oversee the centre's work.[248] This frenetic activity by the Howe and Fraser institutes, plus work by the Public Policy Forum and the Institute for Research on Public Policy and others, was not driven by what the Canadian public wanted. A

CBC-*Maclean*'s poll just several months earlier asked Canadians "What is the most important issue facing Canada today?" Most respondents answered health and education (29 percent) or unemployment and the economy (25 percent). At the very bottom of the list was Canada–US relations, cited by just one percent of respondents.[249] This was the wrong answer. Canadians would need to be persuaded that relations with the United States was the most pressing issue facing the country. This would be the job of the think tanks. The corporate-sponsored think-tank system was created to convince policy makers and the public that what business wants is the only sensible alternative. Alex Carey saw this as an "elite version of the factory system," in which right-wing think tanks recruit sympathetic intellectuals who convert "millions of corporate dollars into up-market propaganda for corporate interests."[250]

Joseph Coors, head of the largest brewery west of the Mississippi River, was not a member of the Business Roundtable, but he was "stirred up" after reading the Powell memorandum. Like Powell, he was convinced American business was "ignoring a crisis" and invested $250,000 to fund a new policy research institute sponsored by conservative Republicans in Congress and members of their legislative staff. This organization was soon named the Heritage Foundation. Conservative billionaire Richard Mellon Scaife kicked in another $900,000 over the first three years and became Heritage's largest foundation supporter for the next three decades.[251]

Like the Howe and Fraser, the network of lavishly-funded think tanks established in the 1970s by Scaife, Coors, and other wealthy backers could promote the objectives of business without being seen as directly tied to business interests. These organizations had little interest in dispassionate intellectual inquiry. Heritage Foundation senior vice-president Burton Pines called his think tank the "intellectual shock troops of the conservative revolution."[252] The system was an immediate success. In less than a decade, "a tidal wave of money, ideas and self-promotion . . . carried the Reaganites to power" and unravelled many social and economic gains of the past half-century, *Nation* media columnist Eric Alterman observes.[253]

Business supported both libertarian and neoconservative think tanks, the ideologies most capable of being impressed into service for business interests. Libertarian think tanks, such as the Cato, Reason, and Fraser institutes, are based on the ideas of Ludwig von Mises, Friedrich Hayek, and Milton Friedman. They are called variously classical liberals, neoliberals, or libertarians. They hold that individual freedom and liberty are the highest achievements of civilization, higher even than the collective accomplishments of civilization itself. Freedom and liberty are to be achieved and protected by a system of strong private-property rights, free markets, and free trade, goals highly desired by business. The state should not be involved in the economy except to use its power to preserve private-property rights and market institutions. The proposition that markets can solve all our problems is crucial to the business interest but has been taken to such extreme lengths by its proponents that it has been dubbed "market fundamentalism."[254]

In 1947, just as movements to establish social and economic rights were gathering momentum, Hayek formed the Mont Pelerin Society (MPS), to keep his ideas alive during the looming "dark age" of the welfare state. Market fundamentalism should have remained a fringe movement, but it provided an intellectual patina the corporate elite needed to justify its goals for lower taxes, less regulation, and small, ineffective government. As David Harvey points out, "it was a minor society but got a lot of support from wealthy contributors and corporations to polemicize on the ideas it held."[255] The expenses of the ten Americans who attended the first meeting at the fashionable resort at Mont Pelerin, Switzerland, were paid by the William Volker Fund, whose financial resources derived from a Kansas City household furnishings multimillionaire. This fund "enabled extreme market ideologues . . . to come together to plot change," writes Australian environmentalist Sharon Beder. It brought Hayek to the University of Chicago, supported libertarian economists such as Mises and Aaron Director who couldn't obtain positions at American universities, and sponsored lectures by Milton and Rose Friedman.[256]

A key figure in spreading libertarian-style think tanks was British industrialist Antony Fisher, who met Hayek after the war. Fisher was inspired by Hayek's *The Road to Serfdom*, which prophesied state intervention — even of a modest social democratic variety — would inevitably lead to slavery and serfdom.[257] Fisher wanted to go into politics to defeat the Labour government. Hayek counselled instead to work to change the prevailing climate of ideas in the universities, colleges, media, and politics, anticipating Powell's manifesto by a quarter-century. Fisher became wealthy by creating the largest poultry-processing plant in Europe. He later sold his interests, providing the financial resources he needed to implement Hayek's plan. In 1955 Fisher set up the Institute for Economic Affairs (IEA) in London, the world's first libertarian think tank.

The IEA became the model for the dozens of think tanks that followed Powell's 1971 call to arms. The institute courted credibility by publishing papers, pamphlets, and books for an intellectual audience. The books would be reviewed by journalists in the financial and general news press. The books would be sold to universities, schools, and the general public.[258] Authors were found among the membership of MPS. Taxpayer money would not be used to finance the operation. And Fisher warned corporate donors the institute wouldn't necessarily publish what the donors wanted, but if the institute wasn't publishing what the donors wanted, why would they contribute to the exercise? Left-wing criticism of IEA publications sparked interest within the corporate world — if the left is criticizing the IEA, it must be doing something we want to support — and the donations began to flow. A second function of the IEA was to act as a meeting place for the small but growing band of libertarians. Monthly lunches and other get-togethers were on the agenda. Persistence and focus eventually paid off. When Margaret Thatcher won the 1979 election, she wrote Fisher, crediting the IEA with "creating the climate of opinion which made our victory possible."[259]

Before Thatcher's and Reagan's victories, when Lewis Powell's memo was circulating among the business elite, Fisher helped establish three new North American think tanks, including the Fraser Institute. In the early 1970s, businessmen in British Columbia were doubly alarmed.

They panicked at the progressive initiatives of the Trudeau government in Ottawa, and they faced the government of New Democratic premier Dave Barrett in Victoria, which had implemented many controversial measures. Most distressing were the Land Commission Act, which froze the conversion of agricultural land to urban uses, and the Residential Tenancy Act, which introduced rent controls, initiatives that imposed constraints on the unfettered rights of property owners in order to protect the interests of tenants and the public.[260] Noranda chairman Alf Powis, who would help organize the Business Council on National Issues two years later, felt "what was needed was a think-tank that would re-establish the dominance of free enterprise ideas, the values of the market, and property rights."[261]

Economist Michael Walker counted Milton Friedman as a close friend. Walker was working at the Bank of Canada and the Department of Finance, pushing the bank to adopt Friedman's monetary policies. A vice-president at logging giant MacMillan Bloedel learned of Walker's interests through a MacBlo economist who had roomed with Walker at the University of Western Ontario and brought Walker to Vancouver. Walker pitched the idea of a Hayek-type think tank in the mould of the Institute for Economic Analysis, and they brought Fisher to Vancouver to set up a similar organization.[262] The name came from the Fraser River, aping the New York–based Hudson Institute, another venerable conservative think tank, which was near the Hudson River. A geographical, rather than ideological, focus — Hayek Institute? — was preferable in the quest for respectability. They would succeed only if they could get access to corporate boardrooms and the $500,000 a year they estimated would be necessary to run the operation. But funding wasn't a problem. Several senior corporate executives stepped up to the plate. The institute's first-year budget was $420,000, and it hit the $500,000 mark in the third year, by which time corporations were clamouring to get on board.[263]

When the Fraser Institute opened its doors with Walker at the helm, it had twenty-eight corporate and eight individual members. The members included all five big banks and major corporations of the day, such as Canadian Pacific, MacMillan Bloedel, John Labatt, and Molson

Companies. Two years later corporate memberships swelled to 175, and individual memberships to more than fifty. The Fraser made big inroads in the real estate and oil and gas industries.[264] Following the IEA model, the Fraser held conferences, commissioned academics to write papers, published the results in book form and distributed the books to high schools, colleges, universities, the media, politicians, libraries, and the general public. Walker worked hard to ensure media coverage was off the business pages so that the institute was not just speaking to the converted.

To heighten the international and academic cachet of its work, a board of academic advisors was set up and given prominence in institute literature, deliberately overshadowing the board of trustees, which was the real power and the source of the corporate funds behind the organization. With a mandate to oversee the research and editorial activities of the institute, this second publicly visible board consisted of a carefully selected panel of international libertarian and conservative scholars. These included two prominent Canadian economists, Herbert Grubel of Simon Fraser University and Tom Courchene of the University of Western Ontario. The international scholars included Alan Walters — Margaret Thatcher's economics advisor — and Hayek himself. Armen Alchian of the University of California at Los Angeles, who popularized the idea that humans are rational, self-seeking economic beings, so we can apply economic principles to every human activity, appropriate or not, was an advisor. Another scholar on the advisory board was James Buchanan, who founded the public choice school of economics, which allows little space for government in public affairs.[265]

Fisher received requests from businessmen around the world to set up think tanks in their countries that could help bring democracy to heel. In 1981 he established the Atlas Economic Research Foundation to automate the process of establishing and running think tanks. Atlas is based in Arlington, Virginia, and was named after Ayn Rand's libertarian screed *Atlas Shrugged*.[266] Today it works with more than 200 market fundamentalist — Atlas calls them "market-oriented" — think tanks around the world.[267] Atlas's executive director, Alex Chafuen, is a long-standing Fraser Institute trustee. When Atlas celebrated its 25th anniversary in 2006, it could boast of affiliated think tanks in six Canadian provinces, forty-four American states, nearly every country in Central and South America, eleven African and Middle Eastern countries, every country in Greater Europe except Latvia, the Netherlands, and Bosnia and Herzegovina, and most countries of South and Southeast Asia.[268] It was an instructive display of global corporate power. But, as was the intention of the project, corporate power was masked behind a facade of independence.

The emblematic libertarian project is the *Economic Freedom of the World Index*. This annual publication "measures the degree to which the policies and institutions of countries support economic freedom." According to this publication, economic freedom consists of "personal choice, voluntary exchange, freedom to compete and security of privately owned property." But in a world dominated by global corporations, these values seem quaintly old-fashioned. The libertarians claim there is a connection between economic freedom and democracy, but the rankings demonstrate this is not the case. The most economically free jurisdictions in the world according to the index are the city-states of Hong Kong and Singapore, places that do not spring to top of mind when thinking about democracy and human rights.[269] Economic freedom was the brainchild of Milton Friedman, and he and Michael Walker created the project in the 1990s. They recruited libertarian economists in over a hundred countries. The Fraser Institute manages the project; country data are provided by think tanks in each country, many of which are affiliated with the Atlas network. IEA is the UK representative, and co-publishers range from the Albanian Center for Economic Research to the Zambia Institute for Public Policy Analysis.[270]

Business also supported a network of neoconservative think tanks. Unlike libertarian or market-fundamentalist institutes, which emphasize the market and small government, neoconservative think tanks delve into social and defence policy and international affairs as well as economic policy. They are based on the teachings of another European refugee, Leo Strauss, as translated by former Trotskyites like Irving

Kristol, who moved to the right during the 1950s and '60s. Strauss was a German-Jewish philosopher who fled Nazi Germany in the 1930s and taught at the University of Chicago — Milton Friedman's home base — for several decades. He developed a following of students and disciples who achieved enormous influence in academia and government. Strauss died two years after Lewis Powell delivered his manifesto to the Chamber of Commerce in 1971, so he did not participate in setting up the first neoconservative think tanks, as Hayek did with the libertarian ones. Nor would he have agreed to this project, given his preoccupation with secrecy. But some of his followers exploited his ideas for their own ends and impressed them into the service of the business elite. Inspired by Strauss's idea of the "noble lie," they aggressively promoted a conservative agenda at home and abroad.

Strauss believed in the inherent inequality of humanity. Most people are too stupid to make informed decisions about their political affairs. Allowing people to govern themselves will lead inevitably to terror and tyranny, in the same way that Germany's Weimar Republic succumbed to the Nazi dictatorship, an event Strauss witnessed firsthand. A ruling elite of political philosophers must make decisions about governance because it is the only group smart enough. It must resort to deception to protect citizens from themselves. The "superior few" — Strauss's students — must rule over the ordinary people, "not honestly or with candid veracity," writes Strauss critic Shadia Drury, "but by duping, deceiving and manipulating them."[271]

Strauss didn't want to be understood by anyone except his students. His legacy would live on through them. He was content to write books in obscurity and convey the ideas in them to a few students over the years. These students carried on the work, teaching Strauss to their students and creating a growing network of Straussians in American and Canadian colleges and universities and in government. But Strauss also attracted dabblers in conservative and reactionary thought — people who saw a chance to change the world order. During the Reagan years, they grabbed ownership of social policy and pushed it to the right; during the Bush years, foreign and defence policy became their field of operation. At the turn of the century, Straussians were the most powerful, most organized, and best-funded scholars in the United States. Libertarians in academia are mostly economists; neoconservatives are historians, political scientists, and philosophers. They controlled major conservative think tanks, foundations, and media. They had the ear of the White House. And for much of that they could thank Irving Kristol, the first intellectual to call himself a neoconservative.

The term "neoconservative" was coined by American socialist leader and *Dissent* magazine editor Michael Harrington, to describe his former comrades who became first liberals and then conservatives. Longtime student of neoconservatism Gary Dorrien defines it "as an intellectual movement originated by former leftists that promotes militant anticommunism, capitalist economics, a minimal welfare state, the rule of traditional elites, and a return to traditional cultural values."[272] Kristol was an entrepreneur of ideas who, like Antony Fisher, operationalized the Powell memorandum. "I raise money for conservative think tanks," Kristol explained. "I am a liaison to some degree between intellectuals and the business community."[273] He is recognized as "the Godfather" of neoconservatism.[274] Kristol's teachers were Strauss and Donald Kagan, a Yale historian who wasn't a Straussian but moved sharply to the right with them in the 1970s.

Kristol complained that business executives on college and university boards were raising money to finance "left-wing humanities and social sciences departments, 'women's studies' programs that are candid proselytizers for lesbianism, programs in 'safe sex' that promote homosexuality, 'environmental studies' that are, at bottom, anti-capitalist propaganda, and other such activities of which they surely disapprove."[275] These trustees tried to be non-ideological and avoid confrontation, but they were contributing to America's subversion. Kristol told businessmen they needed to "defund" socialist and Marxist academics and recruit their own intellectuals.[276] Business needed to defend its interests by subsidizing the work and careers of ideologically sympathetic intellectuals who believe in the preservation of a strong private sector.[277]

In 1978, Kristol teamed up with William Simon, another business-intellectual proselytizer, to found the Institute for Educational Affairs, whose goal was to recapture institutions of higher learning from the "liberals, socialists and Marxists." The institute would accomplish this goal by linking corporate funders with sympathetic scholars. According to the progressive organization People for the American Way, the institute sought out "promising Ph.D. candidates and undergraduates leaders, [helped] them to establish themselves through grants and fellowships and then [helped] them get jobs with activist organizations, research projects, student publications, federal agencies, or leading periodicals."[278]

To launch the neoconservative project, business and conservative foundations snatched the American Enterprise Institute (AEI) from middle-of-the-road obscurity and transformed it into a smoothly functioning neoconservative vehicle for corporate propaganda. The AEI was founded in 1943 by industrialist Lewis Brown, who hoped to create a conservative organization that could match the influence of Robert S. Brookings of the liberal Brookings Institution. Under Kristol's direction, the AEI grew from twelve resident "thinkers" in the mid-1970s into a sophisticated, well-funded organization in 2005 with 145 resident scholars, 80 adjunct scholars and a large supporting staff. Kristol was AEI's star resident scholar for more than twenty-five years. Another star AEI scholar was Strauss student Walter Berns, who taught Calgary School and other Canadian political scientists when he was at the University of Toronto during the 1970s. Kristol helped the institute's budget mushroom from $1 million in 1970 to $10 million in 1981 to $28.4 million in 2006.[279]

The American Enterprise Institute, Heritage Foundation, and the rest of the libertarian and neoconservative think tanks require a steady flow of funds to achieve their goals. Most money comes from businesses and conservative philanthropic foundations. In addition, some think tanks, such as Heritage, depend on direct-mail donations from thousands of individuals. Nevertheless, a few conservative foundations set the agenda for the corporate project, shaping research and public policy by focusing on a few think tanks and scholars. The National Committee on Responsive Philanthropy examined grants made by conservative foundations to conservative think tanks between 1999 and 2001. It found

that 79 foundations made grants worth $250 million, but five founda-
tions provided half the funding. They are the Sarah Scaife, Lynde and
Harry Bradley, John M. Olin, Shelby Cullom Davis, and Richard and
Helen DeVos foundations.[280] Former Straussian Anne Norton says that
some foundations — Olin, Scaife, Bradley, and Earhart — prefer students of Strauss in their grant-making:

> They fund fellowships and internships for graduate students,
> postdoctoral fellowships and fellowships for senior scholars.
> There are book subsidies, honoraria, fellowships designed to
> give young conservative scholars time to write, fellowships
> reserved for conservative scholarship and the advancement of
> conservative ideas, and subsidies offered to presses — and stu-
> dent newspapers — to represent the "conservative point of
> view." They provide research funds, book subsidies and money
> for conferences.[281]

While many conservative foundations support conservative scholars,
the Olin Foundation was most focused on this mission. John Olin's
fortune came from his holdings in pharmaceuticals (Olin Chemical)
and the Winchester Group, which manufactures rifles and ammunition for the Department of Defense. Over twenty years, under the guidance of William Simon, Olin handed out $325 million. Olin was a big
funder of neoconservative books such as Abigail and Stephan
Thernstrom's anti-affirmative action tome *America in Black and White:
One Nation Indivisible* and Dinesh D'Souza's best-selling books *Illiberal
Education, The End of Racism* and *Ronald Reagan: How an Ordinary Man
Became an Extraordinary Leader*[282] while he was in residence at the
American Enterprise Institute. In the 1980s, Olin provided $750,000 to
Irving Kristol to start a new neoconservative foreign policy journal, the
National Interest. Olin supported Straussian scholar Francis Fukuyama's
article, "The End of History," which was published in the *National
Interest* and was later expanded into a well-publicized book.

Olin's largest think-tank grants went to Heritage ($9 million) and
AEI ($7 million), while an even larger amount — $26 million — went

to conservative scholars at Harvard University (for the Olin Center for Law, Economics and Business, the Institute for Strategic Studies, and the Program on Education, Policy and Governance). Another $21 million went to the University of Chicago, where for two decades Olin financed the Center for Inquiry into the Theory and Practice of Democracy.[283] This centre was run by former students of Leo Strauss, led by Allan Bloom (who died in 1992) and Nathan Tarcov, who was an advisor to Alexander Haig, Ronald Reagan's chief of staff. In 2001, the centre made Strauss's major book, *Natural Right and History*, a focus of study.[284] The centre closed its doors in 2005, the year Olin used up all its money, a plan designed to prevent the foundation from falling into the hands of liberals. The final conference considered the question whether, if the United States is becoming a worldwide empire, it can still have freedom at home, a topic of great theoretical and practical interest to the Straussian elite.[285]

Before the foundation shut down, some Olin money trickled into Canada. It provided $32,000 a year for 15 years to the University of Toronto for a lecture series and graduate student fellowships under the direction of Straussians Clifford Orwin and Thomas Pangle. (Orwin and Pangle also received money from the Earhart and Bradley foundations.) And Olin provided over $500,000 to the Faculty of Law's law and economics program, which applies libertarian economics principles to legal issues. Olin also financed a lecture series, directed by Calgary Schoolers Ted Morton and Barry Cooper, attacking so-called judicial activism.[286]

But American foundation influence on Canadian scholarship was easily surpassed by the Donner Canadian Foundation. It's safe to say the corporate project would not have achieved such great success in Canada without Donner's support. Steel magnate William Donner set up the foundation in 1950 and, when he died three years later, most of his money went to the foundation. Through four decades, primary funding targets were medical research and other good works. In 1962, the family established a separate American granting operation in New York City called the William H. Donner Foundation. The American foundation was administered from Canada and followed the same good-works policy. During the Reagan presidency, the west coast, more right-wing branch of the family gained control of the American foundation and adopted the agenda-driven activism of the major conservative foundations such as Olin and Bradley. In the early 1990s, the family decided to move the Canadian foundation to the right by creating a national network of libertarians and neoconservatives paralleling the highly structured networks in the United States.[287] By then, Donner's Canadian endowment was about $135 million, making it one of the largest in the country.[288]

With its new grant-making program in place, Donner poured $2–3 million a year into conservative efforts. With business support, Donner set up three new regional think tanks, the Atlantic Institute for Market Studies (AIMS) in Halifax, the Montreal Economic Institute (MEI), and the Frontier Centre for Public Policy in Winnipeg. The Fraser Institute received more than $2 million from Donner during the nineties. It set up a branch office in Calgary to tap into oil money and the Calgary School; later established a Toronto satellite office to support the work of the Harris government; and in 2007 opened a branch office in Montreal to ride the neoliberal wave in that province. As well as the multi-issue think tanks, Donner helped establish single-issue conservative advocacy organizations such as the Dominion Institute (traditional study of history), Energy Probe (privatization of public utilities and of medicare through medical savings accounts), Work Research Foundation (anti-union studies), Society for the Advancement of Excellence in Education (charter schools), and National Foundation for Family Research and Education (private daycare). It also provided nearly $2 million for two conservative magazines, *The Next City* and *Gravitas*.

Some of Donner's significant academic grants were:[289]

- $450,000 to the University of Victoria, to establish a Centre for Municipal Studies to promote privatization and contracting out of municipal services;
- $400,000 to the Centre for the Study of State and Market at the University of Toronto, to investigate how to best privatize state

institutions; and
- $125,000 to the University of Toronto for a Workers Compensation "Reform" study, which recommended partial privatization.

In 1999 Donner cut back its funding for conservative efforts when some family members decided they wanted more input into the granting process. Before, about two-thirds of the annual funding went to right-wing causes. After the change, it continued funding conservative projects at a level of about $1 million a year, or 25 percent of total granting.[290] It provided between $250,000 and $300,000 a year to each of the four libertarian think tanks plus another $200,000 a year to the Fraser Institute for its awards for social-service delivery. The year Donner cut back its conservative funding, it added Ken Whyte to its board. Whyte had just started his job as editor of Conrad Black's long-awaited radical-conservative paper, the *National Post*. This dual appointment permitted effective dissemination of Donner-funded propaganda, even at the reduced level of support. As noted earlier, Donner provided about $200,000 to support the C.D. Howe's Border Papers series and its promotion of deeper integration with the United States. The *National Post* struck a deal with Howe to publish exclusive commentaries. Whyte was an insider in funding and promoting the series. What better way to ensure its success than by publicizing it?

Money is also supplied by other conservative foundations such as Max Bell and Galen Weston and by corporate Canada. Few Canadian think tanks reveal their corporate backers. They are not required to under the Income Tax Act. The Fraser hasn't released its corporate members since the 1980s and never revealed how much members contributed. However, a partial understanding of corporate backing can be gained by examining think tank boards. The Fraser's board of trustees includes a representative from Pfizer, the world's largest multinational drug company. Just coincidentally, since Michael Walker claims no trustee can tell the staff what to do, the Fraser has a pharmaceutical policy division that attacks Internet pharmacies that provide cheaper drugs for Americans, disparages critics of drug company policies regarding distribution of HIV/AIDs drugs in Africa, attacks generic drugs, and opposes the ban on direct-to-consumer advertising of prescription drugs. All of these programs benefit Pfizer. The board also includes financial investors from Vancouver and Toronto; cutting corporate and income taxes is a Fraser mainstay. There's big and small oil and gas money from Calgary represented on the board; the Fraser has supported so-called climate change sceptics for a decade. With its pockets bulging with cash and its sympathies lying with conservative policies, big oil can be expected to boost its support for the Fraser and other think tanks in the coming years.

The same coincidental links between the interests of board members and institute activities can be found at most think tanks. The Halifax-based Atlantic Institute for Market Studies proposes privatizing New Brunswick Power and allowing electricity rates to rise. Coincidentally, the president of Emera Inc., the largest private utility in the region, which would be the prime beneficiary of the policy, is chair of the AIMS board. AIMS proposes "modernizing" the Newfoundland fishery by allowing industry to shut down "inefficient" plants. The president of Fishery Products International, which owns dozens of these inefficient plants, is on the board. And AIMS proposes doing away with zoning and planning regulations on land development. The CEO of Empire Co., an owner of shopping malls and office buildings and a residential land developer, is on the advisory council.[291]

The Montreal Economic Institute (MEI) specializes in attacking medicare and promoting greater participation in health care by the private insurance industry.[292] Just coincidentally, MEI's most prominent backer is the Desmarais family, Canada's sixth wealthiest family through its control of Power Corp. Helene Desmarais, wife of Power co-CEO Paul Desmarais, Jr., is an MEI founder and board member. Power Corp. owns three life-insurance companies, including Great-West Life, the largest provider of supplementary health insurance in Canada. Extending private health-care coverage to customers who might already be purchasing Great West life insurance for non-medicare services would be a natural fit for the company.

Not only are corporate and foundation sponsors fighting the battles of today, they're preparing for the struggles of tomorrow by training the next generation of scholars and activists. The Fraser Institute's student programs comprise four interrelated initiatives through which the institute says it is "cultivating a network of thousands of young people who are informed and passionate about free-market ideas and who are actively engaging in the country's policy debate."[293] The programs are separately funded but work together as a comprehensive package of recruitment and indoctrination. Over 17,000 students have come in contact with at least one program since 1988, the institute claims. "Developing talented students sympathetic to competitive markets and limited government" through these programs "is one important way that the Fraser Institute is working towards changing the climate of opinion in Canada."[294]

The student seminar is the initial recruitment tool. The net is cast wide for promising candidates, with up to a dozen day-long seminars held in cities across Canada each year on the full range of libertarian topics: how the market protects the environment, how smaller government leads to greater prosperity, and why we need to privatize health care to save it. A big draw is that the seminars, including coffee and lunch, are free and held in prominent downtown hotels. Seminars are free because they are sponsored by the institute's corporate and foundation backers: Lotte and John Hecht Memorial Foundation (BC seminars), W. Garfield Weston Foundation (Toronto), EnCana Corp. (Calgary), and Canwest Global (Winnipeg). Individuals and companies can sponsor specific components: one student costs $120, lunch is $1,875, coffee break, $500, speakers' travel and accommodation, $4,000. An entire seminar can be sponsored for a tax-deductible donation of $17,000.

The seminars mix lectures and small-group discussions presented from a narrow ideological perspective. Discussion groups are led by staffers from the Fraser or its sister think tanks like the Montreal Economic Institute. Lecturers are senior fellows at the institutes or executives from the National Citizens Coalition and the Canadian Taxpayers Federation. Featured guest speakers run the gamut from Tony Clement, then-Minister of Health in the Mike Harris government, to *National Post* columnist Colby Cosh, to Brian Day, head of the

Canadian Medical Association and president of the private Cambie Surgery Clinic in Vancouver. In short, the range of expertise presented at the seminars runs from right to far right.

Students, in contrast, cover the political spectrum — there is no way the institute can weed out college and high school students with progressive views who attend, often out of curiosity. But that doesn't matter. The sceptical ones can participate and have a free lunch. At the end of the day they are offered a warm "thanks for coming and participating," and are never contacted again. Those whose views are approved by the institute, in contrast, are identified for further orientation, writes journalist Patti Edgar, who attended a seminar as a University of Victoria student in 2000.[295] They might be asked to enter the student essay competition, which is sponsored by the Manning Centre for Building Democracy. Recent topics have ranged from "How can property rights protect the environment?" to "The Canadian healthcare system: Why is it broken and how can it be fixed?" to "Eliminating world poverty: what is the best approach?" The winners in this last contest all argued that "economic freedom" beats foreign aid hands down. This outcome is not surprising, given that, to ensure students come up with the right answer, the institute provides lists of resources, which are restricted largely to libertarian publications and Web sites.[296] Students will receive no credit for critiquing the topic. The best essay receives $1,000, second prize is $500 and there's a separate $250 prize for the best high school essay. Winning essays are published in the institute's *Canadian Student Review*. This 12- to 24-page quarterly publication showcases short articles by conservative students. Each year nearly 50,000 copies are distributed free of charge (thanks to the Hecht Foundation) to campuses across Canada by sympathetic professors and student organizations.

Promising students are further identified through the Student Leaders Colloquium. This is an annual weekend conference for "advanced-level" students to discuss and debate complex economic policy issues. Over 120 "keen students" from the one-day seminars are invited to apply by writing a brief essay on why they would like to attend the colloquium. The twenty best essays earn their authors the opportunity to come to Vancouver. Student responses are provided in the Fraser Institute's annual report:

> I found out how powerful market forces are and how capable they are of solving a diverse range of problems.
>
> I no longer see the government as a necessary evil — I now question its legitimacy as a provider of education and health care.[297]

The linchpin in the recruitment and indoctrination process is the internship program. About 400 university and college students apply each year for ten intern positions in Vancouver, Calgary, Montreal, and Toronto offices. Successful applicants are paid between $2,000 and $2,500 a month for four months to train as junior policy analysts. They work with policy or program directors on specific projects that will lead to publishable reports. The program, which costs about $100,000 a year, is financed partly by the Donner and Max Bell foundations. Interns participate in policy briefings and a weekly discussion club, develop their presentation skills, and are plugged into networks of right-wing experts in their field of research. In 2005, interns worked on a variety of projects such as the school report card, the annual mining survey, and some new "products," like the Regulatory Process Transparency Index for states and provinces, which will measure the "burden of regulation," undoubtedly proving that Canadian provinces rank dead last in North America with Alberta being the best of a bad lot. In 2006, one intern worked on an economic sustainability index; another worked on a project to prove private schools are better for the poor than public schools; and a third worked on the annual edition of government failure in Canada. In 2007, a new product was open to internship applications: a profile of successful private-sector elementary and secondary school chains.[298]

Over the twenty years the Fraser has operated its student programs, graduates have spread into politics, media, think tanks, and academia. A growing contingent of academics was helped on its way by the institute's student programs. They have joined the ranks of hundreds of scholars who were helped by other think tanks. Thanks to the efforts of the corporate project over three decades, it no longer seems to matter who wins elections, be it in Canada or the United States. The issues discussed and the range of opinions considered legitimate will be a far cry from the issues on the public agenda in Pierre Trudeau or Ralph Nader's heyday. Business and the wealthy can thank Lewis Powell for providing a blueprint for regaining control. And it's not over yet. As a result of policies promoted by the business-backed think tanks, the wealthy are richer than ever, and they're pumping millions of dollars into the machine, identifying and nurturing future generations of conservative scholars.

9

POWER AND KNOWLEDGE: THE PRECARIOUSNESS OF FREE INQUIRY

Shadia B. Drury

Ironically, we live in an information age with no reliable information. The monopolistic practices of extraordinarily wealthy CEOs such as Conrad Black, Rupert Murdoch, and Israel Asper (and sons) have undermined the reliability, diversity, authority, prestige, and independence of news in the mainstream media. As a result, public confidence has been destroyed and the mainstream media has been dubbed with a dismissive label — the "corporate media." Increasingly, citizens are turning to the Internet as a source of information. Even though Internet bloggers have no professional training, abide by no rules of evidence, and wear their biases on their sleeves, they have the virtue of not being in the service of the corporate elite. In other words, the concentration of the traditional journalistic sources in fewer and fewer hands has backfired. In the age of information, all information has about as much legitimacy as *Fox News*. Every justice is someone's justice and every truth is someone's truth. How did this foxification of the world come about? Can anything be done about it? And is it healthy to return to the old days when science, truth, and knowledge were revered instead of being regarded with suspicion?

In what follows, I will argue that the triumph of neoconservatism and postmodernism has unwittingly created an atmosphere in which all claims to knowledge are suspect. Far from being mutually exclusive antagonists in the culture wars, neoconservatism and postmodernism are mutually sustaining and affirming. Also, the collusion of power and knowledge is neither unprecedented nor as dire as it may appear. It certainly does not spell the death knell of the academic quest for truth, which has always been subject to the pressures of the powerful.

THE DAWN OF THE UNIVERSITIES IN THE WEST

Since the dawn of the universities in the High Middle Ages (the twelfth and thirteenth centuries), there have been efforts to mobilize the universities for some agenda or other. The emergence of the universities in the West was one of the unintended consequences of the Crusades. The latter created a Western hunger for the intellectual life available in the Muslim world. The result was that learning could no longer be restricted to the clergy in the monasteries and the cathedral schools. Exciting and independent thinkers such as Peter Abelard (1079–1142) broke off from the cathedral schools to set up their own autonomous centres of learning. Hordes of students arrived at centres of learning in Paris, Bologna, and Naples.[299] The Catholic Church jumped on the bandwagon in the hope that all this learning would lend support to her dogmas and enhance her authority and prestige. The popes invested massive funds in support of the fledgling universities and made every effort to control the curriculum. They outlawed the reading of Aristotle because of the dual threat posed by a pagan rationalist whose work was discussed, admired, and translated into Latin by Averroës, Avicenna, and other Islamic infidels.

The new universities were not institutions of free inquiry. The chancellor of the University of Paris was a papal legate with absolute power to decide who had permission to teach and who would be censured, banished, or burned. In 1270, the bishop of Paris, Stephen Tempier, condemned thirteen propositions espoused by members of the Faculty of Arts at the University of Paris. In 1277, more condemnations were issued — as many as 219 propositions were condemned. Heterodox thinkers were accused of heresy, excommunicated, banished, silenced, or killed. Despite the overwhelming opposition of the faculty members at the University of Paris, the pope appointed lackeys such as Thomas Aquinas to teach in the Faculty of Arts — Aquinas could be trusted to do the pope's bidding and to defend the Inquisition.[300]

Interestingly, the church's ban on Aristotle was not sustainable, because the church was not the only money-wielding power around. Emperors and other secular authorities would not allow themselves to be left out. The University of Naples was instituted and protected by the Hohenstaufen emperor, Frederick II, who hoped to transcend the barbarism of the church and its Inquisition by bringing back Greek rationalism and Roman law. The ban on reading Aristotle was irrelevant in Naples. Not surprisingly, the University of Paris and other universities under papal control could not continue the ban without being relegated to irrelevance. Once the works of Aristotle were admitted into the University of Paris, scholars such as Siger of Brabant, began to ask difficult questions. For example, how can the soul experience the flames of Hell if it is immaterial?[301] These were reasonable questions for philosophers to consider, but they got scholars into deep trouble. Siger was accused of heresy; he tried to escape, but died under mysterious circumstances in 1277 at the age of forty. Thankfully, the Catholic Church is not as powerful as it once was, though the universities continue to be the locus of the culture wars of society. But the intimidation of scholars is more subtle.

THE NEWEST ENEMIES OF FREEDOM

The neoconservatives who dominate the Republican Party in the United States and the Conservative Party in Canada are the newest enemies of freedom. They are staunchly opposed to freedom of speech, freedom of information, and freedom of inquiry. They believe that a free media, coupled with the freedom of academics to question and criticize every hallowed principle and every government policy, poses unparalleled threats to the safety, well-being, and security of the nation — any nation. Leo Strauss, Allan Bloom, and Irving Kristol are the intellectual gurus of the neoconservatives. They have a huge following *within* the academy that is critical of the openness and liberality of the universities. They worry that freedom of thought and speech invites dissent, threatens the collective consciousness, and undermines the absolute loyalty, ardent devotion, and unquestioning commitment that every nation needs for political and military success.

For Strauss, the universities have an important political role — namely, the education of a savvy political elite. In his view, the problem is how to educate the elite in institutions designed for mass education. It is not feasible to have two sets of classrooms — one for the leaders and another for the followers. Strauss's solution was to rely on "the great books" of Western Civilization; supposedly, these books contain a dual teaching — one for the few, the other for the many. One is esoteric, secret, and morally subversive, while the other is exoteric, salutary, theocratic, and morally conventional. The esoteric teaching is intended for the statesmen of the future and their advisors, while the exoteric or salutary message is intended for the mass of citizens.[302] The elite few must be taught the dark truth about society — namely, that it is built on myths, illusions, and noble lies; there is no God and no rational foundation for morality. In contrast, ordinary citizens must be taught to believe in a God who punishes the wicked and rewards the virtuous. They must be taught to believe in the absolute inviolability of moral truths. They must be taught to defend their honour with their lives. They must be taught to believe in the unqualified goodness of their nation; they must be taught to believe that it is the best country in the world, that its values are superior to all others, that it is beloved by God, and that its enemies are wicked, Satanic, and uncivilized. These myths are necessary to inspire great sacrifices for the nation. People must have unquestioning commitment to the nobility and magnificence of their country in order to be willing to kill, fight, and die for it.[303] The role of the universities is to inculcate these "noble lies" and "pious frauds."[304] The trouble is that Strauss sees only the positive consequences of this "salutary" deception. He is oblivious to the fanatical nationalism and aggressive militarism that it involves. I will focus on the education of ordinary citizens, before turning to the education of the political elite.

PROPAGANDA FOR THE MASSES

In his best-selling but poorly understood book, *The Closing of the American Mind*, Allan Bloom, the most famous student of Leo Strauss, focuses mainly on the failure of the universities to educate the many. He maintains that the open-minded embrace of other cultures and values within the academy is destructive to the wholehearted faith in the superiority of the values of the West.[305] He heaps abuse on professors who think their task is to encourage students to think critically. He compares them to the smart aleck who told him there was no Santa Claus.[306] He argues that the role of the universities is to inculcate the necessary myths. They must convince people that the values of the West are the best in the world and that other cultures are inferior at best and enemies of civilization at worst.

The power of the neoconservatives was never more manifest than during the administration of George W. Bush. As a result, his speeches echoed their sentiments exactly. In one speech Bush said, "The hand of God is guiding the affairs of this nation."[307] In another speech, he declared that America is God's country, and her enemies are on the side of Satan. By conquering all her enemies, she will conquer evil. Those who are not willing to support America are "complicit in a war against civilization."[308]

Freedom of the press and the academy are obstacles to this sort of theological militarism. Critical thinking undermines the unquestioning faith in the nation and its imperial presidency. Once the questions are raised, the theological edifice begins to crumble. Can unprovoked wars of aggression involving massive civilian casualties, as is the case in Iraq, be considered just? If there is a God, would he want us to kill and pillage in his name? Are these wars in the long-term interest of the nation? Have they made the nation more secure? Do we have a right to defend our way of life when that way of life requires the plundering of the resources of others by force and fraud? Should Canada become entangled in American wars of aggression? These questions threaten the sort of resolute and unthinking commitment that the neoconservatives long for.

Once the universities are turned into instruments of political propaganda, censorship and intimidation become the order of the day. Hence, the creation of organizations such as the infamous Campus Watch project by Daniel Pipes that encourages students to report on professors who are critical of Israeli or American foreign policy. The American Council of Trustees and Alumni, which was established by Lynne Cheney (wife of Vice-president Dick Cheney) and Senator Joseph Lieberman, is intended to identify professors who are unpatriotic and un-American. The triumph of this new McCarthyism is not surprising, since the neoconservatives have always been staunch defenders of Senator Joseph McCarthy.[309] Irving Kristol tells us that he and his fellow neoconservatives abandoned their leftist views when Senator Joseph McCarthy made them realize that the world is a very dangerous place and that leftists and liberals are simpletons who cannot grasp the harsh realities of political existence.

Unfortunately, this new McCarthyism is not restricted to the United States. It threatens Canadian universities, as well. For example, Lakehead University's contract with Google to provide email for students and staff threatens privacy and academic freedom because Google preserves the right to disclose the content of emails to the American government. This would make Canadian professors subject to the same surveillance as American ones.[310]

It is important to recognize that neoconservatives are not simply interested in giving conservative ideas a greater voice within the academy. Nothing is more inimical to the spirit of neoconservatism in theory and practice than truth and the free flow of ideas. The new conservatism is not committed to plurality. It is interested in dominance. As a result, the media and the universities are its targets. The universities must be purged of liberal-minded intellectuals with their naïve quest for truth and their belief in open debate, civil liberties, social justice, and other puerile notions. The neoconservative strategy is to discredit liberal academics the same way the distinguished journalist, Dan Rather of CBS, was discredited. The ploy is to accuse them of liberal bias, denounce them as tenured radicals, and then replace them with an academic version of *Fox News*.[311] Only then can the universities become useful instruments in the dissemination of the appropriate propaganda for the masses — the propaganda about God and nation that the neoconservatives are convinced is necessary for political survival in a hostile world. When the education of the many is a form of indoctrination, then citizens become sheep who are easily controlled by a deceptive and manipulative elite.

EDUCATING A MACHIAVELLIAN ELITE

In contrast to the education of ordinary citizens, the education of the political elite of statesmen and their advisors is to be conducted with utmost secrecy and circumspection. Strauss's esoteric teaching must be imparted with great care and subtlety. Politically speaking, the secret "tyrannical teaching" advocates the rule of the wise independent of law, and even contrary to law. The idea is to teach the elite that where politics and war are concerned, there are no rules. They must be taught that the state and the statesman are beyond good and evil. The custodians of the ship of state cannot afford to be morally squeamish about killing — not just the enemy but their own citizens. The cause of the nation, its security, stability, and survival, trumps all other considerations. So understood, the education of future statesmen and their advisors is a process of brutalization. It is the sort of education that Machiavelli prescribed for the prince. But instead of appealing to Machiavelli, Strauss denounced him as a "teacher of evil," and appeals to Socrates instead. When accused of corrupting the young, Straussians in the academy are smug and contemptuously dismissive of the charge. They are delighted to be in the company of Socrates.[312] The latter has, over the centuries, acquired the status of a Jesus figure, so no one is likely to suspect that the "tyrannical teaching" involves levels of treachery, deceit, and chicanery that would make Machiavelli blush.

Unlike other critics, I have never criticized Strauss for being elitist, anti-democratic, or anti-liberal. I have criticized him for cultivating a secretive, duplicitous, treacherous, and morally unscrupulous elite — an elite that has made its way into the corridors of power in the United States: Paul Wolfowitz, Scooter Libby, Abram Shulsky, and William Kristol were the best known Straussians in the administration of George W. Bush. As deputy secretary of defense and assistant to Vice-president Dick Cheney, Wolfowitz was one of the key architects of the invasion of Iraq. As the invasion proved disastrous, he was rewarded by being made chairman of the World Bank. But he was soon forced to leave that post in disgrace, due to lies and illegal activities. Scooter Libby was Vice-president Cheney's chief of staff, until he was convicted on several counts of fraud, obstruction of justice, and lying to the FBI. Abram Shulsky was the director of the Office of Special Plans, which was created by Secretary of Defense Donald Rumsfeld. Shulsky was responsible for finding intelligence that would help to make the case for the invasion of Iraq. We know that the intelligence was misleading, exaggerated, and even false. My point is that Strauss has cultivated the sort of elite that cannot be trusted with power. It is no wonder this elite has fuelled endless speculation by citizens that the attacks of September 11, 2001, were an inside job. The Straussians in power invite this sort of suspicion. In a famous document, they tell us that a catastrophe comparable to Pearl Harbour is necessary to implement their daring policies.[313]

In a recent book, Thomas Flanagan, advisor to Stephen Harper, made a similar claim. He compared the neoconservative policies of the Reform Party with hard medicine. Even though he extolled their beauty, he warned that they require a crisis if they are to be fully implemented.[314] In the absence of some calamity, Flanagan advises the Conservatives to moderate their reforms and expectations. He tells them they must proceed with great care and circumspection, if they hope to hang on to power. Flanagan is astute enough to recognize that neoconservative policies are difficult to implement in the absence of a state of siege.

What is the nature of the strong medicine? Why is such strong medicine required? What is the disease that the strong medicine is supposed to cure? Why is so much care and circumspection needed? Why are lies, deception, and the manipulation of public opinion necessary for this medicine to be administered? Is the public unwilling to accept a medicine that would eventually result in some benefit? Are people too puerile to choose what is good for them in the long run? Or, are perpetual hardship, adversity, and privation precisely what ordinary people need? I have argued elsewhere that endless war is integral to neoconservative social policy. In that case, the medical analogy is misleading and neoconservative policies are more accurately compared to

poison. The hardships of endless war bring only death, not the antici-
pation of a cure.[315]

The secrecy on which Strauss and his disciples rely encourages the
cultivation of feeble-minded clones. Dogmas inculcated without
scrutiny or debate, but only with winks and nudges, are harmful and
noxious doctrines, not profound or unassailable truths. Strauss,
Bloom, and their fellow travellers exploited the intellectual insecurity
of their students. They turn their students into pawns to be shaped by
their supposedly discerning wisdom. The result is docile and subservient young men (they are invariably men) who imagine themselves
to be leaders. But their docility is often concealed behind an exterior
facade of confident aggression, which they acquire once they are flat-
tered into believing they belong to a rarefied fraction of humanity — a
special elite fit for the dark truth that ordinary mortals cannot withstand. This sort of flattery does not deserve the name "education." It is
a betrayal of trust; it is an abdication of responsibility; it is a perversion
of the veracity that liberal education requires. In truth, the education of
the "elite" produces individuals that are just as docile and gullible as
the masses, but more dangerous.

If universities accomplish anything at all, they must nurture people
who can think — people who are not easily bamboozled by lies and
propaganda. Thinking invariably makes people better. Evil is closely
connected to stupidity and the inability of people to think clearly or to
think for themselves. These thoughtless people are the sort of people
on which tyrannies thrive. They buy into the ideologies, lies, and propaganda that the state dishes out. The worse a state is, the more lies it
must dish out. The more the people are enmeshed in falsehood, the
more difficult it is to untangle the lies. In these circumstances, thoughtless people are easily recruited to become the "desk murderers" of the
state. Political philosopher Hannah Arendt described Eichmann, the
Nazi minister of transportation, as such a man. Chalmers Johnson
described George W. Bush, Dick Cheney, Donald Rumsfeld, and
Condoleezza Rice as "desk murderers."[316]

STRAUSSIAN ANECDOTES FROM THE ACADEMY

I did not know Strauss personally, but I knew a political theorist who, as a young man, was appointed to the Department of Political Science at the University of Chicago during the time that Strauss taught there. Naturally, he went to introduce himself to the great man. Strauss was rolling a cigarette in his office as the young man chatted with him. In what looked like a deliberate act, Strauss dropped the cigarette, and waited. The young man did not pick it up. Later, the young man discovered that he could not depend on the cooperation of the secretaries, and could not even acquire department letterhead. He failed the test for subservience.

Sometimes subservience is induced by less subtle means of intimidation. A tutorial leader and graduate student of one of the most famous Straussians failed to understand the importance of subtlety. He came in to class on the first day and told the undergraduates that if they didn't accept Aristotle's argument in favour of slavery, they could not get more than a "C" in the course. The accidental veracity of the graduate student allowed the undergraduates to become aware of the professor's more subtle project of indoctrination. A few years later, the same professor complained in the pages of the *New York Times* that students are not as pliant as they used to be. I am inclined to attribute this good news to the clumsiness and lack of subtlety of the graduate student who unwittingly provided the undergraduates with the awareness that they were pawns, which helped them to resist. But in the hands of more masterful indoctrinators, awareness of manipulation is not easy to detect.

Shortly after I published my first book on Leo Strauss, I received a letter from a graduate student at the University of Chicago. He had just finished his doctoral thesis on Aristotle when he happened upon my book. On reading the chapter on Strauss's interpretation of Aristotle, he was stunned. He had never read Strauss. Yet his thesis contained Strauss's interpretation of Aristotle in all its details. He was mystified and dismayed to discover that he had been led by the nose, all the while believing that his was a unique and original account. He felt cheated, manipulated, and controlled by an "education" that led him unawares to conclusions whose significance he had not fully understood.

A student at the University of Calgary had a similar experience. One day, after hearing my lecture on neoconservatism in a course on political ideologies, the student came by to tell me that he had taken a course on North American political thought that he now realized was really a course on neoconservatism. All the books on the course were by neoconservatives, but the term "neoconservatism" was never used. The student assumed that the neoconservative way of thinking was just the way intelligent people thought. When all the authorities converge on the same truths and interpretations, a student who makes any effort to escape will have to disagree with all the venerated authorities on the subject. Efforts to escape the intellectual captivity become proof of inadequacy and could result in failure. Unhappily, Strauss has bequeathed to the North American academic community a style of teaching that was perfected by Heidegger, whereby students are enmeshed and encircled by a homogeneous set of ideas presented as the totality of human wisdom. This was the reason that the denazification committee prohibited Heidegger from teaching after the war — they did not think the students were strong enough to endure his seduction with their characters intact. It is a style of teaching that turns students into captives in a web from which there is little hope for escape. In contrast, a good education in the liberal arts is one that recognizes that the wise disagree and that the great questions have been, and continue to be, contested by the great thinkers even within the Western tradition.

The Straussian approach to education depends not on debate, discourse, and persuasion but on subtle intimidation and censorship. A former student of mine who was studying at the University of Toronto reported to me that all my books have been listed as "lost" at the University of Toronto library. It may be a coincidence that my books are missing at a university where there is a strong Straussian presence. To successfully indoctrinate students, it is necessary to shield them from any exposure to opposing points of view. Straussian students who discover my work accidentally in a bookstore, invariably send me letters and gifts in gratitude. Some of the gifts include unpublished papers by Strauss circulated among the faithful with clear instructions saying: Do not distribute to suspicious persons. By sending them to a well-known critic, they have transgressed the rules of the secret society and begun the process of recovery.

In my travels, I encounter many students and young professors who describe themselves as "recovering" Straussians. It is a sad state of affairs that students encounter at university the sort of "education" from which they need to recover.

POSTMODERNISM AND THE SHAPING OF REALITY

Unhappily, the universities lack the backbone with which to resist the abuses of the Straussian "education." The value-free social sciences are impotent and in no position to come to the rescue. The same is true of postmodernism, which has invented the sexiest version of relativism in history. Postmodern philosophers maintain that there is no truth: all is interpretation. Reason has no access to impartial knowledge, because there is no such thing. Power and knowledge are inseparable. The quest for knowledge that is uncontaminated with power is chimerical. Despite its self-understanding as being on the left of the political spectrum, postmodernism provides the perfect atmosphere in which neoconservatism can thrive.

In a world where truth is construction, lying is a creative activity. After all, a great lie gives form to the void, imposes order on chaos, and creates the world out of whole cloth. Politics provides the best opportunity for the art of shaping reality. Politics is no longer the domain of judicious lying, or of lying to the enemy to ensure survival or avert annihilation. Lying has become synonymous with politics. Politics can no longer be distinguished from propaganda. Democracy has become a child of marketing, which is to say, the use of psychology for the purposes of control. Our leaders are increasingly relying on image-makers, spin doctors, political scientists, psychologists, and other masters of manipulation.

The administration of George W. Bush was confident in its ability to shape reality. A senior member of the administration explained to a journalist that "guys like you" are steeped in the "reality-based community." You study the world and try to understand it. But "that's not the way the world really works any more," he said; "We're an empire now, and when we act, we create our own reality. And while you are studying that reality, . . . we'll act again creating other new realities which you can study too. And that's how things will sort out. We're history's actors . . . and you, all of you, will be just left to study what we do."[317]

The neoconservatives' efforts to shape reality were not limited to the home front. They made every effort to shape the opinions of their enemies — so much so that the Bush administration conducted what it called "perception management" operations intended to win the hearts and minds of the people of Iraq, Afghanistan, and the Muslim world. A report from the Advisory Group on Public Diplomacy for the Arab and Muslim World[318] tried to explain why they have not been successful in improving the American image in the Muslim world. They surmised it was lack of funds and lack of research into the vagaries of the Muslim mind. The report sounds as postmodern and Nietzschean as Strauss. It reads as if reality is irrelevant.[319] It reads as if the world is made of primordial stuff on which the strongest, the most ingenious, or the most galling can impose their own order, their own truth, and their own justice.

Needless to say, not everyone is equal in the art of creative lying. Those who excel will no doubt subvert the truths of the defeated. In the end, the claim that there is no truth collapses. Instead, we have a doctrine of nature as eternal and immutable, where truth and justice are invariably invented by the strong. In nature, the superior few will always triumph, and truth is simply the interest of the stronger — the most creative liars, the most astute manipulators, and the shrewdest operators. In this way, the supposed contradiction at the heart of Nietzsche's philosophy evaporates. The claim that there is no truth becomes indistinguishable from the claim that the natural order of things is one in which the strong define the true, the good, and the just, which is another way of saying that the natural state of affairs is one in which the strong rule over the weak.

In a classically postmodern analysis of the war between Israel and Hezbollah in the summer of 2006, David Frum attributes the success of Hezbollah not to its tenacity, its organization, or its appetite for martyrdom but to its capacity to wield information, construct reality out of whole cloth, and manipulate the press: "Hezbollah's most effective weapon was not its rockets or bunkers, but its falsified photographs and film clips. These images shaped world opinion to Israel's detriment, giving the country's enemies something close to a veto over Israel's tactics."[320]

Hezbollah supposedly lured journalists into "flood-the-zone coverage of Lebanese civilian casualties, producing false reports on the [July 30, 2006] Qana bombing, doctored photographs and news stories that were arranged and directed by Hezbollah."[321] It turned Qana into a "grotesque film set on which a macabre drama was played out to a willing and complicit media." Frum is no doubt part of the postmodern quest to shape reality. He would like the world to see the war simply as a case where Israel was compelled to defend itself against a villainous terrorist aggressor. Frum laments the fact that Israel has failed to bequeath its version of reality to the world. He concludes that Israel has been victimized by the stronger party, which is Hezbollah. The implication is that in the postmodern world, "the strong" must be defined or redefined as those who are most skilled in the art of shaping reality. The upshot of the matter is that in the age of information the facts are irrelevant. In this way, postmodernism and neoconservatism, the great antagonists in the culture wars, are mutually affirming and sustaining.

CONCLUSION

Even though I have painted a dire picture in which all claims to truth are but the manifestations of the will to power, there is no reason to despair. In the first place, postmodernism has created a welcome suspicion regarding the alliance of power and knowledge. It is healthy to abandon the old reverence for science, truth, and knowledge. It is salutary to keep in mind the fact that the nexus of power and knowledge, and the precarious state of free inquiry, is the perennial problem of higher education. However, contrary to some postmodern claims, the close relationship between power and knowledge is no proof that knowledge always remains a servant of the power that made it possible. No one expects Canada's Fraser Institute to point to the shortcomings of unregulated capitalism. No one expects the American Enterprise Institute to criticize the policies of the Republican Party. Everyone knows that these unthinking tanks are the instruments of the special interests that created them. But there is a difference between universities and the unthinking tanks. Unlike the latter, the former are capable of turning against the powers that sustain them. They are capable of pointing to the shortcomings of the order they are supposed to champion. This is why the universities are more than just instruments of power and propaganda. The neoconservative effort to co-opt the universities into their scheme of propaganda is bound to backfire. However, new enemies of free inquiry will no doubt emerge.

From the dawn of the universities in the Middle Ages, their history has been the story of the perennial quest for freedom of inquiry. The failure of the Catholic Church to control the institutions of higher learning that were intended to lend it support and give it legitimacy is a reason for optimism. No amount of progress in the techniques of psychological manipulation and control can outdo the shrewd cunning of the Catholic Church. If the latter could not control the universities, then no one else is likely to succeed in making them the lackeys of the powers that be. This is not to say that the enemies of free inquiry are not capable of inflicting a great deal of harm. But in time, their dogmas and their lies are bound to be exposed, no matter how "noble" or "pious" they may appear.

IV. OUTSIDE POLITICS INSIDE THE UNIVERSITY

10

TEMPERS OF THE TIMES: THE POLITICIZATION OF MIDDLE EASTERN STUDIES

Marcus Harvey

One would be hard-pressed to find a corner of the American academy that is more tensely engaged in contemporary debates over academic freedom and professorial authority than the field of Middle Eastern studies. Indeed, any scholars whose work impinges on the politics of the region are likely to find themselves the subject of considerable, and seldom welcome, public interest. It is not difficult to understand why the public might be particularly interested in the modern Middle East, its peoples, and its politics at this historical juncture. What is much less obvious are the myriad ways in which that interest is channelled and deployed for particular ends. It is no coincidence that those American academics who are best positioned to reveal, analyse, expose, and critique the operation of political power in the Middle East are the very same individuals who now find themselves at the centre of the culture wars on America's university campuses. How this situation developed in the aftermath of 9/11 and what it means for our society and institutions of higher education are the subjects of this chapter.

Deep political fault lines were, of course, evident in the study of the Middle East well before the attacks on the World Trade Center and Pentagon. Consider the reverberations made by that rock Edward Said threw in the summer of 2000. Responding to the clamour for Said to be disciplined, or even dismissed, the provost of Columbia University offered instead a ringing defence of academic freedom.[322]

The magnitude of the reaction to Said's political gesture, in itself, however, reflects the significant attention that was being paid by the broader public to the actions and utterances of individual scholars of the
Middle East well before 9/11.

The same might be said of the field in its entirety, though it should
be added that one of the key critiques of Middle Eastern studies —
Edward Said's *Orientalism* — is itself a seminal text in the field and the
starting point for much of the criticism that followed its publication in
1978.[323] Of those most hostile to what might be called the academic
approach to Middle Eastern studies has been Martin Kramer, whose
Ivory Towers on Sand had been several years in the making but coincidentally appeared on shelves within a few weeks of the hijackers'
attacks.[324] Kramer's timing could hardly have been more propitious for
his stinging critique and accounts for the attention the book received.
As one reviewer put it: "Were it not for the attacks of September 11, the
controversies occasioned by his short book would be confined to the
academic world, where it has been noted that the fights are so bitter
because the stakes are so small."[325] Indeed, 9/11 and its attendant anx-
ieties provided extraordinary traction to all those who would counter-
poise academia's complex Middle East with a more ideologically
convenient region, one congruent with American foreign policy and
mainstream cultural assumptions.

Within three weeks of the collapse of the twin towers, an alert contributor to the *New York Times* observed that "the terrorist attacks of
Sept. 11 and the nation's prospective response have begun to reignite
the culture wars that divided university campuses more than a decade
ago."[326] Of course, the politico-cultural "wars" over higher education
had never died out altogether: the fight over the Western canon simply
fed into and merged with the campaign to out "political correctness"
through the 1990s.[327] With the nation moving swiftly to embrace both
the rhetoric and reality of war in 2001, however, academics became
increasingly vulnerable to a resurgent critique of what one might call
egghead treason. Given the cultural stereotypes about absent-minded
professors and mad scientists, dark times make it relatively easy for academics to be simultaneously trivialized (for naivety, irrelevance, and

foolishness) and vilified (for disloyalty, ingratitude, and sedition).

If debate over the literary canon and due regard for the narrative of Western "progress" lay at the heart of the old culture wars, it quickly became apparent that loyalty and support for America's military policies would define the new. Indicative of the shift was the American Council of Trustees and Alumni (ACTA)'s publication *Defending Civilization: How Our Universities Are Failing America and What Can Be Done About It. Defending Civilization* first appeared in November 2001, and recounted well over 100 examples of anti-Americanism on US campuses. By Chris Lehmann's count, the report called out some fifty-four individual professors, a surprisingly small number given ACTA's generosity in compiling errors of commission and omission and its willingness to speculate broadly on the insufficiency of the academy's patriotic zeal: "Rarely did professors publicly mention heroism, rarely did they discuss the difference between good and evil, the nature of Western political order or the virtue of a free society. Indeed, the message of many in academe was clear: BLAME AMERICA FIRST." The revised report (the only one still readily available online) substantively added little to the original beyond a half-hearted retroactive anonymity, which it provided by excising individuals' names (but not their institutions or quotations). There is little doubt that in "patriotic correctness," ACTA had found a more urgent and inspiring call to arms than the decline of Shakespeare or insufficient celebration of America's history.[328]

Among the ideologues who have sustained a critique of academic disloyalty in the years since September 11, 2001, one must reckon David Horowitz and Daniel Pipes, both of whom were quick to recognize the power of the Internet to promote and amplify political ideas.[329] Of the two, Pipes was the first to provoke widespread alarm among academics,[330] principally because of his tactical decision to target individual scholars. Under his leadership, the Middle East Forum launched its campus-watch.org Web site to expose anti-American scholars and to encourage students to report on their professors. The Web site initially identified eight faculty members by name, including Juan Cole at the University of Michigan, Rashid Khalidi at Chicago, and John Esposito, who teaches at Georgetown University. The black-list has a long and bitter history in America and, as ACTA had been compelled to do with its *Defending Civilization* report, Pipes ultimately pulled the offending profiles from the Campus Watch Web site. The site does still provide a "white list" of recommended professors.[331]

Underlying the various accusations that faculty members are typical-ly, disproportionately, or unfairly disloyal to the United States is the perception — a legacy of the Vietnam War — that America's scholars and universities tend to line up on the wrong side of a fight. The American public, which has proven abstemious where dissent is con-cerned, has shown little appetite for self-reflection, either. With the open deployment of combat soldiers to Afghanistan (and later to Iraq), it became ever easier to condemn academics for lending aid and com-fort to the "enemy" and/or betraying "our troops" when professors sought to explain the motivations of America's foes, pointed out American policies or (in)actions that may have precipitated hostility, criticized the decision to go to war, or questioned specific strategies. We will never know how effective this cynical use of patriotism may have been in curbing academics' pronouncements or behaviours, but there can be little doubt that it increased public hostility towards the profes-soriate in general. In the context of a previous debacle, similar criti-cisms of the academy led Senator J. William Fulbright to remind his readers of the importance of criticism to a democracy: "The scholar can ask what is wrong with the 'other side,' but he must not fail to ask as well what is wrong with our side, remembering always that the highest devotion we can give is not to our country as it is, but to a concept of what we would like it to be."[332]

In Fulbright's day, the "other side," of course, was the communist menace abroad and socialism at home. With the demise of the Soviet empire and the dismantling of the New Deal state, one might have thought that America's mainstream could afford to shed some of its insecurity and find a little room for charitable nuance. It didn't. The Manichean thinking against which Fulbright railed is as much in evi-dence today as it was then, only now — thanks in good measure to the indefatigable Pipes and Horowitzes of the world — it is the Islamic terrorist abroad and his sympathizers at home who keep middle America awake at night.

The consequence of this emerging menace for the academy has been an intense, or "hyper," politicization of Middle Eastern studies. This is evident in the heightened public awareness of the work coming out of Middle Eastern studies departments, generally, as well as an untoward interest in the loyalties and activities of the field's practitioners.[333] Unlike the stereotypical faculty member quietly labouring in happy obscurity, those whose work impinges on the Middle East can harbour little hope of anonymity.

Take the case of Nadia Abu El-Haj at Barnard College. Her book on Israeli archaeology proved enormously controversial, in large measure because of its perceived implications for Israel's territorial claims and national identity.[334] Despite her clear preference to avoid publicity, her tenure candidacy made the *New York Times* and a campaign and petition urging the college to deny her tenure garnered thousands of virtual signatures.[335] El-Haj ultimately received tenure, but, as one of her detractors on the blogosphere noted with satisfaction: "All this notoriety should have made her extra cautious about what kind of theories she advances in the future. She is going to be challenged for every sentence she writes which she cannot nail down."[336]

This public scrutiny of El-Haj's qualifications as a scholar suggests how easily the academy's micropolitics meld with broader political currents where the Middle East is concerned; however, the extent to which careers can be derailed by the hyperpoliticization of the field is perhaps best illustrated by the case of Norman Finkelstein at DePaul University. Finkelstein has made no efforts to shun publicity or controversy in his academic life, and his infamous exchanges with Harvard's Alan Dershowitz spare no quarter.[337]

Indeed, it was Finkelstein's "tone" that underlay the rationale given by DePaul's administrators for the decision to reject Finkelstein's tenure bid. In a memorandum on Finkelstein's suitability for tenure, his dean described "the tone and substance of [Finkelstein's] scholarship . . . [as] inconsistent with DePaul's Vincentian values." Those values, Dean Suchar explained, included "respect" for "the dignity of the individual . . . the rights of others to hold and express different intellectual positions[, and] . . . our commitment to diversity."[338]

A subsequent letter from DePaul's president explaining why he would not overturn the decision to deny Finkelstein tenure took a similar tack.

> In the opinion of those opposing tenure, your unprofessional personal attacks divert the conversation away from consideration of ideas, and polarize and simplify conversations that deserve layered and subtle consideration. As such they believe your work not only shifts toward advocacy and away from scholarship, but also fails to meet the most basic standards governing scholarly discourse within the academic community.

Such an admonition must have pleased Alan Dershowitz, who had taken the extraordinary step of lobbying members of the DePaul community about Finkelstein's candidacy. Nonetheless, President Holtschneider's letter assured Finkelstein that "much as some would like to create the impression that our process and decision have been influenced by outside interests, they are mistaken."[339] Given the circumstances in Finkelstein's case, this statement seems implausible precisely because hyperpoliticized academics like Finkelstein, even when they are being dealt with by other scholars, cannot easily be separated from the broader socio-cultural eddies they create.

For those who are sensitive to the "publish or perish" ethic in our universities, the oddest thing about the denial of tenure to Finkelstein must be the failure to reward this man's astounding productivity. Leaving aside his many contributions to the popular press, Finkelstein has authored three scholarly books, *Image and Reality of the Israel-Palestine Conflict* (1995); *The Holocaust Industry: Reflections on the Exploitation of Jewish Suffering* (2000); and *Beyond Chutzpah: On the Misuse of Anti-Semitism and the Abuse of History* (2005); and co-authored another with Ruth Bettina Birn, *A Nation on Trial: The Goldhagen Thesis and Historical Truth* (1998). Because it is so politically controversial, Finkelstein's scholarship has had to withstand intense scrutiny and a barrage of criticisms but continues to have a significant impact in his field. These are exactly the measures typically employed to assess a candidate's suitability for tenure, and so it is not surprising that DePaul's did not link the denial of tenure to Finkelstein's productivity as a researcher.

Instead, the university focused on Finkelstein's character and collegial relationships. This approach also proved perverse. It is, for example, striking that the excellence of Finkelstein's teaching and his popularity with his students could be affirmed by his dean and by the university board on promotion and tenure, that Finkelstein's immediate (departmental) colleagues could support his tenure bid by a three-to-one margin, and that his college's faculty panel could vote unanimously for tenure, and yet the primary rationale for denying tenure could boil down to concerns about Finkelstein's collegiality and the university's reputation.[340] Collegiality with whom? Reputation among whom? Only worries over the perceptions of those *outside* the university's walls would seem to explain this particular decision. As Finkelstein's opponents warned in the preamble to an electronic petition: "In our opinion, Finkelstein's association with DePaul University will damage DePaul's reputation. DePaul will be seen as a school that fosters irresponsible scholarship, extremism and childish, hateful debate."[341] These seem to have been the "opinion" makers who weighed most heavily in the thoughts of DePaul's administrators in the spring and summer of 2007.

One wonders what factors informed President Holtschneider's decision in the far less visible case of Mehrene Larudee. Larudee, an assistant professor of international studies at DePaul, had been openly supportive of Finkelstein, her own candidacy all but assured. The news that Larudee had also been denied tenure came, therefore, as a shock to the members of her department, a department that had unanimously recommended her for promotion.[342] For those who live and breathe the culture wars, the denial of tenure to Larudee must have seemed a tactical error. Regardless of its particulars, Larudee's situation could only lend credence to those challenging Finkelstein's dismissal as a politically motivated effort to silence a controversial figure. Not surprisingly, Horowitz's Web site picked up and amplified a quality-based rationale for dismissing Larudee. The following quotation from his *FrontPage Magazine*, for example, appeared (word for word, except for the "Well") as part of an anonymous comment posted to an article in the independent student daily newspaper of the University of Wisconsin, Madison.[343]

> Well, DePaul fired Norman Finkelstein for pseudo-scholarship and bigotry and also canned Finkelstein's ally Mehrene Larudee, who failed to get tenure as an economist, having tried to get it mainly on the basis of her Marxist screeds.[344]

The reference to Larudee in this commentary was a necessary after-thought, a loose end to be tied up before one tripped over it. The real quarry for the neoconservatives culture warriors are those hyperpoliti-cized scholars like Finkelstein and Ward Churchill whose names are well-known beyond academic circles, names that have become metanyms for the radical leftist academy of hippie libertines, freeload-ing peaceniks, and multi-hued subversives.[345] While one might reason-ably maintain that the much-feared Commuversity has never actually existed, the idea of it enjoys continued currency, in part because it is true that academics have historically enjoyed a privileged vantage point from which to comment on social mores and practices. This capacity to criti-cize and debunk has seldom sat well with those in power, and besides, nobody likes a Cassandra. Consequently, the neoconservative assault on the academy and its values has had some success undermining what little cultural authority university professors once enjoyed. Put simply, professors are not dangerous because they line up to the left or right but because they can cut through the bafflegab and hypocrisy that masks and protects bad policy and self-serving arguments.

Despite this potential, the sad reality is that academics have proven politically sluggish. They were, for example, easily beaten off the mark by a handful of neocons with designs on the academy. As a result, we are seeing a wholesale refashioning of the public conception of the aca-demic enterprise, with non-academics — voters and legislators alike —

coming to parrot the neoconservative line: the views of the faculty
should (statistically) reflect public opinion, academic departments
should be "balanced" in terms of faculty members' political affiliations, and individual professors should be apolitical in their professional lives. Concerned by the potential for faculty members to influence Mideast policy, Martin Kramer wrote the following:

> Yes, academics are entitled to their views like anyone else, and
> they are entitled to demonstrate for them in the streets, hob-
> nob with policymakers to express them, or even take a leave of
> absence to work as practitioners. What they are not entitled to
> do is inflict them on either their students or the readers of
> their academic work.[346]

Aside from recognizing the stunningly unself-reflexive quality of this
assertion, it is worth pondering for a moment how one would effectively immunize one's pedagogical and scholarly activities from one's
"views" on the subject under consideration. Indeed, it has been the
neoconservatives' singular triumph to get such facile — but politically
useful — ideas into broad circulation, a triumph that reflects both their
cleverness and their sensitivity to language. Due in large part to a sustained campaign aimed to identify and rectify political "bias" in higher education, public attention has been directed away from the substantive work done by faculty members and redirected toward a more
generalized notion that such work must always reflect individuals'
political biases (narrowly defined), rather than the fruits of professional expertise and study.[347]

The success of the neoconservatives' campaign must also be attributed in some measure to the hyperpoliticization of Middle Eastern
studies and the availability of highly visible academics to provide
demonstrable evidence of faculty radicalism. Indeed, the evidentiary
basis for asserting that higher education suffers from a systemic political "bias" boils down to a handful of questionable surveys showing
that faculty members are more likely to vote Democrat than
Republican,[348] and this is vastly less compelling than the anecdotal

horror stories of faculty members run amok. As portrayed by neoconservatives, the typical faculty member is a Frankensteinian composite
stitched together from bits and pieces of Ward Churchill, Norm
Finkelstein, Columbia University, UCLA's "Dirty Thirty," and so on.[349]
To paraphrase David Horowitz, the academy is hopelessly partisan
because it provides a home for Ward Churchill and the other hundred
"most dangerous academics" in America.[350]

An earlier example of the political conflation of an individual "rad-
ical" with his/her employing institution and profession can be seen in
Roger Kimball's response to the so-called Intifada curriculum in 2002.
At issue was the appearance of a graduate student's syllabus describing
a course offered by the Department of English at the University of
California, Berkeley. Entitled "The Politics and Poetics of Palestinian
Resistance," the course became notorious for a warning in its syllabus
that "conservative thinkers are encouraged to seek other sections."
News of this Politics and Poetics travelled fast and far.[351] In the pages
of the *Wall Street Journal*, Kimball wrote that "by allowing such courses, Berkeley further erodes that line that once separated academic life
from the hurly-burly world of political affairs. The integrity of that line
has earned universities a special status as places apart in our society —
and tax-exempt because their inquiry was not merely partisan."[352]

In an open letter to the president of the University of California on
the matter, Robert Post, who was then a member of the Boalt Hall law
faculty at Berkeley, reasoned that the political nature of the course did
not make it illegitimate on its face. "We seek to inculcate skills that are
relevant to a world of engaged and sometimes tempestuous citizen-
ship," Post argued, "and in that context the controversial nature of the
reading list of 'The Politics and Poetics of Palestinian Resistance' can
actually be seen as an asset rather than a liability." Acknowledging that
"what made the original draft of the course description so coarse and
unacceptable was its nearly explicit suggestion that the graduate student instructor would not tolerate student perspectives that differed
from his own," Post pointed out that the course as approved by the
academic senate no longer contained the objectionable exclusion.
Further, this professional oversight — "this principle that evaluation of

scholarship and teaching is to be entrusted to the judgement of competent professionals, in the form of the corporate body of the faculty" — ensures that political content is a legitimate reflection of scholarly inquiry and not merely propaganda. In this view, the dual mechanisms of peer review and faculty governance provide credibility to the academic enterprise and thereby underpin "the academic freedom of the entire university."[353]

Considered thusly, the political engagement of faculty members must be seen as an appropriate function of their work. "Scholarship," Post wrote, "requires an open mind, but this does not mean that faculty members are unprofessional if they reach definite conclusions" or prove themselves "urgently committed to a definite point of view." Rather, the litmus test for legitimate scholarly engagement is, at its heart, methodological rather than material: provided that scholars "stand ready to revise their conclusions in light of new evidence or further discussion," "exercise . . . disinterested reason," and "form their point of view by applying professional standards of inquiry rather than by succumbing to external and illegitimate incentives such as monetary gain or political coercion," then the results of their inquiry and the content of their pedagogy, regardless of how political it may seem, have legitimacy.[354]

Senator Fulbright would doubtless have agreed. Arguing for informed and healthy dissent within the polity, Fulbright affirmed that the university ought not to be confined or bound by existing social priorities and policies.

> The university, it is true, cannot separate itself from the society of which it is a part, but neither can the community of scholars accept existing public policies as if they set limits on "responsible" inquiry, as if the scholar's proper function, and only proper function, were to devise the technical means of carrying these policies out.[355]

Fulbright was no wild-eyed radical seeking to topple American institutions or lessen American power worldwide. He simply recognized the potential of faculty members to influence public opinion and policy. Through Fulbright's eyes, the infusion of ideas from the academy would have a salutary impact on the body politic. Today's neoconservatives may be similarly sensitive to the potential influence of the professoriate; however, unlike Fulbright, their preference would be to curtail that influence, and they have pursued a variety of strategies to achieve that end.

Consider the circumstances surrounding publication of the quickly famous essay on "The Israel Lobby and U.S. Foreign Policy" by John J. Mearsheimer at the University of Chicago and Stephen M. Walt at Harvard's John F. Kennedy School of Government.[356] Claiming that there is something extraordinary about the relationship between Israel and the United States, Mearsheimer and Walt asserted that extremely effective lobbying by a variety of individuals and organizations, generically described as "the Israel Lobby," had resulted in policy outcomes that seemed contrary to America's economic and security interests and even to the long-term interests of Israel itself.

Following Fulbright's reasoning, one might argue that this sort of work — diagnosing problems and assessing the actions of the polity — is exactly what our distinguished political scientists should be doing. The essay's reception was, however, far from celebratory. For starters, the *Atlantic Monthly*, which had initially approached Mearsheimer and Walt about writing a piece on the Israel Lobby, declined to publish their article, despite having already spent several years collaborating on it with the two professors. A little more than a year after the *Atlantic Monthly* withdrew its support from the project, the *London Review of Books* published a revised version of the paper, "a fully documented version" posted online. In the authors' words, "response to the essay was breathtaking."[357]

As a result of their analysis, John Mearsheimer and Stephen Walt saw their motives impugned and their characters attacked. They had speaking engagements cancelled and the integrity of their research questioned.[358] The *American Thinker* was certainly not atypical when it ran a piece describing Mearsheimer and Walt's essay as "a work without a trace of balance . . . no more than an angry polemic disguised as academic research . . . a long, bitter, op-ed piece given a patina of respectability because of where the authors are employed." In short, the response to "The Israel Lobby" starkly confirmed the authors' assertion that "the Lobby also monitors what professors write and teach."359

One unfortunate consequence of such monitoring has been a tendency toward vituperation and academic character assassination.360 With Mearsheimer and Walt, efforts to direct attention from the substance of their arguments to the character of the men themselves ranged from Alan Dershowitz's careful insinuations (posted in his response to Mearsheimer and Walt on the Web page of the Kennedy school's Faculty Research Working Paper Series) to myriad rants and accusations in the blogosphere's echo chamber.361

> . . . These guys are jew-haters through and through. I, for one, do not understand why one of the authors should continue to hold a chair endowed by a Jew. I also do not understand why Jews do not take a leaf from Muslim tactics; Muslims are suing Danish and French newspapers for publishing caricatures of Mohammed — so why should not Jews sue the *London Review of Books*? Any number of grounds are conceivable, and it would serve to tarnish the authors and publisher with the facts of their bigotry.
>
> With what little claim I have to being among the academe [*sic*], I hereby disavow any association with these slanderous anti-Semites.362

Charges of anti-Semitism, Mearsheimer and Walt note, "have been an all too common response to anyone who criticizes Israel, questions US support for Israel, or challenges the lobby itself." One might point to numerous others who have been or (more frequently in these litigious times) had their work and activities excoriated for being bigoted or anti-Semitic. Sometimes the rhetoric of the accusations is so overblown as to be comedic, perhaps the most entertaining example being a Horowitz article entitled simply, "Jimmy Carter: Jew-Hater, Genocide-Enabler, Liar."363 However, for most academics, it is probably fair to say that being accused of anti-Semitism or bigotry is both distressing and distracting.

Following various small showings of the David Project's film *Columbia Unbecoming*, a film in which Columbia University's Department of Middle East and South Asian languages and cultures (MEALAC) and its faculty are portrayed as hostile to Jewish students and to supporters of Israel, an indignant Joseph Massad claimed that such attacks were "aim[ed] to stifle pluralism, academic freedom, and the freedom of expression on university campuses in order to ensure that only one opinion is permitted, that of uncritical support for the state of Israel."[364] Massad, an assistant professor in the MEALAC department, had been especially put upon in the months following the film's showings with increasing pressure being exerted on Columbia to dismiss him.[365] In a press release dated October 21, 2004, US Representative Anthony D. Weiner is quoted as having written to Columbia's president, Lee Bollinger, as follows:

> I write to request that you fire Professor Massad for his displays of anti-Semitism. . . . Recent events continue to suggest a disturbing trend in which Columbia's administration has not been sensitive to issues of race. By publicly rebuking anti-Semitic events on campus and terminating Professor Massad, Columbia would make a brave statement in support of tolerance and academic freedom.[366]

Given the energies being expended to very specifically silence *his* voice, it should come as no surprise that Massad would see such censorship as *the* principal objective of the pro-Israel groups with which he was contending. "In their fantasy world, the offending academics must be silenced, dismissed from their jobs, and their offending publications heaped and burned in an auto-da-fé."[367] While this may be a reasonable assessment of the most extreme advocates, such definitive outcomes have not proven necessary for the achievement of many political goals by those on the right. What has come to be called "the Israel Lobby" is, by common admission, an amorphous collection of organizations and individuals in pursuit of various objectives and, while some pro-Israel voices may try to silence their opponents completely, others seem to realize that it is not particularly advantageous to suppress one's opponents utterly, provided that key decision makers are predisposed to your arguments. And, since 9/11, one such group in "the Lobby," the neoconservatives, have enjoyed a virtual stranglehold on US foreign policy. With neoconservatism ascendant, there has been little danger of academic voices exerting any countervailing influence on America's "deciders."[368] There has remained, however, a lingering danger that such voices might move public opinion in ways that would be undesirable to either the neocons at home or the perceived interests of Israel abroad.

Given the cultural impracticality of silencing large numbers of academics, neoconservatives have sought to nullify or blunt potential critiques coming from the ivory tower. In 2003, for example, Stanley Kurtz spearheaded a lobbying effort around Congressional reauthorization of funding for regional and area studies. Arguing that faculty members, especially those involved with Middle Eastern studies, are often hostile to America and its security interests, Kurtz helped persuade members of the US House of Representatives to pass (unanimously) a bill that would create advisory boards to oversee programs receiving federal funds.[369] In addition to the creation of a new advisory board, this oversight would have included new requirements to "take into account the degree to which [the] activities of centers, programs, and fellowships at institutions of higher education advance national interests, generate and disseminate information, and foster debate on American foreign policy from diverse perspectives."[370] That bill ultimately died in a Senate committee, but current legislation relating to Title VI of the Higher Education Act still echoes Kurtz's criticisms.[371]

Within the academy itself, a new disciplinary society, the Association for the Study of the Middle East and Africa (ASMEA), was established in the autumn of 2007 with a number of well-known conservatives (George P. Shultz, former Secretary of State under Ronald Reagan among them) at the helm. Although ASMEA's first president is quoted as having claimed the organization was "not neoconservative at all," the roster of the founding academic council and officers would suggest otherwise. Certainly, the presence of an organizational competitor to the Middle Eastern Studies Association (MESA) provides yet another vantage point from which to critique the field of Middle Eastern studies in general.[372]

Both the lobbying effort directed at area studies programs and the creation of an organizational shadow to MESA seem less concerned with the suppression or censorship of individuals than the neutralization of the academy as a source of coherent and sustained criticism. Such efforts ought not to be confused with the quasi-dialectical process that, ideally, characterizes all academic debate: one articulates an initial position that is subsequently refined and revised as new evidence, arguments, or insights arise. Legislating "balance" or creating parallel scholarly apparatus does not advance knowledge — only agendas. The intended effect might be likened to the destructive interference that results from the collision of two equal, but opposite sound waves. Calibrated perfectly, destructive interference leaves only silence or, in this case, its policy equivalent, which is stasis.

Furthermore, a shadow academy, even if it promotes only positions and ideas based on pre-existing ideological commitments, helps to imbue those ideas and positions with greater credibility. This is the genius underlying Horowitz's campaigns. By making reasonable sounding appeals to fairness and by pressing for "balanced" debate and discussion, Horowitz and others like him make their politically calibrated views seem (by virtue of their contestation within the academy) commensurate with positions and arguments emerging legitimately from within the academy. The corollary to this approach, noted earlier, is that it has the added benefit of predisposing the public to dismiss the arguments of academics as the assertions of partisan bias rather than the pronouncements of individuals with particular expertise.

In times of crisis and conflict, there is little value in either an anodyne academy skirting political controversies altogether or one intent on winnowing all positions down to the impoverished binaries (left–right, Republican-Democrat) that characterize contemporary American discourse. Implicit in Robert Post's response to the "Intifada Curriculum" is a rationale for privileging the real academy over its politicized shadow. Far from being a carte blanche for political posturing, academic freedom is an assurance of quality that is grounded in the professional standards and processes of the academy. In the words of the American Association of University Professors' "1915 Declaration of Principles on Academic Freedom and Academic Tenure":

> The liberty of the scholar within the university to set forth his conclusions, be they what they may, is conditioned by their being conclusions gained by a scholar's method and held in a scholar's spirit; that is to say, they must be the fruits of competent and patient and sincere inquiry.[373]

Despite efforts by some to characterize peer review as a precondition for "liberal groupthink,"[374] the reality is that academics must conform to rigorous standards of documentation and argument or face repudiation by their peers. This self-policing of the academy serves as a guarantee to the public that the research, teaching, and other scholarly activities taking place in our universities are both reliable and honest, and that they are, in fact, "not echoes of the opinions of the lay public, or of the individuals who endow or manage universities."[375]

What we need now is more, not less, political engagement from the academy. To put it in Objectivist terms, faculty must stop shrugging so much and engage aggressively in that "hurly burly" of politics, not as partisans and advocates but rather as professionals and experts, defending the appropriateness and the social wisdom of harnessing the specialized knowledge of our faculty members to more fully serve the common good.

11

THE RIGHT'S WAR ON ACADEME AND THE POLITICS OF TRUTH

Kevin Mattson

The conservatives, as a minority, are the new radicals. The evidence is overwhelming.

— William Buckley[377]

There's a reason the recent Arizona version of the Academic Bill of Rights (ABOR)[378] has attracted so much attention: it's particularly egregious. The legislation would, in the words of *Inside Higher Education*, "require public colleges to provide students with 'alternative coursework' if a student finds the assigned material 'personally offensive,' which is defined as something that 'conflicts with the student's beliefs or practices in sex, morality, or religion.'"[379] Even the national leader of the movement for the Academic Bill of Rights, David Horowitz, has opposed this particular version.

But no matter Horowitz's opposition, the Arizona ABOR is emblematic of a world view that the American right has been pushing and that ABOR and Horowitz's own arguments help nurture. Though the right has always distrusted the professoriate, this latest attack on academe alters the battleground dramatically. What's so strange about it is just how postmodernist and relativistic the right has become in waging it. The ABOR is clearly on the cutting edge of a wider set of culture wars that the right is fighting today. Consider, for instance, the defence of intelligent design, a perspective that many proponents argue should be taught just like scientific perspectives, or the attack on objectivity in journalism, an ideal now seen as so dubious and impossible that citizens need only consult overtly political press sources like Fox, Limbaugh, or opinionated Web sites. Together with these fronts, the ABOR stands as one of the most important developments in the American right's cultural warfare.

To understand the right's world view and its implications requires a brief trip through a strange and often overlooked chapter in American intellectual history — the relationship between American conservatives and academia. American conservatives have always distrusted modern intellectuals (consider Whittaker Chambers's "derision of" the "poisonous puddles of the intellectuals" [380]). Intellectuals represent the much maligned tradition of Western Enlightenment; they live deracinated lives and criticize the religious and traditional beliefs of ordinary citizens. The modern university simply focuses the conservative critique of the mind. But now the suspicion has changed — reflecting certain developments during the 1960s — and has become increasingly destructive.

By exploring the relationship between conservatives and academe during the postwar period in American history (1945 to the present), we will get a much better understanding of the Academic Bill of Rights sponsored by David Horowitz. We will be able to notice what has changed in conservative attitudes about academe and what has not over the course of the last fifty years. We will also move the debates from the narrow confines of higher education to the wider world of politics and intellectual life. The Student Bill of Rights has both a longer history behind it and wider ramifications than suggested by a discussion of just America's colleges and universities. Understanding this helps us raise the stakes of the debate that this book prompts.

THE UBER-TEXT: GOD AND MAN AT YALE

The history of the American right and academe would have been very different indeed if William F. Buckley had not attended Yale University. But of course, Buckley's pedigree demanded a Yale education. As his biographer points out, Buckley's father had made the decision for him to attend Yale "a decade earlier" than when the young man entered. After Buckley served in the Army during World War II, he walked into the hallowed halls of America's premiere Ivy League institution and sought the sort of education his family expected.[381]

He recoiled at what he saw there. For sure, he enjoyed cutting his teeth in the debating club and on the university's newspaper. But when he walked into his classes he was aghast at what he found. Throughout the courses he took, Buckley was confronted over and over by teachers who tried to "subvert religion and individualism."[382] Part of his reaction might have owed to being a lonely Catholic in a sea of Protestants. It was also, undoubtedly, Buckley's youthfulness — his biographer called him an "obnoxious brat" — that drove him on to make fierce criticisms of his elders.[383] He thrilled at the youthful rebellion of lambasting his professors, calling out one history professor, for instance, for his "bigoted atheism."[384] He enjoyed thumbing his nose at the administration for lying to the alumni about what was being taught at Yale. And he wanted to cause a sensational splash in making his criticisms known not just to Yalies but to the wider world.

This became the basis for Buckley's first book, *God and Man at Yale*. The book's fame and sensation were due in part to its simplicity. Nowhere did Buckley explain why Yale should be teaching its students two key cornerstones of his own personal faith — entrepreneurial, free-market capitalism (what he labelled "enterprise" and "self-reliance") and Christianity.[385] He just asserted that the institution should, no questions asked. Any teacher of good character would recognize this fact. What shocked Buckley, as he pored over class content, textbooks, lecture notes, and exams, was just how many of his professors embraced Keynesian economics and atheism instead.

The logic of the argument was airtight, especially evidenced in Buckley's concluding policy suggestions. The president of the university, he reasoned, should see teachers as "intermediaries." Since the "president of a university cannot transmit to the students his own values directly," professors must "do the job."[386] Alumni should pressure the president to see to this task. If professors refused to serve as intermediaries of the alums or the president, well, then, Buckley argued, they "ought to be discharged."[387] The idea that professors could or should be protected by some conception of academic freedom seemed to him absurd.

All of this came down to Buckley's own version of conservatism, the ideology that he would take with him to form the *National Review* a few years later. The real culprit — that of other conservatives like Richard Weaver and Whittaker Chambers, too — was a radical relativism that was creeping into the American consciousness and that grew out of a liberal and Enlightenment tradition. Buckley called this the "widespread academic reliance on relativism, pragmatism, and utilitarianism," especially the dangerous thinking of John Dewey.[388] Believing in a universal and objective theory of values, Buckley situated his critique of Yale within the much more important battle of the Cold War erupting everywhere around him. Only an objective faith in free markets and Christianity could serve as the requisite ammunition capable of doing battle not just against the atheistic Keynesians at Yale but communism abroad.

Reactions to *God and Man at Yale* were, not surprisingly, critical. Liberals didn't like the book for obvious reasons. But surprisingly enough, Buckley found attacks coming from his right flank as well. Russell Kirk, editor of the *Modern Age* and eventually a contributor to the *National Review*, would take issue with Buckley's conception of the professor as servant to the president. This offended Kirk's conception of the scholar as independent of political pressures. The scholar didn't have all the rights in the world but certainly had the right to self-governance. After all, "scholars and teachers are not traffickers in a market, but members of the clerisy."[389] They shouldn't be seen, as was obvious from Kirk's belief in the godliness of academic work, merely as "intermediaries."

But there was another reaction to Buckley, one a bit more predictable. It was mostly heard from other Yalies, especially the top administrators recoiling at the young hotshot making news. As Buckley explained it, many at Yale characterized him as a "black reactionary."[390] Though a self-professed conservative, he was perceived as a radical who shook up the status quo. At first, Buckley might have been shocked to learn that the leftist Dwight Macdonald celebrated his "brisk, brash, indecorous" style and saw, in the words of Macdonald's biographer, "the earmarks of the campus radical" in Buckley.[391] But if Buckley was surprised by this praise from the left, he didn't show it. After all, Buckley pronounced conservatives like himself the "new radicals" on America's campuses.[392] He had hit upon a conceptualization that would come back in spades decades later: The Conservative as Cutting-Edge Radical.

THE 1960S AS A TIME OF WOE

It wasn't the Bill Buckleys of the world who stormed the university during the decade after his book appeared. It was the New Left. Even though the scraggly students of the New Left and Bill Buckley didn't look or sound the same, they did in fact share a mutual enemy: the federal government. It wasn't the size of the federal government (or the belief that power should reside in the states making up the American union) that upset the New Left the way it did conservatives. Rather, it was the government's decision to embark on the Vietnam War and to co-opt the modern university into the "war machine" necessary to do so. Universities pursued research for the war machine and provided cover — in the form of "expertise" — to fight what was perceived by a growing number of students throughout the 1960s as an unjust war.

When students took over Columbia University in 1968, inhabiting the president's office and numerous other buildings, they expressed anger at the university's plan to expand into a poorer neighborhood. But they also demanded that the university "disaffiliate from a defense institute involved in research on the Vietnam War."[393] As their occupation heated up before the police were finally called in to clear out the buildings, a local leader, Mark Rudd, explained that the students were putting the New Left principle of "participatory democracy" into "practice."[394] Sometimes this radicalism took on even more desperate and frustrated tones. Two years after Columbia, for instance, bombs went off at "an Army math research project" located at the University of Wisconsin. Chaos had come to the ivory tower.[395]

Conservatives were aghast at these acts, but it's also important to remember that so too were liberals. Richard Hofstadter, a prominent historian and liberal critic of the New Left, sympathized with some of his students' demands at Columbia but chastised their style of protest (which he believed to be therapeutic and dramatic rather than effective or reformist). In the takeover, he saw a dangerous incivility, a pathological outcome of the ideal of participatory democracy. The university needed to preserve its autonomy from political pressures — no matter if they came from the right or left. As Hofstadter's biographer describes his attitude, "In the nation's present crisis [of the late 1960s], universities were needed more than ever as voices of reason. At their best, they offered sanctuary to intellectual heretics wary of popular prejudices and suspicious of concentrated power."[396] Carving out a middle ground between far right and far left, Hofstadter upheld a liberal ideal of the university's independence from political pressures and a defence of its professional standards that stood above the pressures of mob rule. The stance won him few friends among the New Left; one student compared him to "the French aristocrats" during the French "revolution."[397]

Hofstadter's concern would soon be crowded out by a chorus of neoconservative voices. This group of predominantly Jewish and once liberal intellectuals recoiled at the excesses of the 1960s, including student protest and disobedience. They also explained student unrest as part of a wider social breakdown. For neoconservatives, higher education had helped nurture a "new class" of educated people who constituted what was called an "adversary culture." In the words of the leading neoconservative Irving Kristol, the "new class" educated at America's premiere institutions wound up developing "hedonistic life styles" and "emphasized individualistic self-expression which undermined communal and personal restraints, the essential elements for an orderly society and social progress."[398] The new class simply emulated the counterculture and campus rebels of the 1960s as they lived on into the 1970s and 1980s.

Neoconservatives developed a long-range view of politics and cultural transformation. But at no point, no matter how far history proceeded from the time, did the 1960s drop out of the picture for them.

Perhaps the clearest expression of this was Allan Bloom's book, *The Closing of the American Mind*, which came out almost twenty years after the Columbia takeover. During the late 1960s, Bloom was teaching at Cornell University, where he grew shocked at the powerful influence of black students and feminists. He moved on to the University of Chicago, and it was here that he wrote his book. It was written as if the decade of the 1960s was still playing itself out.

Bloom described the 1960s as an "unmitigated disaster."[399] Indeed, he compared the student protestors of the 1960s to the student fascists of 1930s Germany. Bloom believed the New Left's protests prompted "the same dismantling of the structure of rational inquiry as had the German university in the thirties."[400] Following Buckley (who himself had followed Richard Weaver), Bloom lashed out at a pervasive relativism that was the source of all things bad in America's colleges. He described the threat of "openness." The philosophy guiding American higher education was "open to all kinds of men, all kinds of life-styles, all ideologies. There is no enemy other than the man who is not open to everything. But when there are no shared goals or vision of the public good, is the social contract any longer possible?"[401] The question might have been intended as rhetorical, but the answers were extremely straightforward.

The New Left had destroyed the academy. So too had the counterculture and its love of rock music, free sex, and drugs. Bloom sought out the philosophical roots for these movements, and he found them in the German philosopher Friedrich Nietzsche. Bloom's students had embraced a Dionysian "lifestyle." Student protests had died out by the time Bloom wrote the book, but he believed students were still self-centred and lacked any sense of commitment to universal values that transcended their personal desires. Their politics were a simplistic expression of what became known during the late 1980s as "political correctness." Students learned to question any claim to truth as simply a smokescreen for self-interest and domination. Scratch the claims of the Founding Fathers or Western philosophers declaring truth, for instance, and Bloom's students would always find racism or power or some other evil.

Bloom sounded like an old-fashioned reactionary. His story about American higher education was a tale told by many neoconservatives — one of decline. He wanted a return to the Great Books tradition, hoping his students might once again pursue a close reading of Plato and other classics in the Western canon. The battle could be won by changing reading lists. Bloom personified the conservative as crusty curmudgeon at least in the realm of ideas. (His own colourful personality suggested otherwise.) His reaction against the culture of the American academy was a powerful tendency in neoconservative political thinking. But it was only one reaction and certainly not the most important.

THE OTHER 1960S

The conservative as curmudgeon had its limits for those wanting to win political influence. Besides, during the 1990s, growing numbers of conservatives started to think of themselves as hip and cool, far from stuffy and curmudgeonly. They wanted to be seen as something more than just the defenders of an older society that the New Left had torn down. As David Brooks put it in his anthology of mid-1990s conservative thinking, *Backward and Upwards*, conservatives didn't need to be "the heavies" nor did they need to embrace "puritanism." He recounts how he tried to refuse having his picture taken with his arms crossed and looking tough and sinister, because that wasn't the impression he wanted to make. And the social criticism he became known for — *Bobos in Paradise*, for instance — was more funny than stern or moralistic.[402]

Conservatives were quickly becoming hip — referring to themselves as "South Park conservatives" (who enjoyed watching the television show by that name) and "crunchy cons" (who shopped at organic food chains and dressed like hipsters).[403] Conservatives even thought of themselves as rebels, as Fred Barnes explains in his recent celebration of George W. Bush's presidency. Barnes describes Bush as "edgy, blunt" and "scornful of the conventional wisdom." No longer, for Barnes, did the conservative have to appear like William Buckley, who defined conservatism as the need to "stand athwart history, yelling, 'Stop.'" Instead, the conservative could be the defiant rebel — much in the mold of the rebels of the 1960s.[404]

It's here where we must locate the leading exponent of the Academic Bill of Rights, David Horowitz. I have no idea if he's a crunchy con or hip conservative. One thing's for certain: He has made a reputation for attacking the "destructive generation" of the 1960s. In a book with Peter Collier, he sounds much like other neoconservatives, associating "feminized poverty, AIDS, drugs, and drug related crime" of the 1980s with "the heedless assault on The System that took place in the Sixties."[405] But after trying to purge his soul of the bad things he himself did in the 1960s — including associating with the Black Panther Party, which might have had something to do with the murder of a friend of his — he claims the sixties style still lives on in him.

In *The Art of Political War*, one of Horowitz's most provocative books, he cites his "fellow columnist at *Salon*," Camille Paglia. Paglia seemed to be a creature of the 1960s with her celebrations of the Rolling Stones (a band that Bloom detested). But she also became known for her staunch criticism of the feminist movement's political correctness. And in this, she's the perfect champion of Horowitz. Paglia writes that she respects Horowitz "as one of America's most original and courageous political analysts. He has the true 1960s spirit — audacious and irreverent, yet passionately engaged and committed to social change."[406] Horowitz proudly accepted this line of praise.

Horowitz has taken the political content out of the 1960s protest movements — a critique of American power abroad and an alliance with the voices of America's minorities — and has whittled the decade's legacy down to style. This is what Paglia means by his inheritance of the "true 1960s spirit." So when he calls for students to take up the ABOR, he cites historical precedence. "I encourage [students] to use the language that the left has deployed so effectively on behalf of its own agendas. Radical professors have created a 'hostile learning' environment for conservative students. . . . The university should be an 'inclusive' and intellectually 'diverse' community."[407] Here's where the Academic Bill of Rights comes in. It successfully grafts his 1960s style to his conservative politics.

In taking this tack, Horowitz has decided to leave behind any claim to objective, universal knowledge — the sort that Buckley, Weaver, and Bloom defended. Instead, Horowitz now sounds a note of postmodernism, if we associate that academic term with contemporary theories about the indeterminacy of knowledge (for instance, post-structuralism and the French philosopher Michel Foucault's radical critique of the relations between knowledge and power). Take the original ABOR statement: "Human knowledge is a never-ending pursuit of the truth," since "there is no humanly accessible truth that is not in principle open to challenge, and no party or intellectual faction has a monopoly on wisdom."[408] It's in this language that you hear the 1960s spirit swallowing up the right's older faith in objective truth. Buckley, after all, knew just what he wanted taught and how, so too did Bloom.

What carries over from the older conservative tradition is the distrust of intellectuals and the professoriate. But while carried over, it too has changed form. In the past, the right chastised intellectuals for standing in the Western tradition of the Enlightenment, with its break from religious tradition and its critique of organic social hierarchy. Horowitz (an intellectual through and through) distrusts the professoriate for imposing its own political views on college students. In the original words of the ABOR, there is a need for the "protection of students" from "the imposition of any orthodoxy of a political, religious or ideological nature."[409] Here is another radical shift in conservative logic and another inheritance from the 1960s. The ABOR distrusts the authority and competence of the professoriate. How else to explain why Horowitz took the ABOR to state legislatures and supported politicians calling for the monitoring of America's classrooms?[410] A radical distrust of the professoriate — similar to the attacks made on Hofstadter in the late 1960s by his New Left critics — seems to have taken on new form.

To a large extent, Horowitz did inherit the "spirit of the 1960s." The question remains what to make of that spirit. When students of the New Left took over buildings during the late 1960s, they may have had legitimate concerns, but they had also rejected the central principle of political compromise. That's why liberals like Richard Hofstadter criticized them. Liberals pointed out that the university could not become a political football or a battleground for political ideologies. The university would collapse under such pressure.

What's so worrisome about Horowitz's claims today is how much they mirror the radical sentiments of the New Left protestors. Students (or, more accurately, politicians purporting to speak for them) who demand the curriculum better reflect their own ideological orientation and who believe they deserve immediate alternatives if offended are remarkably similar to the uncompromising students of the 1960s. The spirit of demanding one's "rights" and of participatory democracy live on in their demands (or again the demands their surrogates make for them). Both sets of students exert a pressure on an institution that is truly unmanageable. Just try to imagine a university functioning if each professor had to please each student and create a tailor-made curriculum. Imagine a university opening up its classrooms to political legislatures inquiring about "diversity" in political opinion.

These new student demands threaten to make worse one of the most troubling features of higher education today. Since the 1960s, universities have acted like corporations that market themselves to students who act increasingly like consumers. For instance, universities build student fitness centres and then quickly advertise them in publicity literature. Students "shop" for the right college. In filling out course evaluations, they think of themselves as filing consumer reports about what they liked and didn't. The modern university looks like a shopping mall. Is it any surprise that conservative students feel empowered to complain about courses where they have their opinions challenged? The Academic Bill of Rights simply extends these students' logic. And the attitudes of today's conservatives seem remarkably similar to the feel-good therapeutic politics that New Left student protestors engaged in.

This gives you a sense of just how dangerous the ideology surrounding the ABOR really is. It's especially ironic because the conservative voice in higher education debates has historically been in opposition to relativism. Today, conservatives are increasingly the party of relativism and perspectivism. If these debates come down to political power, as Horowitz seems to desire in handing the ABOR over to state legislatures, then we're in real trouble. Horowitz takes Buckley's love of the university presidents' executive power — their ability to fire professors at will — without taking any of his language about objective theories of truth. He also transfers that power from the university's president and places it into the hands of state legislatures. There is no conception of truth operating here, only political power. While conservatives once warned about the dangers of relativism, they now seem willing to use it for the sake of winning the culture wars.

It would seem the appropriate response is to uphold not some objective conception of truth but the institutional mechanism of professionalism, which includes training students to accept their civic responsibility. We should train young scholars how to pursue truth — not to gain absolute, clear-eyed, definitive truth but to respect the ideals of accuracy and honest explanation of the way the world works (or in my discipline, history, the way the world has and hasn't worked). To uphold this vision of professional training is not to say that there's something like Alan Bloom's Platonic idea of truth. It is rather to say that truth evolves, but also needs institutional mechanisms in which to evolve. It is certainly — contra Horowitz — to point out the possibility of acquiring knowledge outside the strictures of power and dominance.

In the end, we should pose questions back to the anti-academic right: Why would anyone want an education system run on the whims of young people determining their individualized curricula or the decisions of political officials snooping around in America's colleges? Why would anyone want a culture that gives up on the ideal of professional competence and the authority of the professoriate and instead embraces the idea that since truth is so hard to determine, it's best to turn educational matters over to state legislatures? We should be asking those questions today, since the ABOR naturally prompts them. The answers to them should terrify anyone concerned with the future of higher education and the future of democracy.

V. THE DANGERS OF A PRODUCTION-DRIVEN RESEARCH CULTURE

12

PRODUCTION IN THE HUMANITIES

Mary Burgan

Any discussion of the current emphasis on "production" in higher education must confront an anomaly in departments like English, history, fine arts, languages, and philosophy. Faculty members in these fields do not manufacture "products." Like their counterparts in professional schools and science departments, they teach students, but those students rarely become discoverers of new planets or captains of industry. It is true there are some creative areas in which humanities students have been known to produce things: they can write best-selling fiction, create marketable images, compose I-Podable tunes, and some historians even construct blockbuster accounts of the past. By and large, however, the humanities are on the margins precisely because they cannot promise miracle drugs, solve global warming, or deconstruct DNA. The situation of the liberal arts major has been epitomized by the American humorist Garrison Keillor in his mock radio commercials for the "Professional Organization of English Majors" (POEM): "Majesty and elegance and depth of feeling. (PIANO CHORDS) Other majors offer you superficial skills — (COMPUTER BEEPS) but English major opens up the landscape of the human heart (SWORD FIGHTING, SHOUTS, HORSES WHINNY, GALLOPING, TRUMPET CALL)."[411]

As a former English major myself, and as a former professor of English, I approach the issue of "production-driven research" in the humanities somewhat narrowly: I cannot speak at first hand of the conditions in every discipline in the humanities, but since English tends to have links with many of the programs in the humanities, my account should give some notion of the problems many of their faculty confront in their scholarship. Perhaps the greatest difference between English and the science and technology fields is that English, like the foreign languages (and even mathematics), is responsible for teaching masses of undergraduate students in labour-intensive courses. A great deal of the English department's productive value for the academy lies in its service teaching rather than its research, even though in the current value system of most institutions research is supported far more heavily than teaching. And so, just as graduates from departments in the humanities are likely to spend some of their lives taking orders from the drive-up window, their teachers find themselves overworked and underpaid in performing the service work of the academy — teaching undergraduates in remedial and basic skills like writing, learning languages, reading difficult texts, and gaining elementary understandings of complicated concepts. This work is essential and worthy, but one of the most pernicious results of our research-driven culture is that teaching is minimized, if not debased, both because it can be performed cheaply by non–research faculty and because it does not garner the profitability or the bragging rights of successful research. The most important gauge of this value system in the academy today is the relegation of many of the faculty in the humanities at research institutions to second-class positions — frequently without tenure and without the time and money needed to pursue their own inquiries. It is important to note that the values of the leading research schools tend to set the values everywhere in higher education.

Partly because of its lack of immediate application, research as well as teaching in humanities departments is rarely "sponsored," in the phraseology of university administrators. Nevertheless, many faculty members in the humanities have difficulty getting tenure or advancement without producing tangible and measurable research "outcomes," and so the "real" professorial jobs are reserved for researchers. Although the more quantitative criteria of scientific and technological productivity only barely suit the enterprises of humanities scholars, those criteria are applied to them in the academy without thought to providing the kind of support that is expected for research in other areas. A Modern Language Association (MLA) survey of American schools indicates that the average maximum "start-up" grant for new tenure-line faculty in language and literature in 2005 was about $7,000 for research universities, with less than half that amount in schools that offer only masters or baccalaureate degrees.[412]

One reason for the sparsity of humanities research funding may be that the needs of researchers in fields like English differ from those of faculty in more applied fields. Humanities researchers tend to work on their own and publish their findings as single authors, and they seldom require crews of research assistants. Every professor of English, for example, is her own "primary investigator." Humanities researchers do not require laboratories with gas jets and running water, high-powered computers, complicated gadgetry, or adherence to environmental standards. They need only an office, books, a computer that can process words, and a printer. More recently, they also need a hook-up to the Internet, for they appreciate and use the technological advances that provide them with digitized texts, scores, films, and the like. Their research has been enriched by the media culture, even as their practice in responding to it may have remained archaic.[413]

Indeed, so immaterial are the needs of the typical humanist that their simplicity may work against him/her in the modern research environment. When I was English Department chair in an American public university in the 1980s, at the very beginning of the computer revolution, I found myself at a disadvantage in representing the needs of my colleagues because their practical requirements were so primitive. I finally got them to recognize that they must convert from typewriters to personal computers and printers. That was hard enough, but then I couldn't graph the productivity that these pieces of equipment would generate to the satisfaction of the requisite IT dean. Eventually, I resorted to a blueprint diagram of my building with markings for the location of each PC in each office, in an effort to give our needs the materiality that would make them real to the funding office. We were competing with departments that were habituated to the culture of grantsmanship and knew how to do the bar graphs, pie charts, and equations that made their needs tangible to non-humanists. In their kind of competition, I found, a pictograph was worth more than all my words, and we got our PCs.

Though administrators generally understand that humanities faculty members are writers and that their writing is in some ways valuable, they still want to "know" how that writing is valuable, and why. Even though it would be inane to try to chart the work of a humanities professor in terms of vectors on graph lines or calculate it through some kind of complicated equation, the desire to have some measurement of humanities achievement itself is not stupid. All faculty members should be able to justify their positions, and I would argue that in literary studies such justification should include written evidence of a mind at work in communicating subtle and convincing understandings about the imaginative and moral life of humankind. The problem for assessing such humanities research is that the ever-present pressure for measurable achievement tends to rely on quantitative more than qualitative terms in order to satisfy the perceived demands of administrations geared to the standards of science and technology.

Non-humanists are apt to feel themselves unable to judge the esoteric issues that humanities professors seek to resolve, and in their effort to convince themselves that the flourishes of language used by humanists deserve support, they tend to seek less mystifying modes of assessment. In some university tenure committees I have served on, members from the sciences have actually stated their suspicion of the rhetoric they found in humanities dossiers — all those words wrapped around so little. And so they look for models from within their own fields, where the standard has some relation to the *amount* of knowledge that the project adds to what the field already knows. Scientific and technological research is *cumulative*, and although quality counts in its invention and execution, a judgment of that quality tends to be fortified by how much information is added to the pile or how much knowledge is altered when experiments are run and verified, when data sets are created, counted, and analyzed.

The notion of cumulative knowledge remains a daunting one for humanists. No matter how original, research in a field like English literature is hardly validated by the fact that it adds one more to a pile of essays or books. There are many reasons for this. One of them is that research in some humanities fields has played out because of over-cultivation. In my own field of English literature, the classic texts are all established, and although there was a minor industry in editing them in the last half of the 1900s, most of the standard texts have been fully established by now. Technical textual analysis has given way to computer analysis of specific texts, and so the concordances that once kept scholars in business have been turned over to ever more subtle computer programming. Annotating, editing, and even translating — activities that have kept humanities scholars busy, and paid for, in past times, are now relatively obsolete. It seems improbable that the humanities can ever recapture that kind of painstaking, additive labour as a source of some claim to "productivity."

Meanwhile, the texts that form the core of the traditional humanities field have been written about almost endlessly by the hordes of scholars who must produce if they are to have rewarding careers in the academy. The classics are great because, in the view of the English critic, Frank Kermode, they are "patient" and therefore can absorb new meanings with each new age,[414] but Kermode, like many other humanists, admits there are diminishing returns.[415] While new versions of Shakespeare's plays can be produced year after year, the proliferation of books and essays about them in prose, read by only a few experts, is seen to be a waste of energy. A rueful colleague once confessed to me, in a late-night vigil at a local café over his fading book project, that he despaired of ever reading all the articles on Shakespeare. There were already enough of them to circle the globe and then start out for the moon! And in a heated argument about the value of faculty research, I once had the CEO of a major electronics store exclaim that there are "too many articles about Shakespeare!" His frustration actually mirrored the attitude of many non-humanists who are hard to convince that in some fields the possibilities are indeed uncountable. They defy the descriptive power of numbers.

In the natural course of time and change, of course, scholars in the humanities have generated new materials for study. In literature departments, they have discovered unexplored texts and exploited important areas that had been neglected by the focus on masterworks of Western culture. The various movements of the last quarter of the twentieth century to assert gender, ethnic, or class identities helped to uncover "lost" or neglected texts from a variety of sources. Popular literature written by women — frequently melodramatic and sentimental bestsellers in their day — have been resuscitated and analyzed as appropriate texts for humanistic study. Although many of these were written to be transparent to a mass audience, they still need a scholar's gloss to set their significance in their time and place. The same has been the case for such neglected texts as slave narratives, folk art, and mass-produced popular art. One example of this rise of new fields in the humanities is children's literature, a specialty that was once relegated to the ministrations of women when they were a lesser tribe in the humanities. The field has now been legitimated, not only because of its intrinsic interest but also because it offers a variety of new texts and new ways to think about them. In such a field, however, the issue of quantity versus quality is most liable to come to the fore. Academic funders are likely to ask whether the new materials are serious enough to warrant sponsorship. Faculty researchers are equally likely to ask if there are sufficient venues for publication. It is notable that at meetings of the Children's Literature Association in the United States, there are panels devoted to advising attendees on how to market their essays and books so as to have something to show when the time comes for them to be considered for jobs, tenure, or promotion.

Faculty in the humanities have, then, been richly productive in developing fields that begin as subsidiaries of old ones but then branch off to form their own enclaves. They have also sought to declare their independence from traditional interpretative practices by seeking ever new combinations of humanities and the social sciences, the sciences, and even economics and management theory whenever possible. Some of them have even imitated trends in the hard sciences by theorizing their own processes — often in esoteric language that gives their work the aura of scientific impenetrability. In reaction against the old ways, as well as in response to the requirements to create more nuanced and complicated interpretations and strategies, humanities fields in the last quarter of the twentieth century became fixated on a variety of theories from outside — from psychoanalysis to Marxism to linguistic anthropology to evolutionary biology — that enable new thinking as well as new claims to productive publication. In the process, interdisciplinarity has flourished, new journals have sprung up, disciplinary societies have been founded, and conference-going has become one mark of a productive career. Research activity has grown almost exponentially over the past twenty-five years, even as the support for research in the humanities has diminished.

Despite such genuine productivity, however, the humanities have been squeezed very hard by institutions' refusal to support any but the most sellable programs and faculty. The near close-out of jobs for new faculty, the dwindling resources for publication, and the demand for even greater research production have come together in a perfect storm for humanities professors. As they run faster to stay in place in research, their institutional leaders and the general public demand that they not only teach more but commit themselves to service at the same time. And research on higher education shows that rather than rebelling against such acceleration of standards, junior faculty members have actually met them. Their workload has increased dramatically, and many find themselves wondering whether it's worth it. Nevertheless, there have been rumblings about the way growing research demands in the entrepreneurial university conflict with the teaching and service aspects of professorial jobs. In the last ten years, these expressions of discontent have reached the consciousness of many leading scholars in the humanities.

The perfect storm has inspired soul searching in the humanities disciplines themselves. For example, the Modern Language Association, which had been agonizing about the decline in concern about teaching as well as the terrible job market in the humanities for most of the 1990s, initiated a series of related studies and reports about the state of research in the fields of literature and language as the decade ended. The first one, released in 1997, studied the dwindling market for tenure-track — i.e., "research" — faculty and the attendant rise of "casual" faculty throughout the profession in North America.[416] A second report issued in 1998 by the MLA and the Association of Departments of English centred on teaching, teacher preparation, and the need for better integration of departments of English with programs in the secondary schools.[417] A third report, in 2002, was concerned about "The Future of Electronic Publishing,"[418] given the narrowing range of evidence accepted by tenure and promotion committees even as book publication became less financially feasible; that report talked about the traditional "tyranny of the monograph" as a threat to aspiring faculty. The crisis described in the report inspired the then MLA president to write an open letter to the profession asking it to respond to the research crisis.[419] (In light of the controversies about Shakespeare scholarship, it is interesting to note that Stephen Greenblatt was the MLA president who voiced concern about tenure standards. Greenblatt is a Renaissance scholar who later published one more book about Shakespeare[420] — an accessible hardcover that was on the best-seller list of the *New York Times* for nine weeks.)

The project of the MLA committee on electronic publishing had been to urge tenure and promotion committees to accept evidence of research from digital sources, but its report made it clear that the issue of research standards went beyond the question of new media. Thus a new MLA committee — actually a "Task Force" — was formed to study how the humanities now actually do decide about tenure and promotion.

The 2007 report from the MLA's "Task Force on Evaluating Scholarship"[421] set out to survey the range of practices in assessing faculty performance in language and literature departments across the membership of the association. Defining the issues before the professoriate, the task force prefaced its report with a description of the problem, noting that the leadership of the MLA had been "alarmed . . . that a disjunction existed between rising expectations for tenure and diminishing availability of publishing outlets. . . . It was concerned about the narrowing definitions of what constitutes scholarship for tenure and promotion, about the exclusion of new, alternative forms of scholarship, and about the failure to take account of the full range of practices that now constitute the system of scholarly exchange." The ensuing report surveyed a substantial number of departments in the United States. It also plotted out the decline of publishing resources for faculty aspiring to academic tenure. It pointed to the already documented truism that academic competition insists on publication as "the gold standard" of the value of faculty work and that such insistence moves on by the subtle osmosis of ambition to most of the colleges and universities that are not "Research I" in the Carnegie classification of American schools. The report finally set up a list of guidelines for departments that includes contractual clarity about tenure, subventions for start-up research, better mentoring, fairer and more transparent tenure procedures, and openness to new forms of evidence for tenure committees.

With all its good intentions, however, the MLA report fell short of making any really effective suggestions — such as for altering the traditional ratio of weight given to research over teaching/service in the academy's current value system — and there is one glaring reason for the choice of amelioration rather than radical reform. The fact is that the task force seemingly decided to sidestep consideration of the damage the present system does by closing out jobs for a large percentage of aspiring junior faculty who have not been able to penetrate the tenure track. Its analysis of the problem of evaluating faculty mentions the disaster of the job situation in the humanities disciplines with only a passing reference to the "reshaping" of the faculty.[422] Having nodded in the direction of that seismic change, it accepts as unalterable "the multitiered faculty structure in higher education, *which is not likely to change in the foreseeable future. . . .*"[423] (Emphasis mine). The MLA's response to the ravages of the research-driven trajectory in higher education was to ignore its effects on the 40 percent of qualified candidates who never get a chance to use their training, and so to view evaluation only within the narrow area that the winners in the job market inhabit. Indeed, the MLA report is animated by the notion that the newly stratified academy should mend, but not end, the competitive system that tenure now serves.

The MLA reports, like those of such cross-disciplinary organizations as the American Association of University Professors, the American Council on Education, and the now defunct American Association of Higher Education, have pointedly noted the exclusionary focus on research productivity in the disciplines, and contrasted this with the great variety of activities that should be considered when assessing value in our complex system of higher education. That said, no organization has been able to go much further than a broad diagnosis of the problems. It is, for example, widely acknowledged that the "contingent" faculty who work outside the charmed oval of the tenure track provide yeoman service to a vast numbers of students with a great diversity of needs, but much less has been done to explain how we should, fairly and professionally, develop, ensure, or measure the talents of our non-tenure-track colleagues.

Everyone who looks on the wide-ranging works of the humanities and despairs harkens to the call to common sense by Ernest Boyer, whose *Scholarship Reconsidered: Priorities for the Professoriate*, published in 1990, continues to represent the most searching appeal for a change in the value system in higher education.[424] In asserting that research throughout the academy should include the scholarship of "discovery, integration, application, and teaching," Boyer hoped to guide the system to a more sensible and sensitive set of criteria for rewarding faculty. He understood the damage the humanities would do to themselves if they continued accepting the cumulative model of the sciences in measuring excellence, and his idealism seemed like a breath of fresh air to many faculty members and their leaders. Nevertheless, and despite all their recent soul searching, it is very hard to find any structured effort on the part of most disciplinary organizations to change the humanities reward system today.

The question for critics of higher education's research-driven culture is: Why there is no deeper reform when so many internal surveys and reports announce the need for it? The MLA report on evaluating scholarship points to one answer — "Department chairs do not express concern about the current level of demands for tenure; on the contrary, they seem to approve of the status quo. . . ." And, further, "Broad-based support . . . continues to exist for both current publication

requirements and the current balance between publication and teaching. . . ."[425] This finding of contentment with the status quo is borne
out by a 2006 cross-disciplinary survey conducted by a group at the
Center for Studies in Higher Education at the University of California,
Berkeley, in a report entitled *Scholarly Communication: Academic Values
and Sustainable Models*.[426] The motive of this group was similar to that
of the MLA committee on electronic publishing — an exploration of
the possibility of moving e-publishing into the assessment arena for
faculty advancement. In its abstract at the outset, however, the report
states that "approaches that try to 'move' faculty and deeply embedded
value systems directly toward new forms of . . . 'final' publication are
destined largely to failure in the short-term." The California study drew
this conclusion from information across the university rather than
from the humanities only; its interview survey covered five different
areas: English-language literature, chemical engineering, anthropology,
biostatistics, and law and economics. In every one of these disciplines,
it found agreement that the status quo would not be easily changed,
although the rationales for this consensus differed somewhat in
emphasis from those advanced in the MLA reports. The California
report focused on the usefulness of publication as an aid to assessing
not only the quality but the prestige of a faculty member's work. In the
English Department at Berkeley, faculty seemed aware of the MLA
report on electronic publishing, but they found the matter of peer
review for traditional publication decisive in warranting submission to
the status quo. "The chief fear is that electronic publications are not
peer-reviewed and are hence less prestigious and 'tenure-worthy' than
their print counterparts."[427] The connection between the worthiness of
research and its prestige, as displayed by its hard-copy publication,
takes us to a final aspect of the assessment of research in the humanities, namely its role in claiming status and thereby ministering to an
institution's claim to a dominant place in the firmament of higher education. John Lombardi, an administrator who has defended the clarity
of counting such things as publication and grant income as measures
of quality, has put it this way in a comment on MLA's evaluation
report: "Colleges and universities have few ways of defining and

demonstrating their excellence other than presenting various measures of scarcity."[428] Lombardi's mention of "scarcity" invokes an added burden on humanities research; the task is not only to get it all written down, published, and vetted, but to prove that the finished product outranks all the other research turned out by an academic factory that has responded so well to the demand for evidence.

It seems that under demands for quantitative assessment many faculty have simply surrendered the question of quality to experts from outside the home campus. One member of the Berkeley English Department bravely maintained that true, inner-directed quality assessment continues in the field, asserting, "We do this the old-fashioned way. We don't count it. We read it. And that's going to continue to be true."[429] But other comments from his department, as well as from the various MLA reports, suggest far less independence in the faculty's ability to make final decisions about the quality of their colleagues' work on their own. For one thing, our research-driven culture has spawned so many publications that most faculty simply don't have the time to read them all.

John Lombardi is correct in identifying the self-consuming mandate — felt at Berkeley as well as other institutions up and down the line — to maintain prestige through assessing research value by its comparative "scarcity" within the universe of all scholarly production in a particular field. As a matter of fact, many of the comments from the fields surveyed in the California report address the fact that the very productivity of the academy — the proliferation of specialties, the interdisciplinary ventures, and the mass of writing — comes close to prohibiting genuine internal review: "Peer review is the hallmark of quality that results from external and independent valuation. It also functions as an effective means of winnowing the papers that a researcher needs to examine in the course of his/her research."[430] Most faculty would agree that, in an ideal world, assessment of their work should command serious time and energy on the part of their colleagues, accepting the proposition that approbation from outside an institution is helpful in judging it. But it seems that the array of publications that have been generated, at least partially, by the self-protective drive to publish, presents too serious a challenge to detailed collegial review. Thus, in the risk-averse, quantity-driven culture of many humanities departments, reliance on an outside opinion has become a shortcut to decision making. Tenure decisions have become, in some cases, insanely mandarin and ultimately dependent on the opinions of strangers.

No matter how new the combinations of interests and practices in the humanities, interpretation is still the primary skill they promulgate, and interpretation is more a process than a product. And so the real problem with the productivity model for the humanities is not simply that it can be faddish, ambitious for material success, and neglectful of the hidden virtues of pure cogitation, it just doesn't fit the work that humanities professors do. As Ernest Boyer rightly insisted, it is not only discovery that must be rewarded, but integration of the insights of one field with many others, application of them to actual situations, and, especially, communicating them to students. The most depressing thing about the suppression of this range of important processes in the humanities is that so many of the tenured faculty members and their departmental leaders actually accept the values that now drive much academic research. Indeed, the most important effect of the imposition of science and technology criteria on the humanities has been the willingness of the humanities, by and large, to serve them. Despite their efforts to avoid the fallacy of misplaced concreteness in the quantity-as-quality assessment equation, the humanities have in fact set ever higher standards of publication for new academicians to meet.

I have written elsewhere about the humanities' engagement in competition for research honours, suggesting that it has turned the academy into a kind of Super Bowl or Final Four contest.[431] Faculty aspirants hustle and show their wares like car salespersons vying for Seller of the Month, and every department wants to claim that it has at least one superstar on its roster. Moreover, given the decline in tenure-track positions, as well as the overproduction of publication in the humanities, the emphasis has had to be reset on fame, as well as numbers; scarcity, as well as quality, has intensified. The addition of fame, or notoriety, intensifies what one pair of economists has called a "winner-take-all" culture.[432] In such a culture, there is no room for the merely "good" faculty member; only a very few can place in the top five, or ten, or twenty — or whatever catchment an institution can claim to be a part of. The others are to be either kept in place as non-tenured faculty or sent back to the service economy as lawyers, social workers, or tired radio performers. Or they become associate professors, who may now be charged with performing so much of the housekeeping of humanities departments that they can never work their way to the publishing heights where live the truly blest.

POSTSCRIPT

Having criticized the dismal situation of research as a driving factor in the humanities, I must now avoid the temerity I have noted in studies of it on the part of concerned, and involved, academics themselves. I will end by listing some specific strategies that seem to me critical for changing the culture:

Teaching

Of course, teaching needs to be taken seriously as a critical feature of faculty work, but since ideal principles abound, I would move to implement real change in the teaching/research balance by insisting that all researchers teach undergraduates as a regular part of their assignment. It is very difficult to police course assignments, although at least one politician who suspected rampant slackerdom in the academy walked the halls at one of the Penn State campuses several years ago, stopping students to ask how much they interact with faculty. But the faculty itself must become more aware of the configuration of its teaching profile. I recommend, then, that every department report annually on senior/tenure-track faculty participation in undergraduate teaching by name. And to make sure the entire faculty understands who is doing the teaching, departments should also issue annual rosters that list all the teaching personnel, tenure and non–tenure line. Ideally, courses that senior faculty teach should include the department's bread-and-butter introductory courses for non-majors. If all faculty members had to serve time in such courses, they might rebel against the increased enrollment of first- and second-year students in massive introductory lectures. Under my plan, the research faculty who teach those mass courses would be monitored in their willingness to meet with and mentor their assistants — TAs, "lab assistants," and undergraduate "peer" tutors. Giving value to teaching will never succeed unless teaching is shared in equity across department ranks and across the teaching staff, and not in graduate courses only.

Tenure

I agree that the severity of requirements for tenure has become part of the problem in the humanities' depressed job market. But I would also reject the elimination of tenure; not only does it protect the academic freedom of faculty in research and teaching but also it enacts a personnel system that works better than any other to keep the faculty self-aware and, yes, productive. Rather than ending tenure, as some critics have suggested, I would work to extend it. I advocate granting the protections of tenure, if not the title, to all casualized instructors who have served satisfactorily for a monitored, probationary period as provided in each contract. My proposal might be criticized as an unworkable form of amnesty for non-tenure-track faculty. I realize that legitimating a large cadre of mainly teaching faculty might finally undermine the whole notion of research in the humanities, but I can see no other way to open up the profession to deserving candidates for the academy's teaching and service work. Obviously, if an amnesty program were enacted, I would insist on the continuation of reasonable and exacting evaluation for all faculty.

Administration

Any radical change in the current value system will require changes in administrative funding habits as well as competitive attitudes. University budgets have become more and more attached to entrepreneurial profit- or prestige-making ventures at the expense of the central work of basic research and instruction. I would revoke those current budgeting systems that cede budgetary authority to individual programs and would assign the over-all management of resources as the prime mandate of a central authority that has the wisdom to safeguard what is essential as its first order of business.

Governance

Since I believe that the faculty itself must have some better say in the way their colleges and universities evaluate their work, I believe they must conduct their collectivity more effectively. Traditionally, they have organized their affairs through varieties of faculty senates, but these have become archaic debating societies on many campuses — essentially because they have no power. I believe the only really powerful mode of faculty organization is unionization, and that faculty should surrender their fears of collective bargaining in order to govern themselves in the most powerful and equitable way available. My proposal would not seem strange in a country like Canada, where almost all faculty members are unionized, but even there, faculty can be disdainful of the union's efforts, failing to give their organizations the active support they deserve. A faculty union without faculty participation is not, of course, the answer I envision. The decision to engage in collective bargaining in the United States is so enmeshed in legal barriers that organizing is almost impossible when an employer opposes it. Nevertheless, the faculties that have unionized in North America seem to me to be more responsive to the dangers of the mono-valence of research than those on more "traditional" campuses. Given the crisis in American higher education today, non-unionized professors should consider their lack of power and seek to regain it through intensive collective governance guided by the experience of academic collective bargaining colleagues.

Change of Heart

Changes of heart are required for any genuine reform. I know they are not predictable or probable in an environment that values the material, the concrete, the countable. But the mission of the humanities is to probe, interpret, criticize, even exhort. Asking their professors for a change of heart is asking them to practice what they preach.

VI. PERILS OF RUNNING A UNIVERSITY IN THE CORPORATE WAY

13

UNRAVELLING THE FABRIC OF ACADEME: THE MANAGERIALIST UNIVERSITY AND ITS IMPLICATIONS FOR THE INTEGRITY OF ACADEMIC WORK

Rosemary Deem

INTRODUCTION

This chapter enquires into the extent to which the impact of current management practices in higher education on the integrity of academic work resembles the frequent unravelling of Penelope's weaving in Greek mythology.[433] Recent research on the management of higher education is examined, focusing in particular on the phenomenon known as "new managerialism" (an ideological approach to the management of publicly funded services in Western societies particularly prominent in the 1980s and 1990s) and its implications for the integrity of academic work. Although the analysis draws principally on research conducted in the United Kingdom, it is recognized that this is a distinctive and culturally specific set of higher education systems.[434] There are, nevertheless, many aspects of new managerialism which are more widely applicable to other higher education systems and which will be recognizable to many academics, wherever they work.

We first offer a definition of what is meant by new managerialism, before considering the findings of a UK Economic and Social Research Council-funded study investigating how UK academics, manager-academics, and career administrators perceive the management of higher education and the extent to which it is perceived to have been permeated by new managerialism.[435] This research was conducted at Lancaster University, England, in eleven learned societies and sixteen UK universities between 1998 and 2000. It is augmented here by reference to some current research on university leadership and management, particularly focusing on the roles of vice-chancellors (presidents/chief executives) and their deputies. The discussion then moves on to an examination of some of the consequences of new managerialism for the integrity of academic work. Three separate examples of this are provided: the explicit management of research activity in universities; external quality evaluation of teaching standards; and the shift of doctoral degree programs from a primarily academic concern to the subject of local and national monitoring and surveillance. Finally, we analyze early impressions from the higher education element of a current UK-based project that is investigating public service modernization, organizational leadership, and change agency.[436] In this study, leaders in universities are being compared with the leaders in publicly funded hospitals, primary (community-based) health care, and secondary schools. We conclude by asking who is involved in the unravelling on the fabric on the academic loom, and consider how, in future, we can work towards sustaining rather than destroying the integrity of the fabric of academic life.

WHAT IS NEW MANAGERIALISM?

Academic debates about the growth of new managerialism in public services in Western societies and its effects both on those working in public-service organizations and on service provision itself became particularly predominant in the 1990s, although new managerialism well predates this period.[437] By the 1990s, new managerialism looked as though it was becoming a firm ideological choice for many Western governments in overseeing the running of publicly funded organizations. The roots of new managerialism lay in 1980s cuts in public expenditure, the introduction of quasi-markets to public services, and examination of the so-called producer-dominance of public services organizations, as part of a more general shift to neoliberalism in many

Western societies.[438] Many academic writers use the terms "new managerialism" and "new public management" interchangeably — and indeed some of their alleged features overlap — but theoretically and conceptually, the two have quite different origins. Thus, while new public management arose out of public choice theory and has become seen as a new technocratic orthodoxy for public-service organizations regardless of the dominant political ideology of the country concerned, new managerialism is much more unashamedly ideological when applied by policy makers, with the private sector seen as providing the efficient and effective organizational model that public services must emulate.[439]

The characteristics of new managerialism vary somewhat by sector but include an emphasis on the primacy of management over all other functions and a concentration on "doing more with less." As Trow noted in a commentary on trends in the management of UK higher education in the 1990s, there is often an underlying assumption that somehow efficient management can be a substitute for resources.[440] Managerialism is a hierarchical form of organizing practice and so is very different from the collegial self-governance traditional among academics[441] and some other public-service professionals. New managerialism focuses on monitoring the achievement of targets (both at the organizational level and in devolved budgetary sub-units) and the performance of individual employees. Greater competition both between organizations providing the same service and between sub-units in the same organization is encouraged. So, for example, universities must compete not only for students and staff as they have long done but also for scarce research funding and positioning in national and international league tables such as those published by Shanghai Jiao Tong University or the *Times Higher Education Supplement*,[442] while different disciplines in the same university are expected to vie with each other for money and even survival. Thus, recently in England, some universities have been closing chemistry departments, as these are expensive to run and there is declining student demand for degrees in a number of institutions.[443] Outsourcing of functions previously carried out in-house is encouraged; in higher education this might include activities like catering and cleaning. The private finance of buildings is also encouraged under new managerialism. In the UK this is termed the "private finance initiative" or PFI, and its assumptions about publicly funded building projects and its long-term liabilities and conse-quences for the public purse and service provision have been subject to considerable criticism, particularly in the UK National Health Service.[444] New managerialism often finds itself in tension with the ways in which professionals are used to working, including not only self-governance and a climate of trust but also the use of discretion.[445] It is also not necessarily a phenomenon that remains stable over time. As Reed has noted, what began as a form of bureau-professionalism that permitted a degree of regulated autonomy (though with neocor-poratist elements) in the 1960s–70s was replaced by neoliberal managerialism by the beginning of the 1980s, which was seen as heralding a revolution in public-service provision. In the late 1990s, neoliberal managerialism was being subordinated by neotechnocratic managerialism, with a greater emphasis on collective organizational learning and attention to service delivery to, and the empowerment of, citizens.[446]

New managerialism has permeated or been imposed on public serv-ices in a variety of ways, including via public funding mechanisms and policies, government reports and recommendations and the use of consultants with private-sector experience.[447] However, while govern-ments and policy makers may expect those in management and lead-ership positions to embrace the tenets of managerialism, no assump-tion is made here that everyone holding a managerial position in pub-lic-service organizations necessarily embraces new managerialism. Some will subvert it or resist it, while others will engage with it whole-heartedly or benefit from the opportunities it offers for widening the range of management positions available, as Ozga and I found in the mid-1990s when studying the experiences of women managers with feminist beliefs who were working in further and higher education.[448] We now turn to examine some of the findings of a research investiga-tion into new managerialism in UK universities.

THE ESRC NEW MANAGERIALISM PROJECT AND THE MANAGEMENT OF UK UNIVERSITIES

This project involved a team of researchers based at Lancaster University. Funded by the UK Economic and Social Research Council (ESRC, award no. R000 27 7661) between 1998 and 2000, the study investigated the extent to which new managerialism had permeated UK universities and analyzed the accounts of careers and management practice provided by a purposive sample of academics holding management positions in the academy (from heads/chairs of departments to heads of institutions). These individuals are termed manager-academics to distinguish them from career managers such as human resource directors. A full account of the project is available elsewhere,[449] so here there is a focus on those elements particularly relevant to the integrity of academic work.

The project fieldwork, using a variety of qualitative methods including interviews, focus groups and institutional case studies, was organized in three phases. In phase one, focus groups based on members of eleven learned societies and professional academic bodies discussed what they thought was happening to the running of higher education. The value of these groups was that they were cross-institutional, included academics, manager-academics, and administrators, and covered a range of academic subjects from physics through arts/humanities and social sciences to business studies. The focus group data suggested that the UK universities were now viewed as highly managerial and bureaucratic, with declining levels of trust between employees and managers and a big reduction in the levels of discretion and self-governance afforded to academics. There was a feeling that some universities now regarded themselves as businesses. Among issues that focus group participants reported concerns about were: high workloads and long hours (and not just for academic staff); decisions made on the basis of monetary considerations, not academic factors; the growth of powerful, unaccountable and uncommunicative senior management teams; and greater pressures for the development of internal and external audit systems for research, teaching, and academic standards. Not everything was negative; some participants mentioned positive changes: more emphasis on teamwork, a greater sense of accountability, and more responsiveness to students.

The second phase of the study involved a cross-section sample of sixteen publicly funded universities with different histories, locations, and missions. The fieldwork consisted mainly of individual interviews with 137 manager-academics (heads of departments, deans, pro- and deputy vice-chancellors/presidents and vice-chancellors/presidents) and a much smaller number of senior career administrators. The interviews were revealing in more ways than we had anticipated, as often when we set out to meet our respondents, the more senior of them proved quite difficult to locate, being surrounded by gatekeepers and not infrequently sequestered away in hidden suites of offices or in buildings where no students were allowed and where few ordinary staff ever went. Our interviewees, like the focus group participants, talked about changes to the environment of higher education (declining public funding, massification of undergraduate enrollment and the growth of research and teaching quality evaluation), but were in general much more positive about recent changes to higher education. This is not surprising, as for many of our interviewees, such changes had made possible or contributed to their careers. Respondents talked about how they had ended up in management roles, emphasizing their personal biographies and the ways that their identities had been defined by teaching, disciplinary commitment, and research. A number of the women manager-academic respondents, who were far fewer on the ground than their male peers in our sixteen institutions (we interviewed pretty much all the female manager-academics we encountered), felt they had been held back by gendered expectations of managers that required different things from women than men, home responsibilities, and/or a lack of positive sponsorship or mentoring.[450]

Among our sample, the motivations for being a manager varied from enjoyment of institutional politics and liking power, through wanting more money, to a desire to protect a discipline or the fear that someone less able to cope would otherwise take on the role. The latter two motivations were particularly found among heads of department. From the manager-academic interviews as a whole we identified three typical routes into management. Career-track managers tended to have found that they enjoyed management at an early stage of their careers and had given up substantial teaching and research commitments soon after. This group were most often found in the post-1992 former polytechnics:

> I rose through the ranks as it were and I was senior lecturer, principal lecturer, course director for the major undergraduate course there, head of postgraduate department. Then dean, I think, unless there was another head of department's job in between. And I had a couple of sort of side trips — I ran what was then the Faculty of Health & Social Sciences for a few months, and I worked as an assistant to the previous director at the Polytechnic, for a short while. Then, as I say, I became dean [at X] and then the pro-vice-chancellor left, so I applied for the job and got it. (Male pro-vice-chancellor, social scientist, post-1992 university.)

At pro-vice-chancellor (PVC) level and above, however, a wider group of our respondents in both types of university than simply career-long manager-academics had set their sights on a management and leadership career path. This was not always straightforward, as in the pre-1992 universities, PVC posts were often rotating and fixed-term, so that those who did not succeed in finding a post as head of another institution might well find themselves back in the academic ranks at the end of their term of office.

A second track of those we termed "reluctant managers," a group already identified in other sectors,[451] were typically found among fixed-term heads of department in established pre-1992 universities. This group tended to strongly reject an identity as a manager and saw themselves instead as academics and academic leaders. Most were planning to return to academic life at the end of their term of office, so were keen to treat their colleagues in a collegial manner. They did not always warm to their management role:

> The previous head of department . . . finished last July. . . .
> One of my colleagues . . . was commissioned by the vice-
> chancellor to sound out members of staff to see who they
> would prefer. . . . They said me. . . . Then I got a letter from
> the VC . . . asking me if I would be head of department. . . .
> I felt completely trapped. . . . I don't think it's fair to refuse to
> do that task — nobody wants to do it as far as I can see. And so
> I said I would, with great misgivings, because it's had a terrible
> effect on my research output. I've got a book that I haven't
> touched for over a year now . . . and I still have a fair bit of
> teaching and my PhD students and so forth. (Female head of
> department, Humanities, pre-1992 university.)

Finally, we identified a small group of "good citizen" manager-academics, who had often entered management at a comparatively late stage in their academic careers. This group were mainly deans or PVCs, and their motivation was often repaying a perceived debt to their university through service in a management role:

> It started simply by other people mentioning it to me. I had no
> ambitions to be a dean. As I said earlier, my main motivation
> is an academic motivation and largely research. So the only,
> the first occasion that I even considered being dean, was about
> ten days before I actually was one. In other words, when the
> process of consultation started, a number of names apparent-
> ly were mentioned, but eventually it was crystallised on one
> individual and that was me, and really that was the first time
> that I had even considered it. . . . I had been asked to be
> dean much earlier in my career by a previous vice-chancellor
> and I turned it down. . . . But it's simply related, I think to
> two factors. One, I'm towards the end of my career. I'm now
> sixty. It sounds very old-fashioned but I perhaps wanted to
> give something back to the university in terms of manage-
> ment. And I did bring an unusual blend of expertise, having
> been out at [a research funding body] you know, for some

time. . . . Secondly, I knew that if I turned it down, a younger
colleague whose career should not be burdened at this stage by
being a dean would have been asked, and would perhaps have
been leant on quite heavily. And this is an individual whose
research career is blossoming at the moment and I simply
didn't want that to be invaded in any way. (Male dean,
Sciences, pre-1992 university.)

We also made some assessment of the state of the UK higher education sectors through the project. Here we drew on models of "new
managerialism" derived from research on the late 1980s reforms to the
UK National Health Service (NHS) done by Ferlie et al. (1996).[452]
Ferlie et al. proposed four models. The efficiency model, "doing more
with less," supported by funding policies and league tables, was perceived as having significantly permeated higher education. We found
no evidence of Ferlie et al.'s "downsizing" model, but there was some
evidence of decentralization in the form of partially devolved budgets
(responsibility for fundraising, control of expenditure, and avoidance
of debt being an integral part of devolved budget units). Often there
was no right to hire staff or spend money, so the devolved element frequently amounted to responsibility without power. The third model,
the learning organization model, was perceived to have some perme-
ation — e.g., endeavours to achieve cultural change (always in the
workers, not in the managers), development of teamwork and some
moves towards planning for strategic activity — but almost no one
thought that staff empowerment had been attempted. It would be ironic if universities showed no indication of being a learning organization. Elements of Ferlie et al.'s fourth model, developing a radical new
approach to public-service provision with a high level of user involvement in the design and provision of services, were not mentioned by
any of our respondents and we saw no other indications of this model.
This may also relate to the fact that quite a few of our respondents, particularly in the established universities, did not appear to think that
they worked in a public service.

In the final phase of the project, we examined the views about university management drawn from a broad range of university employees, from manual workers to contract researchers, in four institutions. Whilst most of our manager-academic respondents told us that they were consultative in their approach to their work, a rather different story emerged from other university staff. Either the consultations had not reached them or the outcomes of these consultations seemed to have been ignored by managers. Employees, especially those in non-academic jobs, were at pains to point out their high loyalty to their institutions (they often said they enjoyed their jobs) but suggested that, in return, they had experienced poor communication from senior management, a failure to listen to staff concerns and problems, slow decision-making, amateur approaches to management, an absence of clearly understood policies, and a growing gap between senior management and everybody else. There was also some mention in a few cases of bullying and (more often) of inappropriate people being put into management roles. This portrait of university management contrasted with the much more upbeat picture of university management given by our manager-academic respondents.

SENIOR MANAGER-ACADEMIC ROLES

There are two major changes that seem to have occurred in the last decade or so, in respect of senior management roles in UK universities. First, there has been a big increase in the number of institutions that have established senior management teams, and the size of these teams is also increasing. This is an international trend, as Marginson and Considine's work on changes to Australian universities demonstrates.[453] In 1998–2000 when we carried out the new managerialism project fieldwork, it was relatively rare for career administrators to be members of these teams, and the teams were quite small. However, in the project we are now doing on public service leadership, career administrators are core members of the senior management team in all the higher education institutions we are researching, and it is clear that all these institutions also have several pro- or deputy vice-chancellors, not just one or two. In some cases, deans are also members of senior management teams.

The role of pro- and deputy vice-chancellors is an interesting one. Their portfolio is often both general (to deputize for the vice-chancellor/president) and specific (a portfolio for research, teaching and learning, resources, staffing, etc.). They rarely have any budgetary or line management responsibilities, and many are still engaged in research or supervise doctoral students. Smith, Adams and Mount's recent work for the UK Leadership Foundation on PVCs[454] has suggested that regardless of portfolio, all PVCs are concerned with similar tasks, including quality standards, compliance and balancing competing pressures, strategic thinking, and dealing with cultural values. Smith et al. also suggest that PVCs act as facilitators at organizational boundaries and as brokers of relationships (rather than operating using executive power). There are few reluctant managers at the PVC level and indeed Gosling, Bolden, and Petrov, in current research on leadership development, in UK universities suggest that, compared to heads of department, institutions often find it relatively easy to recruit to PVC posts, which are well paid and a stepping stone to becoming a vice-chancellor.[455]

Second, although in 1998–2000, external appointment to a management role other than vice-chancellor/president was rare in the established UK universities, it was much more common in the former polytechnics for head of department, dean and pro-vice-chancellor posts. Since then, the role of headhunters (or executive recruitment agencies) has increased,[456] and more jobs, especially at pro-vice-chancellor level, even in established universities, are subject to external recruitment processes. This may have all sorts of other effects: for example, on the social characteristics and backgrounds of those appointed and also on the distancing of the selection process for senior jobs from all other academic-post recruitment processes. The social and academic background of vice-chancellors has certainly been shifting in recent decades,[457] with more social scientists and more women entering from the 1990s on, although there are still fewer than twenty women VCs in the UK, out of well over 120 universities. Given the rise in the number of pro-vice-chancellors and the turbulent environment for higher education in the UK and worldwide, it would not be surprising to find that the role of vice-chancellors is also changing. Though the shift away from being the leading academic towards a more overt concern with being a chief executive was predicted and recommended in the UK as long ago as 1985 by a report looking at how the non-academic decision-making processes of universities could be improved,[458] the job itself has changed more slowly. Even in 2000, in a study that involved work-shadowing vice-chancellors as well as interviewing them, it was noted that their claims to be mainly concerned with strategic activity were often thwarted by their frequent need to deal with crises and react to events.[459] However, rather like their North American counterparts (who have been doing it much longer), more UK VCs are becoming extensively involved in fundraising from alumni, philanthropists, and the private sector. Furthermore, the VC external relations role now involves the entire globe, so that the "airport lounge" VC, distant from and distanced from their staff and students and more familiar with the environs of airports than universities, is now arguably more common in the UK (particularly in the pre-1992 sector) than one who spends a lot of time in their own institution and knows many of the staff and students. Having considered some of the manifestations of new managerialism as revealed in research at the end of the 1990s and the recent trends in recruitment to and roles and composition of senior management teams in universities, we now turn to a consideration of what effects new managerialism may be having on the integrity of academic work.

NEW MANAGERIALISM'S CONSEQUENCES FOR ACADEMIC WORK

As we have seen for the UK (and it is also so for many other higher education systems in the world), there has been a huge investment in management and leadership posts in universities over the last decade or so. Of course, some of this is a consequence of growth in institutional size and complexity. However, in the managerialist focus on efficiency, effectivity, performances, targets, outcomes, markets, audits, and league tables, it is also easy to lose sense of what the academic enterprise is actually about. The creativity of research may be seen as secondary or even as detrimental to a view of research as something that can be overtly '"managed" by others than academics,[460] as a process of generating extra institutional income and as contributing to an international reputation and positioning in world league tables.[461] Similarly, the developmental aspects of education may be replaced by a view of teaching that provides what "consumers" want or mainly offering a form of employability training for students.[462] Academics are notoriously difficult to manage, the process often being referred to as akin to "herding cats," and have frequently proved resistant to managerialism. However, subverting managerialism is time-consuming, and as Leisyte has shown in her comparison of the effects on academics in biotechnology and medieval history of recent changes in research governance in the Netherlands and England,[463] the subversion or distancing is often accompanied by some playing of the "game," too, particularly in relation to research.[464] For example, in Leisyte's study, many academics agreed to undertake research in areas where there is extensive funding available but little intrinsic academic interest, as well as continuing to do "blue skies" research. Others wrote short articles that were published relatively quickly while still working on books that took years, because they felt their credibility and survival depended on doing both.

In many UK universities, research is now thought of as too important to be left to academics; recent studies in Europe suggest this attitude is becoming more widespread.[465] This trend means the whole research process, from intelligence about funding and the development of bids, to the themes that shape research problems, intellectual property rights, and knowledge transfer strategies, is no longer just the preserve of academics. Since 1999, UK academics have been required by their higher education funding councils to fill in a form each term saying how much time they have spent (of a notional and mythical 37.5-hour week) on research, teaching, scholarship, and administration. This is to ensure that research and teaching do not cross-subsidize each other. Despite an apparent rhetoric about integrating research and teaching, for example, via the Higher Education Academy[466] (founded in 2004), which is tasked with enhancing academics' teaching and improving the student experience (the academics' experience apparently being secondary), there is increased pressure to separate the two, not only in the UK but elsewhere as well.[467]

In the UK, research activity is also closely monitored and audited externally via the periodic Research Assessment Exercise in which research-active academics send a small selection of their research outputs and other data about research students, research funding, research culture, and infrastructure, to be quality-assessed by subject-based peer panels. The outcomes of this exercise are then used to drive subsequent funding to institutions from the higher-education funding bodies. The exercise, which uses a range of quantitative and qualitative data but is dependent on academic experts discussing and considering the outputs, is due to be replaced in the period 2010–2013 by a purely metrics-based exercise for science, engineering, and technology subjects, combining this with "light touch" peer review for social sciences and arts/humanities.[468] Currently there is also a plan to assess the citation impact of every paper produced by the academics involved. Internally, university research units and academics with the responsibility for overseeing research activity and strategy examine funding performance and research outputs of academics. Universities may also offer funding or other incentives for undertaking research on particular themes. Research sponsors, from government research councils to private industry, have a big role in shaping research themes and issues. Private industry has long sponsored academic research,[469] but in the contemporary world, there is little choice but to apply for external funding (even if some private funders restrict publication rights or how research data may be utilized) if an academic wants time, equipment, or a research assistant with which to pursue research. Applied research often has the capacity to generate more money than "blue skies" research, so there may be pressure to do more of the former than the latter.[470] In 2007 it was announced that government research councils, which currently fund a good deal of "blue skies" research in the UK, would in future be required to assess the economic impact as well as the academic merit of future grant applications, thus reducing the possibility that curiosity-driven research would be funded.

Managerialism does not only mean considerable interference in research. It also adds significantly to academic workloads, as both the internal requirements and external audit systems work on the basis that academics cannot be trusted to do their work but must continually be checked or show that they have jumped through a series of hoops (for example, by specifying the learning outcomes of a new program before they have ever taught it or by listing and self-evaluating the quality of their own publications on a regular basis). With respect to the evaluation of teaching now being adopted in many countries in the world,[471] the focus is now often more on the paperwork involved than on the actual teaching itself. Furthermore, some academics may become very stressed by the processes involved in the evaluation of their teaching, which is itself an alternative form of governance and a new set of power relations over academic work.[472] In the UK, a government agency, the Quality Assurance Agency (QAA) established in 1997, has sought to impose a series of regulations and codes of practice on higher education, covering everything from the content of undergraduate degrees and the qualifications awarded (with so-called "level descriptors" for bachelor's, master's and doctoral degrees) to overseas collaboration. The QAA carries out regular visits to institutions to inspect their academic standards and, until the early 2000s, also inspected individual subject departments. As with research, the audit culture in teaching has led to the establishment of central quality and academic development units in many universities. It is now much harder for UK academics to make independent decisions about curricula or teaching. Quality audit of teaching is certainly something to which academics have shown strong reactions, as Morley's study shows.[473] A current study of academic attitudes to quality audit of teaching in one research-intensive UK university suggests that a good proportion of respondents think quality audits processes are mostly about paperwork and bureaucracy rather than really being concerned with or affecting the quality of teaching.[474]

A further example of how managerialism has invaded academic life lies in the field of doctoral programs for research students. It is now increasingly rare in Europe (and in many other countries) for doctoral study to simply be left up to academics and their students.[475]

Institutions and agencies are intervening, whether it is in the form of supervisor training, codes of practice for supervisors and students, or determination of policy on doctoral recruitment and selection. Doctoral students are seen as a measure of the research culture, status, and international competitiveness of their institutions.[476] There has been a proliferation of doctoral programs,[477] including variants such as professional doctorates[478] combining significant continuing professional development in the form of taught units with a dissertation. More doctoral students means less individual attention for each one. It also means that many no longer see the doctorate as a preparation for academic employment, so institutions and outside agencies now want to emphasize the importance of the inclusion of generic skills training and consideration of "employability" in doctoral programs Meanwhile supervisors, like teachers, are no longer trusted to do their work properly and are regularly monitored, as are the dropout and completion rates of their students. Supervision is no longer just an academic interaction but may be digitally recorded by students in the event of a future complaint or failure to pass. Supervisors and students are also urged to keep written records of supervisions, partly so these can be used in appeals. Doctoral thesis defences are increasingly also subject to independent chairing by other than an expert examiner or may be digitally recorded. Managerialism removes discretion and trust from academics and replaces it with bureaucracy, distrust, surveillance, and additional paperwork.

As Peters has argued, the contemporary university is fixated on globalization, the market, the world's economy, and student demand.[479] There are, he suggests, two particularly striking variants of this orientation. One is the idea of a "global service university" based on the notion that the publicly funded university, in the face of global changes, needs to take on private-sector, for-profit organizational characteristics in order to contribute to the growth of the world economy and corporations. (Products include the trained graduates and technology transfer, wherein research outcomes are turned into a form useable by industry or commerce.) This model, Peters argues, is closest to that used in the UK's current higher education systems. The second variant is the "hollowed out" university that is stripped down to a core of functions largely focused on meeting student and employers' demands and then aggressively marketed to students around the world. Peters suggests that this is exemplified by the Australian system. The managerialist university would fit happily into either of these templates. But a move is underway, in the UK at least, to drive out managerialism in public services and replace it with a new phenomenon — leadership. Why this change, and what are its implications for the integrity of academic work?

LEADERSHIP AND CHANGE AGENCY IN PUBLICLY FUNDED UNIVERSITIES

Currently I am co-director on a project funded by the UK Economic and Social Research Council, which is examining the New Labour government's endeavours in relation to the modernization and leadership of public services. In particular, we are looking at their effects on those who hold leadership positions in three key public services: health, secondary schools, and universities. An initial critical discourse analysis of key documents from New Labour's term of office from 1997 has suggested that transformational leadership, rather than new managerialism, has become a major aspect of New Labour's reform program for public services.[480] New Labour has also established or supported the establishment of several national leadership development bodies, including one each for the health service, schools, and universities. The body for universities, the Leadership Foundation for Higher Education, founded in 2004, arose out of an initiative between two organizations representing higher education leaders[481] and is not directly financed from the public purse. Nevertheless, it is still heavily dependent on money from the Higher Education Funding Council for England, and a 2006 independent evaluation suggests it is unlikely to be self-funding for several more years.[482] We are interested in whose agendas health, school, and university leaders follow in their efforts to lead and change their organizations, and are also investigating the extent to which leadership development provision supports, is neutral towards, or is critical of government policy. A further concern, particularly in universities, is to find out the extent to which the apparent superseding of new managerialism by inspirational leadership is simply a rhetorical device. Certainly many of the key features of new managerialism, such as national and international league tables, performance management, devolved units, and "doing more with less," still seem to be in place in England's public services. A number of people in bodies allied to UK higher education have objected to the framing of our project, arguing that higher education is not a public service and hence is not comparable with the more overtly publicly funded health service or schools. Yet there is only one completely private university in the UK with the right to award degrees. All the other universities receive a considerable amount of public funding, although there is also an increasing amount of private money from international students, home undergraduate tuition fees, and research and consultancy projects.

In 2007, we interviewed five vice-chancellors (presidents/chief executives) and twenty-four members of their senior management teams in six universities in England. Almost without exception, the academics in these teams described themselves as leaders, not managers. Unlike in North America, none of this group of respondents would think of referring to any of their work as administration — only career managers (such as finance directors or registrars) are happy with such a role identity. However, respondents were also keen to tell us about their distributed management[483] arrangements, which are not consistent with New Labour's emphasis on inspirational leadership:

> I'm a member of the directorate; my portfolio is everything to do with the academic work of the university — all the student facing side of things: academic administration, learning resources, the international office registry, which includes admissions, research degree students, all student support services, and in terms of my more general role with the vice-chancellor. . . . I work closely with the vice-chancellor doing all the things that aren't in that list that are the general things that go on in any university . . . It's a fairly typical PVC role. . . . All of that involves leadership. (Female PVC, Longley, post-1992.)

Distributed leadership is not only about senior management teams sharing responsibility. It was also argued to include academic decision making through committees and the development of devolved budgets to individual units. However, it may be that responsibility is much more widely dispersed than power in such distributed leadership systems. Being on a committee may give an academic a sense of involvement, just as it does for a head of department who has a devolved budget, but if the committee's decisions are overruled or ignored by senior management and if the head of department is not allowed to hire any new staff or spend any surpluses, then the distributed leadership may not mean a great deal.

On the theme of whose agenda for change is being followed in England's higher education system, several interviewees said that they were far from being mere implementers of government policy. What most felt they did was to mediate government changes and policies to fit the circumstances and priorities of their own institutions and also embark on changes of their own:

> When I came here I asked how many faculties there were, and nobody could quite answer the question. It was somewhere between eight and nine; it depended who you asked, and there were eighty-something departments, maybe more, complete chaos, and it's actually not atypical of where universities were, and in fact some still are, and they were in the process of trying to sort out what they should do instead, because they all knew it was nonsense, so I spent a long time with the then eighty heads of department on away days, away weekends, chewing over the strategy for the institution and a structure. We, first of all, worked out the structure, because I insisted we should have a managerial culture, of some sort, that was better than what we had, and that power should be aligned with accountability. All these words were completely foreign to the institution, never heard of, and among Humanities and the Social Science caused apoplexy. . . .
>
> I resent the fact that [because] the government gives us 30

percent of the money, they think they can control 100 percent of what we do. So, I object to that very much, and I'm a very staunch advocate of more autonomy because the more successful universities in the world have the greatest autonomy. (Male VC, Furzedown, pre-1992.)

It is interesting that for this VC, being independent of government nevertheless seemed to involve managerialism.

Several of our other respondents did feel that they were (independent) agents for change:

Implementing government reform? I think I'm responding to it, and there's a whole set of things that I'm doing at the moment . . . [but] I'd hate to be a sort of "kept" change agent on behalf of the government, if you see what I mean. (Male DVC, Furzedown, pre-1992.)

When I was a head of department, one of reasons I got very frustrated . . . is that I didn't seem to be able to act as an agent of change, that I was simply reactive. . . . People told you what to do even though you were supposed to be the person that was making decisions. (Female dean, Parklane.)

One or two respondents, though, had been given cause to reflect on the consequences of leading change without paying sufficient attention to the needs of staff:

When I first came into this job, someone came to see [me] . . . . a chap in tears . . . and said, "Rick I'm packing up, I've had enough. . . . I've worked here twenty-five years, I've never got into trouble, I've worked weekends, done evening work, done the whole lot, and do you know, Rick, in those twenty-five years, nobody has ever said thank you." . . . I learnt an awful lot from that, about valuing people. . . . How often do we say thank you or well done? Far too infrequently, actually. (Male dean, Parklane.)

In the Lancaster managerialism project reported earlier in this chapter, we saw that there were some discrepancies between the allegedly consultative approach to leadership and management noted by those in manager-academic positions and the views of the staff in the same organizations, who suggested there was amateur management and leadership, poor decision making, and a failure to consult. The interviewees in our new project also talked about their consultative approach to leadership:

> I think what would characterize it. . . . is change by persuasion, dialogue, convincing people of the need and how to get there, and the strategies, and building consensus and of course you have to be patient and willing to consider longer time scales if you're going to reach consensus, rather than do it by dictate, but it takes root better. (Male PVC, Hopton.)

> I would say a combination of approaches, really, and whilst on the one hand I like to undertake consultation with people who are going to be involved in the change, it's not. . . . I don't operate, I would say, a strictly democratic approach, towards change. It's taking consultation and then trying to put that together with our own thoughts as to the way to go (Male Associate dean, Littleoaks.)

However, as the last respondent makes clear, consultation and a democratic approach are not the same. Consultation does not mean that leaders will do as their staff suggest. Indeed, too much dissent may be seen as a problem — there have been a number of instances in the UK recently where VCs have disciplined staff who criticize managers.[484]

We are also interested in how far the kinds of leadership development activities senior management teams undergo, reflect government policy or encourage a more independent approach to it. There was a general view among those who had recently experienced such provision, whether from the Leadership Foundation for Higher Education or elsewhere, that no particular line was pursued:

> I mean the thing about the Top Management Programme [run by the LFHE] is really, I mean the best bits of it are about reflection and being exposed to a variety of different ideas, and the other part is just, again, you know, it's the networking thing, sharing common experiences, so no, they didn't promote any particular. . . . I mean they promoted the idea that change was an important thing that you had to deal with, and they said, you know, I can't remember the details of what they expected, the different ways of meeting it. (Male DVC, Furzedown, pre-1992.)

> The main purpose for the week was emphasising that as you moved up the ladder, your role increasingly was to not think of one particular part of the institution in isolation from another, that more and more as you got, as your level got higher, and you essentially were dealing with matters more strategic, you needed to be connecting matters physical with HR, with legal, with marketing, with academic, and so on and so forth. . . . I mean at the end of the week our job was, as a group . . . We were the University of X, and so we were given some constraints about what the task was about, you know, this is the kind of admission, these are the kind of issues your institution deals with, and you have to develop your own mission, and you know, what it is you were going to [do] by way of growth, and physical developments and all the rest of it. (male Senior Management Team Administrator, Valley, pre-1992)

However, we might want to question whether leadership development activities are as innocent of government policy and current orthodoxies about how public-service organizations should be led as some of our respondents have suggested. Both respondents and leadership development providers are deeply immersed, consciously or not, in current ways of doing things, and there is certainly little evidence in England's higher education sector that there has been any significant move away from managerialism, despite the new rhetorical emphasis on inspirational leadership. The hold of the evaluative state is also still strong.[485] We might also want to ask why the dominant approaches to running universities are still being taken for granted by both leaders and leadership development providers, given some of the consequences for staff spelled out in the previous sections.

WHO'S UNRAVELLING THE ACADEMIC FABRIC?

The answer to this puzzle appears to be that it is often academic leaders who are involved in this process, though clearly it does not mean that all of them are implicated, and it is certain that there are examples of academic leaders who are committed to preserving the integrity of academic work. However, we have no real means of knowing the distribution of such leaders compared with those to whom, seemingly, academic work is a necessary evil that must be "managed," curbed, audited, and generally distrusted. At the same time, who is able to defend academic integrity? Individual academics clearly have a role, but any sustainable defence must surely involve collective action. Although the two main UK academic trade unions have recently merged into a single organization, the Universities and Colleges Union, it is not clear from either the limited degree of recent academic support for action (for example, in the summer of 2006 dispute over pay, by refusing to mark exams or other assessed work) or from the response of academic leaders to such action (in some cases docking significant amounts of pay, even though in all other respects academics were working normally) that there remains a strong climate for or tolerance of collective trade union activity among UK academics and their leaders. Without this, the unravelling at the academic loom seems set to continue.

So far, we have established that managerialism appears to be still alive and well in UK higher education (and almost certainly elsewhere too) despite, in the case of England, an attempt by government to supplant (or perhaps to supplement) it by reference to inspirational or transformational leadership. Managerialism also seems to have led to a number of specific consequences for the integrity of academic work. The consequences include, as noted earlier, active intervention in how and on what topics academics conduct research and in the outputs of that research; the development of audit regimes to assess the quality of teaching and learning, which are based on a distrust of academics and a belief that the outcomes of teaching can be predicted in advance; a shift in the axis of doctoral degree from a mainly academic concern to one embroiled in a whole range of intrusive quality measures and bureaucratic devices and changes to doctoral programs and viva procedures, with students also displaying a consumerist attitude to their studies (for example, by recording supervisions in case they ever need to appeal against the failure to award the degree). Manager-academics and academic leaders may claim they are consultative, but their colleagues do not always think so.[486] As we have seen from our current ESRC study on leadership development and public-service modernization, academic leaders often perceive that they are following their own change agendas, but in practice they are still significantly constrained by the audit compliance culture and an "evaluative state."[487] The state's role in this process can often lead to contradictory government policies, such as the English emphasis on all institutions engaging in widening the social basis of higher education participation (itself an important political project) but accompanied with a quest for world class status[488] by universities via their excellence in research and a requirement that all higher education institutions demonstrate the economic impact of their activities, with the social and cultural impact being very much secondary. These activities pull institutions in different directions. In this context, it is important to think through what action academics can still take to preserve the integrity of their academic work.

CONCLUSION

We have seen that the managerial university and the evaluative state are alive and well in the higher education institutions of the UK's four countries, despite an apparent recent attempt to replace new managerialism by an emphasis instead on inspirational leadership. Undoubtedly similar regimes are at work in other higher education systems, too. While not all manager-academics and academic leaders have embraced new managerialism, many of them have. The consequences of new managerialism's grip over academics and their work can be seen in a climate of distrust in universities and overt performance management of academics, together with institutions that are "hollowed out" or focus too much on their "global service" function to the exclusion of all else. As a result, the creative aspects of research and the developmental elements of teaching and learning are being subordinated to other considerations such as the focus on applied research for large companies (even if this research has problematic ethical elements or never produces outcomes that are placed in the public domain) and the emphasis on job training and employability skills for students. Can the integrity of academic work survive this onslaught?

What follows are some suggestions on how academics and those of their leaders who are committed to maintaining the academic integrity of their teaching and research work might approach this task in the current climate. The first point is that we need to (re)learn to trust academics to teach and research without constant audit trails and a compliance culture. This is not to deny that those who are in receipt of public money should be accountable for what they do, but there is a big difference between academics taking steps to do their work professionally and with due regard to the investment of public money in higher education and no academics being trusted to do their work well without constant intrusive surveillance. Secondly, in terms of academic leadership, there are two possibilities. One is to only appoint academic leaders/managers to temporary posts so that those who are more managerially inclined only have a finite remit. At the same time, more attention should be paid to the kind of leadership-development support that leaders and those who aspire to leadership should receive; the cult of the "amateur" manager/leader is not in anyone's interests and neither is an adherence to the belief, in development activities and

elsewhere, that there is only one way to run contemporary higher education institutions. A critical debate among academic leaders on alternatives to managerialism in running universities and a move away by
governments from imposing "what the private sector did ten years ago"
would be two significant steps forward. Academics themselves should
fight for the right to retain an active role in both teaching and research
and ensure that the two parallel activities are firmly connected and
linked,[489] with teaching and research both emphasizing intellectual
engagement and not just training for work or applied research development activities that mainly support — using public resources — the
activities of multinational corporations. Moreover, the climate of
higher education worldwide does not always reflect a genuine belief
in the value of academic work. We should seek ways of retaining free
access to university knowledge without giving it away to commercial
publishers or other big corporations who then make steep charge to
universities to get it back,[490] or — worse — insist on keeping findings
secret. Finally, it might make sense to think of universities as organizations that still retain a vital role in validating and legitimating and
making available knowledge, despite not having a monopoly on that
knowledge.[491]

If we are to overcome the restraints and constraints of the managerial university on the integrity of academic work, then academics, their
trade unions, and their students need to be in the forefront of those
endeavours. Otherwise, there is a real danger that both the integrity
and the value of academic work will be lost.

14

FROM THE MONKISH SCRIBE TO THE DIGITAL AGE: THE UNIVERSITY BOTH CONTINUOUS AND TRANSFORMED

Michael W. Higgins

This chapter may strike you as quirky and exotic. Perhaps a trifle irenic. Hopefully, not arcane. When a few of my Association of Universities and Colleges of Canada colleagues first heard I was participating in a Canadian Association of University Teachers (CAUT) conference, it was clear confirmation to them of early onset of dementia. I hope, however, not to validate their anxiety by providing empirical evidence.

I know something personally about academic freedom — its perils, consequences, and challenges. Over the past ten years I have authored or co-authored numerous books, including *Heretic Blood, Power and Peril, The Jesuit Mystique, The Muted Voice*, etc. Although the substance of these works should have been sufficient to stimulate the censors of opinion to action, it was only when I wrote a column for the *Toronto Star* on the matter of Hindu dancing that I found myself the subject of a North American whirlpool of criticism and intrigue. Monitoring bodies as far away as San Diego, California, with their particularly zealous orthodoxy police, made me realize that fear over interfaith inquiry and meaningful dialogue constitutes for many a genuine threat to the very integrity of the tradition they treasure and, in turn, inspires them to respond in vituperative and irrational terms.

A president-colleague friend from Minnesota commented that he couldn't quite get his head around the furor generated by this column, when a number of books that I have written in no small part stretched the limits of establishment acceptance and managed to successfully skirt controversy. Go figure.

But all of these controversies, whether they are generated and driven by learned commentaries or popular columns, speak directly to the integrity of one's scholarship and to the fact that it is inextricably linked to the integrity one provides in terms of institutional leadership.

Although references to Roman Catholicism — direct or oblique — have been peppered generously throughout this volume by other contributors (David Healy's "banned in Ireland," Brian Alters's right-wing Michigan Christian institution, Ave Maria University; Shadia Drury's palpable relief that she is not for burning, although on a contemporary Catholic campus she is more likely to be canonized; and Marcus Harvey's reference to Finkelstein's undoing via Vincentian politics in Chicago), I am going to draw upon this very same, although richly diverse tradition, to suggest some possible directions for recovering the essence or special charism of the university *qua* university.

A major resource on higher education, arguably a Canadian classic, is Prof. James M. Cameron's *On the Idea of a University*, a series of lectures delivered on the occasion of the sesquicentennial of the University of Toronto and the 125th anniversary of St. Michael's College. These essays trace the genesis and evolution of the university from its inception in medieval Europe. Undoubtedly, education is not a unique or exclusive preserve of the Christian west. Quite the contrary, in fact. But the university iterations that we have experienced in the West find their prototype in Christendom, and to that end, Professor Cameron begins his lectures by looking closely at the historical roots. He notes:

> Universitates were originally mere guilds or clubs of masters or undergraduate students. They began to serve as adjuncts of the studium generale [This means a "place where students from all parts are received," that is, an institution of higher learning . . . an ecumenical institution, a place of general resort for

students from the entire civilized world; and the existence, often troubled and tumultuous, of the many "nations" living side by side in the European universities of the Middle Ages, vividly illustrates this.], first in Paris and Bologna, and later, by migration or infection, in other universities, until in the end it was normal for the affairs of the studium generale to be largely conducted by the universitas of masters, or of students, or by some arrangement between the two. The derived term "university" means, then, the self-government of students, or masters, or both, in the conduct of the affairs of the studium generale.[492]

As you can see, then, the functioning of universities is largely a matter of self-governance responding to the practical needs of societies through the study of specific disciplines, assembling magistri and pupils with the express desire to encourage the development of the critical spirit, and all this done for the clear purpose of ensuring appropriate independence from both the imperium and the sacerdotium. Has it changed all that much since the Middle Ages?

Certainly, Professor Cameron appreciates not only the fact that the university must maintain a certain extraterritoriality about its composition and intellectual range but also that it must ensure a reigning hermeneutic of suspicion. After all, as Cameron observes, the real business of the university and the conditions under which it is pursued are not easy to explain to a public that stands outside the university world. Things may be thought to happen for the best when those who hold political power are themselves reflective about their own educational experiences and are prepared, if they are convinced they ought, to stand by the interests of the universities without falling into the debased rhetoric that goes with much public talk about education. This rhetoric takes the form not so much of nonsense as of what I can only call para-sense.[493]

Cameron is persistent in outlining the unique and discrete character of the university in sharp contrast with the state. At the same time, however, he recognizes that the universities, particularly in the context of Commonwealth and European universities, although independent of the state, are in some very important ways inextricably linked with the state. He writes:

> Universities, then, independent of the State, but always linked with it and inevitably and rightly under its pressure, largely financed from public funds but not thereby required to furnish in return just what the community may from time to time happen to want, internally diversified through colleges and other devices for breaking down the larger institution into smaller, more intimate groups with their own degree of independence over against the university considered as a single power, such seems to be in rough outline the requirements, approved by good sense and our historical experience, for universities now. How far what seems desirable is in the darkness of our time possible is another question.[494]

One way out of the darkness, for me at least, can be found in the writings of Newman — and I don't mean the Seinfeld character. John Henry Newman wrote extensively about education throughout his long life and knew from direct experience what a demanding task it was to tutor the young. A fellow and tutor at Oriel College, Oxford, a teacher and administrator of the Oratory School at Birmingham, the founder and first rector of the Catholic University of Ireland in Dublin, Newman was also the author of what evolved into a three-volume work on university education: *Discourses on the Scope and Nature of University Education Addressed to the Catholics of Dublin* (1852), *Office and Works of Universities* (1856), and *Lectures and Essays on University Subjects* (1859).[495]

Although some of his writings on the role of a liberal arts education and the function of a university betray the biases and limitations of his age and personal disposition, much of his "educational" writing has about it a timeless relevance. Of course, he could change his mind. Or more precisely, nuance it. Or more precisely still, make the necessary historical accommodations.

In the preface to *Discourses on the Scope and Nature of University Education*, he observes that "when the Church founds a university, she is not cherishing talent, genius, or knowledge for their own sake, but for the sake of her children, with a view to their spiritual welfare and their religious influence and usefulness, with the object of training them to fill their respective posts in life better, and of making them more intelligent, capable, active members of society."[496]

Newman proceeds to a distinction between academics and universities and between the quite distinct functions of discovering and teaching. This was the time, however, of his own direct involvement in the establishment of such a university in Dublin, a task which proved much more complicated than he could have anticipated. It was to serve as his rough entrée into the world of ecclesiastical politics, hierarchical prerogatives, jurisdictional squabbles, and clerical anti-intellectualism. His years as founder and rector were fraught with intrigue, misperception, distrust, and pettiness.

Newman was called principally by Paul Cullen, Archbishop of Armagh and eventually Cardinal Archbishop of Dublin, to undertake the onerous task of establishing a Catholic university in Ireland. It was a project designed to offset the damage anticipated by the Queen's University of Ireland initiatives of Sir Robert Peel with its secular, non-denominational, and mixed education components. From the outset, he was persuaded of the primary involvement of the laity.

Newman was resolved that he should be appointed rector and that the management of the new university should not be in his hands only, but shared with the professoriate, the majority of whom would be laymen. In part, this structure would establish its essential difference from the national seminary of Maynooth, and remind all who needed reminding that a university is not a clerical enclosure. Newman's troubles with Cullen are legendary, and the protracted negotiations drained the English convert of much of his valuable energy. Still resident most of the year at his Birmingham Oratory, Newman was compelled to travel constantly to satisfy his several commitments, and the tardiness and anxiety of the Irish hierarchy compounded greatly the already considerable labours of founding and directing a university.

In his *Autobiographical Writings* Newman speaks of his realization that the basic cause of friction between Cullen and himself is to be found in his earnest "desire . . . to make the laity a substantive power in the university."[497] After all, Newman was convinced the financial governance of the university should be in the hands of those for whom it was intended. But he was aware that this notion runs counter to the less venerable Irish clerical tradition which, as he notes in *Letters and Diaries,* would have the laity "treated like good little boys . . . told to shut their eyes and open their mouths."[498] Newman's resolve to appoint honorary members of the university to be drawn from the laity in Ireland and elsewhere and his resolve to appoint competent laymen to all the professorial chairs save theology, in sharp opposition to the preferred convention of appointing inferior priests, were efforts destined to elicit Cullen's ire and raise a few other episcopal eyebrows as well.

Persuaded of the need to contain the clerical presence at the university rather than to expand it, Newman found himself, and not for the first time, at odds with the general thinking of his ecclesiastical superiors. It is not that Newman had an exaggerated respect for the lay state or a penchant for cleric-bashing, it is simply that he held to a historical perspective that refused to suppress the charism or uniqueness of the lay vocation in the interests of a clericalized ecclesiology.

Newman entertained notions of a university that are at marked variance with the prevailing views of our contemporaries — the bureaucrats, the planners, the pedagogues. He seems the purveyor of deliciously arcane ideas, fully suited for the British nobility, nouveau riche, and clever aspirants to the leisure class. After all, it is Newman who defines liberal education as the very maker of the gentleman:

> It is well to be a gentleman, it is well to have a cultivated intellect, a delicate taste, a candid, equitable, dispassionate mind, a noble and courteous bearing in the conduct of life — these are the connatural qualities of a large knowledge; they are the objects of a university; I am advocating, I shall illustrate and insist upon them; but still, I repeat, they are no guarantee of

sanctity or even for conscientiousness, they may attach to the
man of the world, to the profligate, to the heartless — pleasant,
alas, and attractive as he shows when decked out in them.[499]

The utter bankruptcy of an education that does not touch the moral
fibre of a person has been dramatically etched for us moderns in the
terrifying apotheosis of twentieth-century barbarism: the Wagner-lov-
ing, Goethe-reading culture of the supreme automaton: the concentration camp commander. George Steiner, Eli Mandel, Hannah Arendt,
and Thomas Merton have analyzed with profoundly unnerving honesty the severe limitations of reason. But this is our knowledge, our
experience, and not Newman's.

The university, then, is for the enlargement of the sensibility, the cultivation of the mind, and the uncompromised pursuit of intellectual
excellence. But these are not bodiless exploits, somehow untouched by
the personal, the pastoral, and the moral. Newman fully understood
the irreplaceable value of human interaction, for "an academical system without the personal influence of teachers upon pupils is an arctic
winter; it will create an ice-bound, petrified, cast-iron university."[500]

The university has as its function intellectual culture: "to open the
mind, to correct it, to refine it, to enable it to know, and to digest, master, rule, and use its knowledge, to give it power over its own faculties,
application, flexibility, method, critical exactness, sagacity, resource,
address, eloquent expression."[501] This very culture, so essential for the
right governing of a nation and for its prosperity, rings an elitist note
discordant to our egalitarian ears.

Increasingly conscious of the rank utilitarianism of nineteenth-
century political culture, Newman saw the university as a sanctuary
wherein the intellect is cultivated, "disciplined for its own sake," and
not held hostage to the exigencies of the moment, the demands of
economic pragmatism, and the whims of calculating politicos.

For such as these insist that education should be confined to
some particular and narrow end, and should issue in some
definite work, which can be weighed and measured. They

argue as if everything, as well as every person, had its price; and where there has been a great outlay they have a right to expect a return in kind. This they call making education and instruction "useful," and "utility" becomes their watchword. With a fundamental principle of this nature, they very naturally go on to ask what there is to show for the expense of a university; what is the real worth in the market of the article called a liberal education, on the supposition that it does not teach us definitely how to advance our manufacturers, or how to improve our lands, or to better our civic economy; or again, if it does not at once make this man a lawyer, that an engineer, and that a surgeon; or at least if it does not lead to discoveries in chemistry, astronomy, geology, magnetism, and science of every kind.[502]

Who has not heard this before? As John Henry Newman would answer, the university is not a recruitment centre, a storage hold from which can be drawn a fully equipped work force. It is rather, "according to the usual designation, an Alma Mater, knowing her children one by one, not a foundry, or a mint, or a treadmill."[503]

One way of preserving the personal quality of university life is by means of the collegiate system. Now there have been many permutations — some salutary and some deleterious — over the centuries, and Canada, which has traditionally acknowledged the worth of the collegiate principle in the structuring of its universities, has attached special importance to the denominational character of the vast majority of its affiliated and federated colleges.

Keeping in mind Newman's celebration of the disinterestedness of learning, of the pastoral role of the teacher, and of the oneness, the integrity of knowledge — "for its subject matter is one . . . the universe in its length and breadth" — we can appreciate the appropriateness of Newman's insights for our contemporary Canadian educational scene. We need to affirm again and again the value of non-utilitarian learning, as well as affirming the critical importance of the truly personal in the world of the anonymous, the truly communal in the world of the collectivity.

We must cultivate the intellect in order that our graduates can submit to unmuddled scrutiny the ideological biases, spurious presuppositions, and quasi-authentic analyses that proffer an easy wisdom in an age hell-bent on the instant remedy for headache and ennui.

It is the job — the indispensable, necessary job — of education to produce fair critics of both received and of untried ideas. If we cannot rely on our universities to provide an environment wherein an exacting and disinterested search for the ontology is conducted, we have every reason to fear for the future of our society.

The university must do its job; it is a guarantor of our freedom. Still, the prevalent view both in political chambers and in the halls of industry clearly runs counter to the Newman model.

How do we recover an earlier model that is not encased in nostalgia, restorationism, or romanticism?

I would argue that the principal way of recovering an earlier but utterly credible and malleable model is to look at the two key concepts of collegiality and subsidiarity. These two key concepts provide together a critical antidote to creeping managerialism and can, by means of an imaginative re-appropriation, provide the foundation stones for genuine co-responsibility in academic governance. Collegiality in its specifically theological, as opposed to political, meaning is a serious dimension of *communio* or *koinonia*. In other words, collegiality both implies and gives expression to genuine communion of conviction and life. Subsidiarity is a social and political concept that first emerged with Pius XI in his encyclical *Quadragesimo Anno* (1931),[504] in which he identifies this term in such a way as to serve as an adumbration of what contemporary social theorists now refer to as civil society. Subsidiarity is conceived of as a defence of the autonomy of intermediary bodies and corporate enterprises and is largely thought of as a means of redress or correction to inequitable power relationships: "It is an injustice, a grave evil and the disturbance of right order for a larger and higher association to arrogate to itself functions which can be performed efficiently by smaller and lower societies."[505] Although the language used to define subsidiarity is redolent of a hierarchial mode of discourse, the purpose of subsidiarity is largely to ensure the appropriate independence, institutional integrity, and freedom of choice inherent in a corporate body that is neither subservient to nor wholly disengaged from a larger accountability.

Combined together, collegiality and subsidiarity, as principles of governance and as modes of operation, guarantee that the university engage in the larger social enterprise of creating a wisdom culture.

By way of conclusion, then, it seems to me that the digital age university has the unique opportunity of recapturing the particular genius of the past, of incorporating aspects of an earlier teaching modality, and of rethinking the function of knowledge creation in ways that are supportive of a more deeply enriched human enterprise. Knowledge transmission via the Internet provides a wonderful opportunity to reconceive the role of the tutor/mentor as opposed to the narrowly defined definition of magister currently employed in our institutions of higher education. The teacher is more than an instructor; the teacher in the digital age is a mentor and guide. The challenges facing Western universities in terms of a reconfiguration of post-secondary education goals can, if left only to the mandarins of industry and government, result in a commodification of learning and not in the making of a wisdom culture. To help effect the creation of this culture, presidents and principals of institutions of higher learning should themselves be seen as public intellectuals, and universities as sanctuaries. The only way we can provide a meaningfully credible definition of the university in the twenty-first century is to dig deeply into our past, unearth concepts that can be revitalized and re-contextualized, respond to the learning of the ancients in ways that speak to the timeless dimension of knowledge, and re-democratize university governance not by straining to implement a model that best works in civil and entrepreneurial society but by resuscitating those structures of the past that can serve us in the present and help define us for the future.

This is not a reactionary exercise; it is an exercise in creative rediscovery.

15

RESTRUCTURING ACADEMIC WORK

James L. Turk

INTRODUCTION

The quality of North American post-secondary education is being threatened, access is being diminished, and the roles and jobs of faculty and other academic staff are being undermined by a series of profound economic and social changes in the past three decades. Richard Moser accurately locates their origin in the economic shift beginning in the mid-1970s when "the accumulated costs of industry and war had become a significant obstacle to maximizing profits and business leaders sought to shift or externalize those costs."[506]

The effect of calls for lower taxes, a reduced role for governments, and greater reliance on user-pay for post-secondary education has been a gradual but relentless decline in public funding, an embrace of corporate management models, and a continuing shift of costs onto students and their families. As part of these changes, university and college administrators began restructuring the academic workforce along the lines pioneered in the retail and industrial sectors, with a greater reliance on a contingent workforce and more managerial control.

THE CONTINGENT PROFESSOR

The casualization of academic work in North America can be sketched with some precision for the United States but not for Canada, where data are primarily anecdotal[507] due to the inability of Statistics Canada to gather reliable data on part-time faculty.[508] The changes in the United States are striking.

Between 1976 and 2005, there was a 233-percent increase in the number of full-time non-tenure-track faculty and a 214-percent increase in the number of part-time faculty, whereas the percentage increase of tenured and tenure-track faculty was only 17 percent (Figure 15.1).[509]

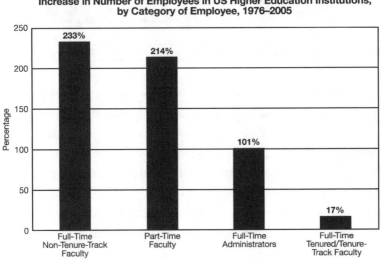

Figure 15.1
Increase in Number of Employees in US Higher Education Institutions, by Category of Employee, 1976–2005

In 1975, 56.8 percent of faculty at American degree-granting institutions were full-time tenured or tenure-track while 13 percent were full-time non-tenure-track and 30.2 percent were part-time. By 2005, fewer than one-third of American faculty were tenured or tenure-track (see Figure 15.2).[510]

The implications of these trends for academic staff and for their students are significant. Those with part-time or limited-term full-time

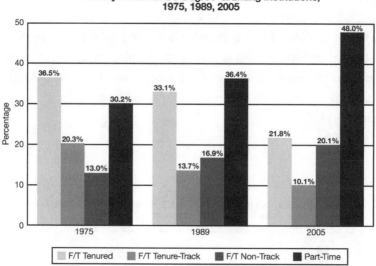

Figure 15.2
Faculty Status at US Degree-Granting Institutions,
1975, 1989, 2005

contracts (contract academic staff[511]) share many disadvantages — poor pay; few, if any benefits; little or no job security; and denial of support for research and service — two of the three responsibilities of a traditional academic. Contract academic staff feel marginalized as, typically, they do not have proper offices, are not seen as part of the academic collective, and have little role in institutional governance, whether at the departmental, faculty, or institution level, and are thus denied a role in curriculum planning and development.

UNDERFUNDING AND RESTRUCTURING

The decline in tenured and tenure-track positions and concomitant growth in contingent academic staff has to be understood in the context of the embrace of corporate management models by university and college administrations and boards intertwined with the pull-back in public funding for post-secondary education. In Canada, the share of the federal transfer nominally earmarked for post-secondary education was increased for 2008–09 by $800 million to $3.2 billion. While a significant increase, it falls more than $1.2 billion short of what would be needed just to restore funding to 1992–93 levels adjusted for inflation and population growth. To restore federal funding to 0.5 percent of Canada's gross domestic product (the level of support in the late 1970s and early 1980s) would require the federal government to boost funding by more than $4 billion annually.[512]

Looking at overall federal and provincial government funding for university teaching and non-sponsored research in Canada, there was a decline from more than $17,900 per student in 1980–81 to $9,900 in 2006–07.[513]

In the face of real-dollar funding cuts, university and college administrations have increasing turned to private-sector managerial models that prize lower labour costs and greater managerial "flexibility" achieved through a restructuring of the academic labour process. The origins of reducing costs by cheapening labour can be traced to Charles Babbage's nineteenth-century writings about dividing an artisan's tasks so that highly skilled workers (who are highly paid) do only highly skilled work, allowing less skilled tasks to be performed by less skilled (and cheaper) workers.[514] Another strand was popularized at the turn of the twentieth century by Frederick Taylor in his advocacy of scientific management, where managers took control of the work process, breaking it down into its key elements and tightly controlling the assignment of work and how it was to be done.[515]

Harry Braverman's influential writings later in the twentieth century argued that work was being deskilled through management control of the labour process and effective use of technology.[516] David Noble, in his brilliant critique of technological determinism, showed that the design of technologies was directed to give priority to managerial control of workers, not to increased productivity, when a choice had to be made between those two priorities.[517] Others followed these leads by examining the deskilling of most work.[518]

All of these changes seemed charmingly irrelevant to academics, as their work arguably defied deskilling and cheapening. Regrettably, they underestimated the determination of academic managers, assisted ably by various higher education experts who recognized that academic work could be unbundled and new technologies could replace academic labour, thereby cheapening the cost of post-secondary educational labour and giving greater control to academic managers.

William F. Massy and Robert Zemsky, two of North America's most distinguished authorities on higher education,[519] more than a decade ago discussed how to proceed. Massy and Zemsky point out that information technologies (IT) offer the possibility of "a departure from the traditional handicraft mode of education, where faculty learning curves (for the production of learning) are shallow and capital offers little leverage beyond the traditional physical plant."[520] In language strikingly similar to that of Babbage, Massy and Zemsky argue that academic work can be subdivided and cheapened through the use of information technologies, allowing productivity gains.[521]

A major theme in the literature on learning technologies is how they allow an "unbundling" of the faculty member's job. John Daniel, when he was vice-chancellor of UK's Open University, noted that "Division of labour means some people develop learning materials, others support students, yet others provide logistic support, and so on." He attempted to mystify what is going on with the aphorism: "The tradition in the university is that the individual teacher teaches. The future is that the university teaches."[522]

One form of "the university teaches" is easy to imagine: the institution arranges for an internationally recognized scholar to "create" the course (the actual work can be subcontracted to a graduate student), and then the university markets it under the faculty member's name in the same way that Nike markets "Michael Jordan" shoes. Imagine "Stephen Hawking Physics 101." The course could then be maintained by a series of poorly paid contract and support staff who do the tutoring, grading, answering of emails, and the periodic updating.

A version of this is already in place in some Ontario community colleges where electronic courses are bought "off-the-shelf" (or prepared by last year's instructor), and the only staff person in the classroom is a member of support staff who oversees the technology, takes attendance, and deals with any computer problems. The University of Toronto recently posted an instructor's position in introductory philosophy. In describing what the instructor would do, the posting said: "Instructor in this course will NOT be lecturing. Lectures are to be broadcast on the Web; times listed represent mandatory 1-hr tutorials, which the instructor will lead (each student attending twice a week)" (Emphasis in the original).[523]

Unbundling the components of academic jobs is designed to increase productivity by facilitating the substitution of cheap labour for expensive labour and by allowing the elimination of some labour altogether. Proper use of IT in post-secondary education, according to Massy and Zemsky, means substituting capital for labour, even where there is no justification in terms of immediate cost benefits:

> [T]echnology provides more flexibility than traditional teaching methods once one moves beyond minor changes that can be instituted by individual professors. The "career" of a workstation may well be less than five years, whereas that of a professor often exceeds 30 years. Workstations don't get tenure, and delegations are less likely to wait on the provost when particular equipment items are 'laid off.' The 'retraining' of IT equipment (for example, reprogramming), while not inexpensive, is easier and more predictable than retraining a tenured professor. Within limits, departments will gain a larger zone of flexibility as the capital-labor ratio grows. The benefits of shifting away from handicraft methods, coupled with scale economies and increased flexibility, argue for the adoption of IT even when one cannot demonstrate immediate cost advantages. For example, the ability to break even during the first few years provides strong justification for going ahead with an IT solution, provided the effects on quality are not harmful.[524]

Of course, this is not for everyone. Massy and Zemsky note that, in this re-engineered post-secondary educational system, the elite will still have access to "traditional handicraft-oriented instruction that has been the hallmark of our system" — an approach "too expensive for massified higher education."[525]

In a document prepared for the World Bank, Bruce Johnstone warns against viewing technologies simply as a supplement to existing teaching practices: "There is a risk that technology continues to be incorporated by individual faculty, mainly as 'add-ons' to conventional teaching and curricula, without the accompanying changes in the instructional production function that are required to realize useful productivity gains."[526]

In the current economic and political context, the only way to understand the rampant casualization and the large and growing investment in educational technologies is an administrative desire to restructure post-secondary education to increase "productivity" by reducing the role of the traditional academic workforce. The World Bank document is very clear about this:

> Radical change, or restructuring, of an institution of higher education means either fewer and/or different faculty, professional staff, and support workers. This means lay-offs, forced early retirements, or major retraining and reassignment, as in: the closure of inefficient or ineffective institutions; the merger of quality institutions that merely lack the critical mass of operations to make them cost-effective; and the radical alteration of the mission and production function of an institution — which means radically altering who the faculty are, how they behave, the way they are organized, and the way they work and are compensated.[527]

THE RESTRUCTURED ACADEMY

The 1990s visions of Massy, Zemsky, and Johnstone are increasingly visible in North American universities and colleges a decade later. In universities, there is a two-tier professoriate. As noted above, less than one-third in the United States are in the top tier — tenured or tenure-track academics who have decent pay, benefits and pensions, and time and support for research and service; control what they teach; have academic freedom; have an office; and play a role in university governance. The two-thirds in the bottom tier lack all or most of these advantages of their top-tier colleagues, as they are poorly paid, without benefits or pensions, denied support or time to do research or service, have little control of what they teach and little or no voice in curriculum decisions or academic governance. Most even lack an office, and academic freedom, if it is available at all, lasts only until their contract expires.

The eminent American anthropologist, Clifford Geertz, in reflecting on his long career and the state of the university today, summed up the situation:

> Is such a life and such a career [as I have had in academe] available now? In the Age of Adjuncts? When graduate students refer to themselves as "the pre-unemployed"? . . . All I know is that, up until just a few years ago, I blithely, and perhaps a bit fatuously, used to tell students and younger colleagues who asked how to get ahead in our odd occupation that they should stay loose, take risks, resist the cleared path, avoid careerism, go their own way, and that if they did so, if they kept at it and remained alert, optimistic, and loyal to the truth, my experience was that they could get away with murder, could do as they wish, have a valuable life, and nonetheless prosper. I don't do that any more.[528]

In the restructured academy, there will always be a place for the "traditional handicraft-oriented instruction" and with it, academic freedom, shared governance, and academic control of academic decision making. That place, like the rain forests in Brazil, is being relentlessly cut back to an ever smaller domain — relentlessly in community colleges and private for-profit universities, and variably elsewhere. While some may feel that elite universities will be an oasis, the most recent *Contingent Faculty Index* published by the American Association of University Professors shows that, even within many elite institutions, the percentage of contingent faculty is already substantial — as at Harvard and Yale, where they constitute 32.2 percent and 44.2 percent, respectively, of the instructional faculty.[529]

The number of non-contingent faculty is still noteworthy, although declining steadily, at public and non-profit doctoral (51.8 percent), master's (38.9 percent), and baccalaureate (44.9 percent) institutions compared to associate degree colleges — public, private, and for-profit — where two-thirds of faculty are part-time and 80 percent of all faculty are contingent. At all categories of for-profit universities and colleges in the United States, virtually 100 percent of faculty are contingent.[530]

It is at these for-profit institutions that one sees the full flowering of the re-engineered academy — institutions that can properly be characterized as academic factories, where managers control curriculum and all aspects of academic work, with academic staff relegated to being managed production workers.[531]

There is a real possibility that the for-profit colleges and universities foretell the future for all post-secondary institutions, save for locally favoured academic program areas in non-elite universities and a wider range of academic and professional programs in the elite institutions.

SHAPING THE FUTURE

That need not be the case, as the future is not determined by inexorable trends but by the actions of people in the situations in which they find themselves. Long-standing traditions of collegial or shared governance and of academic freedom provide a basis for faculty to resist the corporatization of their institutions and the imposition of academic factory conditions and unbundled, increasingly deskilled work.

Some university leaders are openly questioning this production model and point to ways to resist. Former Harvard president Derek Bok, in his somber examination of commercialization in American universities, suggests that trustees "could take pains to establish criteria for evaluating the president that include not only a demonstrated capacity to accomplish goals costing large amounts of money, but also a consistent respect for academic standards even when they conflict with the quest for more resources."[532] Even more importantly, he notes that "faculty members are in the best position to appreciate academic values and insist on their observance."[533]

Traditionally, the place for faculty to be able to "insist" and to be able to protect the integrity of academic values and academic work has supposed to have been in the academic senate — the senior academic body within most universities that has the power to make academic decisions for the institution.[534] Unfortunately, most university senates fail to reflect the voice of academic staff and seem to be more a rubber stamp for the senior administration.

In one of the few comprehensive studies of senates in Canadian universities, Glen Jones notes that, compared to the findings of his research on members of governing boards:[535]

> Senate members indicated less satisfaction with the overall work of the senate and there were indications of discordance between the role that they believed the senate should play and the role that they believe the senate does play within university governance. Less than half of senate members view the senate as an "effective" decision making body, though 64 percent indicated that it plays an important role as a forum for discussing issues.[536]

The subtitle of Robert Birnbaum's famous article on university senates in the United States is quite apt: "Why Senates Do Not Work But Will Not Go Away."[537] Even with the weakness of senates as a power base for faculty, university and college administrators, spurred by demands to be more "business-like" in their management style, are increasingly calling into question the traditional structures of collegial governance.[538]

From an academic-staff perspective, renunciation of senates is neither practical nor desirable. Senates provide academic staff an opportunity to discuss and decide matters that could not be dealt with otherwise: for example, decisions about new programs and about curriculum content. Senates also provide a public space and public theatre. It is here that the administration is obligated to inform the academic community about its academic and financial plans. It is also in senate that academic concerns within the whole academic community — including academic staff, students, non-academic staff, and members at large — can be discussed in a public forum. While this public forum may be effectively under the control of senior administrators, the performance of rituals of public accountability is nonetheless significant.

That said, unless academic staff have another vehicle, the seemingly inexorable transformation of post-secondary institutions into academic factories cannot be stopped. There has been only one consistently effective means by which academic staff can sit down as equals with the administration to shape the nature of their university or college, and that has been through unionization and collective bargaining. At its heart, collective bargaining is about limiting the unilateral powers of the employer. In all workplaces, the employer has all the rights, except those that are taken away by statute or by collective agreements. With the growing concentration of power and control in the offices of the central administration of universities and colleges, the only way that faculty can, as Bok urges, effectively insist on upholding academic values is through their collective strength at the bargaining table.

Across North America, there are many examples of academic staff unions that have entrenched academic values and practices in collective agreement clauses on academic freedom, promotion and tenure, intellectual property, procedures for selection of senior administrators, workload, staff complement, appointment of academic staff, discipline, and employment equity.[539] The ability to protect those rights is enshrined in grievance and arbitration procedures spelled out in the same agreements.

CONCLUSION

Universities and colleges are now contested terrain. On the one hand, many are places where boards of governors and senior administration are actively working, with considerable success, to transform academic work and the goals and values of the institutions along market-friendly lines.[540] On the other, these initiatives are being resisted by faculty and students in internal academic bodies and through academic staff unionization and bargaining.[541]

Turning universities and colleges into servants of the market and of commerce and eliminating the "handicraft mode of production" that characterizes traditional academic work are intertwined initiatives. Successful resistance to the latter requires resistance to the former as well. Reasonable assurance that universities and colleges can fulfill their role in democratic society — offering high quality education to their students and undertaking valuable scholarship for the benefit of their communities and society — requires an empowered academic staff that has not been reduced to closely managed production workers. This means they have to have academic freedom, academic control of academic decision making, job security (a system of tenure), and a mission that goes beyond the bottom line and beyond fulfilling government and industry forecasts (usually incorrectly) of tomorrow's vocational needs.

At her inauguration as president of Harvard in 2007, Drew Faust had the courage to remind her audience of the proper vision of the university in this age of market supremacy:

> A university is not about results in the next quarter; it is not even about who a student has become by graduation. It is about learning that molds a lifetime, learning that transmits the heritage of millennia; learning that shapes the future. . . . Universities make commitments to the timeless, and these investments have yields we cannot predict and often cannot measure . . . [that] we pursue . . . in part "for their own sake," because they define what has over centuries made us human, not because they can enhance our global competitiveness.[542]

We cannot protect the integrity of our work as academics unless we embrace that vision for all universities and colleges and unless academic staff have a means to effectively ensure the realization of that vision in their own universities and colleges. For without such a vision and without the means to implement it, we are consigned to a rearguard action of trying to forestall the advance of the academic factory, where our work as scholars and teachers is undermined and devalued and the ability of our students to get a good education is sacrificed.

VII. CONCLUSION

16

ACADEMIC INTEGRITY AND THE PUBLIC INTEREST

Jon H. Thompson

Instead of dividing the human race into artificial categories, such as Greeks and Barbarians, it is better to employ as a division criterion the qualities of virtue and dishonesty. Many Greeks are dishonest and many Barbarians enjoy a refined civilization.

— Eratosthenes, c. 230 BC[544]

THE PROBLEM AND ITS SOURCES

By the late 1980s, concern over integrity in research had risen to the extent that the American National Academies of Science, Engineering and Medicine convened a "blue ribbon" panel to undertake a comprehensive study. The panel's two-volume report, *Responsible Science: Ensuring the Integrity of the Research Process*, was published in 1992 and included a series of policy recommendations.[545] At the same time in Canada, the federal research granting councils and the CAUT encouraged policy development in this area. In addition to several widely publicized cases of research misconduct in the United States, general concerns were that existing policies had become outdated, or applied mainly to research in biomedical fields.

Among the results of the renewed interest in policy were the CAUT *Policy Statement on Fraud and Other Misconduct in Research* (1992), the essence of which was soon incorporated into faculty collective agreements across the country, and the *Tri-Council Policy Statement: Ethical Conduct for Research Involving Human Subjects* (TCPS, 1998) to which all universities receiving funds from the councils were required to adhere.

By the end of the 1990s, universities across the continent had policies on research integrity that covered all disciplines. Despite this, losses of academic integrity became more extensive and serious during the past two decades, as is clear from the essays in the present volume. Why did this happen? What can be done about it?

The increasing losses of integrity happened for several reasons. They are interconnected, but it is convenient to separate them as follows, in order from the specific to the general:

a. Administrators have sometimes been reluctant to confront serious research misconduct by individuals. This reluctance may be more damaging to academic integrity than many cases of individual misconduct.

b. The policies designed and implemented during the 1980s and 1990s focused on the conduct of individuals or small groups. Policy-makers did not address the possibility of more widespread corrosion of integrity, even though significant instances were already on the public record.

c. Government policy changes that began around 1980 drew universities more extensively into the marketplace, during a time of increasing deregulation of the marketplace itself.

d. For most of the past century, ever-increasing productivity has been a central objective of the dominant political economies. The resulting social pressures have been intensified by the rise of neoliberalism with its emphasis on wealth concentration and social atomization.

Therefore, it should not have come as a surprise to see production-driven research cultures in the academy and increasing losses of academic integrity.

This is not to suggest that it is inappropriate for academics to be involved in public service, commercialization, productivity, or the world generally. They have been throughout history.[546] Much of the modern world depends on commercialized discoveries or technologies that originated in universities.

Universities have always been embedded in their communities, but often in times past they were able to maintain sufficient autonomy to preserve academic freedom and integrity. What is new is the scope of commercial engagement, together with the accompanying inducements to relax standards of integrity. During the past decade, works documenting the extent of resulting problems began to appear, including *The Anti-Depressant Era* (1997), *Science, Money and Politics* (2001), *Universities in the Marketplace* (2003), and *University Inc.* (2005).[547]

Despite these influences, a high level of integrity remains in much of the academy, as well as a determination to protect and strengthen it. For instance, in climatology, the great majority of scientists has resisted pressure from governments and bribes from the private sector to suppress findings on global climate change.[548] Thanks to the courageous efforts of professors such as Nancy Olivieri and David Healy, the corrosive influences of drug companies on much of academic medicine — and on health care generally — have become widely known. Issues such as those they identified are discussed in a number of recent books: *Science in the Private Interest, Let Them Eat Prozac, The Truth About the Drug Companies, Overdosed America, On the Take*, and *Selling Sickness* — all published between 2003 and 2005.[549]

A discussion of the main sources of the problem and how these operated in specific instances can suggest ways of addressing it. However, it is useful first to place the issue in its general context.

ACADEMIC INTEGRITY AND THE PUBLIC INTEREST

Both university autonomy and academic integrity have been subjected to increasing pressures arising from corporate agendas and government policies reflective of these agendas. Thus the problem of declining integrity cannot be fully addressed within the confines of the academy. The only possible sources of external countervailing pressures lie with society at large, whose interests often diverge from corporate interests. This means engagement with the general public will be required.

There is an implicit compact between the academy and society.[550]

Universities receive financial support and the institutional autonomy needed to protect academic freedom. In return, the public benefits from education, research, and the reservoirs of independent knowledge in universities. It is academic freedom that guarantees the independence (and thus the integrity) of university research on which the public relies. For instance, the public relies on professors to provide critical information on a great variety of matters, including public health and safety, the environment, climate, history, justice, the media, government policy, and corporate actions or agendas.

The reciprocal reliance of academics and members of the public has long been understood. As Albert Einstein expressed it, "The right to search for truth implies also a duty; one must not conceal any part of what one has recognized to be true."[551] Noam Chomsky later expressed the point more directly, "It is the responsibility of intellectuals to speak the truth and to expose lies."[552]

Academic freedom and academic integrity are fundamentally related, and their relationship is an integral part of the most widely accepted definition of academic freedom, that of UNESCO, which reads in part:

> Academic freedom carries with it the duty to use that freedom in a manner consistent with the scholarly obligation to base research on an honest search for truth . . . in full accordance with ethical and professional standards . . . with due respect for evidence, impartial reasoning and honesty in reporting.[553]

There are many practical and historical reasons for the linkage. For example, important instances of academic dishonesty by professors have only come to light through exercise of academic freedom by other professors. Also, times when academic integrity is in decline are also times when academic freedom is under attack.

Academic freedom is much better protected in some countries, such as Canada and the United States, than in others, although the protection is not uniformly strong even there. There are two reasons why academic freedom is as well protected as it is. One is the effort by professors and their organizations during the past century to defend this right. The other is that the general public supports the right to academic freedom for professors. The result is legal enforceability of the right. Public support is reflected in the wording of Supreme Court decisions in both the United States and Canada, notably:

> Our nation is deeply committed to safeguarding academic freedom, which is of transcendent value to all of us and not merely the teachers concerned.[554]

> The preservation of academic freedom is . . . an issue of pressing and substantial importance . . . necessary to the maintenance of academic excellence which is or should be the hallmark of a university.[555]

In recent decades, the widespread adoption by faculty associations of collective bargaining has resulted in Canada's having the best protection for academic freedom among all countries. The standards of protection are reasonably uniform across Canada because of common features in labour legislation among the provinces, in contrast to the high degree of variability in labour legislation across the United States. Thus, in Canada, the right of faculty to academic freedom has been strengthened as a result of efforts in the wider society to establish rights of association with broad applicability. Collective bargaining rights were not created in the universities, but academics were granted access to them, and under the stronger industrial-relations labour codes rather than the weaker public-service labour codes.

A more recent instance of public support for academic freedom is the *Recommendation* adopted by UNESCO in 1997 (cited above) that provides a definition equivalent to the CAUT definition. The drafting and negotiations were led by Donald C. Savage of CAUT; and his efforts succeeded in significant measure because the project was supported by the Council of Ministers of Education, Canada (CMEC). Although not in itself legally enforceable, the UNESCO *Recommendation* is widely used as a basis for promoting or defending academic freedom.[556]

Even before the advent of faculty collective bargaining, the most widely accepted definition of academic freedom in Canada (the CAUT definition) went beyond its American counterpart by expressly including the right to criticize the university administration. The CAUT definition is now incorporated in faculty collective agreements across Canada, giving it legal force. A significant instance of the practical application of this protection is the award by an arbitrator in the academic freedom grievance of David Noble at York University in 2007.[557]

University professors occupy a position of trust, a point plainly illustrated by the case of Gideon Koren at the University of Toronto in 2000, discussed later in this chapter. He was disciplined publicly for harassment of colleagues and for dishonesty. The disciplinary letter issued to him by his employers cited, among other things, infringement of academic freedom and abuse of trust:

> Academic freedom cannot flourish in an environment in which unwarranted attacks are made on colleagues' personal and professional integrity. . . . You occupy a position of great trust. You have great responsibilities. . . . You did not tell the truth when you felt untruth would serve you better. Your lying triggered an expensive investigation. You abused the trust reposed in you and you failed to live up to your responsibilities.[558]

Unfortunately, Professor Koren was neither the first nor the last academic to have abused the trust reposed in him by his university and the public.

RELUCTANCE TO CONFRONT MISCONDUCT — THREE CASES

The failure by some senior administrators to exercise their responsibilities is a significant factor in the growing loss of academic integrity.[559] Ultimately, it is they who are charged with supporting integrity, as well as addressing misconduct. It is not sufficient to blame rogue professors, however misguided or dishonest some individuals may be. Where administrators are seen to be excessively lenient with those engaged in serious misconduct, or where they fail to support — or worse still, mistreat — those who have acted with integrity, a strong negative signal is sent to the whole community.

The following examples show that lapses in academic integrity and reluctance to confront misconduct can occur anywhere and at any level. They also show that, in some cases, integrity will only be upheld or restored where individual faculty members or members of the public insist on it. Improvements in policy may help, but if policies are not respected or enforced, integrity is lost. Nevertheless, the ways in which the misconduct was eventually confronted and addressed in these cases give reasons for optimism, as well as pessimism.

DR. VALERY FABRIKANT, ENGINEERING, CONCORDIA UNIVERSITY

One day in 1992, Valery Fabrikant murdered four colleagues and wounded a secretary. He alone was responsible, and he was convicted and sentenced to life in prison for these crimes. However, this extraordinary event happened in a context relevant to our topic. Fabrikant and three senior academic patrons had been engaged in dubious activity within a "production-driven research culture," and the murders followed an escalating dispute between him and his patrons.[560] The escalation was fuelled in part by the failure of senior university administrators to investigate effectively the serious allegations he had made against his three patrons. Later, administrative reluctance to address misconduct extended significantly beyond the Concordia administration of 1992.

Fabrikant had been employed in Concordia's Faculty of Engineering and Computer Science for more than a decade, under the patronage of the dean, the chair of a department, and one of that department's leading researchers. He was very productive in publications, several of which listed one or more of his patrons as co-authors. His productivity was a factor in the success of the department's leading research group in attracting large grants and contracts. In the political economy of this faculty, "authorship (and contracts) came to serve as a valued currency. . . . Those with copious credits and large contracts general-ly enjoyed research funding, prestige and influence."[561]

However, in his view, Fabrikant himself did not enjoy such benefits, or even job security, as he was employed in a series of limited-term appointments. He became increasingly irascible and eventually retali-ated against his patrons by alleging publicly that they had engaged in research misconduct. After the university dismissed his allegations, he made additional allegations, supported by extensive documentation. These allegations were also were dismissed by the university. Fabrikant then took his allegations to the funding agencies, including the Natural Sciences and Engineering Research Council (NSERC), which asked Concordia for a response. During the same time period, his pursuit of tenure was again frustrated. Subsequently, he committed the murders.

Two years later, an independent inquiry chaired by H.W. Arthurs "confirmed the validity of a number of Dr. Fabrikant's more specific allegations" of research misconduct and professional misconduct by his patrons, and also found that he himself had willingly engaged in some of the misconduct with them.[562] The inquiry report concluded: "The two [Concordia] administrative investigations were clearly and seriously deficient. . . . We are . . . unable to understand why they should have been as inadequate as they were. Equally, we are unable to understand why their obvious inadequacies were not immediately challenged and corrected."[563]

A later review of the case published by CAUT suggested a possible factor contributing to these administrative failures: "The administra-tion at Concordia treated the three professors [Fabrikant's patrons] now at the centre of the storm as stars of the university whose activities in securing research funds should be emulated by others."[564]

Initially, representatives of Concordia's board of governors, which had commissioned the report, were displeased with its findings. However, they had given a written undertaking that it would be pub-lished. Following its publication and the reports of other independent inquiries in 1994,[565] the university's board of governors summarily dismissed the rector, and two vice-rectors left their posts. Of Fabrikant's three academic patrons, two retired early and one resigned from the university. Subsequently, in response to concerns over lack of due process, the board's dismissal of the rector was rescinded and he resigned instead.

NSERC also acted promptly against Fabrikant's three patrons by removing their grant eligibility, but two years later reversed itself and restored it to them. Correspondence from NSERC to members of the committee of inquiry suggested that the reasons for the reversal were that any misappropriation of university funds or resources they may have committed did not involve NSERC funds, and misappropriation of authorial credit in scientific articles did not give rise to "a need for NSERC to impose any administrative sanctions."[566] The NSERC responses themselves raised general concerns that were discussed in a lengthy newspaper article based on a reporter's interviews with members of the committee of inquiry.[567]

At around the same time as NSERC's reconsideration, the new rector of Concordia approached members of the committee of inquiry with the suggestion that they should reconsider their findings of academic misconduct concerning Fabrikant's three patrons. The committee members found no reason to alter their report. Subsequently, in a published letter to a magazine editor, the new rector cited the committee of inquiry's findings of academic misconduct, but he only mentioned Fabrikant's conduct, terming it "intellectual dishonesty."[568] In his published letter, the rector omitted the fact that Fabrikant's three patrons had co-authored with Fabrikant the articles in question.

In 1994, when the inquiry reports were released, it was suggested by some that such academic misconduct and administrative mismanagement could only happen in a relatively new university like Concordia, not in an older, well-established institution. The events occurred "in a flawed, not-first-class university," one commentator said.[569]

DR. GIDEON KOREN, MEDICINE, UNIVERSITY OF TORONTO

Gideon Koren was a central figure in a dispute involving hematologist Nancy Olivieri, the University of Toronto, the Hospital for Sick Children (one of the University's fully affiliated health care institutions) and the pharmaceutical manufacturer Apotex Inc. By the mid-1990s, Olivieri was an internationally recognized authority in genetic blood disorders. She was the principal investigator in clinical trials of an Apotex drug, and Koren was a co-investigator. He was a clinical toxicologist and a prolific author of journal articles, with administrative positions in the hospital and in the university's medical faculty. The dispute arose during a period when the University of Toronto was engaged in negotiations with Apotex for a multi-million dollar donation to the university and affiliated teaching hospitals.

In 1996 Olivieri identified an unexpected risk of the drug (loss of efficacy over time — a very serious matter for patients with the disease she was treating). When she moved to fulfill her ethical obligation and disclose the risk to patients enrolled in the trials, Apotex immediately and prematurely terminated the trials. The company also issued warnings of legal action against her should she disclose the risk to patients or anyone. Neither the university nor the hospital provided Olivieri with effective support against the company. However, with the support of leading medical experts from abroad and the Canadian Medical Protective Association, she informed her patients and published her findings.

During the next few years, Olivieri came under a series of attacks on her scientific work and personal character by the company, by the hospital, and by Koren. The most serious attacks were based on "false and seriously neglectful testimony" by Koren.[570] His testimony was used against her by senior hospital administrators, and their subsequent actions against her were cited by Apotex in its efforts to gain marketing licences for the drug.[571] Koren had received substantial research funding from Apotex for the period immediately after the termination of the trials and appeared as a co-author on publications favourable to the drug, including two that had been drafted by company staff.

During the same period, Koren also conducted an anonymous-letter campaign against Olivieri.

Actions by the hospital might have destroyed Olivieri's career. However, she was fully exonerated by independent inquiries,[572] and with the assistance of CAUT and the University of Toronto Faculty Association, she negotiated substantial settlements of her grievances against the university and the hospital. A legal dispute between her and Apotex continues. Attempts to discredit her have also continued.

Koren was eventually found guilty of serious academic and professional misconduct for some of his actions, and disciplined. The contrast between the extensive procedural fairness accorded to him was in marked contrast with the highly unfair treatment accorded to Olivieri. Of relevance to the present discussion is that no administrative action was taken against Koren until after his proven misconduct became a public scandal widely covered in the media.

KOREN'S ANONYMOUS LETTER CAMPAIGN AGAINST OLIVIERI

This campaign extended over a number of months in 1998–1999. It ended only after Olivieri and several supporters (also targeted in the campaign) obtained, at their own expense, forensic evidence that unambiguously identified Koren as the author and sender of the letters and brought this evidence to the hospital and the university. However, Koren denied responsibility and instead of accepting the forensic evidence, the hospital engaged its own expert whose investigation went on for seven months, until December 1999. By then, Olivieri and her supporters had obtained genetic evidence from the saliva on the stamps and envelopes of the anonymous letters that matched genetic material from another letter, one that had been signed and sent by Koren.

After being advised of the genetic identification, Koren admitted to having written and sent the anonymous letters. About a week later, the investigator engaged by the hospital submitted her report, with the finding that he was solely responsible for the anonymous letter campaign. She also found that Koren had provided "false and misleading information" to her in an effort to conceal his responsibility.[573] These events received extensive media coverage.

An apparent reflection of the official hospital perspective at the time was an article in a Toronto newspaper by Alexander Aird, chair of the hospital's board of trustees, trivializing Koren's conduct as merely forwarding "unwanted anonymous mail."[574] The board chair also suggested that the victims of Koren's campaign bore responsibility for his conduct, thus apparently accepting Koren's own explanation.

While Koren's conduct and the institutional response continued in the public eye, disciplinary hearings were commenced. Several months later, the hospital and the university imposed sanctions on him. The disciplinary letter issued to Koren in April 2000 said, "You have provided no acceptable explanation for your misconduct" and

> Your conduct in sending the anonymous letters and in repeatedly lying to Ms. Humphrey [the hospital's investigator] demonstrates lack of fair and ethical dealing with colleagues, irresponsibility and reckless dereliction of duty. . . . You did not tell the truth when you felt untruth would serve your better. . . . Your actions constitute gross misconduct and provide sufficient grounds for dismissal.[575]

Nevertheless, the hospital and the university did not dismiss Koren, citing among mitigating factors his research productivity, and imposing lesser penalties instead.

Two weeks later, in a move that placed her career and livelihood in jeopardy, the hospital referred allegations of misconduct against Olivieri to the College of Physicians and Surgeons of Ontario (CPSO), the provincial licensing body. These allegations were based on testimony by Koren, whom they had just disciplined for lying in regard to other attacks on her. As noted above, Olivieri was fully exonerated by the CPSO's formal inquiry.

The CPSO exhibited reluctance to confront serious, proven misconduct in the case of Koren. Olivieri's three colleagues who also were victims of his anonymous letter campaign lodged a complaint against him, but the CPSO chose not to refer the matter to its discipline committee. The complainants then brought the matter to the Ontario Health Professions Appeal and Review Board, whose membership includes ordinary citizens. In its October 2001 decision, the appeal board found that the CPSO had erred in not referring Koren's conduct to its discipline committee for action. The appeal board held that Koren's anonymous letters were "shocking and outrageous, and constitute serious professional misconduct," and directed the CPSO to refer the matter for discipline. Ultimately, in a decision released in May 2003, the CPSO disciplined Koren for professional misconduct.

Koren's Research Misconduct

In 1997 Koren appeared as senior author of two conference abstracts that had been drafted by Apotex staff. This was one of several scientific venues where Apotex had attempted by legal warnings to prevent Olivieri from presenting her findings of risks associated with the company's drug. The abstracts on which Koren's name appeared as senior author suggested the drug was safe and effective.

In 1999 Koren and two of his Apotex-funded research students published an article in a journal reporting favourably on the efficacy of the company's drug. The article was based on data generated by Olivieri and two American colleagues, but used data only up to "the middle of 1995," even though the clinical trial continued until May 1996, when it was terminated prematurely by Apotex. The article by Koren et al. "does not explain why data collected later than the middle of 1995 were not included." However, it was documented in trial data that the number of patients for whom drug was losing efficacy to the extent of placing them at risk, increased with time.[576]

Olivieri, who was not consulted on this publication despite being principal investigator for the trial, filed a complaint of research misconduct against Koren with the Faculty of Medicine. It is clear to any reader that: (1) the contributions of Olivieri and her American collaborators were not acknowledged, (2) the article did not disclose that Apotex funded the research, and (3) the article did not cite published work by Olivieri and others on a second risk of the drug (liver toxicity). Thus, the article was in plain violation of university policy, as well as widely accepted norms for publication in biomedical fields. An investigating committee was established under faculty procedures. The committee reported in September 2000, but it was not until April 2002 that the dean of medicine disclosed any of its findings to the faculty council.

The dean announced a finding of misconduct against Koren, but only on one ground, that he had published the data "without obtaining consent, review or participation by Dr. Olivieri" or either of her two American collaborators.[577] The dean's report made no mention of the other two clear breaches of research integrity: Apotex's financial support was not disclosed, and published findings of risk of the drug were not cited. These omissions are curious, because the work concerned an experimental drug used to treat a potentially life-threatening condition. Regardless of the dean's intent, omission of these serious matters from his public report arguably diminished the significance of Koren's misconduct. It also bolstered the thesis put forward by the dean in his report that the misconduct had to be understood as arising from an "extraordinarily bitter dispute"[578] between Olivieri and Koren.

The dean did announce disciplinary action against Koren, including a requirement that he write to the journal "to request of the editor that the offending article be deleted from the scientific record through appropriate notification of indexing services."[579] Koren did write to the editor, as directed by the dean, but the editor declined to delete the article from the scientific record.

In its May 2003 statement, the CPSO announced disciplinary action against Koren for his misconduct both in the matter of the anonymous letter campaign and in the matter of the journal publication. Regarding the latter, the CPSO Discipline Committee in its accompanying report cited only one finding, that contained in the dean's report to the faculty council in April 2002. It is not known whether the discipline imposed by the CPSO might have been different had the dean's report included a discussion of the other elements of Koren's research misconduct in connection with this publication.

ANDREI SHLEIFER, ECONOMICS, HARVARD UNIVERSITY

In late 1992 Harvard University was awarded a US government contract to advise the Yeltsin administration in Moscow on privatization of state assets. The contract required project staff to provide disinterested advice — they were not to become speculators and profit from the projects they advised on. The project was directed by Andrei Shleifer, a prominent American economist and Harvard faculty member. Since his undergraduate days, Shleifer had been a protégé of Lawrence Summers, who was chief economist of the World Bank during 1991–1993 and subsequently a cabinet officer in the Clinton administration in Washington. At the time when Harvard was awarded the contract, Shleifer was working in Moscow on behalf of the World Bank.

Serious problems with the Harvard project surfaced a few years later, amid allegations that Shleifer and his associates in the project were engaged in financial transactions that breached terms of the US government contract with Harvard. The project became an embarrassment, and the US government terminated it in 1997. The government later took legal action against Harvard, Shleifer, and several of Shleifer's associates in an effort to recover the millions of dollars it had spent on the project.

Meanwhile, Summers was shortlisted for the presidency of Harvard, and Shleifer was one of the faculty actively campaigning for Summers, who was appointed president in 2001. Throughout his presidential tenure, Summers was a figure of controversy because of views he expressed and because of his administrative approach. For instance, in 2002 he suggested disinvestment proposals by a group of Harvard and MIT faculty members (a number of whom were Jewish) protesting policies of the government of Israel were "anti-Semitic in their effect if not their intent."[580] A much wider controversy broke out in 2005, when Summers spoke at a conference on diversity in the academic world and suggested that women had less innate ability in scientific fields than men. Dissatisfaction with his leadership mounted to the extent that the Faculty of Arts and Sciences passed a motion of lack of confidence in his presidency. This was followed by a motion of censure that passed by a larger majority.

Several months later, after court findings that Shleifer had not complied with the US government contract's conflict-of-interest rules for the Russia project and had "engaged in apparent self-dealing," a settlement was reached.[581] Under the terms of settlement, "Harvard was required to pay $26.5 million to the US government, Shleifer $2 million."[582] Details of the Harvard project and Shleifer's involvement became public in January 2006 in a magazine article, "How Harvard lost Russia," by an investigative journalist, David McClintick. The article reported that, in a court deposition, Summers acknowledged he had intervened with the dean, who was concerned about Shleifer's conduct in the Russia project. The article also noted the long-term personal friendship between Summers and Shleifer.

The revelations in McClintick's article came as additional disputes between the faculty and Summers erupted. A faculty meeting was scheduled for February 2006, at which another lack-of-confidence motion was widely expected to pass. Shortly before the meeting, Summers announced his resignation from the presidency. Later in 2006, following an investigation of Shleifer's conduct by a Harvard faculty committee, Shleifer was deprived of the endowed professorship he had held since 2001, although he retained his regular faculty position.

To summarize, in each of these three cases, at Concordia, Toronto, and Harvard, there was reluctance to confront proven misconduct, at one or more levels. Nevertheless, ultimately, significant action was taken in each case. Also in each case, there were codes of academic conduct in place, and the misconduct was ultimately addressed following the facts that: (i) concerned faculty members from the university, or from other universities, intervened to identify the misconduct, or to demand that it be addressed, and (ii) wide publicity was given to the misconduct by mainstream media outlets. In each case, some commentators argued the disciplinary actions taken were too lenient, while others argued they were too severe. However, this is less important than the result that existing standards of academic integrity were upheld in the end, with the public imposition of disciplinary action.

LOSS OF INTEGRITY ON A WIDER SCALE

Individual cases, no matter how spectacular, are less damaging to the public interest than the wider corrosion of academic integrity they reflect. Losses of integrity on a wider scale are more difficult to address, as they reflect fundamental, systemic problems requiring broad-based attitudinal and policy changes. This is not possible without a cultural shift among practitioners of a discipline or across an entire university system. Also necessary are effective means for managing the adverse influences of powerful financial and political forces that are dominant in any country. However, the task is not impossible, as past events show.

The policy developments of the 1980s and 1990s, focusing on individual conduct, were led by major American agencies such as the National Academy of Sciences and the National Institutes of Health. Their approaches had a significant influence on policy in Canada as well as the United States.

The view of faculty associations at the time was that existing policies on professional duties and responsibilities already provided quite adequate means for defining appropriate conduct and addressing misconduct by individuals. However, the associations recognized that the momentum generated by major research funding agencies in favour of new policies on research misconduct by individuals was unstoppable. Their immediate concern was that such policies be clearly worded and that they be incorporated into faculty collective agreements or similar documents, in order to ensure application by administrators was subject to fair grievance and arbitration procedures. The obvious danger in the absence of fair procedures was that the careers of individuals who were wrongly accused could be damaged or destroyed. During the course of the next decade, CAUT and its local affiliates ensured a clear definition of research misconduct and fair adjudication procedures would be available for most university faculty in Canada, outside medical schools. For those in Canadian medical schools, efforts to provide corresponding safeguards have only recently been underway.[583]

As noted earlier, these policy evolutions did not address the prospect of losses of integrity across a discipline or in universities generally. Published documents of the agencies leading the policy changes at the time leave the impression that either they were unaware or they were unwilling to acknowledge the possibility of wide-scale problems. It is difficult to believe that the senior scientists on the committees of the American National Academies that produced that two-volume report, *Responsible Science*, in the early 1990s, were unaware of significant instances of wide-scale losses of integrity that had already occurred. There were well-documented examples on the public record at the time, a few of which are noted below. Information published quite recently suggests that at least one influential figure was unwilling to permit public acknowledgement of the possibility of a serious wide-scale problem.

The latter, discussed next, also provides an example of a significant wide-scale problem — the channeling of cancer research strategies into directions favourable to certain business interests by the use of vast sums of taxpayers' money.

NAS PRESIDENT DR. FRANK PRESS AND THE INJUNCTION BY EINSTEIN

The report *Responsible Science* was published with a covering letter by Frank Press, President of the National Academy of Sciences (NAS), one of the three national academies sponsoring it. He outlined the problem addressed by the report as follows:

> The search for truth reflects adherence to ethical standards. In recent years, we have learned that . . . not all scientists adhere to this obligation. Reports of falsified research results and pla-giarism involving both junior and senior scientists have stimu-lated doubts and criticism about the ways in which misconduct in science is addressed by the research community.

Press concluded with the comment, "This letter of transmittal conveys the basic sentiments expressed in the report." Indeed, the report focuses on how researchers, universities, granting councils, and government agencies might best address the problem of research misconduct by individuals or research teams.

Press opened his letter with the words of Albert Einstein on the duty of researchers, "One must not conceal any part of what one has recognized to be true." It has since turned out that this grand opening motto for *Responsible Science* did not fully reflect how Press himself operated as administrative head of the NAS.

A major branch of biomedical science of great significance for the public is research into the nature, causes, and treatment of cancer. This also is a field where private corporations and governments have for decades acted to prevent scientists from fulfilling their duty not to conceal the truth. In addition, this is a field where, for decades, vast government financial resources have been deployed in such a way as to divert scientific attention and public concern away from causes to cures. The diversion was accomplished most notably through the so-called "War on Cancer" declared by US President Nixon in 1971 and implemented since then through the National Cancer Institute (NCI) and corresponding agencies in other countries. The focus on cures also has enjoyed much well-intentioned financial and political support by the less-than-fully informed public.[584]

By the late 1930s it was already determined scientifically that many environmental pollutants are carcinogenic. However, while restricting industrial pollution could therefore reduce the incidence of cancer, such action would also have the effect of restricting the profits of major industries. Governments and business firms have been making concerted efforts ever since to suppress information linking cancer to pollutants. Diverting scientific resources and public attention away from causes and toward cures has been a parallel strategy for several decades, contrary to the public interest. There have been many advances in cancer-related science and in medical management of the disease, and cures have been found for a small number of relatively rare types of cancer. However, the age-adjusted cancer mortality rate for the population of the United States has remained approximately the same since 1950, despite the billions of dollars spent pursing the War on Cancer.[585]

This dual strategy of suppression and diversion is the theme of recent books. One of these is *The Secret History of the War on Cancer* by epidemiologist Devra Davis of the University of Pittsburgh. Beginning in the 1980s when she worked at the NAS, Davis and several colleagues "had published a series of papers showing that cancer had actually increased and it couldn't all be explained by smoking, improved diagnoses or aging. Judged by this standard, the then two-decade-long war on cancer wasn't going well."[586] Their papers were well received scientifically and led to a contract to write a book for general readers. In her preface Davis says:

> It's taken me twenty years to write this book. My first try ended in 1986 after I explained to Frank Press, my boss at the National Academy of Sciences, that I had been offered a hefty advance to write about the fundamental misdirections of the war on cancer. . . . Press . . . nodded as I told him of my plans and then said gravely, "It had better be a good book."
>
> I replied, "I guess I think it will be. They're offering me more than half of my annual salary. That's quite a lot for a first-time author. . . . Of course they expect it to be good. . . . So do I."
>
> "Well," he explained, "It had better be, because you won't be able to work here after you write it. . . . I'm just telling you that you can't write a book critical of the cancer enterprise and hold a senior position in this institution."[587]

As she admits, Davis chose to remain in her NAS position, and so her book did not appear until two decades later, when she held a university faculty position.

In essence, it was tolerable at the NAS that Davis published articles in scientific journals showing that specific factors, such as population aging or better diagnostic methods, could not account for the fact that the cancer incidence and mortality rates were actually increasing during the first decade and a half of the War on Cancer. However, it was intolerable that she write a book for a popular audience that would conclude that "the cancer enterprise," as Press called it, was fundamentally misdirected and that, in effect, the public was being misled.

Psychiatrist David Healy relates a parallel experience in another chapter of this book.

ADDITIONAL INSTANCES OF WIDE-SCALE PROBLEMS

Two types of example are presented, one involving an entire university system, the other involving specific disciplines.

The Early Cold War Period

The most significant and instructive instance occurred during the wave of state-sponsored anti-communist hysteria that engulfed the United States in the first decade of the Cold War.[588] It caused widespread loss of integrity across the American university system, including the effective disappearance of academic freedom in all but the narrowest sense. Although intellectuals and political dissenters from all walks of life were targeted, the universities, where "dissent should have found a sanctuary," engaged in the repression "just like every other institution in American life."[589] Many academic assessments and decisions were made on an improper basis as arbitrary dismissals, blacklists, informers, denunciations, and hearings by rigged tribunals kept all but the most stalwart academics and university administrators in line with official ideology. Some of this hysteria spilled over into Canada, although it was more limited in scope and mainly confined to the late 1940s.[590] A similar phenomenon swept over American universities in 1917–1918, with the state-sponsored anti-German hysteria that was whipped up nationwide in order to facilitate American entry into World War I.[591] The newly formed American Association of University Professors (AAUP) immediately abandoned its principles, while its leaders, including some of the most distinguished American scholars of the day, such as John Dewey, joined in the chorus of condemnation against anti-war colleagues.

In cases where university administrations or boards of governors did stand up to state-sponsored witch hunters, the latter withdrew and faculty dissenters were protected.[592] However, such instances were rare, and typically, once an academic was identified by a government agency as someone with undesirable views or associates, he was dismissed by his university and blacklisted from academic employment across the United States. While "the opportunism and cowardice of boards of trustees and university administrators"[593] deserve blame, the same could be said for many faculty members and other citizens. The faculty and citizen organizations founded to protect academic freedom, or dissent in general, such as the AAUP and the American Civil Liberties Union (ACLU), also failed to act with courage or conviction and became ineffectual.

Much of the overt repression in the United States had dissipated by the late 1950s, one reason being that:

> The academy's enforcement of McCarthyism had silenced an entire generation of radical intellectuals and snuffed out all meaningful opposition to the official version of the Cold War. When . . . the hearings and dismissals tapered off, it was not because they encountered resistance but because they were no longer necessary. All was quiet on the academic front.[594]

However, this was not the whole story. In an increasingly affluent society, the stick could be replaced by the carrot. The 1950s saw a rapid expansion of the academy, because during World War II the American government became convinced of the military and economic usefulness of the expertise in universities and the training of their graduates. When combined with Cold War international competition, this recognition spurred huge government investments in higher education and research, resulting in greater affluence and prestige for the rapidly growing professoriate. In this climate, it was relatively easy for the many to ignore the repression of the few. Surveying the period, biologist R.C. Lewontin wrote: "Although it is a severe blow to their sense of moral righteousness and self-esteem, academics must face the fact that the Via Dolorosa along which many of their colleagues, friends and comrades were dragged to their crucifixions was also the high road to professional prosperity for the majority."[595]

A substantial measure of academic freedom and respect for academic integrity was recovered during the next two decades. The growing importance of academics in the American political economy gave them "an extraordinary degree of control over the conditions of their employment."[596] Science and technology enjoyed the greatest prestige because of their significance in military, health, economic, and other fields. Thus, it is not surprising that academics employed at universities with strong Pentagon connections — such as mathematician Stephen Smale at the University of California, Berkeley, and biologist Salvador Luria and linguist Noam Chomsky at the Massachusetts Institute of Technology — were among the leaders in public dissent against American foreign policy in the 1960s and were tolerated by their universities.

Chomsky's experience during the 1960s was that, "the academic freedom record [of MIT] was quite good by comparative standards," even though MIT "was virtually Pentagon university. Aside from two military labs it ran, about 90 percent of the [MIT operating] budget came from the Pentagon."[597] At other universities, there was still "plenty of repression, and persecution of activists and people on the Left."[598] He attributed the difference "to the fact that MIT was a science-based university, and hence the ideological constraints were much less" than at universities such as Harvard.[599]

By the 1970s, partly because the AAUP and other professional organizations again became more robust, the freedom enjoyed by professors at universities such as MIT and Berkeley became more widespread. As a result, universities re-acquired their reputation in the minds of the public for independence of thought and integrity of work. Of course, this re-established credibility was immediately regarded by some, inside and outside the ivory tower, as a tradable commodity.

Inducements to Lax Academic Integrity

In disciplines relating to fields such as international relations, American foreign policy, and modern political history, the ideological constraints of the early Cold War period persisted and academic integrity has been corrupted through to the present. Chomsky outlined the reasons for this a quarter century ago:[600]

A . . . complex of inducements — access to privilege and prestige, class interest, penalties for straying beyond acceptable limits, and the like — produces a systematic bias in the scholarship that is concerned with foreign policy and its formation, serving to protect the basic system of social, economic and decision-making from scrutiny. . . . It is by no means necessary to yield to these pressures, certainly in a society that lacks the forms of coercion and punishment found elsewhere.[601] But the temptation to do so is considerable, and those who choose a different path often find that opportunities to do their work or reach more than a marginal audience are limited or excluded.

This assessment remains valid. For present purposes, it suffices to mention the relationship between American foreign policy and the domestic and foreign policies of Israel. This has been a taboo topic in the United States for several decades. A recent victim of this taboo is the political scientist Norman Finkelstein, a critic of Israeli government policies, who was denied tenure by DePaul University in 2007.[602] The tenure denial came despite favourable recommendations by departmental and faculty committees, and followed concerted attacks on his work by pro-Israel academics and lobbyists.

Anthropologist Nadia Abu El-Haj met a happier fate at Columbia University, where she was granted tenure, despite similar concerted attacks on her work. Her award-winning scholarly book, *Facts on the Ground*,[603] "looked at the role of archaeology in what was essentially a political project: the Biblical validation for Jewish claims to what is now Israel."[604] The reason she fared better at Columbia than Finkelstein did at DePaul is instructive: Columbia had a modern tradition of respect for academic freedom and robust procedures for defending it, along with decades of successful experience in fending off virulent attacks by pro-Israel extremists on distinguished members of its faculty such as Edward Said.

Things can be become difficult even for very senior, well-established scholars, such as John Mearsheimer of Chicago and Stephen Walt of Harvard. They were unable to get an extensively documented article on what they saw as the adverse influences of the Israel lobby on American foreign policy published in the United States. Ultimately, it was published in England in 2006[605] and when it appeared, "the response was breathtaking . . . a firestorm of criticism . . . and we were denounced as anti-Semites."[606]

Unfortunately, such influences have spread to other disciplines. Thanks to recent books for general audiences, such as those listed at the beginning of this chapter, the "complex of inducements" provided by drug companies that now corrupts much of academic medicine (and adversely influences much of health care generally) is becoming more widely known. Thus there is some hope that rising concern among the general public may translate into active assistance for those medical scientists who are courageously working to restore integrity. The coalition of public interest groups and health care professionals that is currently working to prevent direct-to-consumer advertising of prescription drugs in Canada provides an encouraging example.

As a result of the attitudes of many faculty and administrators created by such inducements, publicly established dishonesty is no bar to academic advancement. From the 1960s there is the example of Arthur M. Schlesinger Jr., who had served as the Kennedy administration's advisor on Latin America. Shortly after he acknowledged to the *New York Times* that he had lied in his published account of the Bay of Pigs incident, Schlesinger was appointed the Albert Schweitzer Professor of Humanities at the City University of New York.[607] Noam Chomsky commented:

> It is of no particular interest that one man is quite happy to lie in behalf of a cause which he knows to be unjust; but it is significant that such events provoke so little response in the intellectual community — no feeling, for example that there is something strange in the offer of a major chair in humanities to a historian who feels it to be his duty to persuade the world that an American-sponsored invasion of a nearby country is nothing of the sort.[608]

Today, so-called terrorism has been installed to replace the defunct

USSR as chief hobgoblin,[609] in order to justify continuation of the political economy of the Cold War. A "complex of inducements" to encourage lax academic integrity remains in place. In addition the billions of dollars of public funds spent on security services and the far larger sums expended on aggressive wars in Afghanistan and Iraq, substantial research grants and contracts have gone to academics for what amounts to production of pro-war propaganda with an academic imprimatur.

For example, law professor Amir Attaran noted in a recent newspaper article that millions of dollars originating with the Department of National Defence (DND) has been going to academics for projects "to shape Canadians' perception of the military and the war [in Afghanistan]." Attaran proposed that "credible public intellectuals owe disclosure [of their funding sources] to their public."[610] A few days later, in the same newspaper, historian Jack Granatstein replied that there was no cause for public concern because the decisions on who is awarded these DND funds "are properly based on their track record in publication and research."[611] In a published response, Attaran said, "It's unfortunate Prof. Granatstein didn't mention that the Conference of Defence Associations gave him an award and $5,000 just last week."[612]

Trading in Credibility — Examples from Other Academic Disciplines

Of course it is not only government military and security agencies, such as defence departments, that use academics and their institutions for propaganda purposes. Two disciplines that attracted increasing public scrutiny in the 1970s (and ever since) because of this practice were the agricultural and forestry sciences. It was by then scientifically determined that some commercial practices were causing severe, irreversible environmental damage and posing significant risks to human health. These included indiscriminate spraying of agricultural crops and forests with toxic chemicals, ostensibly to eliminate insect pests or undesired plant species, and massive clear-cutting of forests. It was known also that these practices were often economically counterproductive, except in the short term. However, many scientists willingly served as apologists for them, and some universities willingly lent their institutional credibility.

For instance in the United States, in order to counter mounting public concern over the use of toxic chemicals in agriculture, major corporations in the chemical and agribusiness industries funded the establishment of two propaganda agencies in the mid-1970s. The committees directing these agencies included leading scientists and administrators of the University of California.[613] In Canada a few years later and at the other end of the continent, the administration of the University of New Brunswick agreed to host in its biology department a government–industry environmental monitoring agency for forest insecticide spraying that had been publicly discredited.[614]

On a positive note, the development and resolution of these two scandals provide grounds for optimism and examples of a way forward in efforts to strengthen integrity. In the UNB case, members of the biology department and the faculty union executive combined forces with local environmental groups, and organized public exposure of the actions of the government–industry agency and the university administration in the national media. This included a half-hour documentary on CBC television. Shortly thereafter, the discredited agency was withdrawn from UNB and disbanded. More importantly, the wider public was thereby encouraged to criticize the massive spraying of forests with neurotoxic chemicals. Partly as a result, within the next few years, forest management practices were changed to become more environmentally sensitive.

In the California case, the scandal was exposed in a book (cited above) written by Robert van den Bosch, head of the entomology department at the Berkeley campus. He also was a leading proponent of agricultural practices that were more environmentally sensitive than those prevailing at the time. By making a national public issue of the problems of indiscriminate pesticide spraying and improper trading in his university's reputation by senior administrators, as well suggesting feasible alternative agricultural practices, he helped bring about changes.

Of course, predictably in the current environment for universities, serious problems have again arisen, at Berkeley and elsewhere. Some of these are discussed in the recent book by Jennifer Washburn (cited earlier). For instance, biologist Ignacio Chapela was denied tenure at Berkeley in 2003, despite favourable recommendations from committees of peers in the university. He had incurred displeasure on two counts. One was his vocal opposition to an arrangement between Berkeley and the multinational chemical manufacturer Novartis, whereby the university appeared to trade some of its autonomy and reputation for $25 million from the company. The other was his article in the journal *Nature* on adverse consequences of using genetically modified crops.[615] However, Berkeley's tenure appeal process was sufficiently robust that the decision against Chapela was reversed.

Finally, regardless of the intent of focusing academic integrity policy on the conduct of individual miscreants, the effect has been to deflect attention away from the much larger and more serious systemic problems, or wide-scale problems, as they are referred to here. A parallel phenomenon can be observed in the commercial and financial sectors. In recent years a relatively small number of high-profile individual corporation heads (such as Bernard Ebbers of Worldcom and Conrad Black of Hollinger) have been convicted of fraud or other financial crimes and sent to prison with extravagant media coverage. However, the political economy that facilitates the swindling of investors, taxpayers, and pensioners out of billions of dollars, with the inflating and deflating of financial bubbles every few years, remains largely untouched.

GOVERNMENT POLICY CHANGES

Government policy changes during the past several decades created circumstances that facilitated corruption of academic integrity, regardless of the original intent. These developments are described in recent publications such as Derek Bok's *Universities in the Marketplace* (cited earlier) and David Healy's *The Creation of Psychopharmacology*.[616]

In the 1970s, government funding for universities was not keeping up with the rapidly rising costs of teaching and research in fields such as medicine, engineering, and the sciences. During the same period,

American economic growth was slowing in the face of industrial competition from Europe and Japan,[617] while universities were generating information and technology with significant commercial potential that was not being immediately realized. Significantly also, the biotech industry had been created in 1976, in California, with the development of recombinant DNA technologies of great potential value to the drug industry.[618] Such considerations led to the Bayh–Dole Act of 1980 "which made it much easier for American universities to own and license patents on discoveries made through research paid for with public funds."[619] In addition, government subsidies for university-industry partnerships became widely available. In Canada also, governments introduced measures to encourage university–industry partnerships, following the American trend.

No realistic assessment appears to have been made, either by legislators or leaders of the academic community, of predictable adverse effects of this trend. Private corporations have fundamentally different missions from universities. The former seek profits for their owners or shareholders and are not constrained by ethical principles; the latter exist to seek the truth and have the duty to communicate it. Corporations use commercial performance criteria to gauge success and legal actions or threats of legal action to protect their intellectual property. Academic freedom and openness are central characteristics of universities. Measures could have been developed and implemented to balance these conflicting interests, but they were not.

The government policy changes affecting universities, inducing them to enter the marketplace, came at a time of increasing deregulation across the Western world. Corporations commonly prefer to operate in unregulated environments. The absence of labour or environmental standards, or of constraints on monopoly formation, is considered good for profits. It suffices to recall the manner in which many American, British, and Canadian corporations have operated in Latin America during the past century, where deregulation has been imposed through direct use of American military power or local military power that acts in accordance with North America corporate agendas.[620] Therefore, no one should have expected wholly benign consequences from the drawing of universities into a deregulated marketplace.

As is now becoming better known, the field most profoundly affect-ed by these changes is medicine, where pharmaceutical manufacturers have gained extraordinary influence and power. Their influence rose very rapidly from the 1980s onward, in parallel with the rise in prof-itability of the drug industry. The profitability was not due to the "qual-ity of the drugs the companies were selling,"[621] but instead to American congressional legislation from 1984 onward extending patent protec-tions for drugs and to new marketing strategies for them.

Medicine is not the only field in which serious problems have aris-en in university-industry partnerships. The Fabrikant affair in Montreal, outlined earlier, arose in the context of such a partnership in an engineering faculty.

PRODUCTION-DRIVEN CULTURES

The common feature of the dominant political economies of the past century (including American capitalism and Soviet communism) is the primacy given to productivity and production. This has been the cause of many wars, much environmental damage and, most recently, adverse climate change. In essence, "countries are more anxious to pro-tect their productivity than their people."[622]

The most pernicious example of excess is the vast quantity of nuclear weapons produced by the United States and the USSR. Already in 1955, this "threaten[ed] the continued existence of mankind," as Bertrand Russell, Albert Einstein, and several other distinguished intel-lectuals wrote at the time.[623] Inadvertent or deliberate nuclear war remains the most acute threat to the survival of the human race, despite the focus of media attention on climate change.

Recently, neoliberalism, a more extreme form of capitalism, has been in the ascendancy, with variants of this ideology embraced in all industrialized countries. In comparison to previously dominant eco-nomic ideologies, the central aim of neoliberalism is to accelerate the rate of concentration of wealth and power in the hands of small groups, at the expense of the general population.[624]

The rise of neoliberalism was not spontaneous. It was the result of a well-financed campaign by wealthy individuals, private corporations, and the US's Central Intelligence Agency to turn the clock back in Western society — to a time before there were effective collective bargaining rights, governmental agencies protecting the environment, and state programs providing significant services to poor and middle-income people. Academics were prominent among the handmaidens of the wealthy in this campaign.[625]

Key methods of neoliberalism are deregulation, tax reduction, militarization, social atomization, and misrepresentation. Militarization makes it easier to channel public funds into relatively few hands as well as to deflect public attention from pressing social and environmental problems. Deregulation makes fraud easier to commit, harder to detect, and harder to prosecute, by opening opportunities for self-dealing and weakening public and private sector oversight bodies. Deregulation also facilitates generation of successive stock market bubbles and crashes that result in prosperity for a few and penury for many, as in the recent sub-prime mortgage fiasco.[626] Tax reduction typically benefits the wealthy and harms the non-wealthy by depriving the state of resources to protect their rights and interests. Social atomization (by such means as anti-union legislation and propaganda celebrating individual self-reliance at the expense of the community) makes it difficult for "ordinary" citizens to resist pernicious changes to national and international political economies.

Finally, the real purposes and effects of neoliberal policies have been misrepresented by their proponents throughout the past quarter century. For example, it was asserted that more wealth for the wealthy was justified because it would result in some largesse trickling down to the masses. Predictably, however, rivers of money flowed upward only, and the poor got poorer while the rich got richer.[627] Although neoliberalism has been spectacularly successful in its central objective — concentrating wealth and power for financial elites — it has been spectacularly unsuccessful as the primary basis for operating national economies. This, too, has been misrepresented, with disastrous failures such as Chile (where the Chicago School of neoliberal economists was given free rein in the early years of the Pinochet dictatorship) declared by the mainstream North American media to be successes for neoliberalism.[628]

Tax reduction combined with increased military spending creates deficits. The deficits in turn are used to justify reductions in state services to all but the wealthy, whose influence shields them.[629] On this basis, university funding was sharply reduced across Canada in the 1990s, helping to accelerate the trend to university–industry partnerships that were also facilitated by targeted public funding. These circumstances continue for universities, despite recent modest improvements in untargeted funding. Thus it was not surprising to see even the president of one of Canada's best-funded universities call for more university–industry partnerships.[630] It was also not surprising that the same president said nothing about the problems these partnerships can cause.

In the English-speaking world, the strongest attacks on academic freedom — and hence academic integrity — in the past two decades have come from proponents of neoliberalism. These include the Thatcher and Major governments in the United Kingdom, as well as private organizations such as the American Council of Trustees and Alumni (ACTA), founded by Lynne Cheney (wife of US Vice-president Dick Cheney) and Senator Joseph Lieberman. ACTA and allied groups make use of the same tactics as the anti-communist witch-hunters of the early Cold War era: for instance, labelling certain professors as "un-American."

A striking feature of the neoliberal age is that greed is celebrated and fraud promoted by the mainstream media. The cases of Enron, Worldcom, and Hollinger International are examples in which there have been criminal convictions of individuals previously held up to the public as role models. Propaganda suggests such cases are anomalous, but they may instead come to be seen as characteristic of our time.

In such an environment, no one should be surprised that increasing numbers of university professors and administrators have failed to live up to standards of academic integrity, or that production-driven research cultures now abound in universities. For example, in so far as Professor Andrei Shleifer had been engaging in improper self-dealing while managing the Harvard Russia project (discussed earlier), he was only acting in the manner of some major financial corporations. Similarly, insofar as some senior university administrators have failed to investigate or address scientific misconduct when presented with substantial evidence, they have only been acting in the manner of public and private regulators in areas such as finance, or food and drugs, who have failed to serve the public interest.

MOVING FORWARD IN THE PUBLIC INTEREST

As discussed in this volume, there are serious losses of integrity in substantial parts of the academy, to the detriment of the public interest. In substantial measure this can be attributed to a complex of inducements to individuals or their universities by government agencies and private corporations. Of course, the presence of inducements does not absolve individual professors or administrators from responsibility. As Chomsky said in his 1986 Managua Lectures (citing specific examples of scholars rewriting the history of the United States' many aggressive wars against the people of Latin America), "There are few limits to the capacity of respected Western intellectuals to interpret brutality, atrocities and racist horrors as exemplifying the highest values and noblest intentions."[631]

A corresponding assessment may be applied, for instance, to respected medical scientists who agree to be listed as "authors" of articles claiming the efficacy or safety of a drug, when the articles were drafted by company staff. These "authors" — sometimes referred to as guest authors when they agree to be listed as co-authors of articles drafted by staff of drug companies or professional writers employed by them (sometimes referred to as ghost authors) — have not had access to all relevant trial data, and the data were not accessible to independent scientists to evaluate the claims. David Healy (this volume and elsewhere) was the first to draw attention to this fundamental corruption of science, in his own field of psychiatric medicine. In April 2008, the *Journal of the American Medical Association* (*JAMA*) published articles showing that similar practices have infected other branches of academic medicine.[632] The editor-in-chief of *JAMA*, Catherine DeAngelis, said that the physicians and academics who become guest authors of ghost-written articles are little more than "prostitutes."[633]

Restricting the availability of inducements would likely reduce the incidence of respected scholars serving as propagandists for governments or manufacturers. Although it may not be possible to resolve such important issues in a comprehensive way, it may be possible to move forward in specific directions. Both the present and the past provide grounds for optimism, in the midst of many grounds for pessimism.

Regarding the present, it is now becoming more widely apparent that neoliberalism is an economic and political, a well as social, disaster. It may not be sustainable much longer in its present form and may begin to be supplanted in the next few years. In a different political economy — even in a less extreme neoliberal political economy than at present — restoration of lost academic integrity may be a less daunting task than at the moment.

Some possible approaches to strengthening academic integrity follow.

ENGAGING THE PUBLIC

Ultimately, the only political force capable of balancing the influence of wealthy individuals and corporations and reorienting government priorities toward the general public interest is the citizenry at large. However, citizens can effectively contend with propaganda, reach independent conclusions, and thereby sustain democracy only when they are well informed. This was the point made to the *New York Times* by NASA's leading climatologist, James Hansen, in the course of explaining his refusal to be silenced by the Bush administration. He said, "Communicating with the public seems to be essential, because public concern is probably the only thing capable of overcoming the special interests that have obfuscated the topic [global warming]."[634]

The suggestions made here apply more broadly but are formulated in the context of medical science. As already noted, published studies (such as those referred to in the present volume) have established that, in this field, academic integrity has been extensively corrupted through the improper influence of pharmaceutical manufacturers. None of the usual counterweights to such influence are very effective. This is because medical schools are inadequately funded by the state, medical journals rely on advertisements, politicians and political parties need campaign donations, and regulatory agencies have been rendered ineffective in many respects by political pressure, lack of resources, or legislative changes.

The result is a worldwide problem for humanity. The collective risk may not be as great in the short term as that posed by accidental or deliberate nuclear war, or in the longer term by climate change. Nevertheless, there is a substantial annual toll, individually and collectively: from inadequately tested drugs that are either toxic or ineffective; from unnecessary drugs; and from the vast expense to public or private health care systems for such drugs that divert funds into the coffers of drug companies — funds otherwise usable for proven methods of care, or disease prevention, or health promotion. In addition, science itself is corrupted and discredited when scientific journals publish articles that are more advertising copy than science.

The problem could be alleviated, if not completely solved, by increasing state funding for medical schools and continuing medical education, channelling most of it through arms-length agencies, and by freeing regulatory agencies from political pressures and increasing their resources. This would require tax increases — a tall order under neoliberalism. However, it is not impossible, provided the general public comes to understand what is actually being inflicted upon millions of vulnerable people for the sake of private profits.

Indeed political changes of the required magnitude have happened in the past, and against considerable odds, as a result of changes in public attitudes and attendant political activism. Such changes do not happen overnight, but they can be made to happen through effective organization and mobilization of public sentiment. The following instances are instructive, particularly those in which academics were prominent among the leaders of movements.

Collective Bargaining Rights

Until the middle of the Great Depression, the power structure in the United States had been virulently and violently opposed to rights for trade unions. For instance, employers often called in the National Guard to brutally suppress strikes and demonstrations. Yet, in 1935, with a changing political climate, Congress passed the National Labor Relations Act (Wagner Act), which provided a modern framework for industrial relations, including rights to bargain collectively and to fair means of dispute resolution. Although gradually weakened in the United States during the decades following World War II, the principles were adopted in Canada, where labour codes continue to follow the spirit of the Wagner Act. University faculty have benefited from the Canadian system ever since their local associations began to unionize in the 1970s.

Improvements in the Status of Women

The English-speaking world had long resisted granting women legal, political, and employment rights comparable to those enjoyed by men. The slow rate of progress accelerated in the late 1960s, with increasing numbers of younger people, men and women, gaining university-level education and the publication of influential works by women writers, some of them academics, such as Germaine Greer. In Canada, by the 1980s, federal and provincial governments and professional associations such as CAUT instituted a variety of measures to improve the status of women. Such measures also have helped make a positive difference.

Socialized Medicine

The provision of medical care, and with it medical education, in Canada underwent a transformation in the mid-1960s when the minority Liberal government passed the Canada Health Act with the help of the New Democratic Party. Many now consider the resulting government service to be the structure that particularly defines Canada. The origins of this legislation lay in the Regina Manifesto, a socialist document from the mid-1930s drafted principally by academics who were political and social activists, with Toronto historian Frank Underhill the main author.[635] While three decades passed before their ideas came to fruition, it should noted that in contrast, nothing of the sort has yet happened in the United States.

Nuclear Weapons Treaties

Perhaps the most significant of major political transformations for present purposes is the one initiated by the Pugwash Movement. It led to the adoption of a series of international treaties, most importantly between the United States and the USSR, placing limitations on weapons of mass destruction. This was a successful political process initiated and led by academics. Its first major achievement — the Partial Test Ban Treaty of 1963 — was reached in only eight years, and it was reached in the face of great odds.[636] The process began in a 1955 London press conference at which Bertrand Russell and Albert Einstein released a manifesto, co-signed by nine other academics, on the dangers to the human race posed by nuclear weapons.

The signatories of the Russell–Einstein Manifesto knew that neither ordinary citizens nor political leaders understood the enormity of the dangers, and hence underestimated them — thereby actually increasing the peril. They understood that a campaign of public education was essential in order to address the problem politically, and called for an international conference of leading scientists to begin the process.

Funding for the conference was provided by industrialist Cyrus Eaton, who hosted it and many subsequent conferences at his boyhood home in Pugwash, Nova Scotia, beginning with the first one in 1957. Scientists from the USSR, United States, United Kingdom, Japan, and several other countries participated. Thus began a successful campaign whose aim was to persuade governments of the need for restrictions on development and deployment of nuclear weapons.

Arguably, the scientists from the West had the more complex task. They had to educate the public so that their cause would become a political issue, and they had to persuade several national governments. The Western public had been terrorized by a decade-long deluge of anti-Soviet propaganda, and in the United States also by the anti-communist witch hunts led by such American icons as Richard M. Nixon (House Un-American Activities Committee), and Joseph R. McCarthy (Senate Permanent Subcommittee on Investigations) with his assistant Robert F. Kennedy. Congress was filled with members who had been elected on the strength of their anti-Soviet rhetoric. The Soviet scientists had mainly to convince the Politburo, which may have been a less difficult task, as it was the United States that started the Cold War and the nuclear arms race for the purpose of trying to intimidate the USSR.[637] However, the scientists on both sides leading the campaign enjoyed a common advantage — nuclear physicists had great prestige with their national governments, precisely because they had developed nuclear weapons. The fact that, recently, the American government has unilaterally announced it no longer considers itself bound by some of the weapons treaties of the 1960s and 1970s serves to emphasize how important these treaties were and how difficult it must have been to negotiate them.

Could the Pugwash Movement be successfully imitated in an effort to restore academic integrity to medical science and place public health foremost? Possibly. Even though the issue does not have the immediacy of nuclear war,[638] it is of major international significance. This is because the corruption of integrity in scientific medicine by the complex of inducements put forward by major corporations represents one of the leading "battlegrounds" in efforts to subjugate humanity to a kind of commercial totalitarianism, the logical conclusion of the neoliberal agenda. It may be possible to identify successors to Russell and Einstein for such a venture, but perhaps more difficult to find an industrialist willing to follow in the footsteps of Cyrus Eaton. However, this is a role that the national faculty associations in several countries might wish to consider taking on, as a consortium.

EDUCATION OF THE PUBLIC

As discussed, education of the public is important. This means not just the members of the public who attend, or have attended universities, but all those who can be reached through the media, personal meetings, formal or informal talks, and accessible books and articles, and through engagement with trade unions, environmental groups, church groups, community groups, and so on.

The importance of this matter has been recognized by the Royal Society of London in its recent report, *Science Information: Survey of Factors Affecting Science Communication by Scientists and Engineers*. In his preface, the Society's president, Martin Rees, wrote:

> Scientists need to engage more fully with the public. The Royal Society recognizes this, and is keen to ensure that such engagement is helpful and effective. . . . We hope the findings [in this report] will be helpful to other funding organizations, universities and research institutions in their efforts to promote and enhance the engagement of scientists with the public.[639]

This is not to suggest that science has all the answers. The scientific method has inherent limitations. Worse, as detailed in this volume, science can be corrupted and used for fraudulent purposes. However, it does provide a method for distinguishing truth from falsehood or superstition.

A case in point, showing what can happen when scientists abandon the field of public education to nonscientists, involves Darwinian evolutionary theory. The robust pockets of unscientific opponents that have long thrived in the United States, and have lately also appeared in Canada, did not emerge spontaneously. The historian of science Ian Hacking notes that by the late nineteenth century in the industrialized world, "an evolutionary account of life was taken for granted" by both religious and nonreligious people, but "then something happened."[640] In the years 1910–1915 and later, a group of Chicago businessmen and organizations they supported, such as the Moody Bible Institute, undertook a well-funded campaign against theories of biological evolution. Their campaign opened with a series of pamphlets titled, "The Fundamentals," and those promoting anti-evolutionary views were henceforth termed "fundamentalists." These campaigns continue to the present, as Brian Alters discusses elsewhere in this volume.

CODES OF ETHICS

Focusing on Individuals

Recently, the British government's chief science advisor, David King, has called for adoption of a universal code of ethics for scientists, analogous to the Hippocratic Oath for physicians, in order "to build trust between scientists and society."[641] His draft code focuses on individual conduct, and the initiative has backing from his government and the Royal Society of Chemistry. A code of ethics is a good thing in principle, and a number of scientific societies in North America have already adopted them (for example, the American Mathematical Society and the Canadian Mathematical Society).

However, existence of a code of ethics does not mean those covered by it actually adhere to it. For instance, in medicine, along with the Hippocratic Oath, there are modern codes of research ethics. The problem is that, at least in part because of the inducements presented by drug companies, many individual scientists pay only lip service to the codes, and the relevant societies seldom do much to enforce them. With growing awareness of the problems, the public has begun to distrust science, scientists, and the meaningfulness of codes of ethics.

This is not to say that professional ethics and formal codification are unimportant. Two illustrations are provided by attitudes toward torture and nuclear weapons. Torture has for some time been widely considered immoral and is prohibited by international law. Despite this, torture is practised by many countries, including the United States. The American Medical, Psychiatric, and Nursing Associations have banned participation in torture as a violation of professional ethics. However, some psychologists consider participation in certain forms of torture to be not inappropriate as a professional activity. At its August 2007 convention, the Council of the American Psychological Association voted to reject a call from the American Civil Liberties Union for "a moratorium on the participation of its members in abusive treatment."[642] The continuing participation by psychologists in torture of prisoners enables the American defence and spy agencies to maintain a veneer of respectability for their practice in defiance of international law.[643]

Defence of torture is not confined to psychologists. Harvard law professor Alan M. Dershowitz argues that torture is appropriate in some circumstances and that laws such as the Geneva Conventions should be changed so as to regulate it.[644] Former Harvard human rights policy professor Michael Ignatieff, now a Liberal member of parliament in Canada, has put forward similar views regarding certain forms of torture — coercive interrogations.[645] These professors suggest torture may be necessary to protect democracy. Their reasoning is fallacious,[646] but much academic work — for instance, any scientific theory — is sooner or later found to be flawed. In this sense, promoting a fallacy does not necessarily imply a lack of academic integrity.

Involvement in the design or production of nuclear weapons came to be widely regarded as immoral. However, the original designers of such weaponry, leading physicists of their day, such as Oppenheimer and Teller in the United States, and Zeldovich and Sakharov in the USSR, considered themselves patriots with the moral objective of saving their nations from disaster — a nuclear attack by Nazi Germany in the former case, a nuclear attack by the United States in the latter. Today many academics in many countries participate in military-related activities widely considered immoral, and such work typically does not permit open access to sources or data. However, there is as yet no consensus as to whether such activities violate academic integrity, and codes of ethics for scientists and engineers do not proscribe them. It will be interesting to see whether the British government-backed initiative of David King will come to grips with such issues.

In essence, however, existing codes of ethics are primarily focused on individual conduct or misconduct. As discussed in this chapter, such a focus deflects attention from more general and systemic or political issues, notably as to the influence of neoliberalism and of the complex of inducements to misconduct that agents of commercial corporations, or governments responsive to corporate demands, place before individuals.

Addressing Systemic Problems

Codes of research ethics can usefully be augmented to address systemic problems. For example, the independent committee of inquiry into the Olivieri case recommended that the Canadian research granting councils "should impose a requirement that universities and health care institutions receiving any funding from the granting councils have in place the policy" stating that:

> All contracts, protocols and investigator agreements for indus-
> trial sponsorship of clinical trials should expressly provide that
> the clinical investigators shall not be prevented by the sponsor
> (or anyone) from informing participants in the study, mem-
> bers of the research group, other physicians administering the
> treatment, research ethics boards, regulatory agencies, and the
> scientific community, of risks to participants that the investi-
> gators identify during the research. The same provisions
> should apply to any risks of a treatment identified following
> the conclusion of a trial in the event there are patients being
> administered the treatment in a non-trial setting.[647]

This would have the advantage of placing responsibility on institutions and trial sponsors as well as on individuals. A convenient way to
implement this recommendation would be to amend the TCPS ethics
code. Indeed, in May 2003, the presidents of the three granting councils expressly referred it to the councils' Panel on Research Ethics,
requesting the panel review it "in light of the need to keep the TCPS
current with modern research ethics needs."[648] The panel began the
review, including consultations with experts and other interested parties, but as of May 2008, the long-promised public consultation paper
with draft recommendations by the panel has not yet materialized.
Unfortunately, this may be another circumstance where no action will
be taken in the absence of concerted pressure from the public at large.
An additional way to address systemic problems in scientific medicine
is to revise codes of ethics for editors of journals and authors of articles

submitted to them, so as to place responsibilities not only on individuals but also on their institutions, the journals, and on the manufacturers of drugs or devices under clinical investigation. A series of proposed clauses for such a revised code was outlined in an editorial in a recent issue of the *Journal of the American Medical Association* (*JAMA*), prefaced with the comment that "Drastic action is essential, and cooperation of everyone involved in medical research, medical editing, medical education, and clinical practice is required for meaningful change to occur."[649]

COLLABORATING WITH NATURE

In summary, active consideration of the public interest must come to the fore, and the academy should engage with the public to help ensure that the genuine public interest is served by university research. It must also be recognized that a vital part of the public interest is a harmonious, respectful balance between humanity and nature. These concerns are exemplified in the approach taken by Mark Winston, an ecologist at Simon Fraser University. He is an expert on bees, studying the ominous collapses of colonies of pollinating bees observed internationally in recent years. As reported in *The Globe and Mail*:

> [Mark Winston] has refocused his teaching. He now preaches bee-like virtues of collaboration and congeniality to undergraduates in a . . . program at SFU that focuses on civic dialogue. "My experience with bees grew into a serious concern about how we teach students to engage with the world."[650]

ABOUT THE AUTHORS

BRIAN ALTERS is the Tomlinson Chair in Science Education at McGill University and also holds an appointment at Harvard University. Dr. Alters was one of five expert witnesses in the largest, most important, and highest profile trial on science education in the past quarter-century — *Kitzmiller, et al. v. Dover Area School District, et al.*, and his testimony was cited twenty times in the decision. This US federal case concerned science education, the nature of science, evolution and intelligent design creationism. Alters's work has been reported worldwide in thousands of journals and media outlets, including *Nature*, ABC, CNN, CBC, MSNBC, Associated Press, the *New York Times*, *Scientific American*, MTV, and a cover story in *Rolling Stone*. Along with producing five books in the past seven years on biology, evolution, religion, and education, Dr. Alters is founder and director of the Evolution Education Research Center, a joint involvement between researchers in science and education at McGill and Harvard. Some of his books include *Biology: Understanding Life* (a university-level biology textbook), *Teaching Biology in Higher Education* (a teaching guide for instructors), and his "bestseller," *Defending Evolution in the Classroom* (with a foreword by Stephen Jay Gould). He recently won McGill University's highest teaching award, the President's Prize for Excellence in Teaching. This year, the CBC recruited Dr. Alters to host a series of prime-time nationally broadcast television shows titled Project X. The series is a science magazine show with the mandate to educate the public about science. It airs on CBC, BBC, and PBS stations and has already been seen by millions.

GARY BAUSLAUGH was editor of the Canadian magazine *Humanist Perspectives* from 2003 to 2008. He has a PhD in chemistry from McGill, taught for four years at Bishop's University, and taught and was an administrator for many years in the British Columbia post-secondary system, most recently as vice-president of Instruction and Planning at Malaspina University College in Nanaimo, BC. Following that, he was CEO of the Centre for Curriculum, Transfer and Technology in Victoria, BC. He has written many articles and papers, including about twenty op-ed articles for the *Vancouver Sun*.

MARY BURGAN, PhD (Illinois), Hon DLett (Marquette), is professor emerita of English, Indiana University-Bloomington. As a faculty member at Indiana University, Burgan served as chair of the English Department, associate dean of the College of Arts and Sciences, and elected leader of the IU-Bloomington and University Faculty Councils. From 1994 to 2004 she served as general secretary of the American Association of University Professors. Among her awards are Indiana University's Distinguished Service Award (1991), the Frances Andrew March Award for Distinguished Service to the Profession of English (awarded by the Association of Departments of English, 2003), and a residency at the Rockefeller Center in Bellagio, Italy (2003). In 1994, she published *Illness, Gender, and Writing: The Case of Katherine Mansfield* (Johns Hopkins University Press). In 2006, she published with the same press *What Ever Happened to the Faculty? Drift and Decision in Higher Education.*

JOANNA E. COHEN, BSc (McGill), MHSc (Toronto), PhD (North Carolina), is director of research and training at the Ontario Tobacco Research Unit; associate professor in the Dalla Lana School of Public Health Sciences at the University of Toronto; and associate scientist, Centre for Addiction and Mental Health, Toronto. Cohen just completed a five-year New Investigator Award from the Canadian Institutes of Health Research and has written extensively on tobacco policy, including papers on the links between tobacco companies and academia. She is a senior editor of *Tobacco Control*, an international journal published by the BMJ Group.

ROSEMARY DEEM, BA, MPhil (Leicester), Ph.D. (Open University), is professor of Education, research director for the Faculty of Social Sciences and Law, and director of strategic development, Graduate School of Education, University of Bristol. Deem taught at North

Staffordshire Polytechnic, Loughborough, York, and the Open and Lancaster universities before moving to Bristol in 2001. At Lancaster she served as head of the Department of Educational Research (1992–1994) and dean of Social Sciences (1994–1997), and was founding director of the University Graduate School (1998–2000). Deem co-authored *Knowledge, Higher Education and the New Managerialism: The Changing Management of UK Universities* (Oxford, 2007).

SHADIA B. DRURY, BA Hons, MA (Queen's, Canada), PhD (York, Canada), is Canada Research Chair in Social Justice, director of the masters program in Social and Political Thought, and professor in the departments of Political Science and Philosophy at the University of Regina. She is a fellow of the Royal Society of Canada. Drury has been a steadfast critic of the gurus of the neoconservatives (Leo Strauss, Allan Bloom, Alexandre Kojève, and Irving Kristol). She is author of *The Political Ideas of Leo Strauss* (updated ed., 2005), *Leo Strauss and the American Right* (1997), and *Alexandre Kojève: The Roots of Postmodern Politics* (1994). Her most recent books have focused on religion and politics. In *Terror and Civilization: Christianity, Politics, and the Western Psyche* (2004), she documents the deleterious influence of Christianity on Western thought, including the thought of Christianity's staunchest critics — Nietzsche and Freud. In *Aquinas and Modernity: The Lost Promise of Natural Law* (2008), she shows how Aquinas betrays the theory of natural law in favour of a politics of salvation, which threatens political order then as now.

BRENDA L. GALLIE, MD, FRCPC, is senior scientist, Division of Applied Molecular Oncology, Ontario Cancer Institute; affiliate scientist, Division of Visual Science, Toronto Western Research Institute; professor of Molecular Genetics, Medical Biophysics and Ophthalmology at the University of Toronto; and head of the Retinoblastoma Program at the Hospital for Sick Children in Toronto. Gallie is a world leader in the basic understanding and clinical application of knowledge of the prototype genetic cancer, retinoblastoma. Her work, for which she received the Distinguished Scientist Award of the Medical Research

Council, has spanned basic research to clinical application in health care. She led the development of a method for detecting gene mutations that enhances care for families with retinoblastoma. Her work to develop precise mutation identification for retinoblastoma families has spawned a new not-for-profit Canadian molecular diagnostics industry while developing the most sensitive and efficient test available. Gallie is vice-president of the Harry Crowe Foundation and a member of the board of directors.

DONALD GUTSTEIN, BArch, MArch (British Columbia), is senior lecturer in the School of Communication, Simon Fraser University, and co-director of NewsWatch Canada. Gutstein teaches in the areas of documentary research, journalism studies, propaganda analysis, and information policy. He writes about think tanks and media for various print and online publications and is author of the forthcoming *Not a Conspiracy Theory: How Business Uses Propaganda to Manipulate Us and What We Can Do About It* (to be published by Key Porter, March 2009).

MARCUS HARVEY, BA (Western), MA (Queens), PhD (Florida), is a professional officer with the Canadian Association of University Teachers. He previously staffed the west coast office of the American Association of University Professors in California and has spoken widely on academic freedom issues. Harvey trained as a historian. His dissertation examined the cultural significance of old age in the southern United States during the nineteenth century.

DAVID HEALY, MD (Dublin), FRCPsych, is professor of Psychological Medicine in Cardiff University, Wales. Healy studied in University College, Dublin, Ireland, and the University of Cambridge, England. He is former secretary of the British Association for Psychopharmacology, and author of over 150 peer-reviewed articles, over 200 other pieces, and 20 books, including *The Antidepressant Era* and *The Creation of Psychopharmacology* from Harvard University Press, *Let Them Eat Prozac* from Lorimer/New York University Press and *Mania* from Johns Hopkins University Press. He has been involved as an expert witness in homicide and suicide trials involving SSRI drugs, and in bringing these problems to the attention of American and British regulators. He has raised awareness of how pharmaceutical companies market drugs by marketing diseases and co-opt academic opinion leaders by ghost writing their articles.

MICHAEL W. HIGGINS is president and vice-chancellor of St. Thomas University, Fredericton, New Brunswick, where he is also a full professor of English and Religious Studies. He is past president of St. Jerome's University in Waterloo, Ontario, and the author and co-author of numerous books including *Thomas Merton: Pilgrim in Process, Women and the Church: A Sourcebook, Portraits of Canadian Catholicism, My Father's Business: The Biography of Gerald Emmett Cardinal Carter, The Jesuit Mystique, Heretic Blood: The Spiritual Geography of Thomas Merton, The Muted Voice: Religion and the Media,* and *Stalking the Holy: In Pursuit of Saint-Making.* Higgins has published many articles and reviews in such scholarly publications as *The American Benedictine Review, Cistercian Studies, Studies in Religion, Journal of American Studies,* and the *Thomas Merton Annual.* He also has a long career as a documentarist and writer for CBC Radio One's *Ideas,* as a scriptwriter for such programs as *Testament* and *Celebration,* and as a consultant and commentator for numerous radio and television series, including CBC's *Sunday Edition,* CTV's *Canada AM,* and TVOntario's *Studio 2.* He served as chief consultant for the six-hour Sir Peter Ustinov's *Inside the Vatican* television series and as a film consultant for *Mariette in Ecstasy* and CBC's *Man Alive.* He is a former columnist for the *Toronto Star* (1986–2006) and a regular contributor to both *The Globe and Mail* and the *Literary Review of Canada.* He sits on several national and international scholarly and administrative boards, served for twelve years as editor of the award-winning *Grail: an Ecumenical Journal,* is a contributor to the official blog of *Commonweal,* writes a monthly column for the *Catholic Register,* and has given numerous named university lecture series, including the Jordan, the Seton, and the Columbus. He has been appointed one of the twenty-five public intellectuals who constitute the "globe.salon" of *The Globe and Mail.*

SHELDON KRIMSKY, BSc (Brooklyn College, CUNY), MSc (Purdue), MPhil, PhD (Boston), is professor of Urban and Environmental Policy and adjunct professor of Public Health and Family Medicine at Tufts University. He is also a fellow of the American Association for the Advancement of Science and a fellow of the Hastings Center on Bioethics. Krimsky has served on the National Institutes of Health's Recombinant DNA Advisory Committee and as a consultant to both the Office of Technology Assessment and to the Presidential Commission for the Study of Ethical Problems in Medicine and Biomedical and Behavioral Research. He participated in the study panel for the American Civil Liberties Union that formulated a policy on civil liberties and scientific research. Krimsky chaired the Committee on Scientific Freedom and Responsibility for the American Association for the Advancement of Science for four years and serves on the board of directors for the Council for Responsible Genetics. In 2003 he published *Science in the Private Interest: Has the Lure of Profits Corrupted Biomedical Research?* Currently, Krimsky serves on the Committee A — Academic Freedom and Tenure — of the American Association of University Professors.

KEVIN MATTSON is Connor Study Professor of Contemporary History at Ohio University and serves as a faculty associate of the Contemporary History Institute. His work examines the intersection between politics and the world of ideas. He is author of *Rebels All! A Short History of the Conservative Mind in Postwar America* (forthcoming, 2008); *Upton Sinclair and the Other American Century* (2006); *When America Was Great: The Fighting Faith of Postwar Liberalism* (2004); *Engaging Youth: Combating the Apathy of Young Americans Towards Politics* (2003); *Intellectuals in Action: The Origins of the New Left and Radical Liberalism, 1945–1970* (2002); and *Creating a Democratic Public: The Struggle for Urban Participatory Democracy During the Progressive Era* (1998). Additionally, he is co-editor of *Liberalism for a New Century* (2007); *Steal This University! The Rise of the Corporate University and the Academic Labor Movement* (2003); and *Democracy's Moment* (2002). He has written essays on a variety of topics for the *New York Times Book*

Review, Washington Post Book World, the *Nation,* the *American Prospect, Common Review,* the *Baffler,* and *Chronicle Review.* He has also appeared on Fox News, German Television, PBS, and NPR. He is presently an affiliated scholar at the Center for American Progress (based in Washington, DC), active in the American Association of University Professors, and on the editorial board of *Dissent* magazine.

HOWARD PAWLEY is an associate professor emeritus at the University of Windsor. From 1993 to 1998 he held the Paul Martin Chair in International Relations and Law and was an associate professor at the University of Windsor from 1990 to 2000. Since then he has been a Stanley Knowles Professor at the University of Waterloo (Fall 2000) and served in both 2001 and 2003 as a visiting professor in Canadian Studies at the Henry Jackson School of International Relations at the University of Washington. Prior to his academic career, he served for nineteen years as a member of the Manitoba Legislature (1969–1988). During that time, he was attorney general (1973–1977) and the minister responsible for the introduction of the Manitoba public auto insurance system. Subsequently, he served as premier of Manitoba (1981–1988). Pawley is a vice-president of the Canadian Civil Liberties Association; executive member of the Public Interest Advocacy Centre, president of the Harry Crowe Foundation, vice-chair of the National Panel of the Canadian Broadcast Standards Council and a patron of the Douglas Coldwell Foundation. He was appointed a Queen's Counsel in 1974, a Privy Councillor by her Majesty Queen Elizabeth II in 1982, Officer of the Order of Manitoba in 2000, Officer of the Order of Canada in 2001, and University of Windsor Social Justice Person of the Year for 2003. Pawley was awarded the Cesar Chavez Black Eagle Award in 2001. He also received a Manitoba Historical Society Award in 2004. He received with his wife, Adele, the Lucile Ono Award in Manitoba in 2005.

ARTHUR SCHAFER, BLitt (Oxford), is professor of philosophy and director of the Centre for Professional and Applied Ethics, University of Manitoba. He is also an ethics consultant for the Department of

Pediatrics and Child Health at the Health Sciences Centre in Winnipeg. He has been a Canadian Commonwealth Scholar, Honorary Woodrow Wilson Scholar, and Canada Council fellow. Schafer has published widely in the fields of moral, social, and political philosophy. He served for a decade as head of the Section of Bio-Medical Ethics in the Faculty of Medicine of the University of Manitoba, and was Visiting Scholar, Green College, Oxford.

BLAIR STONECHILD, BA (McGill), MA, PhD (Regina), is professor of Indigenous Studies, First Nations University of Canada. Stonechild's *Loyal Till Death: Indians and the North-West Rebellion* won the Saskatchewan Book Award and was a finalist for the 1997 Governor General's Literary Award. His most recent book, *The New Buffalo: The Struggle for Aboriginal Post-secondary Education in Canada*, was published by the University of Manitoba Press in 2006.

JON H. THOMPSON is professor emeritus in the Department of Mathematics and Statistics, University of New Brunswick. He chaired the Academic Freedom and Tenure Committee of the Canadian Association of University Teachers from 1985 to 1988. He has been involved in the investigation and resolution of disputes at universities across Canada during the past two decades. He was a member of the Independent Committee of Inquiry into Academic and Scientific Integrity appointed by the board of governors of Concordia University in 1993–1994. He chaired the Independent Committee of Inquiry appointed by CAUT in 1999–2001 whose report led to a resolution of the academic freedom case of Nancy Olivieri at the University of Toronto. In 1993, he received the James B. Milner Memorial Award for contributions to academic freedom.

JAMES L. TURK, BA (Harvard), MA (UC Berkeley), Ph.D. (Toronto), is the executive director of the Canadian Association of University Teachers. Prior to joining CAUT, he was an associate professor of sociology at the University of Toronto, specializing in Canadian Studies, and was director of the Labour Studies Program at University College.

He has also been director of education for the Ontario Federation of Labour. His most recent book, co-edited with Allan Manson, is *Free Speech in Fearful Times: After 9/11 in Canada, the U.S., Australia and Europe*. Turk is a member of the executive and of the board of directors of the Canadian Centre for Policy Alternatives.

PATRICK WALDEN is a research scientist at the TRIUMF cyclotron laboratory in Vancouver, British Columbia. He is currently engaged in running experiments on nuclear astrophysics at TRIUMF's radioactive beam facility, ISAC, studying nuclear reactions pertinent to the stellar nucleosynthesis of the chemical elements of the universe. Orthogonally to his research, he serves as a trustee on the University of British Columbia faculty pension plan board. He has many outside interests, one of which is defending evolution. He has written considerably on the Social Sciences and Humanities Research Council incident, much of which was published in the magazine *Humanist Perspectives*. Dr. Walden received his PhD at Caltech in the field of particle physics in 1972. He worked at the Stanford Linear Accelerator Center (SLAC) in a post-doc position before taking a research position at TRIUMF in 1974.

NOTES

INTRODUCTION

1   Robin S. Harris, *A History of Higher Education in Canada, 1663–1960* (Toronto: University of Toronto Press, 1976), 27.

2   Johann Gottlieb Fichte, the first vice-chancellor of Humboldt University, expressed one crucial aspect of the new German university, ". . . The University exists not to teach information but to inculcate the exercise of critical judgment." Translated by Bill Readings and quoted in Bill Readings, *The University in Ruins* (Cambridge: Harvard University Press, 1996), 6.

3   Harold T. Shapiro, *A Larger Sense of Purpose: Higher Education and Society* (Princeton: Princeton University Press, 2005), 72.

4   The distinctive characteristics of Canadian universities noted by Harris are the existence of general and honours degrees, inclusion of professional courses in the arts and science curriculum, the lack of a American junior college system to provide the first two years of a university degree, and the involvement of almost all small universities in some aspects of professional education (594–7). Harris does note that by 1960 graduate studies in Canada closely resembled the American practice, albeit the development of PhD programs and the pace and range of programs lagged by about twenty years because of Canadian universities not being given similar financial resources (599).

5   The importance of institutional autonomy and academic freedom was affirmed by the overwhelming majority of countries in the world when the 1997 General Conference of the United Nations Educational, Scientific and Cultural Organization (UNESCO) adopted the "Recommendation concerning the Status of Higher Education Teaching Personnel," http://unesdoc.unesco.org/images/0011/001102/110220e.pdf#page=32.

6   Lawrence J. Soley, *Leasing the Ivory Tower: The Corporate Takeover of Academia* (Boston: South End Press, 1995), 145.

7   Jennifer Washburn, University Inc.: *The Corporate Corruption of American Higher Education* (New York: Basic Books, 2005), ix.

8   Derek Bok, *Universities in the Marketplace: The Commercialization of Higher Education* (Princeton: Princeton University Press, 2003).

9   Janice Newson and Howard Buchbinder, *The University Means Business: Universities, Corporations and Academic Work* (Toronto: Garamond Press, 1988). See also James L. Turk ed., *The Corporate Campus: Commercialization and the Dangers to Canada's Colleges and Universities* (Toronto: James Lorimer, 2000).

10   Karl Marx and Friedrich Engels, *The German Ideology*, quoted in Clyde W. Barrow, *Universities and the Capitalist State: Corporate Liberalism and the Reconstruction of American Higher Education, 1894–1928* (Madison: University of Wisconsin Press, 1990), 13.

11   Barrow, *Universities and the Capitalist State*, 14.

12   Thorsten Veblen, *The Higher Learning in America* (New York: Sagamore Press, 1957; originally published 1918), 165.

13   Theodore Roszak, "On Academic Delinquency" in Theodore Roszak, ed., *The Dissenting Academy* (New York: Vintage Books, 1968), 4.

14   University of Toronto, "Purpose of the University," http://www.utoronto.ca/aboutuoft/missionandpurpose.htm.

15   See, for example, Scott Jaschik, "New Plan to Limit Tobacco-Funded Research," *Inside Higher Education*, September 18, 2007, http://www.insidehighered.com/news/2007/09/18/tobacco.

16   See Jon Thompson, Patricia Baird, and Jocelyn Downie, *The Olivieri Report* (Toronto: James Lorimer, 2001); A.M. Viens and J. Savulescu, eds., "The Olivieri Symposium," Special Issue of the *Journal of Medical Ethics* 30, no. 1 (February 2004). Olivieri's story helped inspired John Le Carré's *The Constant Gardener*.

17   http://www.discovery.org/.

18   http://www.discovery.org/fellows/.

19   See Horowtiz's *The Professors: The 101 Most Dangerous Academics in America* (Washington: Regnery, 2006); the David Horowitz Freedom Center Web site http://www.horowitzfreedomcenter.org/ and the ACTA Web site http://www.goacta.org/.

20   H.W. Arthurs, Roger A. Blais, and Jon Thompson, Integrity in Scholarship: A Report to Concordia University by the Independent Committee of Inquiry into Academic and Scientific Integrity, April, 1994, 4, http://archives3.concordia.ca/timeline/histories/Arthurs_report.pdf.

21   Ibid., 5–8. Jon Thompson discusses key aspects of the Fabrikant case on pages 312-314 in the final article in this volume.

CHAPTER 1: PRINCIPLES AND INTEREST: IS THE ACADEMY AN ACCOMPLICE IN A CORPORATE-CAUSED PANDEMIC?

22   R. Peto, A. Lopez, J. Boreham, et al., *Mortality from Smoking in Developed Countries, 1950–2000* (Oxford: Oxford University Press, 1994).

23   Canadian Tobacco Use Monitoring Survey (CTUMS), *Trends in Smoking, 1999* (Ottawa: Health Canada, 1999), http://www.hc-sc.gc.ca/hl-vs/tobac-tabac/research-recherche/stat/_ctums-esutc_fs-if/1999-trends_e.html.

24   Canadian Tobacco Use Monitoring Survey (CTUMS), *Results for 2005* (Ottawa: Health Canada, 2005, http://www.hc-sc.gc.ca/hl-vs/tobac-tabac/research-recherche/stat/ctums-esutc_2005_e.html.

25   Canadian Tobacco Use Monitoring Survey (CTUMS) *Result Highlights* (Ottawa: Health Canada, 2007, http://www.hc-sc.gc.ca/hl-vs/tobac-tabac/research-recherche/stat/ctums-esutc_2007_e.html.

26   J. Rehm, W. Gnam, S. Popova, D. Baliunas, S. Brochu, B. Fischer, et al., "The
      Costs of Alcohol, Illegal Drugs, and Tobacco in Canada, 2002," *Journal of
      Studies on Alcohol and Drugs* 68 (2007): 886–95.

27   J. Mackay, M. Erikson, and O. Shafey. *The Tobacco Atlas*, 2nd ed. (Atlanta:
      American Cancer Society, 2006).

28   C. Orleans and J. Slade, *Nicotine Addiction: Principles and Management* (New
      York: Oxford University Press, 1993).

29   Tobacco Control Legal Consortium, *The Verdict Is In: Findings from United States
      v. Philip Morris, Suppression of Information* (St. Paul: Tobacco Control Legal
      Consortium, 2006), http://www.tobaccolawcenter.org/resources/
      theverdictisin.pdf.

30   Tobacco companies were being sued by the states to recover health care costs
      related to tobacco use. The companies felt it was in their financial interests to
      settle for $250 billion and to release all their internal documents; by settling
      under these conditions they implicitly acknowledged that the result of the law-
      suit would have been much worse for them if they had proceeded to judgment.

31   N. Francey and S. Chapman. "Operation Berkshire: The International Tobacco
      Companies' Conspiracy," *British Medical Journal* 321 (2000): 371–4; S.A. Glantz, J.
      Slade, L.A. Bero, P. Hanauer, D.E. Barnes, eds. *The Cigarette Papers* (Berkeley:
      University of California Press, 1996); N. Hirschhorn, "Shameful Science: Four
      Decades of the German Tobacco Industry's Hidden Research on Smoking and
      Health," *Tobacco Control* 9 (2000): 242–8; E. Smith, "It's Interesting How Few
      People Die from Smoking: Tobacco Industry Efforts to Minimize Risk and
      Discredit Health Promotion," *European Journal of Public Health* 17 (2007): 162–70.

32   D. Barnes and L. Bero, "Why Review Articles on the Health Effects of Passive
      Smoking Reach Different Conclusions," *Journal of the American Medical
      Association* 279 (1998): 1566–70; J. Barnoya and S. Glantz, "Tobacco Industry
      Success in Preventing Regulation of Secondhand Smoke in Latin America: The
      'Latin Project,'" *Tobacco Control* 11 (2002): 305–14; J. Barnoya and S.A. Glantz,
      "The Tobacco Industry's Worldwide ETS Consultants Project: European and
      Asian Components," *European Journal of Public Health* 16 (2006): 69–77; A.
      Bornhauser, J. McCarthy, and S.A. Glantz, "German Tobacco Industry's
      Successful Efforts to Maintain Scientific and Political Respectability to Prevent
      Regulation of Secondhand Smoke," *Tobacco Control* 15 (2006): e1; J. Drope and
      S. Chapman, "Tobacco Industry Efforts at Discrediting Scientific Knowledge of
      Environmental Tobacco Smoke: A Review of Internal Industry Documents,"
      Journal of Epidemiology and Community Health 55 (2001): 588–94; D. Garne, M.
      Watson, S. Chapman, and F. Byrne, "Environmental Tobacco Smoke Research
      Published in the Journal Indoor and Built Environment and Associations with
      the Tobacco Industry," *The Lancet* 365 (2005): 80–89; L.L. Mandel and S.A.
      Glantz, "Hedging Their Bets: Tobacco and Gambling Industries Work Against
      Smoke-Free Policies," *Tobacco Control* 13 (2004): 268–76; M.E. Muggli, J.L.
      Forster, R.D. Hurt, and J.L. Repace, "The Smoke You Don't See: Uncovering
      Tobacco Industry Scientific Strategies Aimed Against Environmental Tobacco
      Smoke Policies," *American Journal of Public Health* 91 (2001): 141–23; M.E.
      Muggli, R.D. Hurt, and D.D. Blanke, "Science for Hire: A Tobacco Industry
      Strategy to Influence Public Opinion on Secondhand Smoke," *Nicotine &*

Tobacco Research 5 (2003): 303–14; M.E. Muggli, R.D. Hurt, and L.B. Becker, "Turning Free Speech into Corporate Speech: Philip Morris' Efforts to Influence U.S. and European Journalists Regarding the U.S. EPA Report on Secondhand Smoke," *Preventive Medicine* 39 (2004): 68–80; M.E. Muggli, R.D. Hurt, and J. Repace, "The Tobacco Industry's Political Efforts to Derail the EPA Report on ETS, *American Journal of Preventive Medicine* 26 (2004): 167–77; E.K. Ong and S.A. Glantz, "Tobacco Industry Efforts Subverting International Agency for Research on Cancer's Second-Hand Smoke Study," *The Lancet* 355 (2000): 1253–9; J.M. Samet and T.A. Burke, "Turning Science into Junk: The Tobacco Industry and Passive Smoking," *American Journal of Public Health* 91 (2001): 1742–4; E.K. Tong, L. England, and S.A. Glantz, "Changing Conclusions on Secondhand Smoke in a Sudden Infant Death Syndrome Review Funded by the Tobacco Industry," *Pediatrics* 115 (2005): e356–66; E. Yano, "Japanese Spousal Smoking Study Revisited: How a Tobacco Industry Funded Paper Reached Erroneous Conclusions," *Tobacco Control* 14 (2005): 227–33.

33 B.C. Alamar and S.A. Glantz, "The Tobacco Industry's Use of Wall Street Analysts in Shaping Policy," *Tobacco Control* 12 (2004): 223–7; S. Chapman and A. Penman, "Can't Stop the Boy: Philip Morris' Use of Healthy Buildings International to Prevent Workplace Smoking Bans in Australia," *Tobacco Control* 12, Suppl. 3 (2003): 107–12; D. Michaels, C. Monforton, "Manufacturing Uncertainty: Contested Science and the Protection of the Public's Health and Environment," *American Journal of Public Health* 95, Suppl. 1 (2005): S39–48; Y. Saloojee and E. Dagli, "Tobacco Industry Tactics for Resisting Public Policy on Health," *Bulletin of the World Health Organization* 78 (2000): 902–10; M. Scollo, A. Lal, A. Hyland, and S.A. Glantz, "Review of the Quality of Studies on the Economic Effects of Smoke-Free Policies on the Hospitality Industry," *Tobacco Control* 12 (2003): 13–20; E.M. Sebrie, S.A. Glantz, "Attempts to Undermine Tobacco Control: Tobacco Industry 'Youth Smoking Prevention' Programs to Undermine Meaningful Tobacco Control in Latin America," *American Journal of Public Health* 97 (2007): 1357–67; T. Szilagyi and S. Chapman, "Tobacco Industry Efforts to Erode Tobacco Advertising Controls in Hungary," *Central European Journal of Public Health* 11 (2003): 223–8.

34 P.A. McDaniel, E.A. Smith, and R.E. Malone, "Philip Morris's Project Sunrise: Weakening Tobacco Control by Working with It," *Tobacco Control* 15 (2006): 215–23; P.A. McDaniel, G. Intinarelli, R.E. Malone, "Tobacco Industry Issues Management Organizations: Creating a Global Corporate Network to Undermine Public Health," *Global Health* 4 (2008): 2; M.E. Muggli and R.D. Hurt, "Tobacco Industry Strategies to Undermine the 8th World Conference on Tobacco OR Health," *Tobacco Control* 12 (2003): 195–202; E.M. Sebrie, S.A. Glantz, "Attempts to Undermine Tobacco Control: Tobacco Industry 'Youth Smoking Prevention' Programs to Undermine Meaningful Tobacco Control in Latin America," *American Journal of Public Health* 97 (2007): 1357–67; E.L. Sweda, Jr., and R.A. Daynard, "Tobacco Industry Tactics," *British Medical Bulletin* 52 (1996): 183–92.

35 L. Bero, D. Barnes, P. Hanauer, J. Slade, and S.A. Glantz, "Lawyer Control of the Tobacco Industry's External Research Program: The Brown and Williamson Documents," *Journal of the American Medical Association* 27 (1995): 241–7; L.C. Friedman, R.A. Daynard and C.N. Banthin, "How Tobacco-Friendly Science Escapes Scrutiny in the Courtroom," *American Journal of Public Health* 95, Suppl.

1 (2005): S16–20; L. Hardell, M.J. Walker, B. Walhjalt, L.S. Friedman, and E.D. Richter, "Secret Ties to Industry and Conflicting Interests in Cancer Research," *American Journal of Industrial Medicine* 50 (2007): 227–33; Erratum in: *American Journal of Industrial Medicine* 50 (2007): 234; N. Hirschhorn, S.A. Bialous, and S. Shatenstein, "The Philip Morris External Research Program: Results from the First Round of Projects," *Tobacco Control* 15 (2006): 267–9; E.K. Ong and S.A. Glantz, "Constructing 'Sound Science' and 'Good Epidemiology': Tobacco, Lawyers, and Public Relations Firms," *American Journal of Public Health* 91 (2001): 1749–57.

36   Ong & Glantz, "Tobacco Industry Efforts," 1253–9 (see note 11).

37   World Health Organization, *Tobacco Industry Strategies to Undermine Tobacco Control Activities at the World Health Organization*, Report of the Committee of Experts on Tobacco Industry Documents, July 2000, http://www.who.int/tobacco/en/who_inquiry.pdf.

38   Ibid., 18.

39   R. Taylor and A. Rieger, "Medicine as Social Science: Rudolf Virchow on the Typhus Epidemic in Upper Silesia," *International Journal of Health Services* 15 no. 4 (1985): 547–59.

40   Ibid.

41   Michael Prideaux, "Meeting Reasonable Public Expectations of a Responsible Tobacco Company," June 21, 2000. Bates: 325049576-325049595, http://tobaccodocuments.org/batco/325049576-9595.html.

42   J.E. Cohen, M.J. Ashley, A.O. Goldstein, R. Ferrence, and J.M. Brewster, "Institutional Addiction to Tobacco," *Tobacco Control* 8, no. 1 (1999): 70–4.

43   H. Waxman, Issues and Legislation: Health — Tobacco, http://www.house.gov/waxman/issues/health/tobacco_leg.htm.

44   S. Boyse, Note On a Special Meeting of the UK Industry on Environmental Tobacco Smoke, London, February 17, 1988. British American Tobacco Company, Bates No. 2063791181/1187, http://legacy.library.ucsf.edu/tid/kur45d00.

45   A. J. Gardiner B.A. Forey, and P.N. Lee, "Avian Exposure and Bronchogenic Carcinoma," *British Medical Journal* 305, no. 6860 (1992): 989–92; P.A. Holst, D. Kromhout, R. Brand, "For Debate: Pet Birds As an Independent Risk Factor for Lung Cancer," *British Medical Journal* 297, no. 6659 (1988): 1319–21; L. Kohlmeier, G. Arminger, S. Bartolomeycik, B. Bellach, J. Rehm, and M. Thamm, "Pet Birds as an Independent Risk Factor for Lung Cancer: Case-control Study," *British Medical Journal* 305, 6860 (1992): 986–9.

46   A. Zivojinovic, "Tobacco Donation Makes a Stink in Corporate Ethics Program," *The* (University of Toronto) *Varsity*, November 28, 2002.

47   John Ralston Saul, "Corporatization of Academia" (2007 C.B. Macpherson Lecture, University of Toronto, Toronto, ON, November 1, 2007).

48   P.E. Kaufman, J.E. Cohen, M.J. Ashley, R. Ferrence, A.L. Halyk, F. Turcotte, et al.,

"Tobacco Industry Links to Faculties of Medicine in Canada," *Canadian Journal of Public Health* 95 (2004): 205–8.

49 S. Glantz, S. Bialous, K. Homer Vagadori. Campaign to Defend Academic Integrity: Universities That Prohibit or Limit Tobacco Industry Funding of Research, http://academic-integrity.com/_wsn/page6.html.

50 G.W. Gau. Why Mccombs Ultimately Said No to Tobacco Money, February 11, 2008, http://www.mccombs.utexas.edu/news/pressreleases/gau_tobacco.asp.

51 Cohen et al., "Institutional Addiction to Tobacco."

52 These journals are the *American Journal of Respiratory and Critical Care Medicine*, the *American Journal of Respiratory Cell and Molecular Biology* and the *Journal of Health Psychology*. See J. Cohen, "Tobacco Money Lights Up a Debate," *Science* 272 (1996): 488–94 and D. Marks, "A Higher Principle Is at Stake Than Simply Freedom of Speech," *British Medical Journal* 312 (1996): 773–4.

53 N. Wander and R.E. Malone, "Selling Off or Selling Out? Medical Schools and Ethical Leadership in Tobacco Stock Divestment," *Academic Medicine* 79 (2004): 1017–26.

54 Barnes & Bero, "Why Review Articles" (see note 11).

55 Cohen et al., "Institutional Addiction to Tobacco."

56 Prof. J. Corbett McDonald to Dr. Dunn, Imperial Tobacco Ltd., October 28, 1988, http://tobaccodocuments.org/mayo_clinic/81000086.html. See full text of the letter in this chapter.

57 G. Harris, "Cigarette Company Paid for Lung Cancer Study," *New York Times*, March 26, 2008, http://www.nytimes.com/2008/03/26/health/research/26lung.html?_r=1&hp=&pagewanted=all.

58 Academic Freedoms / Ethics in Science, May 1998 (est.). Bates: 2078745608-2078745610, http://tobaccodocuments.org/pm/2078745608-5610.html.

59 E.g., S. Chapman, "Tobacco Funding of Academics: Buying Respectability," *British Medical Journal* 312 (1996): 1098–9; S. Chapman and S. Shatenstein, "The Ethics of the Cash Register: Taking Tobacco Research Dollars," *Tobacco Control* 10 (2001): 1–2; J.E. Cohen, "Universities and Tobacco Money: Some Universities are Accomplices in the Tobacco Epidemic," editorial, *British Medical Journal* 323, no. 7303 (2001): 1–2; R.E. Malone and L.A. Bero, "Chasing the Dollar: Why Scientists Should Decline Tobacco Industry Funding," *Journal of Epidemiology and Community Health* 57 (2003): 546–8; M. Parascandola, "Hazardous Effects of Tobacco Industry Funding," *Journal of Epidemiology and Community Health* 57 (2003): 548–9.

CHAPTER 2: THE UNIVERSITY AS CORPORATE HANDMAIDEN: WHO'RE YA GONNA TRUST?

60 Arthur Schafer, "Biomedical Conflicts of Interest: A Defence of the Sequestration Thesis — Learning from the Cases of Nancy Olivieri and David Healy," *Journal*

of Medical Ethics 30, no. 1 (2004): 8–24.

61   Its impact factor, at 44, is almost double that of its nearest rival. See: R. Smith, "Lapses at the New England Journal of Medicine," *Journal of the Royal Society of Medicine. Editorial* 99 (August 2006).

62   C. Bombardier, L. Laine, A. Reicin, et al., "Comparison of Upper Gastrointestinal Toxicity of Rofecoxib and Naproxen in Patients with Rheumatoid Arthritis," *NEJM* 343 (November 23, 2000): 1520–1528.

63   F. Silverstein, G. Faich, J. Goldstein, et al., "Gastrointestinal Toxicity with Celecoxib Vs. Nonsteroidal Anti-Inflammatory Drugs for Osteoarthritis and Rheumatoid Arthritis, the CLASS Study: a Randomized Controlled Trial," *JAMA* 284 (2000): 1247–1255.

64   J.R. Lisse, M. Perlman, G. Johansson, et al., "Gastrointestinal Tolerability and Effectiveness of Rofecoxib versus Naproxen in the Treatment of Osteoarthritis, the ADVANTAGE Study: A Randomized, Controlled Trial," *Annals of Internal Medicine* 139 (2003): 539–564.

65   More than 25 million Americans took Vioxx between 1998 and 2004. The number taking Celebrex was comparably vast. Canadian doctors prescribed these drugs at a rate similar to their American colleagues. See A. Berenson, "Evidence in Vioxx Suits Shows Intervention by Merck Officials," *New York Times*, April 24, 2005.

66   At least 4,600 people or their survivors are suing Merck. See: Berenson, "Evidence in Vioxx Suits." These suits allege death and other damage from the drug. The company does not concede that its drug caused such harm and it has adopted the position of fighting every lawsuit.

67   S. Okie, "Missing Data on Celebrex," *Washington Post*, September 10, 2001.

68   Ibid.

69   http://www.nytimes.com/2004/12/19/business/19drug.html?ei=5094.

70   Ibid.

71   As described by Candis McLean in *Report* magazine, March 19, 2001.

72   See an excellent discussion of the cardiovascular risks posed by Vioxx in Chapter 3 of John Abramson, *Overdosed America: The Broken Promise of American Medicine* (New York: Harper Collins, 2004). Abramson also points out that the subjects of the VIGOR trial were quite unrepresentative of the majority of people for whom doctors prescribed Vioxx. More than half the subjects in the trial were on steroids. This little-noticed fact is of great importance because the study shows significant reductions in risk of serious GI complications only in those patients who were on steroids. For the others, i.e., most of the people who ended up taking Vioxx, there was no statistically significant reduction of GI complications.

73   D. Armstrong, "Bitter Pill: How the New England Journal Missed Warning Signs on Vioxx," *Wall Street Journal*, May 15, 2006, A1. See also: Smith, "Lapses at New England Journal of Medicine" and G.D. Curfman, S. Morrissey, and J.M. Drazen, "Expression of Concern Reaffirmed," *New England Journal of Medicine* 353 (2005): 2813–14.

74   See note 14.

75   Abramson, *Overdosed America*.

76   Theoretically, the ADVANTAGE trial was meant to show that Vioxx caused fewer stomach problems than naproxen, but this had already been demonstrated by the VIGOR study, which had a much larger number of subjects. Dr. Edward M. Scolnick, top Merck scientist between 1985 and 2002, admitted as much in an internal company memo: "Small marketing studies which are intellectually redundant are extremely dangerous," he wrote. See Berenson, "Evidence in Vioxx Suits."

77   See note 17.

78   See note 17.

79   Merck bought 900,000 reprints of the article to use in marketing Vioxx, more than one for every doctor in America. The revenue to the *NEJM* is estimated to be in the range of three quarters of a million dollars. See Smith, "Lapses at the New England Journal."

80   If either the data suppression or the scientifically skewed interpretations were done deliberately, intentionally, or knowingly, then the scientists involved could be seen as corrupt. If these problems arose because of an unconscious desire to please commercial sponsors, then a charge of corruption might not stick. Instead, the researchers would be guilty of unprofessional conduct for allowing themselves to be in the kind of conflict-of-interest situation that tends to undermine research integrity. The conflicts of interest inherent in corporate sponsorship of academic research are now so pervasive that many now regard them as professionally acceptable because unavoidable and because "everyone is doing it."

81   J. Lexchin, K.A. Bero, and B. Djulbegovic, "Pharmaceutical Industry Sponsorship and Research Outcome and Quality: Systematic Review," *British Medical Journal* 326 (2003): 1167–74.

82   I. Kant, "Idea for a Universal History from a Cosmological Perspective" in ed. Pauline Kleingeld, *"Toward Perpetual Peace" and other Writings on Politics, Peace and History* (New Haven: Yale University Press, 2006). Akad. Ed. 8, no. 23: 9.

83   J. Benda, *La Trahison des Clercs* (Paris: Editions de la Nouvelle Revue Francaise, 1928).

84   D. Healy, *Let Them Eat Prozac* (Toronto: James Lorimer, 2003).

85   For a fuller discussion, see Schafer, "Biomedical Conflicts of Interest."

86   E.g., much of the research being done on genetically modified crops is funded by petro-chemical companies, such as Monsanto and Bayer. See A. McIlroy, "Under Siege in the Ivory Tower," *Globe and Mail*, September 8, 2001, for an interview with Professor Ann Clark of Guelph University. Clark describes how fearful her colleagues are, across Canada, when it comes to speaking publicly about genetically modified organisms (GMOs). What they fear, according to Clark, is that their research will lose its funding — in effect, that they will be blackballed by industry. Worse, says Clark, they also fear harassment from their

own universities. Clark then describes her own experiences of serious harassment by Guelph University after she established a Web site critical of GMOs.

87   See, e.g., S. Shulman, *Undermining Science: Suppression and Distortion in the Bush Administration* (Los Angeles: University of California Press, 2006).

88   B. Adeba, "The Politics of Security Studies in Canada: A Look Behind the Centres Studying War and Defence at Canadian Universities, Where They Get Their Funding and Their Political Biases," *Embassy*, February 21, 2007, 20, http://www.embassymag.ca/reports/2007/022107_em.pdf.

89   See, e.g., S. Krimsky, *Science in the Private Interest* (New York: Roman and Littlefield, 2003); M. Mahar, *Money-Driven Medicine* (New York: Collins, 2006); D. Bok, *Universities in the Marketplace* (Princeton, NJ: NP, 2003); M. Angell, *The Truth About the Drug Companies* (New York: Random House, 2004).

90   R.K. Merton, *The Sociology of Science* (Chicago: University of Chicago Press, 1973).

91   See Krimsky, *Science in the Private Interest*; Schafer, "Biomedical Conflicts of Interest."

92   Lexchin et al., "Pharmaceutical Industry Sponsorship," 1169.

93   M. Davis, "Conflict of Interest," *Business and Professional Ethics Journal* 1 (1982): 17–27.

94   J. Dana and G. Lowenstein, "A Social Science Perspective on Gifts to Physicians from Industry," *JAMA* 290 (2003): 252.

95   H.T. Stelfox, G. Chua, K. O'Rourke, et al., "Conflict of interest in the debate over calcium-channel antagonists," *New England Journal of Medicine* 338 (1998): 101–6.

96   See, e.g., J.E. Beckelman, Y. Li, and C.P. Gross, "Scope and Impact of Financial Conflicts of Interest in Biomedical Research, *JAMA* 289 (2003): 454–65.

97   Lexchin et al., "Pharmaceutical Industry Sponsorship."

98   Dana and Lowenstein, "Social Science Perspective on Gifts."

99   See, e.g., M. Angell, *The Truth About The Drug Companies* (New York: Random House, 2004); S. Krimsky, *Science in the Private Interest* (Lanham, MD: Rowman and Littlefield, 2003); J.P. Kassirer, *On the Take* (Oxford: Oxford University Press, 2003); and J. Abramson, *Overdosed America*.

100   Angell, op. cit.

101   Arthur Daemmrich, *Pharmacopolitics: Drug Regulation in the US and Germany* (Chapel Hill, NC: University of North Carolina Press, 2004), cited by Philip Mirowski, "Johnny's in the Basement, Mixin' Up the Medicine: Review of Angell, Avorn, and Daemmrich on the Modern Pharmaceutical Predicament," *Social Studies of Science* 37 (2007): 311.

102   For a range of possible answers to the question "From where will the vast sums of money needed to fund research come?" see Schafer, *Biomedical conflicts of interest*, 22–4.

CHAPTER 3: WHEN SPONSORED RESEARCH FAILS THE ADMISSIONS TEST: A NORMATIVE FRAMEWORK

103   The author wishes to thank Carlos Sonnenschein, Charles Weiner, L.S. Rothenberg, and Kristin-Shrader Frechette for their comments on earlier drafts of this chapter.

104   Sheldon Krimsky, "The Transformation of the American University," *Alternatives* 14 (May/June 1987): 20–9; Sheldon Krimsky, "University Entrepreneurship and Public Purpose," in *Biotechnology: Professional Issues and Social Concerns*, ed. D. DeForest et al, (Washington DC: American Association for the Advancement of Science, 1988); Sheldon Krimsky, "Science and Wall Street," chapter 4 in *Biotechnics and Society*, 64–5 (New York: Praeger, 1991).

105   National Council of University Research Administrators (NCURA) and the Industrial Research Institute, Guiding Principles for University-Industry Endeavors, April 2006, http://www7.nationalacademies.org/guirr/Guiding_Principles.pdf.

106   Sen. John Cornyn (R-TX) and Sen. Joseph Lieberman (D-CT) introduced the *Federal Research Public Access Act of 2006*, S. 2695, which requires federal agencies that fund over $100 million in annual external research to make electronic manuscripts of peer-reviewed journal articles stemming from their research publicly available via the Internet within six months of publication.

107   David B. Resnik, "Industry-sponsored Research: Secrecy Versus Corporate Responsibility," *Business and Society Review* 99 (1999): 32.

108   Krimsky, *Biotechnics and Society*, 38.

109   Drummond Rennie, "Thyroid Storm," *Journal of the American Medical Association*, 277 (April 16, 1997): 1238–43.

110   Henry Miller, "Score 2 for Academic Freedom," *Chronicle of Higher Education* 54 (October 2, 2007): 107.

111   Resnik, "Industry-sponsored Research," 31.

112   Stephanie Saul, "Merck Wrote Drug Studies for Doctors," *New York Times*, April 10, 2008.

113   Edward S. Herman and Robert J. Rutman, "University of Pennsylvania's CB Warfare Controversy," *BioScience* 17, no. 8 (August 1967): 526–9.

114   Charles Weiner, unpublished research notes and personal communications.

115   Paul Thacker, "Vote Postponed on Tobacco Research Ban," *Inside Higher Education* (January 19, 2007).

116   T. Zeltner, D.A. Kessler, A. Martiny, F. Randera, *Tobacco Company Strategies to Undermine Tobacco Control Activities of the World Health Organization*, World Health Organization Report of the Committee of Experts on Tobacco Industry Documents. The International Agency for Research on Cancer (IARC), July 2000.

117   Ibid.

118   David Grimm, "Is Tobacco Research Turning over a New Leaf?" *Science* 307 (January 7, 2005): 37.

119   C. Turner and G.J. Spilich. "Research into Smoking or Nicotine and Human Cognitive Performance: Does the Source of Funding Make a Difference?" *Addiction* 92 (1997): 1423–6.

120   Gardiner Harris, "Cigarette Company Paid for Lung Cancer Study," *New York Times*, March 26, 2008.

121   Joan Wallach Scott, "Academic Freedom and Rejection of Research Funds from Tobacco Corporations," American Association of University Professors, Report of Committee A. 2002–3, *Academe* 89, no. 5 (September–October 2003), http://www.aaup.org/AAUP/comm/rep/A/2002-03Comm-A-report.htm.

122   Grimm, "Is Tobacco Research Turning," 36.

123   Donna Euben (staff council), American Association of University Professors, "Legal Issues in Academic Research," paper presented at the 13th Annual Conference on Legal Issues in Higher Education, October 6, 2003, http://www.aaup.org/AAUP/protect/legal/topics/researchissues.htm.

124   Alan Charles Kors and Harvey A. Silvergate, *The Shadow University: The Betrayal of Liberty on America's Campuses* (New York: The Free Press, 1998), 140.

125   Scott Glassman, "Pioneer Sparks Debate at Delaware," *Daily Pennsylvanian,* September 23, 1994.

126   The American Legacy Foundation states in its instructions under the Small Innovative Grants Program, "Legacy will not award a grant to any applicant that is in current receipt of any grant monies or in-kind contribution from any tobacco manufacturer, distributor, or other tobacco-related entity," http://www.americanlegacy.org/1710.aspx.

127   Resolution of the University of California's Academic Senate, in Grimm, "Is Tobacco Research Turning," 37.

128   Susan Wright, ed., *Preventing a Biological Arms Race* (Cambridge, MA: The MIT Press, 1991).

129   John W. Servos, "The Industrial Relations of Science: Chemical Engineering At MIT: 1900-1939," *ISIS* 71, no. 4 (December 1980): 547.

130   See http://workgroups.Clemson.edu.

131   Colin Macilwain, "Carbon Sequestration Gains Support," *Nature* 407 (October 26, 2000): 932.

132   Sylvia Wright, "Chevron Fuels $25 M Alternative Energy Endeavor," *Dateline UC Davis*, September 22, 2006.

133   Andrew C. Revkin, "Exxon-led Group Is Giving a Climate Grant to Stanford," *New York Times*, November 21, 2002.

134   Sheldon Krimsky, *Science in the Private Interest* (Lanham, MD: Rowman & Littlefield, 2003), 36.

135   Master Agreement between BP Technology Ventures Inc. and The Regents of the University of California, November 9, 2007, http://www.stopbp-berkeley. org/docs/FINAL_Execution_11-9.pdf.

136   Rick DelVecchio, "UC Faculty to Join Talks on Big BP Biofuels Deal," *San Francisco Chronicle*, March 31, 2007.

137   See http://www.stopbp-berkeley.org/corporate.html.

138   See http://EHP.niehs.nih.gov/cfi.pdf.

139   Scott, "Academic Freedom."

CHAPTER 4: COLLEGIALITY LOST

140   H.Z. Noorani, H.N.Khan, B.L. Gallie, A.S. Detsky, "Cost Comparison of Molecular versus Conventional Screening of Relatives at Risk for Retinoblastoma," *American Journal of Human Genetics* 59, no. 2 (1996): 301–7.

141   J. Thompson, P. Baird, J. Downie, *The Olivieri Report* (Toronto: James Lorimer, 2001).

142   N.F. Olivieri, G.M. Brittenham, C.E. McLaren, D.M. Templeton, R.G. Cameron, R.A. McClelland, et al., "Long-term Safety and Effectiveness of Iron-Chelation Therapy with Deferiprone for Thalassemia Major," *New England Journal of Medicine* 339, no. 7 (1998): 17–23.

143   A. Naimark, B. Knoppers, F. Lowy, "Clinical Trials of L1 (Deferiprone) at the Hospital for Sick Children: A Review of the Facts and Circumstances" (Toronto: Hospital for Sick Children, 1998).

144   Thompson et al., *The Olivieri Report*.

CHAPTER 5: ACADEMIC STALKING AND BRAND FASCISM

145   D. Healy, "The Psychopharmacological Era: Notes toward a History," *J Psychopharmacology* 4 (1990): 152–67; D. Healy, "The Marketing of 5HT: Anxiety or Depression," *British J Psychiatry* 158 (1991): 737–42.

146   D. Healy, *The Antidepressant Era* (Cambridge, MA: Harvard University Press, 1997).

147   W. Creaney, I. Murray, D. Healy, "Antidepressant Induced Suicidal Ideation," *Human Psychopharmacology* 6 (1991): 329–32; D. Healy, "The Fluoxetine and Suicide Controversy," *CNS Drugs* 1 (1994): 223–31; D. Healy, M. Savage, "Reserpine Exhumed," *British J Psychiatry* 172 (1998): 376–8; D. Healy, C. Langmaak, M. Savage, "Suicide in the Course of the Treatment of Depression," *J Psychopharmacology* 13 (1999): 94–9.

148   D. Healy, *Psychiatric Drugs Explained*, 5th ed. (Edinburgh: Churchill & Livingstone, 2008), originally published (London: Mosby Yearbooks, 1993).

149   D. Healy, *Let Them Eat Prozac* (Toronto: James Lorimer, 2003).

150   C. Elliott, introduction to *Prozac as a Way of Life*, ed. C. Elliott and T. Chambers (Durham, NC: Duke University Press, 2004). The original articles were P. Kramer, "The Valorization of Sadness: Alienation and Melancholic Temperament," *Hastings Center Report* 30 (2000): 13–19; C. Elliott, "Pursued by Happiness and Beaten Senseless: Prozac and the American Dream," *Hastings Center Report* 30 (2000): 7–12; D. DeGrazia, "Prozac, Enhancement and Self-creation," *Hastings Center Report* 30 (2000): 34–40; J.C. Edwards, "Passion, Activity and 'The Care of the Self,'" *Hastings Center Report* 30 (2000): 31–3; D. Healy, "Good Science or Good Business?" *Hastings Center Report* 30 (2000): 19–22.

151   Cited in C. Elliott (2004), introduction to *Prozac as a Way of Life*, ed. C. Elliott and T. Chambers (Durham, NC: Duke University Press, 2004).

152   D. Healy, "Antidepressant induced Suicidality," *Primary Care Psychiatry* 6 (2000): 23–8.

153   A. McIlroy, "Prozac Critic Sees U of T Job Revoked," *Globe and Mail*, April 14, 2001.

154   J. Coyne, "Healy's Study 'Odd,'" *Bulletin* (University of Toronto), July 23, 2001: 8.

155   http://www.healyprozac.com/AcademicStalking/default.htm.

156   S. Ryder, letter to Robert J. Temple, Director, Office of Drug Evaluations, July 26, 2004, http://www.FDA.gov/ohms/dockets/ac/04/briefing/2004-406561-31-pfizer -letter.pdf, 24–5 (Accessed September 21, 2007). This document is also available at http://www.healyprozac.com/AcademicStalking/Post%203%20- %20Pfizer%20letter%20re%20Healy.pdf.

157   D. Healy, "Contra Pfizer," *Ethical Human Psychology & Psychiatry* 7 (2005): 181–95.

158   J. Coyne, "Lessons in Conflict of Interest: The Construction of the Martyrdom of David Healy and the Dilemma of Bioethics," *American J of Bioethics* 5 (2005): W3–W14.

159   http://www.ahrp.org/cms/content/view/18/87/ and http://www.healyprozac.com/AcademicStalking/default.htm.

160   All correspondence on http://www.healyprozac.com/AcademicStalking/ default.htm.

161   All reviews and the covering letter are available from the author.

162   Further documents can be found on http://www.healyprozac.com/AcademicStalking/default.htm.

163   A. Fugh-Berman, "Doctors Must Not Be Lapdogs to Drug Firms," *BMJ* 333 (2006): 1027.

164   From profile of Peter Pitts on Drugwonks.com.

165   From Drugwonks.com. Posting on September 6, 2007.

166   From http://www.mslpr.com/, accessed January 15, 2008.

167   J. Thompson, P. Baird, and J. Downie, *The Olivieri Report* (Toronto: James Lorimer, 2001).

168   A. Blumsohn, http://scientific-misconduct.blogspot.com/ (2006); A. Blumsohn, "Authorship, Ghost-science, Access to Data and Control of the Pharmaceutical Scientific Literature: Who stands behind the word," *Professional Ethics Report* (American Association for the Advancement of Science) XIX, no. 3 (2006), http://www.aaas.org/spp/sfrl/per/per46.pdf.

169   http://finance.senate.gov/press/Bpress/2007press/prb111507a.pdf.

170   C.M. Beasley, B.E. Dornseif, J.C. Bosomworth, M.E. Sayler, A.H. Rampey, J.H. Heiligenstein, V.I. Thompson, D.J. Murphy, and D.N. Massica, "Fluoxetine and Suicide: A Meta-Analysis of Controlled Trials of Treatment for Depression," *BMJ* 303 (1991): 685–92.

171   I. Oswald, Letter, *BMJ* 303 (1991): 1058.

172   All correspondence is available on http://www.healyprozac.com.

173   D. Healy, Guest Editorial, "A Failure to Warn," *Int J Risk Safety in Medicine* 12 (1999): 151–6.

174   D. Healy, "Antidepressant Induced Suicidality," *Primary Care Psychiatry* 6 (2000): 23–8.

175   D. Healy, and D. Cattell, "The Interface Between Authorship, Industry and Science in the Domain of Therapeutics," *British J Psychiatry* 182 (2003): 22–7.

176   H. Jick, J.A. Kaye, and S.S. Jick, "Antidepressants and the Risk of Suicidal Behaviours," *JAMA* 292 (2004): 338–43.

177   This data is also available on http://www.fda.gov/ohrms/dockets/ac/04/transcripts/2004-4065T2.pdf, 154.

178   D. Fergusson, S. Doucette, K. Cranley-Glass, S. Shapiro, D. Healy, P. Hebert, and B. Hutton, "The Association between Suicide Attempts and SSRIs: A systematic review of 677 randomized controlled trials representing 85,470 participants," *BMJ* 330 (2005): 396–9.

179   D. Healy. "Did Regulators Fail over Selective Serotonin Reuptake Inhibitors?" *BMJ* 333 (2006): 92–5.

180   See http://www.healthyskepticism.org/presentations/2007/Study329.ppt.

181   M.D. Keller, N.D. Ryan, M. Strober, et al. "Efficacy of Paroxetine in the Treatment of Adolescent Major Depression: A randomized, controlled trial," *J Am Acad Child Adolesc Psychiatry* 40 (2001): 762–72.

182   Earlier versions of this paper and correspondence between the company and medical writer, as well as letters to the journal, are available from DH.

183   Email from J. Glanville, editor of *Index on Censorship*, to the author.

184   Editorial, "Depressing Research," *Lancet* 363 (2004): 1335.

185   D. Healy, "Our Censored Journals," in ed. A.R. Singh and S.A. Singh, *Medicine,*

Mental Health, Science, Religion, and Well-being, MSM, 6, (Jan–Dec 2008), n.p.

186   C. De Angelis, "The Influence of Money on Medical Science," *JAMA* 296 (2006): 996–8.

187   J. Carlson, ed., *Banned in Ireland: Censorship and the Irish Writer* (London: Routledge, 1990).

188   J. Cornwell, *The Power to Harm: Mind, Medicine and Murder on Trial* (London: Penguin, 1996).

189   J. Cornwell, *Hitler's Pope: The Secret History of Pius XII* (London: Penguin, 1999).

190   J. Cornwell, personal communication.

191   The term "brand fascism" was coined by Kal Applbaum, author of *The Marketing Era.* See note 55.

192   D. Healy, *Mania: a Short History of Bipolar Disorder* (Baltimore: Johns Hopkins University Press, 2008).

193   United States Patent 4,988,731. Date of Patent Jan 29, 1991; United States Patent 5,212,326. Date of Patent May 18, 1993.

194   United States Patent 5,229,382. Date of Patent May 22, 1992. European patent, EP0,454,436, filed on April 24, 1991.

195   Memo from Leigh Thompson, February 7, 1990. Exhibit 98 in *Forsyth vs. Eli Lilly,* cited in Healy, *Let Them Eat Prozac,* chapter 11.

196   Zyprexa Multidistrict Litigation 1596, Bates page ZY201548772, July 25, 2001.

197   Healy, *Let Them Eat Prozac,* see note 5.

198   D. Healy, "Trussed in Evidence? Ambiguities at the Interface of Clinical Evidence and Clinical Practice 2008," *Transcultural Psychiatry* (In press).

199   R. Moynihan and A. Cassels, *Selling Sickness* (New York: Nation Books, 2005).

200   I. Heath, "Combating Disease Mongering: Daunting but nonetheless essential," *PLoS Medicine* 3 (2006): e146.

201   K. Applbaum, *The Marketing Era* (New York: Routledge, 2004).

202   M. Angell, *The Truth about the Drug Companies: How they deceive us and what to do about it* (New York: Random House, 2005); J. Kassirer, *On the Take: How medicine's complicity with big business can endanger your health* (New York: Oxford University Press, 2005).

203   D. Healy, "The New Engineers of Human Souls and Academia," *Epidemiologia e Psichiatria Sociale* 16 (2007): 205–11.

CHAPTER 6: ACADEMIC FREEDOM AT THE FIRST NATIONS UNIVERSITY OF CANADA

204   Blair Stonechild, *The New Buffalo: The Struggle for Aboriginal Postsecondary*

Education in Canada (Winnipeg: University of Manitoba Press, 2006).

205 First Nations University of Canada, *Collective Agreement*, 2002–2005, University of Regina Faculty Association, Regina, 3–5.

206 Saskatchewan Labour Relations Board, "Hearing in a Matter of an Arbitration Pursuant to a Collective Agreement Between University of Regina Faculty Association (Dr. Blair Stonechild) and First Nations University of Canada," March 25, 26 & 27, 2006, at Regina, Saskatchewan, 17.

207 Queen's Bench for Saskatchewan, 2007 SKQB 179, Regina, Saskatchewan, May 24, 2007, 8.

208 Tina Pelletier, communications officer, "Response to Dr. Blair Stonechild Judgement," First Nations University of Canada, May 29, 2007.

209 For terms of the probation, see Association of Universities and Colleges of Canada, "AUCC Board of Directors Statement on First Nations University of Canada," news release, April 18, 2007, http://www.aucc.ca/publications/media/2007/first_nations_18_04_e.html.

210 Association of Universities and Colleges of Canada, "First Nations University of Canada's Probationary Status Lifted," news release, April 2, 2008, http://www.aucc.ca/publications/statements/2008/FNUC_statement_04_02_e.html.

211 Canadian Association of University Teachers, "Aboriginal Education Ill-Served by AUCC Decision," Ottawa, April 3, 2008.

CHAPTER 7: INTELLIGENT DESIGN AND SSHRC: AN EMBARRASSMENT FOR SCIENCE IN CANADA

212 1987 Supreme Court ruling in *Edwards v. Aguillard*, 482 U.S. 578 (1987) found that creation science violated the Establishment Clause of the First Amendment: http://en.wikipedia.org/wiki/Edwards_v._Aguillard.

213 *Kitzmiller v. Dover Area School District*, Case No. 04cv2688, December 2005. Judge Jones issued his ruling that the Dover mandate was unconstitutional, and barred intelligent design from being taught in Pennsylvania's Middle District public school science classrooms, http://en.wikipedia.org/wiki/Kitzmiller_v._Dover_Area_School_District.

214 Brian Alters, private communication. A facsimile of the original rejection notice can be found at http://tuda.triumf.ca/evolution/Rejection_Letter.pdf.

215 Brian Alters, "The Landmark Trial: Intelligent Design, God, and Evolution," presentation at meeting sponsored by The Royal Society of Canada and McGill University, March 29, 2006. Montreal.

216 All of the Canwest news quotes from Janet Halliwell and Larry Felt can be found in the articles of: Peggy Curran and Randy Boswell, April 5, 2006 and Randy Boswell, April 6, 2006; April 12, 2006; and April 17, 2006.

217 Royal Society of Canada, April 2006, http://www.ncseweb.org/resources/

articles/7403_statements_from_scientific_an_12_19_2002.asp#rsc and
http://tuda.triumf.ca/evolution/RSC_Statement.pdf.

218   http://tuda.triumf.ca/evolution/gaffield_061108.pdf.

219   Louis Marchildon, president of CAP, to Chad Gaffield, president of SSHRC,
       September 11, 2007, https://www.cap.ca/news/briefs/SSHRC.pdf.

220   Ibid.

221   http://www.cap.ca/news/CAP_Bulletin_Dec_2007_en.pdf.

222   During the CAP congress at Laval, Quebec, June 2008, Isabelle Blain, NSERC
       vice-president, Research Grants & Scholarships, reported to CAP council that the
       initiative was still being actively pursued. A new infrastructure will be needed for
       processing joint science education research grants, and the proprietary position
       of the Canadian provinces over educational concerns needs to be considered.

223   http://richarddawkins.net/print.php?id=342&showComments=yes.

224   E.C. Scott, review of The Trouble with Science, Reports of the National Center for
       Science Education, 18, no. 6 (1998), 25.

225   Peter McKnight, "A New Alliance Against Science: The 'Anything Goes' Academic
       Left Is Coming to the Support of the 'God Did It' Religious Right," Vancouver
       Sun, Saturday, April 22, 2006, C5.

CHAPTER 8: CONSERVATIVE THINK TANKS AND THE ACADEMY: CREDIBILITY BY STEALTH?

226   Lorne Gunter, "An Evening with Premiers, Past, Present and Future," National
       Post, October 16, 2004, A13.

227   CBC News, "Klein Leads Tribute to Fraser Institute," Calgary, October 13, 2004,
       http://www.cbc.ca/canada/calgary/story/2004/10/13/ca_fraser20041013.htm.

228   Fraser Institute, "A Salute to the Fraser Institute: 30 Years of Influential Ideas,"
       October 12, 2004. No longer available online.

229   "Yesterday's 'Right Wing' Is Today's Norm," The Province (Vancouver), October 14,
       2004, A20; reprinted as "Daring to Dissent," Ottawa Citizen, October 14, 2004,
       A16; "Fraser Institute Was Right for 30 Years," Windsor Star, October 25, 2004, A7.

230   Gunter, "An Evening with Premiers."

231   Marci McDonald, "The Man behind Stephen Harper," Walrus, October 2004.

232   Thomas Flanagan, First Nations? Second Thoughts (Montreal: McGill-Queen's
       University Press, 2000); Thomas Flanagan, Riel and the Rebellion: 1885
       Reconsidered, 2nd ed. (Toronto: University of Toronto Press, 2000).

233   David Rovinsky, The Ascendancy of Western Canada in Canadian Policymaking
       (Washington, DC: Center for Strategic and International Studies, February 16,
       1998), 2; Brian Mulawka, "Go West, Young Intellectual," Alberta Report, March
       30, 1998, 8.

234   John Ibbitson, "Educating Stephen: What Does the Conservative Party's
       Enigmatic Leader Really Stand For?" *Globe and Mail*, June 26, 2004, F4.

235   Fraser Institute, *2005 Annual Report*, 40, http://www.fraserinstitute.org/files/
       PDFs /annual_reports/2005_Annual_Report.pdf.

236   Fraser Institute, *2006 Annual Report*, 32, http://www.fraserinstitute.org
       /files/ PDFs/annual_reports/2006_Annual_Report.pdf.

237   Lewis F. Powell, Jr., "Confidential Memorandum: Attack of American Free
       Enterprise System," *Media Transparency*, August 23, 1971, http://www.
       mediatransparency.org/story.php?storyID=22.

238   Jerry Landay, "The Powell Manifesto: How a Prominent Lawyer's Attack Memo
       Changed America," *Media Transparency*, August 20, 2002, http://www.
       mediatransparency.org/story.php?storyID=21.

239   Powell, "Confidential Memorandum."

240   Murray Dobbin, *The Myth of the Good Corporate Citizen: Democracy under the Rule
       of Big Business* (Toronto: Stoddart, 1998), 166.

241   David Vogel, *Fluctuating Fortunes: The Political Power of Business in America* (New
       York: Basic Books, 1989), 198; Alex Carey, *Taking the Risk out of Democracy*
       (Urbana: University of Illinois Press, 1997), 92–93.

242   Dobbin, *The Myth*, 166.

243   Jack Mintz, "Government Policy and the Canadian Advantage," *Canadian
       Business Economics* (August 2000): 6–9.

244   "Integrate Economies, CNR Chief Advises," *Edmonton Journal*, December 15,
       2001, H1. See also Paul Tellier, "Integration Calls for Debate on Tough
       Questions Facing Canada," speech to the Canadian Railway Club, Montreal,
       December 14, 2001, *Canadian Speeches*, Jan–Feb 2002.

245   Tom d'Aquino, Security and Prosperity, the Dynamics of a New Canada-United
       States Partnership in North America, presentation to the annual general meeting
       of the CCCE, Toronto, January 14, 2003, http://www.ceocouncil.ca/publications
       /pdf/b10f11c9777f6bcf34fa14e57a594c3c/presentations_2003_01_14.pdf.

246   Bill Dymond and Michael Hart, "Navigating New Trade Routes: The Rise of
       Value Chains, and the Challenges for Canadian Trade Policy," CD Howe
       Institute *Commentary*, no. 259, March 2008, 31,
       http://www.cdhowe.org/pdf/commentary_259.pdf.

247   CD Howe Institute, Ideas that Make a Difference, *Annual Report 2002*, 2,
       http://www.cdhowe.org/pdf/annual_report_2002.pdf.

248   Fraser Institute, "New Fraser Institute research initiative: Centre for Canadian-
       American Relations," *Frontline* 5, no. 1 (February 2006): 1.

249   "Since Sept. 11: The Responses Show How Terrorism and War Have Left Their
       Mark," *Maclean's*, December 31, 2001, 38.

250   Carey, *Taking the Risk*, 89.

251   Robert F. Kaiser and Ira Chinoy, "Scaife: Funding Father of the Right,"
      Washington Post, May 2, 1999, A1.

252   Amy Wilentz, "On the Intellectual Ramparts," *Time*, September 1, 1986,
      http://www.time.com/magazine/article/0,9171,962189,00.html.

253   Eric Alterman, "Fighting Smart," *Mother Jones* (July/August 1994): 59–61.

254   Ruth Rosen, "Challenge Market Fundamentalism," *TomPaine.com*, February 5,
      2007, http://www.tompaine.com/print/challenge_market_fundamentalism.php.

255   Sasha Lilley, "On Neoliberalism: An Interview with David Harvey," *Monthly
      Review*, June 19, 2006, http://mrzine.monthlyreview.org/lilley190606.html.

256   Sharon Beder, *Free Market Missionaries: The Corporate Manipulation of Community
      Values* (London: Earthscan, 2006), 94.

257   Friedrich Hayek, *The Road to Serfdom* (Chicago: University of Chicago Press,
      1944).

258   John Blundell, *Waging the War of Ideas*, 3rd ed. (London: Institute for Economic
      Affairs, 2007), 24, http://www.iea.org.uk/files/upld-book404pdf?.pdf.

259   Ibid., 26.

260   Donald Gutstein, "Corporate Advocacy: The Fraser Institute," *City Magazine*,
      September 1978, 32–39.

261   Murray Dobbin, quoted in Brooke Jeffery, *Hard Right Turn* (Toronto:
      HarperCollins, 1999), 420.

262   Jeffery, *Hard Right Turn*, 421.

263   Fraser Institute, *The Fraser Institute at 30: A Retrospective*, 2004, 2,
      http://www.fraserinstitute.org/files/PDFs/About_Us/30th_Retrospective.pdf;
      Fraser Institute, "Income and Expenditure," *Annual Report 1978*, 13.

264   Fraser Institute, "The Fraser Institute Membership List," March 6, 1979, adden-
      dum to 1978 Annual Report.

265   Fraser Institute, *Annual Report 1978*, ii.

266   Ayn Rand, *Atlas Shrugged* (Random House, 1957).

267   Atlas Economic Research Foundation, "How did Atlas Start?" 2006,
      http://www.atlasusa.org/V2/main/page.php?page_id=319.

268   Atlas Economic Research Foundation, "Atlas: Year-in-Review," *Annual Report*,
      2006, http://www.atlasusa.org/V2/files/pdfs/2006_Fall_YIR.pdf.

269   James Gwartney and Robert Lawson, *Economic Freedom of the World: 2007 Annual
      Report*, Economic Freedom Network (Vancouver: Fraser Institute, 2007),
      http://www.freetheworld.com/2007/EFW2007BOOK2.pdf.

270   Ibid.

271   Shadia Drury, *The Political Ideas of Leo Strauss* (New York: Palgrave, 2005), xiii.

272   Gary Dorrien, *The Neoconservative Mind: Politics, Culture and the War of Ideology* (Philadelphia: Temple University Press, 1993), 8.

273   Ibid., 102.

274   Ibid., 68.

275   Ibid., 101.

276   Eric Alterman, "Neoconning the Media: a Very Short History of Neoconservatism," *Media Transparency*, April 22, 2005, http://www.mediatransparency.org/story.php?storyID=2; Dorrien, *The Neoconservative Mind*, 100.

277   Dorrien, *The Neoconservative Mind*, 101.

278   People for the American Way, "Buying a Movement: Right-wing Foundations and American Politics," 1996, 14, http://www.pfaw.org/pfaw/dfiles/file_33.pdf.

279   American Enterprise Institute, *2007 Annual Report*, December 27, 2007, 43, http://www.aei.org/about/filter.,contentID.20038142214000053/default.

280   National Committee for Responsive Philanthropy, "Axis of Ideology: Conservative Foundations and Public Policy," March 2004, 14.

281   Anne Norton, *Leo Strauss and the Politics of American Empire* (New Haven: Yale University Press, 2004), 11–12.

282   Stephan Thernstrom and Abigail Thernstrom, *America in Black and White: One Nation, Indivisible* (New York: Simon & Schuster, 1997); Dinesh D'Souza, *Illiberal Education: The Politics of Race and Sex on Campus* (New York: Free Press, 1991); Dinesh D'Souza, *The End of Racism: Principles for a Multiracial Society* (New York: Free Press, 1995); Dinesh D'Souza, *Ronald Reagan: How an Ordinary Man Became an Extraordinary Leader* (New York: Free Press, 1997).

283   Media Transparency, "Recipients of Funder: John M. Olin Foundation, Inc.," (n.d.), http://www.mediatransparency.org/recipientsoffunder.php?funderID=7 (accessed September 17, 2007).

284   Leo Strauss, *Natural Right and History* (Chicago: University of Chicago Press, 1953).

285   William Harms, "Olin Center Offers Last Conference on 'Empire and Liberty,'" *Chicago Chronicle* 24, no. 15, (April 28, 2005), http://chronicle.uchicago.edu/050428/olin.shtml; John M. Olin Center for Inquiry into the Theory and Practice of Democracy, "About the Olin Center," January 2, 2000, http://olincenter.uchicago.edu/about_olin.html.

286   Paul Knox, "The Strauss Effect," *Globe and Mail*, July 12, 2003, F9; "Recipient Grants: University of Toronto," *Media Transparency*, (n.d.), http://www.mediatransparency.org/recipientgrants.php?recipientID=338

287   Krishna Rau, "A Million for Your Thoughts," *Canadian Forum* (July 1996): 14.

288   Ibid., 12.

289   Sources for these figures are: Rau, "A Million for Your Thoughts," 16; Thomas Walkom, "Right-wing Causes Find a Rich and Ready Paymaster," *Toronto Star*,

October 25, 1997, E1; and various editions of the *Canadian Directory to Foundations and Grants* (Toronto: Canadian Centre for Philanthropy).

290   Tasha Kheiriddin and Adam Daifallah, "Rescuing Canada's Right," *Western Standard*, November 8, 2004, 29.

291   Atlantic Institute for Market Studies, "Board of directors," 2007, http://www.aims.ca/aboutaims.asp?cmPageID=90 (accessed May 1, 2007).

292   Montreal Economic Institute, "Using Private Insurance to Finance Health Care," *Economic Note*, November 2005, http://www.iedm.org/uploaded/pdf/nov05_en.pdf.

293   Fraser Institute, "The Fraser Institute Challenges 1000's of Young Thinkers," *Frontline* 3, no. 2, (September 2004): 3.

294   Fraser Institute, "Record number of teachers & students learn the value of free markets," *Frontline* 4, no. 1, (February 2005): 4; See also Marjorie Cohen, "Neo-cons on Campus," *This Magazine*, July 1995, 30.

295   Patti Edgar, "A Date with the Fraser Institute," *e.Peak Features* 104, no. 2, (January 17, 2000) reprinted from *The Martlet* (University of Victoria), http://www.peak.sfu.ca/the-peak/2000-1/issue2/fraserinstitute.html.

296   See, for instance, Fraser Institute, "Student Essay Contest: How Can Property Rights Protect the Environment? Free-Market Environmentalism Resource Guide," Fraser Institute, 2005. No longer available online.

297   Fraser Institute, *2002 Annual Report*, 21. http://www.fraserinstitute.org/files/PDFs/annual_reports/2002_Annual_Report.pdf.

298   Fraser Institute, "Summer Internship Program 2005: Research projects, 2005." No longer available online.

CHAPTER 9: POWER AND KNOWLEDGE: THE PRECARIOUSNESS OF FREE INQUIRY

299   See Gabriel Compayré, *Abelard and the Origin and Early History of Universities* (Honolulu: University Press of the Pacific, 2002).

300   See Shadia B. Drury, *Aquinas and Modernity: The Lost Promise of Natural Law* (New York: Rowman & Littlefield, 2008).

301   Siger of Brabant, *On the Eternity of the World*, a translation of *De Aeternitate Mundi* by Lottie H. Kendzierski (Milwaukee: Marquette University Press, 1964).

302   Shadia B. Drury, *The Political Ideas of Leo Strauss*, updated ed. (New York: Palgrave Macmillan, 2005).

303   An excellent example of the sort of individual that the Straussian education aspires to create is the character of Col. Paul Tibbets as played by Robert Taylor in the film *Above and Beyond*, which was based on the life of Tibbets, who dropped the atomic bomb on Hiroshima. In the film, Tibbets was one of many officers who were tested for his appropriateness to launch a secret mission

intended to inflict unprecedented death, carnage, and mayhem on a civilian population. The test consisted of an interview in which the officer was seated before a desk with a large black button. He was asked if he would press that button if by doing so he would kill a few thousand people instantly, but would also end the war and save thousands of American lives. Without a moment of hesitation, and without asking any questions, Tibbets pressed the button. Needless to say, he was selected for the deadly mission. Other officers hesitated. They wanted to know more. But Tibbets did not ask any questions. He did not ask: Is not the massacre of unarmed civilians contrary to the rules of war? Is winning a war by massacring civilians an honourable way to win a war? How do we know this crime is necessary to end the war? How can we be sure the bomb will end the war? Of course, there was no guarantee.

304   Leo Strauss, *Persecution and the Art of Writing* (Chicago: University of Chicago Press, 1952), 35.

305   Allan Bloom, *The Closing of the American Mind* (New York: Simon & Schuster, 1987), 36.

306   Ibid., 42.

307   CNN (documentary), "The Mission of George W. Bush," Sunday, October 11, 2004.

308   Speech delivered in the Philippines, October 19, 2003.

309   William F. Buckley, a traditional Catholic conservative, defended McCarthy in his hugely successful work *God and Man at Yale* (1951). In the opening pages of the book, Buckley paid tribute to his teacher at Yale, Willmoore Kendall, a disciple of Leo Strauss, the German émigré political philosopher. Buckley described a conversation that Kendall had with the janitor at the university. The janitor asked Kendall, "Is it true, professor, dat dere's people in New York City who want to . . . destroy the guvamint of the United States?" To which Kendall replied, "Yes Oliver, that's true." Then Oliver said, "Well, why don't we lock'em up?" After this exchange, Kendall informed the faculty at Yale that the janitor had more political wisdom than all of them put together. I doubt the faculty at Yale was ruffled by someone who regarded Lincoln as the arch enemy of America for having liberated the slaves, as Kendall maintains in *The Conservative Affirmation* (1985). In any case, Buckley agreed with Kendall, and in 1961, edited a large collection of essays in defence of McCarthy, *The Committee and Its Critics: A Calm Review of the Committee on Un-American Activities*. What the story reveals is the simple-mindedness of Kendall, Buckley, and company. Instead of agreeing with Oliver, the professor should have pointed out that in a civilized society, we do not assume, as they did in the barbaric age of the Catholic Inquisition, that anyone who is accused is guilty. And in a society characterized by the rule of law, we do not normally lock people up on the basis of mere suspicion. McCarthy's accusations were based on the flimsiest evidence from anonymous informers. The climate was a haven for grudge informers, scoundrels, and villains of every stripe. Guilt was assumed, and an accusation was enough to destroy a career.

310   *CAUT Bulletin* 54, no. 5 (May 2007): 1.

311   Roger Kimball, *Tenured Radicals: How Politics Has Corrupted Our Higher Education* (New York: Harper & Row, 1990).

312   The suggestion is that the accusation is as preposterous in their case as it was for
       Socrates. But those with some knowledge of the political conditions of ancient
       Athens know that the case against Socrates was not bogus. See I. F. Stone, *The
       Trial of Socrates* (Toronto: Little, Brown, 1988).

313   Straussian-educated William Kristol and his neoconservative colleagues outlined
       what was to become the Bush foreign policy in the Statement of Principles of
       The Project for the New American Century (June 3, 1997) and in a letter to then
       President Bill Clinton, (January 26, 1998), both available at
       http://www.newamericancentury.org/lettersstatements.htm. The ominous state-
       ment about Pearl Harbor is made on p. 51 of Rebuilding America's Defenses:
       Strategy, Forces and Resources For a New Century (A Report of The Project for
       the New American Century, September 2000), http://www.newamericancentury.
       org/RebuildingAmericasDefenses.pdf.

314   Interview with Kathleen Petty of CBC Radio's "The House," September 22, 2007.
       See also Thomas Flanagan, *Harper's Team: Behind the Scenes in the Conservative
       Rise to Power* (Montreal: McGill-Queen's University Press, 2007).

315   See "Straussians in Power: Secrecy, Lies, and Endless War," in Drury, *The Political
       Ideas of Leo Strauss*. See also Shadia B. Drury, "Gurus of Endless War," in *The
       New Humanist* (May/June, 2007).

316   Chalmers Johnson, *Nemesis* (New York: Henry Holt, 2006), 21.

317   Ron Suskind, "Without a Doubt," *New York Times Magazine*, October 17, 2004.

318   U.S. Advisory Group on Diplomacy for the Arab and Muslim World, *Changing
       Minds, Winning Peace*, October 1, 2003, http://www.state.gov/documents/
       organization/24882.pdf.

319   The fact that the United States is invading Muslim countries and killing count-
       less innocent civilians seems irrelevant. The fact that the United States is giving
       unqualified support to Israel despite the latter's violation of dozens of United
       Nations resolutions — violations blessed by the United States — is no obstacle.
       The fact that the United States supplies Israel with billions of dollars' worth of
       military aid that the Israelis use to terrorize and bomb their Palestinian neigh-
       bours, who have no army and no air force, is no problem. More money to
       spend on propaganda will do the trick.

320   David Frum, "Misinformation Warfare," *National Post*, February 2, 2008.

321   Ibid.

CHAPTER 10: TEMPERS OF THE TIMES: THE POLITICIZATION OF MIDDLE EASTERN STUDIES

322   Jonathan R. Cole, "On the Matter of Edward Said," statement from Columbia
       University's Office of the Provost and Dean of Faculties, October 18, 2000;
       Sunnie Kim, "Edward Said Accused of Stoning in South Lebanon," *Columbia
       Spectator*, July 19, 2000, http://www.columbiaspectator.com/node/33458; Aaron
       Matz, "Stone Thrower and Scholar: Edward Said's Ferocious Unity," *New York*

Observer, September 10, 2000, www.observer.com/node/43354; "'Edward Said's Action Protected,' Says Columbia," *Academe*, 87 (January–February, 2001): 3; Dinitia Smith, "A Stone's Throw Is a Freudian Slip," *New York Times*, March 10, 2001, http://query.nytimes.com/gst/fullpage.html?res= 9D06E0D7143AF933A 25750C0A9679C8B63.

323   Said's critique of "Orientalism" was not confined to Anglo-French discourse of the 19th and early 20th century, and he positioned the emergence of the "vast apparatus for research on the Middle East," including the Middle East Studies Association, in the context of American strategic and economic priorities. Indeed, Said expressed misgivings about the prospects for scholarship in any discipline defined "canonically, imperially, or geographically." Edward W. Said, *Orientalism* (New York: Pantheon Books, 1978; New York: Vintage Books, 1979), 295, 326.

324   Martin Kramer, *Ivory Towers on Sand: The Failure of Middle Eastern Studies in America*, Washington Institute for Near East Policy, Policy paper 58 (Washington, D.C., 2001). For an overview and discussion of the criticisms of Middle Eastern studies, see Pinar Bilgin, "What Future for Middle Eastern Studies," Futures 38 (2006), 575–85.

325   F. Gregory Gause III, "Who Lost Middle Eastern Studies?" review of *Ivory Towers on Sand* by Martin Kramer, *Foreign Affairs* 81 (March/April 2002), 164. In the main, Gause finds "Kramer's diagnosis . . . skewed and overly pessimistic," but others, like Stanley Kurtz, are more fulsome in their praise of Kramer's "unsparing new study" of "the intellectual rot in a scholarly field of capital importance to our national well-being." Stanley Kurtz, "The Scandal of Middle East Studies: Bankrupt Scholarship and Foolish Policy Advice," *Weekly Standard*, November 19, 2001, 14.

326   Anemona Hartocollis, "Campus Culture Wars Flare Anew over Tenor of Debate after the Attacks," *New York Times*, September 30, 2001, http://query.nytimes.com/gst/fullpage.html?res=9C02E6DB143DF933A0575AC0 A9679C8B63.

327   Several works detailing the construction of "political correctness" followed the publication of Dinesh D'Sousa's *Illiberal Education: The Politics of Race and Sex on Campus* (New York: The Free Press, 1991). John K. Wilson, *The Myth of Political Correctness: The Conservative Attack on Higher Education* (Durham: Duke University Press, 1995); Richard Feldstein, *Political Correctness: A Response from the Cultural Left* (Minneapolis: University of Minnesota Press, 1997).

328   Jerry L. Martin and Anne D. Neal, "Defending Civilization: How Our Universities Are Failing America and What Can Be Done About It," A project of the Defense of Civilization Fund, Washington, D.C. (February 2002), 3, available at http://govdocs.evergreen.edu/defciv.pdf. On the curious matter of the disappearing names, see Chris Lehmann, "Operation Infinite Jest: The Return of the Culture Wars," *In These Times*, January 4, 2002, http://www.inthesetimes.com/issue/26/04/feature5.shtml. ACTA's earlier publications included *The Shakespeare File: What English Majors are Really Studying* (1996) and *Losing America's Memory: Historical Literacy in the 21st Century* (2000). For an assessment of "patriotic correctness" see John K. Wilson, *Patriotic Correctness: Academic Freedom and its Enemies* (Boulder: Paradigm Publishers, 2007).

329   A great deal of progressive ink has been spilt over these two men. On Pipes, see
       Eyal Press, "Neocon Man," *The Nation*, May 10, 2004,
       http://www.thenation.com/doc/20040510/press; Zachary Lockman, "Critique
       from the Right: The Neo-conservative Assault on Middle Eastern Studies," *CR:
       The New Centennial Review* 5 (Spring 2005), 90–4. On Horowitz, see Jennifer
       Jacobson, "What Makes David Run," *Chronicle of Higher Education*, May 6, 2005,
       http://chronicle.com/weekly/v51/i35/35a00801.htm; Scott Sherman, "David
       Horowitz's Long March," *The Nation*, July 3, 2000,
       http://www.thenation.com/doc/20000703/sherman.

330   Horowitz launched several unsuccessful assaults on the university community
       before starting his Students for Academic Freedom and launching the Academic
       Bill of Rights (ABOR) in 2003. Amongst Horowitz's failures were his "Think
       Twice" campaign aimed at curtailing student protest against the war, and a
       "National Campaign to Take Back Our Campuses." See Bill Berkowitz,
       "Horowitz's Campus Jihads," *Dissident Voice*, October 9–10, 2004, www.dissiden
       tvoice.org/Oct04/Berkowitz1009.htm. The ABOR is treated at length in Stephen
       H. Aby, ed., *The Academic Bill of Rights Debate: A Handbook* (Westport: Praeger,
       2007).

331   In the words of one commentator, "The site's Cold War terminology was clearly
       provocative, [but] the response from academics was equally intemperate." Tim
       Cavanaugh, "Campus Comedy: A Bogus Controversy over McCarthyism
       Continues," *Reason Magazine*, October 28, 2002,
       http://www.reason.com/news/show/32825.html. See also Scott Smallwood,
       "Web Site Lists Professors Accused of Anti-Israel Bias and Asks Students to
       Report on Them," *Chronicle of Higher Education*, September 19, 2002,
       http://chronicle.com/daily/2002/09/2002091902n.htm; Lockman, "Critique,"
       92–4; Kristine McNeil, "The War on Academic Freedom," *The Nation*, November
       11, 2002, http://www.thenation.com/doc/20021125/mcneil; Campus Watch Web
       site, "Recommended Professors," http://www.campus-watch.org/
       recommends.php.

332   J. William Fulbright, *The Arrogance of Power* (New York: Vintage Books, 1966), 43.

333   Joel Beinen and Zachary Lockman have each written on the political pressures
       being brought to bear on the field of Middle Eastern studies. Lockman,
       "Critique," 63–110; Joel Beinen, "The New McCarthyism: Policing Thought
       about the Middle East," in *Academic Freedom after September 11*, ed. B. Doumani
       (New York: Zone Books, 2006), 237–66.

334   Nadia Abu el-Haj, *Facts on the Ground: Archaeological Practice and Territorial Self-
       Fashioning in Israeli Society* (Chicago: University of Chicago Press, 2001); Jacob
       Lassner, "Not Grounded in Fact," review of *Facts on the Ground* by Nadia Abu el-
       Haj, *Middle East Quarterly* 10 (Summer 2003), http://www.meforum.org/article
       /560; Alexander H. Joffe, review of *Facts on the Ground* by Nadia Abu el-Haj,
       Journal of Near Eastern Studies 64 (October 2005), 297–304.

335   Karen W. Arenson, "Fracas Erupts Over Book on Mideast by a Barnard Professor
       Seeking Tenure," *New York Times*, September 10, 2007,
       http://www.nytimes.com/2007/09/10/education/10barnard.html; Scott Jaschik,
       "Barnard Tenures Scholar Opposed by Massive Campaign, *Inside Higher Ed*,
       November 5, 2007, http://insidehighered.com/news/2007/11/05/elhaj. The peti-

tion to deny El-Haj tenure gained more than 2,500 signatures and was still posted online as of April 4, 2008, at the "Deny Nadia Abu El Haj Tenure" Web site,
http://www.nadiaabuelhaj.com. One cannot help but feel impressed at the
effrontery of using El-Haj's own name as the URL for this site.

336   The quotation is from a comment posted on November 1, 2007, by "Noga" to
      the blog of Martin Solomon, who, "like David Horowitz," professes to be a con-
      vert from liberalism: "What triggered the change? I'm sure in great measure it's
      the typical story — 9/11." On Solomon and his blog, see http://www.solomonia
      .com/blog/who.shtml. On the tenure of El-Haj, see
      www.solomonia.com/blog/archive/2007/11/sources-nadia-abu-el-haj-receives
      -tenure.

337   The tenor of the Finkelstein-Dershowitz debate is captured by the following
      titles: Norman G. Finkelstein, "Descent Into Moral Barbarism: Should Alan
      Dershowitz Target Himself for Assassination?" *CounterPunch*, August 12–13,
      2006, http://www.counterpunch.org/finkelstein08122006.html; Alan M.
      Dershowitz, "Finkelstein the Sexist," *FrontPage Magazine*, November 22, 2007,
      http://www.frontpagemag.com/Articles/Read.aspx?GUID=E76479CC-84D
      0-40D7-8B90-500D7691514A; Alan M. Dershowitz, "Finkelstein's Bigotry," *Wall
      Street Journal*, May 4, 2007. On the animus between these two men, see also
      Gary Younge, "Dershowitz vs. Finkelstein," *Salon*, August 12, 2005,
      http://dir.salon.com/story/books/feature/2005/08/12/finkelstein_dershowitz;
      Gary Younge, "J'accuse," *The Guardian*, August 10, 2005,
      http://books.guardian.co.uk/departments/politicsphilosophyandsociety/story/
      0,6000,1545972,00.html.

338   Charles S. Suchar to the University Board on Tenure and Promotion, memoran-
      dum of 22 March 2007, posted on Peter Kirstein's blog,
      http://english.sxu.edu/sites/kirstein/?p=680.

339   Dennis H. Holtschneider to Norman Finkelstein, 8 June 2007, posted on
      Finkelstein's Web site,
      http://www.normanfinkelstein.com/pdf/tenuredenial/Finkelstein,Norman06.08.
      2007.pdf. On Dershowitz's extracurricular efforts — to oppose Finkelstein's
      tenure and, earlier, to try and halt publication of his book, *Beyond Chutzpah* —
      see Jennifer Howard, "Harvard Law Professor Works to Disrupt Tenure Bid of
      Longtime Nemesis at DePaul U.," *Chronicle of Higher Education*, April 5, 2007,
      http://chronicle.com/daily/2007/04/2007040504n.htm; Jon Wiener, "Giving
      Chutzpah New Meaning," The Nation, July 11, 2005,
      http://www.thenation.com/docprint.mhtml?i=20050711&s=wiener.

340   Scott Jaschik, "Furor Over Norm Finkelstein," *Inside Higher Ed*, April 3, 2007,
      http://www.insidehighered.com/news/2007/04/03/finkelstein.

341   Posted to the Solomonia blog, April 11, 2007,
      http://www.solomonia.com/blog/archives/010346.shtml.

342   Sierra Millman, "DePaul Professor Who Supported Finkelstein Also Was Denied
      Tenure," *Chronicle of Higher Education*, June 12, 2007,
      http://chronicle.com/daily/2007/06/2007061204n.htm.

343   Kyle Szarzynski, "Israel Lobby Censors Academic Honesty," *The Badger Herald*,
      September 11, 2007,

http://badgerherald.com/oped/2007/09/11/israel_lobby_censors.php. The idea
that Larudee authored only political tracts rather than serious scholarship was in
circulation before the *FrontPage* article referenced in the following note had
appeared. "Upanishad," for example, commented on the Vincent G. Rinn Law
Library blog at De Paul University that "popular magazine articles and articles
in Marxist magazines and journals do not count as academic publication
(Larudee)," August 29, 2007, http://depaullaw.typepad.com/library/2007/
08/current-finkels.html.

344 Steven Plaut, "The Next Piece of Housekeeping for DePaul?" *FrontPage Magazine*,
     September 6, 2007, http://www.frontpagemag.com/Articles/Read.aspx?
     GUID=b24f5bf9-a8cf-4951-80f5-f9e4b99f7039. Returning to the subject of
     Larudee eleven days later, Plaut shifted his focus from the shrillness of her
     Marxism to her lack of productivity — Marxist or otherwise. "Virtually no one
     had ever heard of her, which turns out to be most of her problem. Her academic
     record was nearly empty. Claiming to be an economist, her publications were
     not enough to get her tenured anywhere." Presumably, eleven days gave Plaut
     enough time to realize that any content-based critique of Larudee would only
     reinforce the arguments of those claiming that tenure denials at DePaul were
     politically motivated. The safest course for the critic was to argue that Larudee
     would have been denied tenure "anywhere." Steven Plaut, "The Passion of
     Norman Finkelstein," *FrontPage Magazine*, 17 September, 2007, http://front-
     pagemag.com/Articles/Read.aspx?GUID=76B162C1-1038-400B-B112-
     87C09C917227.

345 The term "neoconservatism" is freighted with meaning, but is used here to
     denote that strand of (primarily) American ideology and practice that has been
     politically ascendant since the Reagan presidency and is characterized by extreme
     tax reductions, deregulation of markets, corporate subsidies, reckless deficits, the
     erosion of the welfare state, privatization of the public sector, hostility to organ-
     ized labour, exaggerated military expenditures, aggressive foreign policy, support
     for aggressive Israeli foreign policy, military adventurism, high levels of domestic
     consumption, disregard for environmental consequences, shooting friends in the
     face with shotguns, religious fundamentalism, propagandistic media strategies,
     and heightened surveillance by the state. It is, in short, the political antithesis to
     both traditional conservatism and progressive liberalism and, in even shorter
     hand, the triumph of short-term self-interest over all other values.

346 Martin Kramer, "Policy and the Academy: An Illicit Relationship," *Middle East
     Quarterly* 10 (Winter 2003), http://www.meforum.org/article/521.

347 It should come as no surprise that the first salvo in this campaign was fired by
     David Horowitz, whose Center for the Study of Popular Culture (now the David
     Horowitz Freedom Center) commissioned pollster and conservative strategist,
     Frank Luntz, to conduct a study of political bias at eight Ivy League institutions.
     The original study from December 2002 is still available on the Students for
     Academic Freedom Web site at http://www.studentsforacademicfreedom.org
     /news/1902/LUNTZ.html.

348 Several studies along these lines have now been produced, prompting a second
     wave of commentaries and responses, all of which has had the — presumably,
     desired — effect of keeping the "issue" of faculty bias constantly in the news.

One would, of course, search in vain for any corresponding analysis of the political "bias" of university governing boards or alumni donors. Studies promoting the idea of inappropriate faculty biases include: Daniel B. Klein, Charlotta Stern, and Andrew Western, "Documenting the One-Party Campus, *Academic Questions* 18 (Winter 2004–05), 40–52; Daniel B. Klein and Andrew Western, "How Many Democrats per Republican at UC-Berkeley and Stanford? Voter Registration Data Across 23 Academic Departments," *Scandinavian Working Papers in Economics*, no. 54 (November 18, 2004); Stanley Rothman, S. Robert Lichter, and Neil Nevitte, "Politics and Professional Advancement Among College Faculty," *The Forum* 3 (March 14, 2005), http://www.bepress.com/forum/vol3/iss1/art2/. Responses to the initial wave of bias studies include: John Lee, "The 'Faculty Bias' Studies: Science or Propaganda?" on behalf of Free Exchange on Campus (November 2006), http://www.aft.org/pubs-reports/higher_ed/FacultyBiasStudies.pdf; Neil Gross and Solon Simmons, "The Social and Political Views of American Professors," Working paper (September 24, 2007), http://www.wjh.harvard.edu/~ngross/lounsbery_9-25.pdf.

349 As the last academic home of Edward Said and current home to the Department of Middle East and Asian Languages and Culture (MEALAC), Columbia University has been a lightning rod for accusations of bias and disloyalty. The utility of faculty radicals to their critics has been noted by Scott Sherman, who wrote that "for Pipes & Co., Massad is something of a gift." Scott Sherman, "The Mideast Comes to Columbia," *The Nation*, March 16, 2005, http://www.the nation.com/doc/20050404/sherman. The "Dirty Thirty" refers to a Web site dedicated to "Exposing UCLA's Radical Professors." Established by a protege of David Horowitz, the site achieved notoriety for an offer (retracted under pressure) to purchase class notes from students of the University of California, Los Angeles. Despite moving to a voluntary reporting model, the site continued to "out" faculty members for such things as "ardent anti-Israel [sic] and anti-Zionism," "tireless anti-Israel activism," and "biased Palestinian classroom proselytizing." The site was still online as of March 30, 2008, and the "Dirty Thirty" list (of only twenty-eight radicals) is posted at http://www.uclaprofs.com/articles/dirtythirty.html.

350 David Horowitz, *The Professors: The 101 Most Dangerous Academics in America* (Washington: Regnery Publishing, 2006), vii–xxv.

351 Tanya Schevitz, "Cramped Speech at UC Berkeley: Teacher Warns 'Conservative Thinkers,'" *San Francisco Chronicle*, May 10, 2002, http://www.sfgate.com/cgi-bin/article.cgi?f=/c/a/2002/05/10/BA122563.DTL.

352 Roger Kimball, "The Intifada Curriculum," *Wall Street Journal*, May 9, 2002, http://www.campus-watch.org/pf.php?id=6. Kimball is a conservative critic of the academy whose works include: *Tenured Radicals: How Politics Has Corrupted Higher Education* (New York: HarperCollins, 1990) and *The Rape of the Masters: How Political Correctness Sabotages Art* (San Francisco: Encounter Books, 2004).

353 Robert C. Post to President Atkinson, August 12, 2002, partially reprinted as "Academic Freedom and the 'Intifada Curriculum,'" Academe 89 (May–June 2003), 16–20.

354 Ibid., 19.

355   Fulbright, *Arrogance*, 42.

356   "The Israel Lobby and U.S. Foreign Policy" appeared simultaneously in the
       London Review of Books, March 23, 2006,
       http://www.lrb.co.uk/v28/n06/mear01.html and on the John F. Kennedy School
       of Government's Faculty Research Working Paper Series, http://ksgnotes1
       .harvard.edu/Research/wpaper.nsf/rwp/RWP06-011. Any page references that fol-
       low are to this second document.

357   An account of the paper's genesis appears in Mearsheimer and Walt's subse-
       quent book on the subject, John J. Mearsheimer and Stephen M. Walt, preface
       to *The Israel Lobby and U.S. Foreign Policy* (New York: Farrar, Strauss and Giroux,
       2007), vii–viii.

358   See Richard Drake, "On Being Called an Anti-Semite in Montana," *Academe* 93
       (September–October 2007), 44–6; Patricia Cohen, "Backlash Over Book on
       Policy for Israel," *New York Times*, August 16, 2007,
       http://www.nytimes.com/2007/08/16/books/16book.html; Ken Silverstein, "A
       Balancing Act at the Chicago Council on Global Affairs," *Harper's Magazine*,
       August 16, 2007, http://www.harpers.org/archive/2007/08/hbc-90000914;
       Mearsheimer and Walt, "Setting the Record Straight: A Response to Critics of
       'The Israel Lobby,'" http://us.macmillan.com/CMS400/uploadedFiles/FSGAdult/
       Setting_the_Record_Straight.pdf, 2–4.

359   Richard Baehr and Ed Lasky, "Stephen Walt's War with Israel," *American Thinker*,
       March 20, 2006, http://www.americanthinker.com/2006/03/stephen_walts_war_
       with_israel.html; Mearsheimer and Walt, "The Israel Lobby," 22.

360   It is impossible to measure the extent to which public policy is influenced by
       academic research, but a recent essay on the topic stressed the importance of the
       reputation and credibility of the researchers and their backers. Morley
       Gunderson, "How Academic Research Shapes Labor and Social Policy," *Journal
       of Labor Research* 28 (Fall 2007), 577. Deplorable though it may be, demonizing
       and discrediting academics with whom one disagrees is a potentially effective,
       and therefore logical, weapon in the field of political war.

361   Dershowitz's insinuations feel much less careful in the pages of the *New York
       Sun*, which quotes him as seeing little difference between the Protocols of the
       Elders of Zion and the essay by Mearsheimer and Walt, except that "the
       Protocols are a forgery, but ['The Israel Lobby'] is actually written by two big-
       ots." Eli Lake, "David Duke Claims to Be Vindicated by a Harvard Dean," *New
       York Sun*, March 20, 2006, http://www2.nysun.com/article/29380. The paper
       posted on the Faculty Research Working Paper Series Web site is Alan M.
       Dershowitz, "Debunking the Newest — and Oldest — Jewish Conspiracy: A
       Reply to the Mearsheimer-Walt 'Working Paper,'" http://www.hks.harvard.edu/
       research/working_papers/dershowitzreply.pdf.

362   These three comments were posted by various contributors to the Jewish
       Current Issues blog under the March 27, 2006 thread, "Are Walt/Mearsheimer
       Anti-Semitic?" http://jpundit.typepad.com/jci/2006/03/are_waltmearshe.html.
       In order, the comments were posted by "J. Lichty," (March 27, 2006); "Walt
       Sherwin," (April 2, 2006); and Rex Lewis Field, (April 29, 2006).

363   David Horowitz, "Jimmy Carter: Jew-Hater, Genocide-Enabler, Liar," *FrontPage Magazine*, December 14, 2006, http://www.frontpagemag.com/Articles/ Read.aspx?GUID=E064A534-7C85-4E30-AC1C-4AC3E8B56458.

364   Joseph Massad, "Statement in Response to the Intimidation of Columbia University," November 3, 2004, http://www.columbia.edu/cu/mealac/faculty/massad/#intimidation. A video transcript of *Columbia Unbecoming* is available at http://www.columbiaunbecoming.com.

365   Jonathan Cole discusses the Massad incident briefly in a paper published previously in a collection assembled by the Crowe Foundation. Cole, "Academic Freedom on American Campuses in Troubled Times," in *Free Speech in Fearful Times: After 9/11 in Canada, the U.S., Australia & Europe*, ed. J.L. Turk and A. Manson (Toronto: James Lorimer, 2007), 165–7, 168. Massad's own responses to the ad hoc committee charged to investigate these incidents ("Statement to the Ad Hoc Committee," March 14, 2005; "Response to the Ad Hoc Grievance Committee Report," April 4, 2005) are posted on his Web site, http://www.columbia.edu/cu/mealac/faculty/massad/.

366   "Columbia Urged to Fire Professor for Espousing Anti-Semitic Views," press release from the Office of Congressman Anthony D. Weiner, October 21, 2004, http://www.house.gov/list/press/ny09_weiner/102104columbiaurgedtofire.html.

367   Joseph Massad, "Policing the Academy," *Al-Ahram Weekly*, no. 633 (April 10–16 2003), http://weekly.ahram.org.eg/2003/633/op2.htm.

368   Ed Henry and Barbara Starr, "Bush: 'I'm the Decider' on Rumsfeld," *Cable News Network*, April 18, 2006, http://www.cnn.com/2006/POLITICS/04/18/rumsfeld/.

369   Kurtz wrote a number of articles on this subject for the *National Review* through the second half of 2003: Stanley Kurtz, "Studying Title VI: Criticisms of Middle East Studies Get a Congressional Hearing," *National Review*, June 16, 2003, http://www.nationalreview.com/kurtz/kurtz061603.asp; "Hearing Both Sides of Title VI: Middle-east Studies Critics and Defenders Clash on the Hill," *National Review*, 23 June 2003, http://www.nationalreview.com/kurtz/kurtz062303.asp; "All About Defense: A key To the Future of Our National Security Is in Jeopardy," *National Review*, July 1, 2003, http://www.nationalreview.com/script/printpage.p?ref=/kurtz/kurtz070103.asp; "Reforming the Campus: Congress Targets Title VI," *National Review*, October 14, 2003, http://www.nationalreview.com/kurtz/kurtz200310140905.asp; "Opening the Classroom Door: Making Schools Safe for U.S. Foreign Policy," *National Review*, December 4, 2003, http://www.nationalreview.com/kurtz/ kurtz200312040900.asp. Indicative of the response to Kurtz are Juan Cole, "Why Are Arch Conservatives Ganging Up on the Middle East Studies Association?" *History News Network*, January 20, 2003, http://hnn.us/articles/1218.html; Zachary Lockman, "Behind the Battles Over US Middle East Studies," *Middle East Report Online* (January 2004), http://www.merip.org/mero/interventions /lockman_interv.html.

370   Jennifer Jacobson, "The Clash Over Middle East Studies," *Chronicle of Higher Education*, February 6, 2004, http://chronicle.com/weekly/v50/i22/22a00801.

htm. The full text of H.R.3077 is available from the Library of Congress at http://thomas.loc.gov/cgi-bin/ query/z?c108:H.R.3077:.

371   The Senate's bill (S.1642) would insert a requirement, under Title VI "Education and Training Programs," that "activities funded by the grant will reflect diverse perspectives and a wide range of views on world regions and international affairs." The most recent text of S.1642 is available from the Library of Congress at http://thomas.loc.gov/cgi-bin/query/z?c110:S.1642:.

372   Scott Jaschik, "A Different View of the Middle East," *Inside Higher Education*, November 2, 2007, http://www.insidehighered.com/news/2007/11/02/mideast; ASMEA homepage, accessed November 6, 2007, http://www.asmeascholars.org.

373   American Association of University Professors, "1915 Declaration of Principles on Academic Freedom and Academic Tenure," in *AAUP Policy Documents and Reports*, 10th ed. (Baltimore: Johns Hopkins University Press, 2006), 298.

374   Mark Bauerlein, "Liberal Groupthink Is Anti-intellectual," *Chronicle Review*, November 12, 2004, http://chronicle.com/weekly/v51/i12/12b00601.htm.

375   American Association of University Professors, "1915 Declaration," 294.

CHAPTER 11: THE RIGHT'S WAR ON ACADEME AND THE POLITICS OF TRUTH

376   Another version of this essay appeared in *The Academic Bill of Rights Debate: A Handbook*, edited by Stephen Aby (Westport: Praeger, 2007).

377   William Buckley, *God and Man at Yale* (Chicago: Regnery, 1951), 107.

378   Academic Bill of Rights, posted at http://www.studentsforacademicfreedom.org/abor.htm. Some references to the ABOR will cite the "Student Bill of Rights," a term used especially earlier on in Horowitz's work.

379   "Avoid Whatever Offends You," *Inside Higher Education*, http://www.inside highered.com/layout/set/print/news/2006/02/17/ariz

380   Whittaker Chambers, *Cold Friday* (New York: Random House, 1964), 7.

381   John Judis, *William F. Buckley, Jr: Patron Saint of the Conservatives* (New York: Simon and Schuster, 1988), 52.

382   William Buckley, *God and Man at Yale*, xiii.

383   Judis, *William F. Buckley*, 50.

384   Buckley, *God and Man at Yale*, 13.

385   Ibid., 45.

386   Ibid., 172.

387   Ibid., 197.

388   Ibid., 25.

389   Russell Kirk, *Academic Freedom* (Chicago: Regnery, 1955), 122.

390   Buckley, *God and Man at Yale*, 106.

391   Michael Wreszin, *A Rebel in Defense of Tradition: The Life and Politics of Dwight Macdonald* (New York: Basic Books, 1994), 274.

392   Buckley, *God and Man at Yale*, 107.

393   James Miller, *Democracy is in the Streets: From Port Huron to the Siege of Chicago* (New York: Simon and Schuster, 1987), 290.

394   Rudd quoted in Miller, 291.

395   David Farber, *The Age of Great Dreams: America in the 1960s* (New York: Hill and Wang, 1994), 211.

396   David Brown, *Richard Hofstadter* (Chicago: University of Chicago Press, 2006), 184.

397   Quoted in Brown, 185.

398   Kristol quoted in Murray Friedman, *The Neoconservative Revolution: Jewish Intellectuals and the Shaping of Public Policy* (Cambridge: Cambridge University Press, 2005), 188.

399   Allan Bloom, *The Closing of the American Mind* (New York: Simon and Schuster, 1987), 320.

400   Ibid., 313.

401   Ibid., 27.

402   David Brooks in the Introduction to *Backward and Upward* (New York: Vintage, 1995), xi. For more on Brooks, see my "What's the Matter with David Brooks," *Common Review*, Summer 2005, 22–29.

403   Brian Anderson, *South Park Conservatives* (Washington, D.C.: Regnery, 2005) and Rod Dreher, *Crunchy Cons* (New York: Crown, 2006).

404   Fred Barnes, *Rebel-In-Chief* (New York: Crown, 2006), 13, 21.

405   Peter Collier and David Horowitz, *Destructive Generation* (New York: Summit Books, 1990), 266–67.

406   Paglia quoted in David Horowitz, *The Art of Political War* (Dallas: Spence Publishing, 2000), 96.

407   Horowitz quoted in Stanley Fish, "'Intellectual Diversity': The Trojan Horse of a Dark Design," *Chronicle of Higher Education* 50, no. 23 (February 13, 2004): B14.

408   Academic Bill of Rights, posted at http://www.studentsforacademicfreedom.org/abor.htm.

409   Ibid.

410   For more on this, see my "A Student Bill of Fights," *Nation*, April 4, 2005, 16–17.

CHAPTER 12: PRODUCTION IN THE HUMANITIES

411   Garrison Keillor, "English Majors" script, PBS program, *A Prairie Home Companion*, http://prairiehome.publicradio.org/programs/2004/10/23/scripts/english.shtml.

412   MLA Task Force on Evaluating Scholarship for Tenure and Promotion, Report, in *Profession 2007* (New York: MLA, 2007), 48.

413   C. Judson King, Diane Harley, Sarah Earl-Novell, Jennifer Arter, Shannon Lawrence, and Irene Perciali, *Scholarly Communication: Academic Values and Sustainable Models* (Berkeley: Center for Studies in Higher Education, 2006), 29.

414   Frank Kermode, "The Patience of Shakespeare," in *Shakespeare, Spenser, Donne: Renaissance Essays* (London & New York: Routledge, 2005), 149–63.

415   Frank Kermode, "Writing about Shakespeare," *London Review of Books*, December 9, 1999, 3.

416   MLA Task Force on Evaluating Scholarship, 9–71.

417   MLA Ad Hoc Committee on Teaching, Final Report, in *Profession 2001* (New York: MLA, 2001) 225–38, http://www.mla.org/rep_teaching.

418   MLA Ad Hoc Committee on the Future of Scholarly Publishing, "The Future of Scholarly Publishing," in *Profession 2002* (New York: MLA, 2002), 172–86, http://www.mla.org/issues_scholarly_pub.

419   Stephen Greenblatt, "A Special Letter from Stephen Greenblatt," May 28, 2002, http://www.mla.org/resources/documents/rep_scholarly_pub/scholarly_pub.

420   Stephen Greenblatt, *Will in the World: How Shakespeare Became Shakespeare* (New York: W.W. Norton, 2004).

421   MLA Task Force on Evaluating Scholarship, 13.

422   Ibid., 18.

423   Ibid., 19.

424   Ernest L. Boyer, *Scholarship Reconsidered: Priorities for the Professoriate* (Princeton: Carnegie Foundation for the Advancement of Teaching, 1990; reprint, San Francisco: Jossey-Bass, 1997).

425   MLA Task Force on Evaluation Scholarship, 35.

426   King et al., *Scholarly Communication*, 2.

427   Ibid., 30.

428   John Lombardi, "Research Competition and the MLA," *Inside Higher Education*, January 11, 2007, http://www.insidehighered.com/views/2007/01/11/lombardi.

429   King et al., *Scholarly Communication*, 27.

430   Ibid., 4.

431   Mary Burgan,. *What Ever Happened to the Faculty? Drift and Decision in Higher*

Education (Baltimore: Johns Hopkins University Press, 2006).

432   Robert H. Frank and PhilipJ. Cook, *The Winner-Take-All Society: Why the Few at the Top Get So Much More Than the Rest of Us* (1995; reprint, New York: Penguin, 1996).

CHAPTER 13: UNRAVELLING THE FABRIC OF ACADEME: THE MANAGERIALIST UNIVERSITY AND ITS IMPLICATIONS FOR THE INTEGRITY OF ACADEMIC WORK

433   When Penelope's husband Odysseus did not come home from the Trojan War, she was besieged by other potential husbands. However, Penelope still hoped Odysseus would return and so told would-be suitors that she could not remarry until she had completed a woven shroud for Laertes, her husband's father. She spent some of every day weaving the shroud, but each night she would unravel the work on the loom. Eventually a servant told her suitors what she was doing, and they demanded she choose one of them to marry. She declared that she would marry the first suitor who could string Odysseus's bow and shoot an arrow through twelve axes. Meanwhile, Odysseus returned, dressed as a poor man, passed the bow test and then murdered the suitors who had harassed Penelope. See http://www.pantheon.org/articles/p/penelope.html.

434   The UK higher education system is in reality composed of four different national systems: England (the largest), Scotland, Wales and Northern Ireland (the last named is the smallest, with only two universities). Higher education policy is largely a devolved power, though confusingly, science policy — including the Research Assessment Exercise — is UK-wide.

435   R. Deem, O. Fulton, R. Johnson, S. Hillyard, et al., *New Managerialism and the Management of UK Universities*, End of Award Report (Swindon: Economic and Social Research Council, 2001),
http://www.esrcsocietytoday.ac.uk/ESRCInfoCentre/ViewAwardPage.aspx?data=a ysN67OSmH%2f4mKibNqyEcPaU2MSTsPt6VIWlBC%2f7QiiZy5R4Ny5FWZ5Z5 Q9b7dqmcsFjyRRkdvp3Y4Qs5T20rjWvCB5OhNjQwqH5bzvzFv21RGde9Q2was dGaAPh5%2bTZLDDuX3pxbOQ%3d&xu=&isAwardHolder=&isProfiled=&Awar dHolderID=&Sector=; R. Deem, S. Hillyard, and M. Reed, *Knowledge, Higher Education and the New Managerialism: The Changing Management of UK Universities* (Oxford: Oxford University Press, 2007).

436   This project, "Developing Organisation Leaders as Change Agents in the Public Services" is funded by the UK Economic and Social Research Council (Award No RES-000-23-1136), from May 2006 to April 2009 and is a collaboration involving the author and three professors from Cardiff University Business School, namely Mike Reed, Jon Morris, and Mike Wallace.

437   M. Reed, "New Managerialism and Public Services Reform: From regulated autonomy to institutionalised distrust," in *Knowledge, Higher Education and the New Managerialism* (see note 3), 1–28; R. Deem, "The Knowledge Worker, the Manager-academic and the Contemporary UK University: New and old forms of public management," *Financial Accountability and Management* 20 (2 May 2004):

107–28.

438   J. Clarke and J. Newman, *The Managerial State: Power, politics and ideology in the remaking of social welfare* (London: Sage, 1997); M. Exworthy and S. Halford, eds., *Professionals and the New Managerialism in the Public Sector* (Buckingham: Open University Press, 1999); W. Enteman, *Managerialism: The Emergence of a New Ideology* (Madison WI: University of Wisconsin Press, 1993).

439   R. Deem and K. J. Brehony, "Management as Ideology: The case of 'new managerialism' in higher education," *Oxford Review of Education* 31 no. 2 (2005): 213–31.

440   M. Trow, "More Trouble than It's Worth," *Times Higher Education*, Supplement, October 24, 1997, 26; M. Trow, "Managerialism and the Academic Profession: The case of England," *Higher Education Policy* 7, no. 2 (1994): 11–18.

441   B. Kehm and U. Lanzendorf, eds., Reforming *University Governance: Changing conditions for research in four European countries*. (Bonn: Lemmens/Verlag, 2006).

442   J. Merisotis and J. Sadlak, "Higher Education Ranking: Evolution, acceptance, and dialogue," *Higher Education in Europe* 30, no. 2 (2005): 97–101; S. Marginson and E. Sawir, "University Leaders' Strategies in the Global Environment: A comparative study of Universitas Indonesia and the Australian National University," *Higher Education* 52, no. 2 (2006): 343–73; N.C. Liu and Y. Cheng, "Academic Ranking of World Universities — Methodologies and problems," *Higher Education in Europe* 30, no. 2 (2005): 127–36.

443   P. Curtis, "Dire Warnings as Chemistry Departments Close," *Guardian*, February 2, 2004, http://education.guardian.co.uk/universitiesincrisis/story/0,,1137231,00.html.

444   D. Saint-Martin, "The New Managerialism and the Policy Influence of Consultants in Government: An historical-institutionalist analysis of Britain, Canada and France," *Governance: An International journal of policy and administration* 11, no. 3 (1998): 319–56; A. Pollock, *NHS PLC: The Privatisation of our Healthcare* (London: Verso, 2004); A. Pollock, J. Shaoul, and N. Vickers, "Private Finance and 'Value for Money' in NHS Hospitals: A policy in search of a rationale?" *British Medical Journal* 324, no. 7347 (May 18, 2002): 1205–9.

445   M. Exworthy and S. Halford, eds. *Professionals and the New Managerialism in the Public Sector* (Buckingham: Open University Press, 1999); C. Farrell and J. Morris, "The 'Neo-Bureaucratic' State: Professionals, managers and professional managers in schools, general practices and social work," *Organization* 10, no. 1 (2003): 129–56.

446   M. Reed, "Beyond the Iron Cage? Bureaucracy and democracy in the knowledge economy and society," in *Defending Bureaucracy*, ed. P. Du Gay (Oxford: Oxford University Press, 2004); M. Reed, "New Managerialism and Public Services Reform: From regulated autonomy to institutionalised distrust," in *Knowledge, Higher Education and the New Managerialism*, ed. R. Deem, S. Hillyard, and M. Reed (Oxford: Oxford University Press, 2007), 1–28.

447   Saint-Martin, "The New Managerialism."

448   R. Deem, and J. Ozga, "Women Managing for Diversity in a Post Modern

World," in *Feminist Critical Policy Analysis: A perspective from post secondary education*, ed. C. Marshall (London and New York: Falmer, 1997), 25–40; R. Deem and J. Ozga, "Transforming Post Compulsory Education? Femocrats at work in the academy," *Women's Studies International Forum* 23, no. 2 (2000): 153–66; J.T. Ozga and R. Deem, "Colluded Selves, New Times and Engendered Organizational Cultures: The experiences of feminist women managers in UK higher and further education," *Discourse* 21, no. 2 (2000): 141–54.

449   R. Deem, S. Hillyard, and M. Reed, *Knowledge, Higher Education and the New Managerialism: The changing management of UK universities* (Oxford: Oxford University Press, 2007).

450   R. Deem, "Gender, Organizational Cultures and the Practices of Manager-academics in UK Universities," *Gender, Work and Organization* 10, no. 2 (2003): 239–59.

451   R. Scase and R. Goffee, *Reluctant Managers: Their work and lifestyles* (London: Unwin Hyman, 1989).

452   E. Ferlie, L. Ashburner, L. Fitzgerald, and A. Pettigrew, *The New Public Management in Action* (Oxford: Oxford University Press, 1996).

453   S. Marginson and M. Considine, *Enterprise University in Australia: Governance, strategy and reinvention* (Cambridge: Cambridge University Press, 2000).

454   D. Smith, and J. Adams, "Changing Roles of the Pro-vice Chancellor," *Engage* no. 7 (2007): 14; D. Smith, J. Adams, and D. Mount, *UK Universities and Executive Officers: The changing role of pro-vice chancellors*. Leadership Foundation for Higher Education: Research and Development Series (London: Leadership Foundation for Higher Education, 2007).

455   G. Petrov, R. Bolden, and J. Gosling, *Developing Collective Leadership In Higher Education*, Interim Report Summary, Exeter, UK: University of Exeter, Leadership Foundation for Higher Education, 2006, http://www.lfhe.ac.uk/research/projects/goslingsummary1.pdf/; G. Petrov, "No More Heroes? Rhetoric and Reality of Distributed Leadership in Higher Education" (paper presented to the South West Higher Education Research Network, University of Bristol, Graduate School of Education, June 19, 2007), http://www.bristol.ac.uk/education/research/networks/henetsw.

456   M. Newman, "Alarm at Lack of Players in VC Hiring," *Times Higher Education*, Supplement, November 30, 2007, http://www.timeshighereducation.co.uk/story.asp?sectioncode=26&storycode =311279.

457   D. Farnham and J. Jones, "Who are the Vice-chancellors? An analysis of their professional and social backgrounds 1990-1997," *Higher Education Review* 30, no. 3 (1998): 42–58; A. Fazackerley, "Will the Face at the Top Ever Really Change?" *Times Higher Education*, Supplement, July 28, 2006 http://www.timeshighereducation.co.uk/story.asp?storyCode=204538& sectioncode=26.

458   A. Jarratt, *Report of the Steering Committee for Efficiency Studies in Universities* (London: Committee of Vice Chancellors and Principals, 1985).

459   C. Bargh, J. Bocock, P. Scott, and D. Smith, *University Leadership: The role of the chief executive* (Buckingham: Open University Press, 2000).

460   R. Deem, *Managing Academic Research in Universities or Cat-herding for Beginners: The case of the UK* (paper presented to the Research Mission of the University conference of the Consortium of Higher Education Researchers, University College, Belfield, Dublin, August 31, 2007).

461   K. H. Mok, R. Deem, and L. Lucas, "Transforming Higher Education in Whose Image? Exploring the concept of the 'world-class' university in Europe and Asia," *Higher Education Policy* 21 (2008). (In press)

462   R. Naidoo, "The Commodified University: Pitfalls and possibilities (seminar paper), Graduate School of Education, University of Bristol, CLIO seminar, November 19, (2003); R. Naidoo and I. Jamieson, "Empowering Participants or Corroding Learning? Towards a research agenda on the impact of student consumerism in higher education," *Journal of Education Policy* 20, no. 3 (2005): 267–81.

463   L. Leisyte, *University Governance and Academic Research* (PhD diss., Centre for Higher Education Policy Studies, University of Twente, Enschede, the Netherlands, 2007).

464   L. Lucas, *The Research Game in Academic Life* (Maidenhead: Open University Press and Society for Research into Higher Education, 2006).

465   B. Kehm and U. Lanzendorf, eds., *Reforming University Governance: Changing conditions for research in four European countries* (Bonn: Lemmens/Verlag, 2006).

466   A. Jenkins, *Guide to the Research Evidence on Teaching-Research Relations* (The Higher Education Academy, 2005), http://www.heacademy.ac.uk/resources/detail/id383_guide_to_research_evidence_on_teaching_research_relations.

467   R. Deem, "Conceptions of Contemporary European Universities: To do research or not to do research?" *European Journal of Education* 41, no. 2 (2006): 281–304; R. Deem and L. Lucas, "Research and Teaching Cultures in Two Contrasting UK Policy Locations: Academic life in education departments in five English and Scottish universities," *Higher Education* 54, no. 1 (2007): 115–33.

468   Higher Education Funding Council for England, *Research Excellence Framework: Consultation on the assessment and funding of higher education post-2008* (Higher Education Funding Council for England, November 2007), http://www.hefce.ac.uk/news/hefce/2007/ref.asp; B. Bekhradnia, *Evaluating and Funding Research through the Proposed "Research Excellence Framework"* (Higher Education Policy Institute, 2007), http://www.hepi.ac.uk/pubdetail.asp?ID=246&DOC=reports.

469   A. Nelson, "Nationalism, Internationalism, and the Institutionalization of Research in the Early American Republic: The case of plant science, 1780–1815," (paper presented to the Critical Perspectives on Realizing the Global University workshop, London, November 14, 2007), http://www.wun.ac.uk/theglobal university/workshop.html.

470   L. Leisyte, "University Governance and Academic Research" (PhD diss., Centre for Higher Education Policy Studies, University of Twente, Enschede, the Netherlands, 2007).

471   S. Shah and J. Brennan, "Quality Assessment and Institutional Change:

Experiences from 14 countries," *Higher Education* 40, no. 3 (2000): 331–49.

472 L. Morley, *Quality and Power in Higher Education* (Buckingham: Open University Press, 2003).

473 Ibid.

474 M. Cheng, "The Perceived Impacts of Quality Audit on the Work of Academics: A Case Study of a Research-Intensive Pre-1992 University in England," unpublished PhD dissertation, Graduate School of Education, University of Bristol, Bristol, UK., 2008).

475 B. Kehm, *Doctoral Education — Quo Vadis?* (plenary address, Research Mission of the University conference of the Consortium of Higher Education Researchers, University College, Dublin, August 31, 2007).

476 P. Cunningham, *Guardians of Knowledge, Drivers of Change — Universities serving society* (plenary address), Research Mission of the University conference of the Consortium of Higher Education Researchers, University College, Dublin. September 1, (2007).

477 S. Powell and H. Green, *The Doctorate WorldWide*, Maidenhead: Open University Press, (2007).

478 UK Council for Graduate Education, *The Professional Doctorate*, UK Council for Graduate Education 2002, http://www.ukcge.ac.uk/NR/rdonlyres/53BE34C8-EBDD-47E1-B1C7-F80B45D25E20/0/ProfessionalDoctorates2002.pdf; J. Taylor, "Quality and Standards: The challenge of the professional doctorate (paper presented to the Critical Perspectives on Realizing the Global University workshop, London November 14, 2007), http://www.wun.ac.uk/theglobaluniversity/workshop.html.

479 M. Peters, "Re-imagining the University in the Global Era," Worldwide University Network seminar series, Ideas and Universities: *The Purpose of Universities: Ideals and Realities*, 2007, http://www.wun.ac.uk/ideasanduniversities/seminars/archive/2007_programme/index.html.

480 D. O'Reilly, M. Wallace, R. Deem, J. Morris, et al., "The Discursive Representations of Leadership Development in the Reform of UK Health and Education Public Services" (paper presented to the Political Studies Association, University of Bath, April 11–13, 2007).

481 Universities UK and Standing Conference of Principals, *Business Case for the Leadership Foundation for Higher Education*, Universities UK and Standing Conference of Principals, (from steering group chaired by Adrian Smith, 2003), http://www.universitiesuk.ac.uk/mediareleases/downloads/LFBusinessCase.pdf.

482 Oakleigh Consulting, *Final Report: Interim Evaluation of the Leadership Foundation for Higher Education* (Manchester: Oakleigh Consulting, 2006), http://www.lfhe.ac.uk/about/history/evaluation.html.

483 P. Gronn, "Distributed Properties: A new architecture for leadership," *Educational Management and Administration* 28 (2000): 317–8; P.C. Gronn, "Distributed Leadership as a Unit of Analysis," *Leadership Quarterly*, 13, no. 4 (2002): 423–51.

484   M. Newman, "Reprimand for Keele Lecturer over Open Letter," *Times Higher Education* Supplement, no. 1827, January 10–16, 2008, 16.

485   L. Leisyte, H.F. de Boer, and J. Enders, "England: The Prototype of the 'Evaluative State,'" in *Reforming University Governance: Changing conditions for research in four European countries.* eds. B. Kehm and U. Lanzendorf (Bonn: Lemmens/Verlag, 2006), 21–58.

486   R. Deem and R.J. Johnson, "Managerialism and University Managers: Building new academic communities or disrupting old ones?" *Higher Education and its Communities,* ed. I. McNay (Buckingham: Open University Press, 2000), 6–84; R. Deem, "Managing to exclude? Manager-academic and staff communities in contemporary UK universities," in *International Perspectives on Higher Education Research: Access and Inclusion* ed. M. Tight (Amsterdam and London: Elsevier Science JAI, 2003), 103–25.

487   H.F. de Boer, L. Leisyte, and J. Enders, "The Netherlands: 'Steering from a distance,'" in *Reforming University Governance: Changing conditions for research in four European countries,* ed. B. Kehm and U. Lanzendorf (Bonn: Lemmens/Verlag, 2006), 59–96.

488   Mok, Deem, and Lucas, "Transforming Higher Education" (see note 28).

489   A. Brew, *Research and Teaching: Beyond the divide* (Basingstoke: Palgrave Macmillan, 2006).

490   P. Ciancanelli, "Re/producing Universities: Knowledge dissemination, market power and the global knowledge commons," in *Geographies of Knowledge, Geometries of Power: Higher education in the 21st century,* World Year Book of Education 2008, ed. D. Epstein, R. Boden, R. Deem, F. Rizvi, and S. Wright (London: Routledge Falmer, 2007), 67–84.

491   S. Fuller, "University Leadership in the Twenty-first Century: The case for academic Caesarism," in *Geographies of Knowledge* (see note 57), 50–66.

CHAPTER 14: FROM THE MONKISH SCRIBE TO THE DIGITAL AGE: THE UNIVERSITY BOTH CONTINUOUS AND TRANSFORMED

492   J.J. Cameron, *On the Idea of a University* (Toronto: University of Toronto Press, 1978), 26–7.

493   Ibid., 33.

494   Ibid., 44.

495   John Henry Newman, *Discourses on the Scope and Nature of University Education* (London: Dent, 1965). The 1856 and 1859 volumes have been out of print since the nineteenth century.

496   Newman, *Discourses,* xxxi.

497   Charles Stephen Dessain, ed.,*The Letters and Diaries of John Henry Newman* (Oxford: Oxford University Press, 1966), vol. xvi, 68.

498   Henry Tristam, ed., *John Henry Newman: Autobiographical Writings* (New York: Sheed and Ward, 1957), 327.

499   Ibid., 99.

500   Ian Ker, *John Henry Newman: A Biography* (Oxford: Clarendon Press, 1988).

501   Newman, *Discourses*, 101.

502   Ibid., 129–30.

503   Ibid., 122.

504   Pius XI writes: "As history abundantly proves, it is true that on account of changed conditions many things which were done by small associations in former times cannot be done now save by larger associations. Still, that most weighty principle, which cannot be set aside or changed, remains fixed and unshaken in social philosophy: Just as it is gravely wrong to take from individuals what they can accomplish by their own initiative and industry and give it to the community, so also it is an injustice and at the same time a grave evil and disturbance of right order to assign to a greater and higher association what lesser and subordinate organizations can do." (*Quadragesimo Anno*, section # 79, 1931). The text is: Michael Walsh and Brian Davies, eds., *Proclaiming Justice and Peace: Papal Documents from Rerum novarum through Centesimus annus* (Mystic, CT: Twenty-Third Publications, 1991), 62. The principle of subsidary function or subsidiarity has been regularly invoked by John XXIII, Paul VI and John Paul II.

505   Adrian Hasting, *The Oxford Companion to Christian Thought* (Oxford: Oxford University Press, 2000), 687.

CHAPTER 15: RESTRUCTURING ACADEMIC WORK

506   Richard Moser, "The New Academic Labor System" (Washington: American Association of University Professors, 2001), 1, http://www.aaup.org/AAUP/issues/contingent/moserlabor.htm.

507   John Harp reported that a survey he did at Carleton University in the late 1990s indicated that more than half of all undergraduate course titles were taught by non-tenured, non-tenure-track faculty (personal communication). Numerous departments at major research universities confirm that the majority of undergraduate teaching is done by those off the tenure track.

508   Statistics Canada surveys of part-time faculty in the 1990s were rendered of little value, as a number of major universities chose not to complete the questionnaires.

509   American Association of University Professors, "The Annual Report on the Economic Status of the Profession, 2007–2008," *Academe* 94, no. 2 (March–April 2008): 16.

510   American Association of University Professors, Research Department, 2007, compiled from the U.S. Department of Education, IPEDS Fall Staff Survey, http://www.aaup.org/AAUP/issues/contingent.

511   The term "contract academic staff" has come into usage to describe all those off
        the tenure-track, because nomenclature for different types of contingent posi-
        tions varies widely. They are variously called "sessionals," "adjuncts," "limited-
        term," "stipendiaries," and "part-timers." The defining characteristic of their sit-
        uation is that all are on term contracts, whether part-time or full-time, which is
        why "contract academic staff" is used as the generic descriptor.

512   CAUT, *Statement to the House of Commons Standing Committee on Finance regard-
        ing the 2007 Pre-Budget Consultations*, August, 2007, http://www.caut.ca/pages.
        asp?page=584&lang=1.

513   Association of Universities and Colleges of Canada, *Trends in Higher Education,
        vol. 3: Finance* (Ottawa: AUCC, 2008), 29, http://www.aucc.ca/_pdf/english/
        publications/trends_2008_vol3_e.pdf

514   Charles Babbage, *On the Economy of Machinery and Manufactures* (Fairfield, NJ:
        A.M. Kelley, 1986.)

515   Frederick Winslow Taylor, *The Principles of Scientific Management* (New York:
        Norton, 1967).

516   Harry Braverman, *Labor and Monopoly Capital: The Degradation of Work in the
        Twentieth Century* (New York: Monthly Review Press, 1974).

517   David F. Noble, *Forces of Production: A Social History of Industrial Automation*
        (New York: Knopf, 1984).

518   See, for example, Philip Kraft, *Programmers and Managers: The Routinization of
        Computer Programming in the United States* (New York: Springer-Verlag, 1977);
        Andrew Zimbalist, ed., *Case Studies in the Labor Process* (New York: Monthly
        Review Press, 1979).

519   William F. Massy is professor emeritus of education and business administration
        at Stanford University and former director of the Stanford Institute for Higher
        Education Research. Robert Zemsky is professor of education at the University
        of Pennsylvania, chair of the Higher Education Division, and director of the
        Institute for Research on Higher Education.

520   William F. Massy and Robert Zemsky, "Using Information Technology to
        Enhance Academic Productivity,"
        http://www.educause.edu/ir/library/html/nli0004.html.

521   Ibid., 4.

522   John Daniel, "Distance Learning in the Era of Networks," *Bulletin of the
        Association of Commonwealth Universities*, no. 138 (2000): 9.

523   Job Posting: University of Toronto Instructorships in Philosophy, posted on
        Monday, January 28, 2008. Positions: PHL 201 H1F — Introduction to
        Philosophy.

524   Massy and Zemsky, 7.

525   "A small core of traditional institutions will probably remain buffered from
        these changes: these are the well-endowed institutions with many more appli-
        cants than student places. A small core of traditional learners, those who can

afford it and those whose abilities are rewarded with scholarships, will continue to seek out the traditional handicraft-oriented education that has been the hallmark of our system. For these students, traditional education provides acculturation as well as learning. The public has begun to question, however, whether this model is extendible to the whole of higher education. Already the criticism of higher education's rising costs suggests that society finds this educational model too expensive for massified higher education." Ibid, 9.

526   D. Bruce Johnstone with Alka Arora and William Experton, *The Financing and Management of Higher Education: A Status Report on Worldwide Reforms* (Washington: The World Bank, 1998), 26.

527   Ibid., 22.

528   Clifford Geertz, *Available Light: Anthropological Reflections on Philosophical Topics* (Princeton, NJ: Princeton University Press, 2000), 10–11.

529   *AAUP Contingent Faculty Index 2006, Appendix 1: Doctoral and Research Universities.* The *Index* is based on figures submitted by institutions to the US Department of Education's IPEDS database for fall 2005. The Index is available at http://www.aaup.org/AAUP/pubsres/research/conind2006.htm.

530   John W. Curtis and Monica F. Jacobe, "Consequences: An Increasingly Contingent Faculty," *AAUP Contingent Faculty Index 2006,* 18 (see note 25).

531   Sam Dillon, "Troubles Grow for a University Built on Profits," *New York Times,* February 11, 2007. http://www.nytimes.com/2007/02/11/education/11phoenix.html?ex=132885000 0&en=5c8573d57de4bffe&ei=5088

532   Derek Bok, *Universities in the Marketplace: The Commercialization of Higher Education* (Princeton: Princeton University Press, 2003), 187.

533   Ibid., 189.

534   Senior academic bodies, to the extent that they exist in community colleges, rarely have the statutory authority of many of their university counterparts to make academic decisions. Rather they are advisory to the board of governors.

535   Glen Jones and Michael Skolnik, "Governing Boards in Canadian Universities," *Review of Higher Education* 20, no. 3 (1997), 277–95.

536   Glen A. Jones, "The Structure of University Governance in Canada: A Policy Network Approach" in Alberto Amaral, Glen A. Jones and Berit Karseth, *Governing Higher Education: National Perspectives on Institutional Governance* (Dordrecht/Boston/London: Kluwer Academic Publishers, 2002), 213–234.

537   Robert Birnbaum, "The Latent Organizational Functions of the Academic Senate: Why Senates Do Not Work But Will Not Go Away," *Journal of Higher Education* 60, no. 4 (July–August 1989): 423–443.

538   One of the most interesting cases was the Oxford vice-chancellor's unsuccessful multi-year fight to end the university's system in which faculty have final authority in governance of the institution. See Jessica Shepherd, "Hood faces questions over rejection of Oxford reform plans," *Guardian,* January 23, 2007,

http://education.guardian.co.uk/administration/story/0,,1996270,00.html.

539   CAUT, *CAUT Policy on Governance: Where We Have Been and Where We Should Go*, November 2004, http://www.caut.ca/uploads/governance.pdf.

540   See, for example, Henry Giroux, *The University in Chains: Confronting the Military-Industrial-Academic Complex*, (Boulder, CO: Paradigm, 2007); Rosemary Deem, Sam Hillyard and Michael Reed, *Knowledge, Higher Education and the New Managerialism: The Changing Management of UK Universities*, (Oxford: Oxford University Press, 2007); Jennifer Washburn, University Inc.: *The Corporate Corruption of Higher Education*, (New York: Basic Books, 2005); Sheila Slaughter and Larry Leslie, *Academic Capitalism and the New Economy: Policy, Politics and the Entrepreneurial University*, (Baltimore: Johns Hopkins University Press, 1997).

541   Over the past eight years, for example, the Canadian Association of University Teachers has successfully organized into academic staff unions thousands of unorganized contingent faculty so as to be able to begin to reverse their exploitation and the undermining of academic labour. Similar initiatives are being undertaken by the American Federation of Teachers, the American Association of University Professors and the National Education Association in the United States.

542   Drew Faust, "Unleashing Our Most Ambitious Imaginings" (speech at her inauguration as President of Harvard, October 12, 2007), http://www.president. harvard.edu/speeches/faust/071012_installation.html.

CHAPTER 16: ACADEMIC INTEGRITY AND THE PUBLIC INTEREST

543   The writer thanks Donald C. Savage and Vladimir Tasiç for helpful discussions.

544   This opinion is attributed to Eratosthenes by Strabo, in *Geographikon*, 1.4.9, published in Greek and English translation as *The Geography of Strabo* (London: W. Heinemann, 1917), 247–9. See Alberto Manguel, *The City of Words* (Toronto: Anansi, 2007), 49, 152, for the particular English wording used here (from the 1960 Heinemann edition).

545   Panel on Scientific Responsibility and the Conduct of Research, *Responsible Science: Ensuring the Integrity of the Research Process* (Washington: National Academy Press, Volume I, 1992, and Volume II, 1993).

546   Legend has it that Archimedes designed war engines to defend Syracuse against the Romans (as recorded in Plutarch's *Life of Marcellus*). Much of the scholarly work by Eratosthenes and other scholars at the Museum of Alexandria was of political or economic significance. Copernicus, Newton, and Laplace held senior government posts during parts of their careers. Kelvin became wealthy from consulting fees and royalties on his patents. (He was, among other things, chief consulting engineer for the first trans-Atlantic cable.)

547   David Healy, *The Anti-depressant Era* (Cambridge, MA: Harvard University Press, 1997); Daniel S. Greenberg, *Science, Money and Politics* (Chicago: University of Chicago Press, 2001); Derek Bok, *Universities in the Marketplace* (Princeton:

Princeton University Press, 2003); Jennifer Washburn, *University Inc.* (New York: Basic Books, 2005).

548   Andrew C. Revkin, "Climate Expert Says NASA Tried to Silence Him," *New York Times*, January 29, 2006; Ian Sample, "Scientists offered cash to dispute climate study," *Guardian*, February 2, 2007, http://environment.guardian.co.uk/print/ 0,329703480-121568,00.html.

549   Sheldon Krimsky, *Science in the Private Interest* (Lanham, MD: Rowman & Littlefield, 2003); David Healy, *Let Them Eat Prozac* (Toronto: James Lorimer, 2003); Marcia Angell, *The Truth About Drug Companies* (New York: Random House, 2004); John Abramson, *Overdosed America* (New York: Harper-Collins, 2004), Jerome P. Kassirer, *On the Take* (New York: Oxford University Press, 2005); Ray Moynihan and Alan Cassels, *Selling Sickness* (Vancouver: Greystone, 2005).

550   Jonathan R. Cole, "Academic Freedom on American Campuses in Troubled Times," in James L. Turk and Alan Manson (eds.), *Free Speech in Fearful Times* (Toronto: James Lorimer, 2007), 195.

551   This statement by Einstein is inscribed on the statue of him located in front of the National Academy of Sciences in Washington, D.C.

552   Noam Chomsky, *American Power and the New Mandarins* (New York: Pantheon Books, 1969 (first printing 1967)), 325.

553   United Nations Educational, Scientific and Cultural Organization, *Recommendation Concerning the Status of Higher-Education Teaching Personnel*, November 11, 1997, section VII, paragraphs 33 and 34 (c), at http://portal.unesco.org/en/ev.php-URL_ID=13144&URL_DO=DO_ TOPIC&URL_SECTION=201.html

554   Brennan J, Supreme Court of the United States, for the majority in *Keyishian v. Board of Regents*, 385 U.S. 589 (1967), 174.

555   La Forest J, for the majority in *McKinney v. University of Guelph* (1990), 76 D.L.R. (4th) 545 (S.C.C.), 649.

556   News report, *CAUT Bulletin*, December 2007, 1, http://www.cautbulletin.ca/default.asp?vol=7&no=44

557   Professor Noble publicly issued a document criticizing the administration of York University, alleging it had "clamped down" on campus activities by students who were pro-Palestinian because of "the presence and influence of staunch pro-Israel lobbyists, activists, and fundraising agencies" on the university's own fundraising body. In effect, he alleged that the university had ceded some of its administrative autonomy to certain wealthy private supporters and their allies in moving inappropriately to limit freedom of expression on campus. In response, the university issued an official public statement denouncing Professor Noble's document as representing "racism" and "bigotry," although Professor Noble is himself Jewish. He filed a grievance, alleging that his academic freedom and other rights had been violated by the university's denunciation. The arbitrator found that the university had violated Professor Noble's academic freedom and awarded him a remedy. (Russell Goodfellow, arbitration

award in *York University and York University Faculty Association* [grievance of David Noble], 2007 CanLII 50108 [ON L.A.], http://www.canlii.org/en/on/onla/doc /2007/2007canlii50108/2007canlii50108.html.)

558   Jon Thompson, Patricia Baird, and Jocelyn Downie, *The Olivieri Report: The Complete Text of the Report of the Independent Inquiry Commissioned by the Canadian Association of University Teachers* (Toronto: James Lorimer, 2001), 400–401 (quoting from the disciplinary letter sent to Gideon Koren by Robert Prichard and Michael Strofolino, representing Koren's university and hospital employers).

559   That this factor remains insufficiently appreciated can be seen from a recent list of recommendations for restoring integrity in medical science put forward by the editors of a leading journal. Two of the eleven recommendations propose that offenders be reported to the dean of their medical school. However, the editors offer no guidance for circumstances in which the dean, or the president, or administrators of federal granting or regulatory agencies may be part of the problem, as illustrated by the cases discussed here. (cf. Catherine D. DeAngelis and Phil B. Fontanarosa, "Impugning the Integrity of Medical Science: The Adverse Effects of Industry Influence," *Journal of the American Medical Association*, 299, no. 15 [April 16, 2008], 1833–5).

560   H.W. Arthurs, Roger A. Blais, and Jon Thompson, *Integrity in Scholarship* (Montreal: Concordia University, 1994), 4–9.

561   Ibid., 13.

562   Ibid., 69.

563   Ibid., 39–40.

564   Joyce Lorimer, "Inquiries at Concordia University," CAUT Memorandum 94:46, August 15, 1994, 3.

565   There were three independent inquiries at Concordia in the aftermath of the murders by Fabrikant: i) by H.W. Arthurs et al. into Fabrikant's allegations of misconduct by his three patrons, ii) by J.S. Cowan into Fabrikant's employment history in the University, and iii) by P.C. Levi, a forensic auditor. The Cowan inquiry found that the university administration had repeatedly mishandled matters involving Fabrikant, including unfair treatment of him in promotion and tenure considerations, and failure to address his increasingly menacing conduct. The Levi report confirmed that there had been significant misappropriation of university funds and resources by some of Fabrikant's patrons.

566   Letters from NSERC president T.A. Brzustowski to committee of inquiry chair H.W. Arthurs, July 8, 2006 and September 23,1996; Jennifer Lewington, "Fabrikant story gets new twist," *Globe and Mail*, February 18,1997, A6.

567   Jennifer Lewington, "Fabrikant story gets new twist," *Globe and Mail*, 18 February 1997.

568   Frederick Lowy and Donat J. Taddeo, "For Shame," letter to the editor, *University Affairs* June–July 1996.

569   Morris Wolfe, "Dr. Fabrikant's Solution," *Saturday Night*, July–August 1994, 59.

570   Thompson et al., *The Olivieri Report*, 32.

571   Thompson et al., *The Olivieri Report*, 32, 368 (note 151), 393–4, 405–12.

572   Two independent inquiries exonerated Olivieri in their reports, one commis-
      sioned by CAUT (Jon Thompson et al., *The Olivieri Report*, published October
      26, 2001, cited in endnotes), the other commissioned by the College of
      Physicians and Surgeons of Ontario (*CPSO Complaints Committee Report on a
      Complaint by Dr. L. Becker [Chair of the Medical Advisory Committee of the Hospital
      for Sick Children] Concerning Dr. N. Olivieri*, published December 19, 2001).

573   Hospital for Sick Children, report of forensic investigator, quoted in Jon
      Thompson et al., *The Olivieri Report*, 398.

574   Alexander Aird, opinion article, *Globe and Mail*, December 31, 1999, cited in Jon
      Thompson et al., *The Olivieri Report*, 399.

575   Disciplinary letter written by the hospital and university presidents to Gideon
      Koren, April 11, 2000, cited in Jon Thompson et al., *The Olivieri Report*, 401.

576   Jon Thompson et al., *The Olivieri Report*, 404.

577   David Naylor, Dean's statement, University of Toronto Faculty of Medicine, min-
      utes of the Faculty Council meeting held 22 April 2002.

578   Ibid.

579   Ibid.

580   Judith Butler, "No, It's Not Anti-Semitic," *London Review of Books*, August 21,
      2003, 25, 16, www.lrb.co.uk/v25/n16/print/but102_.html.

581   David McClintick, "How Harvard Lost Russia," *Institutional Investor*, January
      2006, 22, www.dailyii.com/print.asp?ArticleID=1039086

582   McClintick, "How Harvard Lost Russia," 23.

583   The case of Nancy Olivieri in the medical school at the University of Toronto
      provides a dramatic example of what can happen in the absence of fair proce-
      dures. As discussed earlier in this chapter, her career was nearly destroyed by
      false allegations of research misconduct brought by Gideon Koren. Only the
      intervention by scientists and organizations external to the university ensured
      procedural fairness and exoneration for her, enabling her to continue her career.

584   Since President Nixon's declaration in 1971, the annual budget of the NCI has
      increased thirty-fold and is now approximately $5 billion, while that of the
      American Cancer Society has increased to approximately $800 million.

585   John C. Bailar and Heather L. Gornik, "Cancer Undefeated," *New England
      Journal of Medicine* 336, no. 22, (May 29,1997), 1569–75; Samuel S. Epstein,
      Cancer-gate: How to Win the Losing Cancer War (Amityville, NY: Baywood
      Publishing, 2005).

586   Devra Davis, *The Secret History of the War on Cancer* (New York: Basic Books,
      2007), x.

587   Ibid. It is hard to believe that Frank Press was isolated in his attitude toward the

public interest. Having been science advisor to President Carter (1977–80) and then chair of the National Research Council, as well as president of the NAS (1981–93), he was at the pinnacle of the American scientific establishment.

588   The political repression of this period (mid-1940s to late 1950s) is often inaccurately referred to as McCarthyism. The organized repression was a campaign by business interests and politicians that began several years before Senator Joseph McCarthy joined in with his own crusade, and lasted several years beyond his ignominious fall from official grace. The campaign had two related purposes. One was to turn the USSR from vital ally into feared enemy, in order to justify continuation of the military-Keynesian economy that had proved so successful and profitable during WW II. The other was to renew efforts "to undermine unions, working-class culture and independent thought" that had pre-dated the war (Noam Chomsky, *Deterring Democracy* [New York: Hill and Wang, 1992]. See Ellen W. Schrecker, *Many Were the Crimes* [Toronto: Little, Brown, 1998] for a survey of this period.)

589   Ellen W. Schrecker, *No Ivory Tower* (New York: Oxford University Press, 1986).

590   Michiel Horn, *Academic Freedom in Canada* (Toronto: University of Toronto Press, 1999).

591   Robert Hofstader and Walter P. Metzger, *The Development of Academic Freedom in the United States* (New York: Columbia University Press, 1955).

592   Schrecker, *No Ivory Tower*, 113; Horn, *Academic Freedom in Canada*, 186.

593   Richard C. Lewontin, "The Cold War and the Transformation of the Academy," in *The Cold War and the University*, ed. André Schiffrin (New York: The New Press, 1997), 20.

594   Schrecker, *No Ivory Tower*, 341.

595   Lewontin, "The Cold War," 2.

596   Ibid.

597   Noam Chomsky, "The Cold War and the University," in *The Cold War and the University* (see note 40), 179.

598   Ibid.

599   Ibid., 178.

600   Noam Chomsky, *Towards a New Cold War* (New York: Pantheon, 1982), 14.

601   "Elsewhere," for example, in the USSR under Stalin, intellectuals or Soviet citizens generally who deviated from ideological norms could be summarily deprived of their privileges, or freedom, or even their lives. Orthodoxy extended even into fields such as biology, where it was illegal to dissent from the theories of Trofim Lysenko. It was not until a decade after Stalin's death that Pyotr Kapitsa and several other nuclear physicists succeeded in exposing Lysenko's work as fraudulent. It has been fashionable in the more affluent and free West to view such events condescendingly. However, as we are now beginning to understand more fully, inducements are as effective in imposing fraudulent orthodoxies in the neoliberal West as coercion was in the Stalinist East.

Chomsky (above) was writing about political orthodoxy, but as noted in this and other chapters of the present volume, the same virulent processes have infected much of Western medical science. The most recent revelations of fraudulent science appeared in the issue of the *Journal of the American Medical Association* dated April 16, 2008, cited elsewhere in this chapter.

602 http://en.wikipedia.org/wiki/Norman_Finkelstein.

603 Nadia Abu El-Haj, *Facts on the Ground* (Chicago: University of Chicago Press, 2001).

604 Jane Kramer, "The Petition," *The New Yorker*, April 14, 2008, 50–59.

605 John Mearsheimer and Stephen Walt, "The Israel Lobby," *London Review of Books*, March 23, 2006, http://www.lrb.co.uk/v28/n06/mear01_.html.

606 John J. Mearsheimer and Stephen J. Walt, *The Israel Lobby and U.S. Foreign Policy* (New York: Farrar, Straus and Giroux, 2007), viii.

607 The same phenomenon was observed in Canada four decades later. As discussed earlier, Gideon Koren was disciplined for professional misconduct, including repeated lying, and for research misconduct. One of the disciplinary penalties was that he was removed from the CIBC-Wood Gundy Children's Miracle Foundation Chair in Child Health Research he held, although he retained his regular faculty and clinical positions in Toronto. Shortly after these highly publicized events, Koren was awarded the Ivey Chair in Molecular Toxicology at the University of Western Ontario.

608 Noam Chomsky, *American Power and the New Mandarins* (New York: Pantheon, 1969), 325

609 "The whole aim of practical politics is to keep the populace alarmed by menacing it with an endless series of hobgoblins, all of them imaginary." – H.L. Mencken, quoted in Howard K. Zinn, *A People's History of the United States* (New York: Harper Collins, 2003), 647.

610 Amir Attaran, "When Think Tanks Produce Propaganda," *Globe and Mail*, February 21, 2008, A13.

611 Jack Granatstein, "There's Nothing Improper about Educating Canadians on Defence," Globe and Mail, February 27, 2008, A13.

612 Amir Attaran, letter to the editor, *Globe and Mail*, Toronto, February 28, 2008.

613 Robert van den Bosch, *The Pesticide Conspiracy* (Garden City: Doubleday, 1978), 119–28.

614 "The EMOFICO Affair," *CAUT Bulletin*, April 1980, 1.

615 Washburn, *University Inc.* (see note 3), 4, 14–16.

616 David Healy, *The Anti-depressant Era*, 257; David Healy, *The Creation of Psychopharmacology* (Cambridge MA: Harvard University Press, 2002), 371–2; David Healy, this volume.

617 It is relevant to note in the present context that Japanese economic productivity began to rival American not just because it adopted a different model for its

national economy but also because it gained enormously from its role as the main staging area for America's long, aggressive war against the people of Indochina. As with other American wars of aggression, before and since, leading intellectuals generated much of the propaganda for this illegal war of genocidal proportions.

618   Steven Shapin, "I'm a Surfer," *London Review of Books*, March 20, 2008, 5.

619   Derek Bok, *Universities in the Marketplace* (see note 3), 11.

620   Eduardo Galeano, *Open Veins of Latin America* (New York: Monthly Review Press, 1973); Noam Chomsky, Year 501 (Montreal: Black Rose Books, 1993).

621   Marcia Angell, *The Truth About Drug Companies* (see note 5), 3.

622   Elias Canetti, *Crowds and Power* (New York: Farrar Straus Giroux, 1984), 466 (German original: *Masse und Macht*, 1960).

623   The Russell-Einstein Manifesto, issued in London, July 9, 1955, http://www.geocities.com/CapitolHill/3778/manifest.html?20085.

624   David Harvey, *A Brief History of Neoliberalism* (New York: Oxford University Press, 2005), 19. This rationalization of avarice is the latest revival of an ideology decried by Adam Smith: "All for ourselves and nothing for other people, seems, in every age of the world, to have been the vile maxim of the masters of mankind." (*The Wealth of Nations* [Toronto: Penguin Books, 1999; first printed 1776], III, 512.)

625   Lewis H. Lapham, "Tentacles of Rage," *Harper's Magazine*, September 2004, 31–41; Pierre Bourdieu, *Acts of Resistance* (New York: The New Press, 1998), 29–44; Noam Chomsky, *Profit Over People* (New York: Seven Stories Press, 1999).

626   Eric Janszen, "The Next Bubble," *Harper's Magazine*, February 2008.

627   Pam Martens, "The Obama Bubble Agenda," http://www.counterpunch.org/martens05062008.html ; Michael Valpy, "The Canadian Dream?" *Globe and Mail*, May 2, 2008, A1, A10 (reporting on results of the 2006 Census)

628   Noam Chomsky, *What We Say Goes* (New York: Metropolitan Books, 2007), 51–52.

629   Walter Russell Mead, "Why the Deficit is a Godsend," *Harper's Magazine*, May 1993, 56–62.

630   Indira Samarasekera, "Partnerships Are the Order of the Day," *Globe and Mail*, January 21, 2008, A13.

631   Noam Chomsky, *On Power and Ideology: The Managua Lectures* (Boston: South End Press, 1987), 69.

632   Joseph S. Ross, Kevin P. Hill, David S. Egilman, and Harlam M. Krumholz, "Guest Authorship and Ghostwriting in Publications Related to Rofecoxib," *Journal of the American Medical Association*, 299, no. 15 (April 16, 2007), 1800–1812; Bruce M. Psaty and Richard A. Kronmal, "Reporting Mortality

Findings in Trials of Rofecoxib for Alzheimer Disease or Cognitive Impairment," *Journal of the American Medical Association*, 299, no. 15 (April 16, 2007), 1813–17.

633   Paul Taylor, "Merck 'Misrepresented' Risks and Ghost-Authored Papers: Studies," *Globe and Mail*, April 16, 2008, L1, L4.

634   Andrew C. Revkin, "Climate Expert Says NASA Tried to Silence Him," *New York Times*, January 29, 2006.

635   Michiel Horn, *Academic Freedom in Canada* (Toronto: University of Toronto Press, 1999), 93–4.

636   Not least of the obstacles was the sharp escalation in mutual threats and suspicion occasioned by the Cuban Missile Crisis of 1962, during which nuclear war was barely averted. (cf. James Blight and Philip Bremer, *Sad and Luminous Days* [Lanham, MD: Rowman and Littlefield, 2002]).

637   P.M.S. Blackett, *Fear, War and the Bomb* (New York: McGraw-Hill, 1948); Greg Herken, *The Winning Weapon* (New York: Alfred A. Knopf, 1980).

638   The one thing on which Henry Kissinger and Noam Chomsky agree is the imminent danger posed by nuclear weapons, cf. George P. Shultz et al., "Toward a Nuclear-Free World," *Wall Street Journal*, January 15, 2008, and Noam Chomsky, *Failed States* (New York: Metropolitan Books, 2006), chapter 1.

639   Martin Rees, preface to *Science Information: Survey of Factors Affecting Science Communication by Scientists and Engineers* (London: The Royal Society, June 2006).

640   Ian Hacking, "Root and Branch," *The Nation*, October 8, 2007, http://www.the nation.com/doc/20071008/hacking.

641   Anne McIlroy, "A Hippocratic Oath for Science," *Globe and Mail*, December 15, 2007, F9.

642   Stephen Soldz, "Why Mary Pipher Returned Her APA Award," http://www.cou nterpunch.org/soldz08252007.html.

643   Stephen Soldz, "Abusive Interrogations," at http://www.counterpunch.org/soldz12122006.html; interview with Dr. Mary Pipher, *The Current* (radio show), CBC, September 25, 2007.

644   Alan M. Dershowitz, "Should we Fight Terror with Torture?" The Independent, July 3, 2006, http://news.independent.co.uk/world/americas/article1154084.ece.

645   Michael Ignatieff, "Lesser Evils," *New York Times Magazine*, May 2, 2004.

646   Rather than required to protect democracy, torture is, to the contrary, the "essential feature" of totalitarian rule, as W.G. Sebald observed in an essay in the collection, *On the Natural History of Destruction* (Toronto: Vintage Canada, 2004), 153.

647   Thompson et al., *The Olivieri Report*, 41.

648   Memorandum from the presidents of the Canadian research granting councils titled "Reference from the Granting Agencies to the Interagency Panel on Research Ethics: TCPS Research Ethics Matters Raised by the Olivieri Report," May 2003.

649   Catherine D. DeAngelis and Phil B. Fontanarosa, "Impugning the Integrity of
      Medical Science: The Adverse Effects of Industry Influence," *Journal of the
      American Medical Association*, 299, no. 15 (April 16, 2008), 1834. The *JAMA* edi-
      tors propose that, "All clinical trials must be prospectively listed in registries
      accepted by the International Committee of Medical Journal Editors (ICMJE)
      prior to patient enrollment, and the name(s) of the principal investigator(s)
      should be included as a required data element in the trial registration record,"
      and that, "Medical education courses should not condone or tolerate for-profit
      companies having any input into the content of educational materials or pro-
      viding funding or sponsorship for medical education programs."

650   Andrew Nikiforuk, "Is the Bee Virus Bunk?" *Globe and Mail*, November 3,
      2007, F10.

INDEX